Let's Meet Blockchain

Let's Meet Blockchain

Technology Changing for Working, Creating, and Playing

Sylvain Metz

Let's Meet Blockchain: Technology Changing for Working, Creating, and Playing

Copyright © Business Expert Press, LLC, 2024

Cover design and graphics by Funda Öner Metz

Sylvain's Photo by Christine Oetter and Gary Edgington

Interior design by Exeter Premedia Services Private Ltd., Chennai, India

First published in 2023 by
Business Expert Press, LLC
222 East 46th Street, New York, NY 10017
www.businessexpertpress.com

ISBN-13: 978-1-63742-535-0 (paperback)
ISBN-13: 978-1-63742-536-7 (e-book)

Business Expert Press Collaborative Intelligence Collection

First edition: 2023

10 9 8 7 6 5 4 3 2 1

To my wife, Funda, my daughter, Eliane, and my late parents, Gilbert and Louise Metz.

Description

A quiet revolution is taking place within the computer ecosystem; one that will change the way we do business on the Internet.

It's called blockchain, and it promises to disrupt the way people interact with one another online, whether its messaging, banking, keeping up with medical records, land records, booking a vacation, socializing, or voting. Programs are also being developed to use blockchain to serve as one's identity *papers*.

Blockchain technology is based on the idea that all online transactions should be between two people without the need for public or private third-party oversight. Blockchain technology developers believe thoughts and ideas should be shared, not quashed. It's a world where Web platforms are governed by their members, not a board of directors; privacy comes first, and one's personal information is kept private, not for third parties to take and sell as they, please.

Blockchain technology offers everyone opportunities to take part. Anyone can participate in the fast-growing world using NFTs, where works of art, music, literature, and poetry can be tokenized and sold or traded on a blockchain.

These components comprise the next generation of the World Wide Web, which is referred to as Web 3.0. Billions of dollars are being spent to create infrastructure to create a viable framework to mainstream blockchain.

This book offers a peek into this new world, with examples of how this technology is being used today as well as the hurdles, including legal challenges, it must overcome to be viable.

So, if you're ready, let's meet blockchain.

Keywords

blockchain; encryption; peer-to-peer; bitcoin; proof-of-work; centralized authority; decentralized authority; smart contract; digital identity; digitized token; cryptocurrency; NFTs; cryptocurrency wallet; digital assets; decentralized funding; Web 3.0; artificial intelligence; machine learning; internet of things; net neutrality; free speech; trustless; decentralized funding; privacy; transparent ledger

Contents

Acknowledgments...xiii

Introduction xv

Privacy Through the Ages..1

What Is Blockchain?..9

Blockchain: Nuts and Bolts 27

PoW's Dirty Reputation 47

Blockchain and the Supply Chain 53

Blockchain and Health Care...61

Blockchain and Identity 71

Blockchain and Government...81

Blockchain, Banks, and Financial Institutions 95

Blockchain and Real Estate...101

Blockchain and Print Media 105

Blockchain and the Practice of Law 111

Blockchain: Travel and Entertainment..................................117

What's Ahead for Blockchain? 123

Cryptocurrency... 125

Introduction...127

From Cows to Crypto: The Evolution of the Swap.............133

The Age of Cryptocurrency 143

A Token Economy...151

Tools for Trading..167

Risk and Regulation 175

Do I Need This?...185

NFTs 187

What Are NFTs? 189

NFTs: Art, Music, and Those Adorable Collectibles 191

NFTs and Gaming 205

NFTs as Real Estate..209

NFT Pros and Cons 215

Web 3.0 The Next Generation... 219

Web 3.0 The Next Generation 221

A Brief History of the World Wide Web..227

Web 3.0: Under the Hood..235

Web 3.0 Today 247

Web3: The Battle for Control...253

Resources 257

Bibliography..259

About the Author...309

Index 311

"Why, sometimes I've believed as many as six impossible things before breakfast."

Alice's Adventures in Wonderland
—Lewis Carroll

Acknowledgments

I want to thank Sherif Abushadi with NEAR Foundation, a nonprofit that supports programs for building onto the blockchain ecosystem, for awarding me a fellowship to begin learning about blockchain technology. He granted me the fellowship with the idea of expanding the blockchain conversation outside of the tech world through a series of e-books and articles told through the eyes of writers and artists. That idea was the genesis of this book. I thank my wife, Funda, a talented artist, designer, and architect, for designing the cover and providing the diagrams. A special thank you to my former editor at The Clarion-Ledger, Deborah Skipper Solis, who graciously agreed to edit the original drafts of the first two sections, and taught me how to look for the answers to questions before being asked. I want to offer a special thank you to my former college professor Dr. Michael Mitias, Emeritus Professor of Philosophy at Millsaps College, Jackson, MS, for graciously offering his scholarly insights that contributed greatly to the discussion of NFT art and aesthetics. I want to thank Christine Oetter and Gary Edgington, a gifted photography duo who bring life to all photos they make for taking my portrait. Finally, I'd like to recognize all those writers, reporters, bloggers, videographers, storytellers, and researchers worldwide whose commitment to blockchain technology, cryptocurrency, nonfungible tokens, and Web3 helped me to weave this tapestry together. Their zeal for this technology is inspiring.

Introduction

If you ask anyone about blockchain, most likely, you will be met with silence. Mention bitcoin; just about everyone can tell you something, although that will most likely be negative based on what they have heard before the conversation turns to another topic.

Yet, no matter how hard one tries to ignore it, blockchain keeps popping up. In addition to the news stories about the dangers of using cryptocurrency, we are treated to crazy stories about unique digital art selling for hundreds of thousands, if not millions, of dollars for something called NFTs.

While the public rolls its eyes with disinterest, while talking heads scream in disgust, a large group of computer scientists, programmers, engineers, self-described cyberpunks, and the like are building a new infrastructure dedicated to creating the next generation of Internet experience.

Blockchain technology, first used to create and transfer cryptocurrency, serves as the engine driving changes to the Internet. Under this new paradigm, consumers, not third parties, control who uses their personal information. Under this new system, privacy is consideration number one.

It's no pipe dream. Blockchain technology and other key elements to drive that change are in use now. In addition to moving cryptocurrency and creating NFTs, blockchain technology is being used to facilitate private banking for those in countries where none exists, store land and health records, vote, and book vacations—with transparency, speed, and privacy. Startups are also creating programs incorporating blockchain technology to replace our official *papers* with digital identities. No longer will people be asked to hand over fistfuls of identification documents. Their digital identity will be more than enough to suffice.

It's not a fad or a technology that is here today and gone tomorrow. Referred to by many as the *great disruptor*, blockchain technology could drastically alter if not in some cases replace the institutions the world relies upon today. If blockchain delivers what it promises, you will no longer have to rely on traditional financial institutions to process or monitor your transactions or provide you with loans. You won't need others to prove your identity. All of this, and more, will rest in your hands.

Governments and corporations worldwide are taking notice, spending billions on developing and implementing blockchain technology. Combined spending came to U.S.$6.6 billion in 2021, up 50 percent from the previous year. By 2024, that figure is expected to reach U.S. $19 billion.[1]

Forbes magazine, known for its list of the world's wealthiest people, started a new list in 2019 of the top 50 companies with revenues of U.S.$1 billion or more in sales planning to incorporate blockchain technology.[2]

Globally, the blockchain market was worth U.S.$4.8 billion in 2021,[3] then grew to U.S.$11.7 billion in 2022.[4] By 2030, that figure is expected to reach U.S.$69 billion.[5]

Let's Meet Blockchain

The assumption is you know little, if anything, about blockchain technology other than what you have heard, read, or seen on television

---

[1] IDC. *Global Spending on Blockchain.* www.businesswire.com/news/home/20210419005059/en/Global-Spending-on-Blockchain-Solutions-Forecast-to-be-Nearly-19-Billion-in-2024-According-to-New-IDC-Spending-Guide.

[2] ConcenSys. *Companies Exploring Blockchain.* https://consensys.net/blog/enterprise-blockchain/forbes-releases-top-50-billion-dollar-companies-exploring-blockchain-over-half-are-working-with-ethereum/2021.

[3] Custom Market Insights. *Global Blockchain Technology Market Worth $69 Billion by 2030.* www.globenewswire.com/en/news-release/2022/08/25/2504745/0/en/Global-Blockchain-Technology-Market-Size-Worth-69-Billion-by-2030-at-a-68-CAGR-Check-Blockchain-Industry-Share-Growth-Trends-Value-Analysis-Custom-Market-Insights.html#:~:text=The%20blockchain%20technology%20market%20size,a%20number%20of%20driving%20factors.

[4] Tuwiner. *Blockchain Statistics.* https://buybitcoinworldwide.com/blockchain-statistics/.

[5] Custom Market Insights. *Global Blockchain Technology Market Size Worth $69 Billion.* www.globenewswire.com/en/news-release/2022/08/25/2504745/0/en/Global-Blockchain-Technology-Market-Size-Worth-69-Billion-by-2030-at-a-68-CAGR-Check-Blockchain-Industry-Share-Growth-Trends-Value-Analysis-Custom-Market-Insights.html#:~:text=The%20blockchain%20technology%20market%20size,a%20number%20of%20driving%20factors.

about cryptocurrency. Regardless, you may be surprised that blockchain technology has already filtered into your life. Whether you are in government or a medical, legal, or business professional, blockchain technology is now being used to manage your records. If you are an artist, musician, or writer, it's being used to showcase your work. If you plan leisure time, it's being used to help you make your plans. No matter where you are in the world or what you do, it's becoming a part of your life.

The purpose of this book is to act as an introduction that will, in the most straightforward language possible, help shed light on this technology with examples of how it works, how it is being used today, and the hurdles it faces to be successful. It also contains a bit of history as to how we got here. This book does not endorse the use of blockchain technology or its components. By the end of the book, which incorporates redundancy, you will have a general understanding of what blockchain is and how it is employed. By the end, hopefully you will gain a greater appreciation of this technology, or maybe not. But you will have the benefit of credible information.

The book is divided into four sections, each representing a significant pillar of blockchain technology: blockchain, cryptocurrency, nonfungible tokens (NFTs), and Web 3.0.

The information used is based on a wide array of research: white papers, research papers, journal articles, videos, and the writings of journalists and experts in their fields, all listed in the footnotes and bibliography. If you find a topic that interests you and want to know more, follow the footnote or refer to the bibliography. Please note that, unlike traditional books, online sources can change. Article titles are sometimes changed and updated. Also true is that links can be changed. If that happens, type or copy and paste the title and source into your search engine. If you don't find it, you will find something similar.

Today, you are dipping your toe into the waters of a new world that strives to change how you work, create, and play.

You may be wondering why blockchain is needed at all. Why go to all this trouble?

That's a determination you alone can make once you reach the end of this book.

One of the key tenets of blockchain is privacy. Developers believe your information is private and should remain with you. So, this is where we start with a brief history of privacy.

If you are ready, let's meet blockchain.

Privacy Through the Ages

What Happens in Vegas Stays in Vegas

This slogan, created by the Las Vegas Convention and Visitors Authority in 2003 to promote the gaming capital of the United States as an adult entertainment hub, speaks volumes about privacy. The campaign strikes a chord with those who cherish the belief that the letter we get, the package we open, the bank account we have, the agreements we sign, and the annual doctor's checkup we undergo are private. Like that trip to Vegas, it's no one's business. The contents of that letter, that box, that account, that contract, and that checkup, are between two parties and should remain with those two parties.

A central tenet of blockchain is keeping transactions, agreements, and personal matters confidential.

How did we get to a place where maintaining privacy has evolved into a struggle? Like everything else, it evolved as society modernized, opportunities grew, and technology expanded.

The ambivalence over privacy is not new. The issue has been with us since the advent of civilization. On the one hand, human beings love to share their accomplishments and glory when it suits them. On the other hand, people want their privacy when public scrutiny is uncomfortable.[1]

Privacy From Ancient Days to the Present Era

Periods of war have provided, and continue to give, a large volume of personal information. This includes information from conscripts recorded by their governments. Then, there is the personal information gathered about citizens affected by war, public and private services that take care of those affected by war, and industries that provide war materials.[2]

---

[1] Ferenstein. *Birth and Death of Privacy.* https://medium.com/the-ferenstein-wire/the-birth-and-death-of-privacy-3-000-years-of-history-in-50-images-614c26059e.

[2] Ibid.

In ancient days, personal information was kept within the tribe or community where the person lived, the sum of one's life ultimately etched in symbols on a tombstone.[3] When the ancient Greeks added taxation, there was a need for adding personal information about households.[4]

As civilizations matured, writing became integral to communication in letters and diaries, resulting in more shared personal information.[5]

Skipping forward to the 10th and 11th centuries, as cities in Western Europe prospered from trade and industry, the need for accurate recordkeeping was recognized.[6] Status among the nobility was central, so keeping up with land ownership was crucial. These records also provided a gateway to one's position. They could prove or disprove if one were a nobleman, knight, or courtier.[7]

Keeping one's ledger, journal, or letters private was one thing. Keeping personal matters out of earshot of others was quite another. Eavesdropping on one's private conversation became such a problem that governments passed laws forbidding it. In the 18th century, there are references to *eavesdropping* laws chronicled in William Blackstone's *Commentaries on the Laws of England* (1769), as those who "listen under walls or windows, or the eaves of a house, to hearken after discourse, and thereupon to frame slanderous and mischievous tales, are a common nuisance and presentable at the court-leet."[8] Seen as a *bad habit*, eavesdropping was believed to be perpetrated by women, who, if found guilty, could be fined or *bound over for good behavior*.[9] Eavesdropping, which has evolved to include nefarious electronic eavesdropping in modern times, remains a crime in countries worldwide.

---

[3] Beckles. *History of Personal Data.* https://iapp.org/news/a/from-ancient-to-modern-the-changing-face-of-personal-data/.

[4] Ibid.

[5] Ibid.

[6] Buylaert and Haemers. *Record-Keeping.* https://academic.oup.com/past/article/230/suppl_11/131/2884255.

[7] Ibid.

[8] Ian Porter Museum of Art. *Eavesdropping.* https://digicult.it/articles/sound/eavesdropping-a-collaboration-between-liquid-architecture-and-melbourne-law-school/.

[9] Darby. *The Nuisance of Eavesdroppers.* www.criminalhistorian.com/the-nuisance-of-eavesdroppers/.

The 20th century brought new and unknown challenges to privacy. Early computing, for example, found ways to create methods for mass data storage as well as ways to weaponize it.

In Germany, the Nazis used census technology created by International Business Machines (IBM) to identify, target, and eventually round up Jews for transportation to concentration camps. Census data included religion, making persecution easy.

This punch card system was dreamed up by a young census worker, Herman Hollerith, who worked for both the 1880 and 1890 census.[10] Hollerith, who left the Census Bureau to start the Computing-Tabulating-Recording Company (CTR) in 1911, had the idea of creating electronic tabulators and readable punch cards indicating one's gender, nationality, and occupation, among others.[11] The company changed its name in 1924. IBM Germany, a subsidiary of IBM, worked with the Nazi Party to conduct the 1933 census, which then used that data to locate Jews who were then rounded up and sent to concentration camps.[12]

The U.S. Constitution requires a decennial census that determines congressional representation and allocation of federal funding. By law, census data are confidential, something most Americans believe to be true. In a Pew Research Center poll taken in 2020, 66 percent of the Americans said they were confident the Census Bureau would keep their personal information private. Of those, 18 percent were *very confident*, and 48 percent were *somewhat confident*.[13]

Although most Americans trust the Census Bureau, many undocumented immigrants do not. The polarizing politics and angry rhetoric emanating from the Trump administration (January 20, 2017–January 20, 2021) berating Central and South American inhabitants for attempting

---

[10] U.S. Census History. *Connection Between U.S. Census Bureau and IBM.* www .census.gov/history/www/faqs/innovations_faqs/what_is_the_connection_between_ the_census_bureau_and_ibm.html#:~:text=Hollerith%20left%20the%20Census%20 Bureau,International%20Business%20Machines%20(IBM).&text=company%20 he%20founded%20eventually%20became%20known%20as%20IBM.

[11] Wikipedia. *IBM and the Holocaust.* https://en.wikipedia.org/wiki/IBM_and_ the_Holocaust.

[12] Ibid.

[13] Pew Research Center. *U.S. Census and Privacy Concerns.* www.pewresearch .org/social-trends/2020/02/20/the-u-s-census-and-privacy-concerns/.

to cross into the United States, created fear in that population that the government would use the 2020 census information to round them up and deport them.[14]

While Americans, in a 2020 Pew Research Center poll, said they felt confident in the ability of the government to safeguard their personal information, they were less confident about some private entities that held their personal information. Americans largely agreed that credit card companies could protect their data (66 percent, with 17 percent saying they were very confident). In comparison, 49 percent of those polled expressed confidence in retailers' ability to keep personal information private (6 percent of whom were very confident).[15]

In another Pew research study, 6 in 10 Americans believed businesses and the government were tracking and monitoring their online activities. The poll found 62 percent of respondents believed that companies were tracking them, while 63 percent believed the government was tracking them.[16]

It should be no surprise that Americans had even less trust in social media platforms. Only 23 percent gave these platforms their vote of confidence, of which 4 percent were *very confident* social media protected their privacy.[17]

As centralized platforms began their proliferation at the beginning of the 21st century, governments worldwide were forced to confront the growing threat to privacy. As of 2020, 142 countries had enacted data protection laws.[18]

Chile in 1999 was the first Latin American country to do so, followed by Argentina in 2000. Since then, other Latin American

---

[14] The Conversation. *Undocumented Immigrants Fear Census.* https://theconversation.com/why-undocumented-immigrants-still-fear-the-2020-census-132842.
[15] Ibid.
[16] B. Auxier, L. Rainie, M. Anderson, A. Perrin, M. Kumar, and E. Turner. *Americans and Privacy.* www.pewresearch.org/internet/2019/11/15/americans-and-privacy-concerned-confused-and-feeling-lack-of-control-over-their-personal-information/.
[17] Ibid.
[18] Rodriguez and Alimonti. *Data Protection in Latin America and Spain.* www.eff.org/deeplinks/2020/09/look-back-and-ahead-data-protection-latin-america-and-spain.

countries that followed were Uruguay, Mexico, Peru, Colombia, Brazil, Barbados, and Panama.[19]

The European Union has also passed a myriad of privacy laws going back to the mid-1990s, reiterating a long-standing belief in Europe that the right to privacy is a fundamental right. The right to privacy is part of the 1950 European Convention on Human Rights, which states, "Everyone has the right to respect for (their) private and family life, (their) home and (their) correspondence,"[20] the EU stated.

The concern over data protection led to the EU passage of the General Data Protection Regulation (GDPR) in 2016, which requires organizations to respect the privacy rights of all EU citizens and residents while also safeguarding their personal data. The GDPR, considered the toughest in the world, also applies to organizations outside the EU collecting data on those living in the EU.[21] Violators face stiff fines for noncompliance.

In April 2022, the EU passed the Digital Services Act (DSA), holding social media platforms accountable for misinformation and targeted advertising.[22]

In May 2023, the EU fined Facebook's parent company, Meta, $1.3 billion for transferring European users' personal data to the United States.[23] In addition, the company was ordered to end such practices and come into compliance with EU privacy regulations.

In September 2023, TikTok was fined 345 million euros for failing to protect children's privacy and violating EU privacy rules.

---

[19] Ibid.

[20] GDPR.EU. *What Is GDPR?* https://gdpr.eu/what-is-gdpr/ - :~:text=The%20 General%20Data%20Protection%20Regulation,to%20people%20in%20 the%20EU.

[21] Ibid.

[22] A. Satariano. *E.U. on Social Media's Harms.* www.nytimes.com/2022/04/22/ technology/european-union-social-media-law.html.

[23] Chan. *Meta Fined $1.3 Billion for Privacy Violations.* https://apnews.com/ article/meta-facebook-data-privacy-fine-europe-9aa912200226c3d53aa293dca 8968f84?user_email=f5ff8be8d0fa22bbafcffab811c1fcbb897c1533ead9d83568 2c1e6db1fbf7a7&utm_medium=Morning_Wire&utm_source=Sailthru&utm_ campaign=MorningWire_May22_2023&utm_term=Morning%20Wire%20 Subscribers.

The fines were hefty and significant, but the potential damage to their customers who trusted them was done.

Elsewhere, Africa has seen a rapid increase in digital traffic in recent years due to ongoing investment in local digital infrastructure. These changes have led the government to grapple with privacy laws governing personal digital data.[24] Kenya, Rwanda, and South Africa have adopted elements from the EU's GDPR. However, several proposed data protection laws have specific rules that differ from those in other African countries. Therefore, technology companies working in Africa are advised to keep abreast of those changes.[25]

In Southeast Asia, Malaysia, South Korea, Vietnam, and Singapore enacted strict data privacy laws in the first decade of the 21st century, prompted by consumer concern.[26] As with the EU's GDPR, these privacy laws apply to foreign organizations doing business in the region. Violations can result in hefty fines.

In North America, Canada enacted its stringent Personal Information Protection and Electronic Documents Act on January 1, 2004. The law requires organizations to gain permission from individuals "when they collect, use or disclose that individual's personal information."[27]

Unlike its neighbor to the north, the United States has no singularly structured federal law that protects individuals from data miners, leaving states to tailor their own legislation to protect consumers.[28] As of this writing, 11 states have enacted comprehensive data protection laws: California, Virginia, Connecticut, Colorado, Utah, Iowa, Indiana, Oregon, Montana, Texas, and Tennessee, while six other states have

---

[24] Schneidman, Cooper, Mkhize, Choi, and Naidoo. *Tech Regulation in Africa.* www.insideprivacy.com/data-privacy/tech-regulation-in-africa-recently-enacted-data-protection-laws/.

[25] Ibid.

[26] Hamilton. *Privacy Laws in Southeast Asia.* www.termsfeed.com/blog/privacy-laws-southeast-asia/.

[27] Privacy Commissioner of Canada. *PIPEDA in brief.* www.priv.gc.ca/en/privacy-topics/privacy-laws-in-canada/the-personal-information-protection-and-electronic-documents-act-pipeda/pipeda_brief/.

[28] Klosowski. *U.S. Consumer Data Privacy Laws.* www.nytimes.com/wirecutter/blog/state-of-privacy-laws-in-us/.

"tailored" privacy laws. Another 12 states enacted privacy laws in 2023 with others expected to follow suit.[29]

In the meantime, large online platforms continue to gobble up personal data and sell it to retailers, despite public outcry. Although people complain about violations, they continue patronizing these sites. Researchers refer to this as the privacy paradox. While, on the one hand, people are concerned about their privacy, they do little to protect it.[30]

Let's face it. Our personal information is out there with little hope of reclaiming it through conventional methods. The proponents of block-chain technology say it can be a step in the right direction by allowing private information to remain confidential.

Ultimately, it's up to consumers to decide how much personal information they feel comfortable sharing. No changes to everyday habits are necessary if one doesn't mind being tracked. On the other hand, for those who have had enough and are willing to submit to a learning curve, utilizing platforms built on a blockchain could be the answer.

[29] Bloomberg Law. Updated September 7, 2023. *States With Consumer Data Privacy Laws*. www.nytimes.com/wirecutter/blog/state-of-privacy-laws-in-us/.
[30] Barth and de Jong. *The Privacy Paradox*. www.sciencedirect.com/science/article/pii/S0736585317302022.

What Is Blockchain?

So, what is blockchain?

The textbook answer is that a blockchain is a transparent distributed ledger, or spreadsheet, comprised of a series of data blocks containing verified encrypted digital transactions that cannot be changed or altered, linked together sequentially so that anyone on the network can verify it. This information is stored worldwide on decentralized computer networks.

Blockchain achieves this by incorporating specific sets of technologies and protocols designed to initiate, validate, transfer and store transactions and information safely and securely between interested parties. For example, when two people transact business using blockchain technology, that transaction is recorded and stored on a virtual ledger with other transactions that can be retrieved in perpetuity. The ledger is transparent, meaning anyone can see those transactions. Unlike reports one may find in a filing cabinet or in a computer file, these transactions are encrypted. So, one would need to know the transaction number, sender, and receiver. Again, this information is encrypted.[1] To find transactions, you must go online or download an app, then enter the information on a blockchain explorer. More about this later.

While created to transact business between two people without needing a third party, such as a bank, blockchain technology is used today by several platforms for the same purpose. These platforms include financial, social media, travel, and messaging, all using blockchain to protect one's private information from those who collect and sell it.

Take social media platforms, for example. You are allowed in, but that platform controls the content you receive and has easy access to your personal information, viewing history, and comments. They are called *walled gardens*, in that these centralized platforms control the users' access to their content and services.[2]

---

[1] Moreland. *Reading Blockchain Transaction History*. www.ledger.com/academy/how-to-read-a-blockchains-transaction-history.

[2] Froehlich. *Walled Garden*. www.techtarget.com/searchsecurity/definition/walled-garden#:~:text=On%20the%20internet%2C%20a%20walled,prevent%20access%20to%20other%20material.

Say something pettish on one of these platforms, and you could find yourself temporarily or permanently banned from that site.

In blockchain technology, there's no profit in knowing your personal details and no desire to monitor your speech.

It's not just large platforms looking in on you. Those prying eyes include those fun and convenient apps you use on your electronic devices. You want the download, the information, or the game, so you just agree to accept their conditions without reading the fine print. Even if you did, chances are you would still accept.

The business model that boosts stock portfolio values for these centralized platforms is contrary to blockchain technology that believes your personal data are not theirs to share.

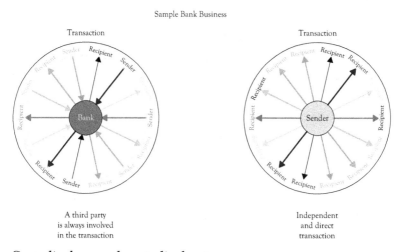

Centralized versus decentralized systems

The Origin of Blockchain

On October 31, 2008, Satoshi Nakamoto released a white paper, *Bitcoin: A Peer-to-Peer Electronic Cash System,*[3] describing a method for sending digital currency from one person to another without a third party, such as a bank. He proposed the creation of a digital currency, which he called bitcoin, to conduct peer-to-peer (P2P) commerce that could be sent in a block of code that included a timestamp to verify when the transaction was created, and a digital signature to verify the transaction's legitimacy.

---

[3] Satoshi. *White Paper.* https://nakamotoinstitute.org/bitcoin/.

The first bitcoin was created in January 2009, paving the way for the creation of digital assets and the way people conduct business.

While Satoshi's white paper was groundbreaking, his proposal was based on years of work by others.

Some trace blockchain's origins back to 1991 when cryptographer and computer scientist Stuart Haber and physicist and scientific researcher W. Scott Stornetta created the digital timestamp to protect the integrity of document creation. More about timestamps later.

In 2002, David Mazières, professor of computer science at Stanford University (CA), and Dennis Shasha, professor of computer science at New York University (NY), conceptualized the block. They advanced the idea of storing data on a multiuser file system in blocks, which was the precursor to today's blockchain.[4]

Another essential element is the concept of proof of work (PoW) necessary to verify blocks of transactions. PoW was the brainchild of cryptographer and security architect Adam Back who in 1997 proposed a way to use hash functions to curb e-mail spam.[5] Simply put, senders would first have to generate a hash using an algorithm program and affix it to e-mails like postage stamps. Then, when that e-mail arrived at the server, the server would recognize the hash and the extra effort (work) that went into sending that e-mail, letting it go through. The reasoning behind the creation he called *Hashcash* was that he believed spammers would not want to go through all that trouble to add a *stamp*.[6]

A hash is a form of security made up of a fixed string of seemingly random numbers and letters. Hashing takes input (information) of variable length and converts it into a fixed length of numbers and letters representing the input. The result is like a fingerprint. Any alteration would result in a different output.[7] There are dozens of hashing programs available today, some online. The most recognized is Secure Hash Algorithm 256-bit

[4] Blockstreet HQ Team. *Distributed Ledger*. https://medium.com/blockstreethq/before-blockchain-there-was-distributed-ledger-technology-319d0295f011.

[5] Back. *A Denial of Service Counter-Measure*. https://nakamotoinstitute.org/static/docs/hashcash.pdf.

[6] Biz Vlogs. *Hashcash*. www.youtube.com/watch?v=YUTwqG6e8LY&ab_channel=BizVlogs.

[7] Sundaramoorthy. *Public Key Cryptography*. https://medium.com/@thyagsundaramoorthy/hashing-and-public-key-cryptography-for-beginners-292aaf14efae.

(SHA-256), an open-source encryption program created by the U.S. National Security Agency, used to mine (create) bitcoin.

Let's see an example. Here's Shakespeare's Sonnet 18. We all know it as it was the one all English textbooks included. It begins, "Shall I compare thee to a summer's day? Thou art more lovely and more temperate:…" Using SHA-256 to create a hash, the entire sonnet is represented as 74ad4c4ff4-41eff450f35badd836722002a9f46c7e6a4fde526e75751cb3e5a9.

H·A·S·H
SHA-256

Shall I compare thee to a summer's day?
Thou art more lovely and more temperate:
Rough winds do shake the darling buds of May,
And summer's lease hath all too short a date;
Sometime too hot the eye of heaven shines,
And often is his gold complexion dimm'd;
And every fair from fair sometime declines,
By chance or nature's changing course untrimm'd;
But thy eternal summer shall not fade,
Nor lose possession of that fair thou ow'st;
Nor shall death brag thou wander'st in his shade,
When in eternal lines to time thou grow'st:
So long as men can breathe or eyes can see,
So long lives this, and this gives life to thee.

74ad4c4ff441eff450f35badd836722002a9f46c7e6a4fde526e75751cb3e5a9

Hashing

That's it, the entire sonnet. No matter how often the sonnet is put through this program, it generates the same 64-character hash. You could download the entire contents of the U.S. Library of Congress and will get a 64-character string that represents its contents.

One caveat. You have to use the same hashing program to get the same results. If you use another SHA-256 program, your output will be different.

Now then, back to our example. If you remove one character, in this case, the colon at the end of the second line of the sonnet, you get this: 192cb743f3485f8f6530718d142546fe60c9044368f7d9531f2d96b-d4a2dd586.

Replace the colon and take out the second *e* in the fourth word, *thee*, and you get dff365d8ac9d4ccba3554bb3bfa3e64b49ee25e50dd-4bae5de60e35f601e34f3.

You see why it's like a fingerprint. Change any part of a message, just one character, and the hash changes completely.

Impressive, but there is no way to convert that hash string without another tool, as hashing is a *one-way* function.[8] You cannot reverse engineer to read the sonnet otherwise. You need an encryption tool to encrypt your hash and then allow a second party to decrypt it. Blockchain technology, borrowing from cryptography, relies on *keys* to do this. Without getting into the weeds, keys are numbers or functions blended with the hash output to create an encrypted message. There are two keys: A public key that identifies the sender (much like an e-mail address), and a private key that proves ownership allowing access, like a PIN.

There are two types of cryptography: symmetrical and asymmetrical. With symmetrical encryption, the sender encrypts a hash with a private key. The only way for the receiver to open it is with the sender's private key. Sending that key with the message, however, raises security issues.

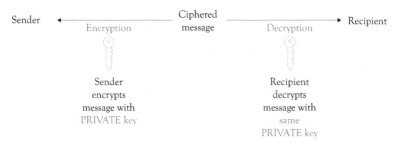

Symmetric encryption

---

[8] Armstrong. *Hashing vs Encryption.* https://nordlocker.com/blog/hashing-vs-encryption/#:~:text=Hashing%20is%20not%20a%20type,the%20case%20with%20encrypted%20messages.

If the key were intercepted, bad actors could use it to decrypt the message and gain access to the sender's account.[9]

Asymmetrical cryptography offers additional security. Rather than one key, two keys are created. One is private and the other public. This *key pair* is used to encrypt the information, while the receiver uses their keys to decrypt it. Private keys are never sent.[10]

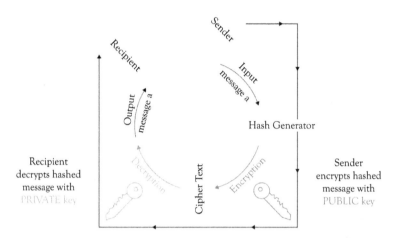

Asymmetrical encryption

But wait, even if the receiver gets an encrypted message from someone they know, how can they be sure they sent it? This is accomplished by creating a unique *signature*. As mentioned earlier, an encrypted message is created with the hash and blended with the sender's private key, creating a unique *digital signature*. The signature, a string of numbers and letters like the hash, is unique because no two messages are identical. Different characters produce different hash outputs.

The encrypted message is then blended with the receiver's public key as part of the message. The receiver uses their private key to decrypt

---

[9] Sundaramoorthy. *Hashing and Public Key Cryptography.* https://medium.com/
@thyagsundaramoorthy/hashing-and-public-key-cryptography-for-beginners-
292aaf14efae.
[10] Ibid.

the message, then uses the sender's public key to verify the information. Remember the sonnet. The receiver can compare the two hashes to ensure the messages are identical.[11]

It is also possible for the sender to encrypt the message with the sender's public key and then be decrypted by the receiver's private key.[12]

Two other vital pieces of the blockchain puzzle were created by Nick Szabo, a computer scientist, cryptographer, and legal scholar who, in 1994, came up with the idea of the *smart contract*. This program acts like a contract that will self-activate if all conditions are met. We will talk more about them in the next chapter. Then in 2005, Szabo had the idea of a blockchain-based currency called *bit gold*, reasoning that fiat (which means formal authorization or decree) money relied on the trust of a *third party* for its value. In this case, the value of money is backed by governments. Given the economic challenges of the 20th century, he believed that reliance on third parties such as banks was not ideal.[13]

On the other hand, precious metals and other collectibles cannot be replicated and are expensive to extract. Therefore, they are valuable commodities that can be used for commerce.[14] However, their use also presents problems. Large amounts of precious metals can be challenging to transport, not to mention risky. They can be lost or stolen. Szabo further reasoned that testing metals to guard against counterfeit metals and metal purity could also be expensive.[15]

Szabo concluded that the best currency would be a digital currency, which he called *bit gold* that could be created online and valued the same way precious metals are valued. The *bit gold* could be autenticated online using *client puzzle function*, *Proof-of-Work function*, or *secure benchmark function*, all of which are forms of hashing, leading to the creation of this bit gold.[16]

---

[11] Ibid.

[12] Preveil. *Public-Private Key Pairs*. www.preveil.com/blog/public-and-private-key/.

[13] Szabo. *Bit Gold*. https://nakamotoinstitute.org/bit-gold/.

[14] Ibid.

[15] Ibid.

[16] Ibid.

The problem Szabo ran up against was the issue of double-spending. At that time, the bits of data created could be copied and spent more than once.[17] Satoshi solved the double-spending problem by introducing peer-to-peer time-stamped transactions broadcast across a decentralized network that could be proved mathematically and displayed sequentially, proving beyond a shadow of a doubt when a bitcoin was spent.[18]

If Szabo's bit gold and Satoshi's bitcoin sound eerily familiar, they are. There is speculation that the two men are one and the same.[19]

Do We Need Blockchain?

Do we need another method to verify and record our transactions? Some argue that we don't, as those mechanisms exist. Banks already do this for us.

We are already used to sharing private information with large institutions we trust to conduct our business.

To operate in today's world, one must share personal or financial information, including the Social Security number (if one lives in the United States), to get credit, open bank accounts, get credit cards, buy property, and vote. All that data are kept in large computer banks to be analyzed, shared, and, in some cases, sold to others. Consumers accept this as the cost of doing business.

The blockchain creators believe these institutions have too much control over personal information. Moreover, institutions like banks, which collect fees, decide what transactions to approve or disapprove, even though it's our money.

Blockchain developers no longer accept the idea of third parties peering over our shoulders, monitoring our business, deciding what to accept, and getting fees for the privilege. No, they say. It's time to remove

---

[17] BlockstreetHQ Team. *Distributed Ledger.* https://medium.com/blockstreethq/before-blockchain-there-was-distributed-ledger-technology-319d0295f011#:~:text=But%20the%20concept%20was%20not,which%20has%20a%20rich%20past.

[18] Ibid.

[19] Roberts. *Did This Man Created Bitcoin.* https://fortune.com/2018/10/31/satoshi-identity/.

the middleman. It's time to reclaim personal privacy while streamlining paperwork.

Blockchain isn't only about finance. It's a way to keep your personal information private.

For example, keeping up with your medical records can be challenging, especially if you have health issues that require specialists. Each office you visit has its own set of medical records based on your visits to their office. With each new doctor comes a new form to be filled out, listing all the medications and treatments you are taking for your condition.

Do you have control over your identity? What do you use to prove who you are? Depending on where you live, you can use documents such as your birth certificate, Social Security number, or photo identification, such as a driver's license, passport, or residence card. When you open a new bank account, apply for a credit card or loan, register to vote, or sign up for some government service, you must provide proper identification and information that those institutions copy and store.

Blockchain technology offers a remedy for these situations, and others, using a decentralized peer-to-peer network that allows you to share your information, store your records, and make transactions without oversight.

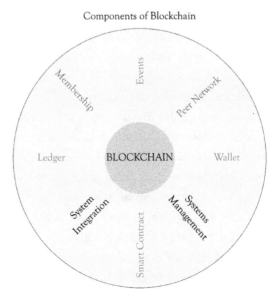

Blockchain components

Blockchain's Pitch

The proponents of blockchain technology claim that this new technology will provide the privacy we require to conduct transactions while protecting our personal information from third parties. We won't need some third party to authorize our dealings. Blockchain technology, they say, offers security, transparency, low cost, and stability.

Security

As discussed, information is hashed and then encrypted by a set of keys—private and public. The private key proves the sender is the owner of the information, while the public key serves as their address. Blending the hash with a private key produces a unique digital signature that cannot be replicated.

After a transaction is initiated, it is sent out or broadcast to nodes, a computer network operated by validators who verify the transaction.

Once validated, the transaction is added to a block containing hundreds, if not thousands, of similar transactions. Miners verify the block using an algorithm before it can be created.

Once created, the miner attaches a hash attesting to its validity, then makes a copy of the blockchain up to that point. Other nodes pick it up, validate the new block verifying the hash, and make their own copies of the blockchain before sending it forward. Once transactions are processed, the contents are delivered to the receivers.

Blocks are immutable (unalterable) and stored on a network of decentralized computers as a chain. Each block includes the hash of the previous and new validators, linking them sequentially.

This is basically how blockchain works. Of course, we'll take a more in-depth look at the entire process in the next chapter.

That's fine, you say, but is blockchain safe? Can't someone in the network steal the contents of those blocks?

Yes, a block can be manipulated, but it isn't easy. What's more, attempts would not go undetected. For one, the hash on the block would change, alerting the network that the block had been compromised. Remember, multiple copies of a blockchain are stored by those who created or validated those blocks. So it is easy to compare the hash of a block tampered with others that have not been corrupted. Recall the example of Shakespeare's sonnet.

The attacker would need to reproduce additional sets of alternate transactions that would have to replace no less than 51 percent of the previously shared block copies to convince the network that their altered transaction is the real deal.[20]

Say Jack wants to impress his friends. So, he goes on the Web and finds a photo of the president of the United States taken at a special event. The photo was sent out over wire services, timestamped with a date, location, and the photographer's name, along with a caption describing the event, including those pictured, to newspapers worldwide. Jack sees the photo and places a picture of himself next to the president. He then copies and pastes this photo into his personal file and sends it out over the network to his friends. It doesn't take long for Jack's photo to be recognized as a fake. Even if his friends are bamboozled, anyone outside his network could easily compare the altered version with the same photo broadcast around the world, making it unlikely he could keep up the ruse for very long.

It's not impossible to take control of a blockchain, but it isn't easy, either.

One would have to convince a simple majority of nodes their block was the real McCoy. They could create another version of that blockchain, reflecting any changes in transactions, such as the amount of cryptocurrency being sent. For this to work, hackers, as noted above, must control 51 percent of the mining process.[21] Why 51 percent? We'll discuss that later. For now, all you need to know is that a simple majority is all that is needed to change a blockchain.

---

[20] Information governance. *Blockchain Can Be Hacked.* www.epiqglobal.com/en-us/resource-center/articles/blockchain-can-be-hacked.
[21] Ibid.

While this is possible, it would require enormous effort. Remember, each node that validates a block makes a copy of the blockchain. The blockchain with the most blocks is seen as valid. The smaller the block-chain, the more susceptible they are to hackers compared to larger, complex blockchains.[22]

Let's go back to our example of Jack and his doctored photograph. To fool his friends, he would need to intercept and manipulate 51 percent of those platforms that held the original photo. Even if he had the necessary computing power and tools, he would still compete with the original, splitting reality in two. In the blockchain world, this is called a *fork*,[23] as in "there's a fork in the road. Which road do we take?" A fork is created when there is a lack of consensus about the information being passed along, creating two blockchains. Consensus will dictate which blockchain is the right one. After a while, people will get wise to Jack's subterfuge and ignore his photo.

One estimate suggested it would cost hackers more than U.S.$260,000 per hour to attack the bitcoin blockchain.[24] The smaller the blockchain, the less expensive it is to attack.[25]

Blockchain can also be exploited due to mistakes or failures by the end users. Some argue that hackers can expose flaws if errors are made during a blockchain's creation.[26] The greater the blockchain's complexity, the greater the possibility of flaws allowing hackers access.[27]

Forks can also occur when, say, the software package used by one node can't *agree* with the results of another software package used by another node.

---

[22] Ibid.

[23] Wikipedia. *Blockchain Fork*. https://en.wikipedia.org/wiki/Fork_(blockchain).

[24] Orcutt. *Blockchains Getting Hacked*. www.technologyreview.com/2019/02/19/239592/once-hailed-as-unhackable-blockchains-are-now-getting-hacked/.

[25] Ibid.

[26] Information governance. *Blockchain Can Be Hacked*. www.epiqglobal.com/en-us/resource-center/articles/blockchain-can-be-hacked.

[27] Orcutt. *Blockchains Getting Hacked*. www.technologyreview.com/2019/02/19/239592/once-hailed-as-unhackable-blockchains-are-now-getting-hacked/.

When there is a *radical* change of protocols[28] (rules defining how information is shared),[29] on the blockchain network, it is referred to as a *hard fork*.

Think of a hard fork like a train on the track. Suddenly, a switch is thrown and a portion of the train is thrown onto another track. It could have been done to save some of the cars from disaster, or it could have been done with malicious intent. In either case, there are now two cars—or in our case, two blockchains. Which blockchain do nodes follow? The one the majority believe to be the correct one. In other words, consensus determines which part of the blockchain to accept. Aside from 51 percent attacks, a lack of security also puts blockchains at risk, as demonstrated by several high-profile hacks of cryptocurrency exchanges in previous years. In December 2021, hackers stole U.S.$200 million in assorted tokens from BitMart Exchange, breaching two different cryptocurrency wallets connected to the Internet that was under their control.[30] In another case, a hacker made off with U.S.$600 million in August 2021, following a successful attack on another network.[31]

Fighting off hackers is a shared problem across the Internet. As with any network or centralized platform, it's always a race to keep ahead of hackers intent on theft and destruction.

Transparency

In today's world of centralized recordkeeping, information can be lost, unrevised, altered, or destroyed. Human error can result in the conveyance of incorrect information. Any one of these circumstances can result in a disagreement among parties regarding what information is correct.

---

[28] CFI Team. *Hard Forks.* https://corporatefinanceinstitute.com/resources/cryptocurrency/hard-fork/.

[29] Geeks for Geeks. *Blockchain Protocols.* www.geeksforgeeks.org/blockchain-protocols-and-their-working/.

[30] Pattnaik. *Hackers Steal From Bitmart Exchange.* www.benzinga.com/markets/cryptocurrency/21/12/24449490/hackers-steal-200m-worth-of-shiba-inu-saitama-and-other-tokens-from-bitmart-exchange.

[31] Ibid.

Because blockchain is an open, transparent digital ledger, all transactions can be viewed by using one of several blockchain explorers to track transactions.[32] One only needs the transaction hash, address, or block number to view specific transactions.[33] While open for all to see, other than the amount sent, all the information relating to the transaction are encrypted.

Cost Reductions

Today financial institutions, such as banks, credit card companies, and other electronic money transfer platforms set daily spending limits while also charging fees for use and transfers. Customers can also be charged to verify documents, paying a bank notary for their stamp and signature. Merchants are charged fees for processing credit cards. There are fees for everything. A study by Capgemini Consulting found blockchain technology could save consumers up to U.S.$16 billion annually.[34]

Financial institutions, also looking to blockchain to reduce their overhead, could save around U.S.$20 billion annually by incorporating blockchain technology, according to a study by Santander Bank.[35] Of course, for those financial institutions to reap those savings, they would need to make a significant capital investment to replace outdated computers and infrastructure.[36]

---

[32] Software Testing Help. *Blockchain Explorer Tutorial.* www.softwaretestinghelp .com/blockchain-explorer-tutorial/#:~:text=A%20blockchain%20explorer%20 is%20a,user%20in%20a%20searchable%20format.

[33] Blockchain Support Center. *Looking Up a Transaction on Blockchain.* https:// support.blockchain.com/hc/en-us/signin?return_to=https%3A%2F%2Fsupport .blockchain.com%2Fhc%2Fen-us%2Farticles%2F211160663-How-can-I-look-up-a-transaction-on-the-blockchain-#:~:text=To%20look%20up%20a%20 bitcoin,your%20search%20query%20will%20display.

[34] Tapscott and Tappscott. *Blockchain Is Changing Finance.* https://hbr.org/ 2017/03/how-blockchain-is-changing-finance.

[35] Ibid.

[36] Di Gregorio. *Blockchain Can Cut Costs.* www.pwc.com/m1/en/media-centre/ articles/blockchain-new-tool-to-cut-costs.html.

Stability

In today's network, if a server goes down or a system goes offline, it can lead to significant headaches not only for the companies but for hundreds of thousands, if not millions, of their customers who find their lives upended by the chaos. In May 2021, for example, air traffic across the country was delayed due to a computer outage. The shutdown was caused by Sabre, a third-party travel reservation company, which affected several airlines. When their reservation platform went down, the airlines could not check people in, print boarding passes, or print bag badges.[37]

Two years earlier, air traffic was halted when a computer system operated by the U.S. Customs and Border Protection agency went offline, forcing major delays across the country.[38]

Other disruptions have occurred over the past years because of cyberattacks, led mainly by foreign powers such as North Korea, China, Iran, and Russia, to spy or spread disinformation. Ransomware is also becoming a significant problem. In these cases, attackers successfully wrest control of a computer or server and then demand money to restore control. These attacks have placed municipalities, hospitals, and a major oil pipeline, Colonial Pipeline,[39] in jeopardy. On October 31, 2023, Mr. Cooper, one of the largest mortgage lenders in the United States, was attacked by cyber criminals, resulting in the disruption of payments and other transactions for its 4.3 million customers.[40]

Imagine if that pipeline network, airline services, or mortgage provider, had decentralized computer networks. In the pipeline case, an attack would require tremendous financial resources to take control of the network. In the case of system crashes, a decentralized system could allow the network to continue without interruption.

---

[37] CBS LA Staff. *Computer Outage Causes Delays at Nationwide Airports.* www .cbsnews.com/losangeles/news/massive-computer-outage-causes-frustrating-delays-at-airport-nationwide-including-lax/.

[38] Alsup, Almasy, and Sands. *US Customs Outage.* https://edition.cnn.com/2019/08/16/politics/us-customs-computers/index.html.

[39] Morrison. *Pipeline Held for Ransom.* www.vox.com/recode/22428774/ransomeware-pipeline-colonial-darkside-gas-prices.

[40] Cowley. *Cyberattack Disrupts Mortgage Payments for Millions of Customers.* www .nytimes.com/2023/11/07/business/cyberattack-mr-cooper-mortgages.html#:~:text=7%2C%202023-,Mr.,31.

Types of Blockchains

There are four categories of blockchain: public, private, consortium, and hybrid.

Public blockchains are open to everyone. No one is restricted from participating.[41] The data are stored on the open ledger and are available for all to see. The verification process requires approval from the nodes, considered *trustless*, whose sole job is to prove that the information contained within the block originated with the sender and no one has tampered with it.

Wait, you are thinking. Isn't the point of blockchain to remove third-party oversight? If that is true, why does blockchain verification rely on those that cannot be trusted? The difference is in the idea of *trustless* nodes. In today's world, we trust institutions to confirm our transactions. They hire people who are loyal to the company. These institutions employ these people to process, accept or reject those transactions, and maintain our personal information. We take it for granted that when we go to the cash machine, the information on the card will give us our money (assuming there's enough in the account). We believe that when we get to the polls, it will be evident that our documents will give us access to a ballot, and that our vote will be counted.

On the other hand, stakeholders are *trustless*. It sounds counterintuitive to place one's faith in a system that relies on someone or something that does not require trust. In the world of blockchain, it means the very opposite. One does not need to trust the nodes that link together to confirm transactions. They have no allegiance to an employer or its practices. They do not receive directives to push this product or deny that application. Their job is to use resources to prove the hash on a block is valid and accepted through consensus. If they attempt to tamper with the block for personal gain, other nodes can quickly discover them, and their work will be separated from the block.[42]

---

[41] Wegrzyn and Wang. *Types of Blockchains*. www.foley.com/en/insights/publications/2021/08/types-of-blockchain-public-private-between.

[42] Kasireddy. *Trustless*. www.preethikasireddy.com/post/what-do-we-mean-by-blockchains-are-trustless.

Public blockchains are used today to verify cryptocurrency transactions.

Private blockchains are controlled by central authorities. Unlike the open participation by nodes, validators are selected and hired by these central authorities, which set up their own blockchain and maintain complete control over them.[43] Hence, the idea of independent consensus is forfeited as the nodes are not independent, resulting in blockchains that are susceptible to *fraud and bad actors*.[44] Private blockchains face another challenge. They can be easier to hack because there are fewer nodes in the network resulting in compromised or stolen data.

Companies using private blockchains include De Beers, which specializes in diamonds, to verify the authenticity of diamonds, and Comcast, which allows advertisers to target viewers with specific advertisements while maintaining the viewer's privacy.[45]

Consortium blockchains are those created and controlled by several organizations instead of just one.[46] The downside is that with several entities involved, it requires cooperation but can also be a logistical nightmare, not to mention the possibility of being charged with antitrust action.[47]

One example of a consortium blockchain is BankChain, a banking consortium designed to improve banking solutions.[48]

Hybrid blockchains, like private blockchains, are controlled by one organization, but the public blockchain performs validation.[49] One notable example of a hybrid blockchain is the IBM food trust, which is dedicated to improving the world's food supply chain. The network

---

[43] Iredale. *Public Vs Private Blockchain*. https://101blockchains.com/public-vs-private-blockchain/.

[44] Wegrzyn and Wang. *Types of Blockchains*. www.foley.com/en/insights/publications/2021/08/types-of-blockchain-public-private-between.

[45] Euromoney Learning. *Rise of Private Blockchains*. www.euromoney.com/learning/blockchain-explained/the-rise-of-private-blockchains.

[46] Wegrzyn and Wang. *Types of Blockchains*. www.foley.com/en/insights/publications/2021/08/types-of-blockchain-public-private-between.

[47] Ibid.

[48] Anwar. *Top 20 Blockchain Consortia*. https://101blockchains.com/blockchain-consortium/.

[49] Wegrzyn and Wang. *Types of Blockchains*. www.foley.com/en/insights/publications/2021/08/types-of-blockchain-public-private-between.

includes all of the stakeholders involved in the production and distribution of food—farmers, wholesalers, distributors, and retailers.[50]

Summing Up

Scores of developers are working worldwide to build on the vision set out by Satoshi. Blockchain is an evolving technology grappling with growing pains and unintended consequences, such as the large amount of data being parked on decentralized computers worldwide. But, like any evolving technology, serious people on both sides of the spectrum are looking at the problems while calling out the hype. It's still, after all, a work in progress.

---

[50] Geroni. *Hybrid Blockchains*. https://101blockchains.com/hybrid-blockchain/.

Blockchain

Nuts and Bolts

This chapter looks at a block's makeup and how blocks are created and added to the blockchain. It's a process and, for the purposes of this book, extra credit. The overview in the previous chapter and related chapters in the cryptocurrency section will more than suffice. So, if you are new to blockchain or tech turns you off, feel free to move on to the next chapter. On the other hand, as you read the following chapters, you will see that blockchain technology is being embraced in a big way by all sectors employing technology that uses the components and steps listed in this chapter. For that reason, you may want to keep reading.

Transparent Distributed Ledgers

A chain of blocks, or blockchain, contains all verified transactions and is openly shared on the network. Because the blocks are linked sequentially, transactions can be traced back to their original starting point by referring to the hash on each block. The hash from a preceding block is also on the following block. The first block is referred to as the Genesis block.

If you are familiar with accounting basics or have watched gangster movies, you know that a ledger is a list of bookkeeping entries of financial transactions—money going in and out. Entries typically include the date, the recipient, and the amount. In the movies, gangsters, who may or may not code for their client's names, always lock their ledgers in a safe.

Elements of a Block

Blockchains, as discussed, are encrypted data blocks containing similar transactions linked together and stored on a network of decentralized computers. Other elements include a hash of all transactions of the previous block, a hash of all transactions in that block, and a timestamp giving the exact time the block was mined and validated.

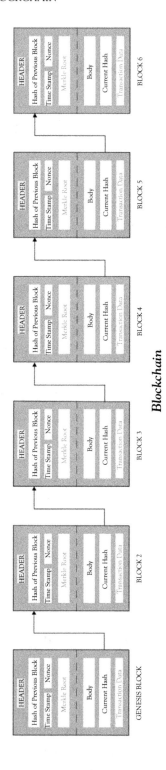

Blockchain

Each transaction includes the addresses of the sender and the recipient, and the amount being sent if it's a financial transaction involving cryptocurrency. It also includes a transaction fee referred to as *gas*. Each transaction also includes a smart contract.

Smart Contracts

As mentioned in the previous chapter, a smart contract is a self-executing agreement that is activated if the conditions set by both the buyer and seller are met.[1]

Think of a smart contract the way you would any traditional contract. When someone enters into a significant financial agreement with another (like buying someone's home), the individual initiating the purchase or agreement will draw up a contract specifying both parties' duties, responsibilities, and obligations. Most likely, that contract is created by attorneys representing one of the two parties. It ends with a signature page (name and date) and a line for the notary who identifies the parties involved and verifies the authenticity of their signatures.

As you recall, the idea for smart contracts was first proposed in 1994 by Nick Szabo.[2] Smart contracts provide a way to protect the integrity of agreements while eliminating the need for a middleman.[3] It gained popularity when Ethereum, the second-largest blockchain, began using them for a wide range of transactions.[4]

Let's say you want to rent an apartment. Instead of going through a rental agency, you register online, putting your information on a

---

[1] Zapotochnyi. *Smart Contracts*. https://blockgeeks.com/guides/smart-contracts/.

[2] Petersson. *History of Smart Contracts*. www.forbes.com/sites/davidpetersson/2018/10/24/how-smart-contracts-started-and-where-they-are-heading/?sh=4fb0539537b6.

[3] Kukkuru. *Smart Contracts*. www.infosys.com/insights/digital-future/smart-contracts.html.

[4] Wikipedia. *Smart Contract*. https://en.wikipedia.org/wiki/Smart_contract#:~:text=Since%20the%202015%20launch%20of,a%20blockchain%20or%20distributed%20ledger.

blockchain created by those renting apartments.[5] If selected, you get access to the apartment once you pay the required amount. Once payment is received, the keys are delivered, or the smart door is unlocked. There's no middleman. There are no extra fees. On the other hand, if the conditions outlined in the contract are not met, the smart contract will reject the transaction, and that door will stay locked.

Another example. Say you want to send crypto. When the transaction is initiated, it includes a smart contract that will not activate if there's insufficient money in your account.

The transaction process is black and white, with no gray area. There's no wiggle room for negotiation, no discussion about a bank deposit that came in a day or two later than expected. It's a computer program that acts on the conditions outlined in the agreement.

Timestamps

Each block is timestamped, verifying the time and date it was created (mined) and validated, which protects the integrity of transactions. Timestamps prevent double-spending.

The timestamp was created in 1991 by cryptographers Stuart Haber and W. Scott Stornetta to protect the integrity of digital documents as to when they were made, changed, or deleted.[6] Despite its promise, timestamps went largely unused until Satoshi advocated its use to make transactions immutable.

The fact information cannot be changed or deleted also means incorrect information, such as a cryptocurrency address (a long string of letters and numbers), cannot be easily corrected. Suppose you send crypto to an incorrect address. It cannot be recovered, which is ironic as the blockchain is an open ledger that can be tracked from start to finish and viewed by anyone on the network. It cannot be

[5] Qi-Long, Rong-Hua, and Fei-Long. *Blockchain-Based Housing Rental System.* www.scitepress.org/Papers/2019/80972/80972.pdf.
[6] Hosoi. *Timestamping.* www.globalsign.com/en/blog/what-is-timestamping-how-does-it-work.

amended if incorrect information is included.[7] On the other hand, you can always copy and paste the address and then recheck it before sending it.

Let's look at a transaction from start to finish to give you a better idea of how blockchain transactions work.

The Transaction

So, Harry wants to send Sally some cryptocurrency. Harry opens his digital wallet (a topic we will get to in the section on cryptocurrency) containing his virtual assets, selects the amount he wants to send Sally, then adds Sally's address. After he has checked everything, Harry clicks the send button, and his wallet does all the work, automatically generating the transaction.

The wallet first unlocks and retrieves the currency using Harry's private key. It then prepares an encrypted transaction.[8] It then digitally signs the transaction by combining its hash with Harry's private key.[9] The wallet then broadcasts the transaction to nodes in the network, which pick up the transaction to verify that Harry is the owner of the assets, and that his wallet has enough currency to send by using his public key.[10]

Digital signatures are never the same. Every time a transaction is generated, the digital signature changes because the information changes, adding to the security of each transaction.[11]

---

[7] Kyle. *Human Error Breeds Catastrophe.* https://medium.com/@Kyle.May/blockchain-issues-2-human-error-breeds-catastrophe-679948072da4.

[8] Coinbase. *Digital Signatures.* www.coinbase.com/de/cloud/discover/dev-foundations/digital-signatures#:~:text=Digital%20signatures%20are%20a%20fundamental,other%20users%20from%20spending%20them.

[9] Cryptopedia Staff. *Public and Private Keys.* www.gemini.com/cryptopedia/public-private-keys-cryptography.

[10] Coinbase. *Digital Signatures.* www.coinbase.com/de/cloud/discover/dev-foundations/digital-signatures#:~:text=Digital%20signatures%20are%20a%20fundamental,other%20users%20from%20spending%20them.

[11] 99Bitcoins. *Digital Bitcoin Signatures.* www.youtube.com/watch?v=hv-nz8jJlTA&ab_channel=99Bitcoins.

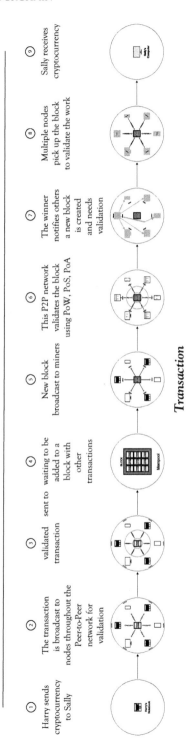

TRANSACTION PROCESS

① Harry sends cryptocurrency to Sally

② The transaction is broadcast to nodes throughout the Peer-to-Peer network for validation

③ validated transaction   sent to

④ waiting to be added to a block with other transactions

⑤ New block broadcast to miners

⑥ This P2P network validates the block using PoW, PoS, PoA

⑦ The winner notifies others a new block is created and needs validation

⑧ Multiple nodes pick up the block to validate the work

⑨ Sally receives cryptocurrency

Transaction

After verifying the transaction, it is sent to a virtual space called a mempool, where it is sorted and placed in a block with hundreds, if not thousands, of other like transactions to await validation.

Mempools

A mempool, or memory pool, is the space where blocks wait to be added to the blockchain.[12] Hundreds of thousands of transactions can be sitting in a mempool at any given moment, waiting to be loaded into a block. The number of transactions per block depends on the size. The average number of transactions can be between 1,000 and 2,000 per block.[13]

Blockchain transactions can be tracked using online sites like blockchainexplorer.com or mempool.space.

A Funny Thing Happened on the Way to the Blockchain

Waiting in the mempool is like waiting for the next city bus. For most, it's about getting to one's destination in time. Some may decide not to get on the bus when it arrives. This is true for transactions. A sender can cancel their transaction before it is approved and moved to a block. A passenger may also decide it would be faster to take a taxi. They pay more but arrive faster. This is also true of mempools. One may choose to pay a higher transaction fee, also known as *gas*, to get their transaction approved faster. Miners earn money from these fees, so naturally they will look for transactions paying higher gas fees.[14]

Other issues that can affect one's transaction include wallets that don't transmit the transaction, nodes dropping the transaction, or the sender being a front-running victim.[15] Front-running is when *bad actors* use technology (like a front-running bot) to monitor blockchain transactions

---

[12] Blocknative. *Mempools*. www.blocknative.com/blog/mempool-intro.

[13] Blockchain.com. *Transaction Time*. www.blockchain.com/charts/n-transactions-per-block.

[14] Blocknative. *Liquidity 2020*. www.youtube.com/watch?v=aZPx7K8XI68&t=932s&ab_channel=Blocknative.

[15] Ibid.

and gas prices, using this *insider information* to manipulate the market in their favor.[16] By tracking gas prices, these bad actors can see when they can pay more for the miner to process their order first to take advantage of major moves in the market that affect market pricing.[17]

While illegal in the stock market, front-running is now legal in blockchain because transactions are transparent. However, the European Parliament, in April 2023, passed comprehensive rules to regulate the cryptocurrency industry. The package includes prohibiting market manipulation tactics like front-running.[18] These new rules go into effect sometime in 2024.

Another problem could arise if a block is, for whatever reason, reorganized or replaced, causing further delays.

Delays happen. You can have a long string of successes moving your assets but then, for whatever reason, discover a transaction you've made countless times before, is uncharacteristically delayed. If this occurs, be patient. If you have concerns, you can always contact your exchange for help. If a transaction fails, your cryptocurrency will be returned to your wallet.

Get a Glimpse

To see the mempool in action, go to mempool.space, an open-sourced platform, or use this QR code to watch blocks move from the mempool (left side) to the blockchain, undergoing various validation stages (right side). Click on any box at the top, then scroll down to see all the transactions in real time. Run your finger or pointer over any box on your computer or smart device, and you will find all the information about that

---

[16] Singh. *What Is Front-Running.* https://cointelegraph.com/explained/what-is-front-running-in-crypto-and-nft-trading.

[17] Ibid.

[18] Dentons. *Dentons Tech Discusses New EU Regulations Governing Cryptocurrency Assets.* www.dentons.com/en/insights/articles/2023/april/26/worldwide-wednes-days-dentons-tech-talks-global-cryptocurrency-laws-mica-regulation-in-the-eu#:~:text=EU%20legislators%20aim%20to%20restore,to%2018-month%20transition%20period.

particular transaction. It's like watching airplane traffic in cyberspace. The site automatically adjusts the language based on your location.

Mempool.space link

Nodes

Think of nodes—computers linked to the blockchain network and those who operate them, the miners or validators, as traffic cops responsible for maintaining the integrity of the blockchain. As discussed, they are the heart of the network that is charged with validating transactions, building, and validating blocks.

There are 10 different types of nodes,[19] some of whose duties overlap. For the purposes of this book, we will only focus on two. They are full nodes and mining nodes.

Full nodes are responsible for validating complete blockchains and copying and maintaining the complete blockchain ledger. They ensure that the rules governing the blockchain are strictly followed.[20] There are anywhere between 13,000 and 83,000 full nodes overseeing bitcoin, alone.[21] Full nodes do not earn monetary rewards for their work.[22]

Mining nodes are those that create and validate blocks. Miners (the operators) gather transactions into blocks and then attempt to produce a predefined algorithm using expensive computing power. The process

---

[19] Becher. *Blockchain Nodes.* https://builtin.com/blockchain/blockchain-node.
[20] CoinTelegraph. *What Is a Bitcoin Node.* https://cointelegraph.com/bitcoin-for-beginners/what-is-a-bitcoin-node-a-beginners-guide-on-blockchain-nodes.
[21] Ibid.
[22] Sharma. *Full Bitcoin Nodes.* www.investopedia.com/news/running-full-bitcoin-node-investors/#:~:text=While%20there%20are%20no%20monetary,bitcoin%20transactions%20in%20a%20day.

of solving the algorithm is called proof-of-work (PoW). If successful, they earn cryptocurrency coins and transaction fees.[23] Mining nodes are highly competitive, racing the clock to solve the algorithm and earn their reward. It has been estimated that more than one million miners are mining bitcoin.[24]

PoW

In the absence of a centralized authority approving transactions (like a bank approving a debit card purchase), Satoshi advocated for a PoW system that solved the problems of verification and concensus.[25]

For verification, Satoshi would rely on a perfect, impartial system that gave a direct answer removed from emotion. He would rely on a mathematical equation derived from an algorithm. One can question the validity of one plus one equals two, but in the end the answer is straight-forward. For this, he turned to the work of cryptographer and security architect Adam Back.

As you recall from the previous chapter, Back conceptualized PoW as a way to use the hash functions to curb e-mail spam.[26] Simply put, senders would first have to generate a hash using an algorithm program and affix it to e-mails like postage stamps. Then, when that e-mail arrived at the server, the server would recognize the hash, and determining no extra effort (work) had gone into sending that e-mail, allow it to go through. The reasoning behind what Back called Hashcash was that spammers would not want to go through all that trouble to add a *stamp*.[27]

---

[23] Becher. *What Are Blockchain Nodes.* https://builtin.com/blockchain/blockchain-node.

[24] "Buy Bitcoin Worldwide." *Number of Bitcoin Miners.* https://buybitcoinworldwide.com/how-many-bitcoins-are-there/#:~:text=How%20Many%20Bitcoin%20Miners%20Are,1%2C000%2C000%20unique%20individuals%20mining%20bitcoins.

[25] Satoshi. *Bitcoin White Paper.* https://nakamotoinstitute.org/bitcoin/.

[26] Back. *Denial of Service Counter-Measure.* https://nakamotoinstitute.org/static/docs/hashcash.pdf.

[27] Biz Vlogs. *HashCash.* www.youtube.com/watch?v=YUTwqG6e8LY&ab_channel=BizVlogs.

NUTS AND BOLTS   37

Satoshi recognized that it was necessary to ensure the integrity of transactions if blockchain was to have credibility. With no third party to approve or disapprove transactions, he turned to Back's work as the best way to validate transactions. It had to be difficult. If it were easy, anyone could do it.

The PoW model would involve using an algorithm program that had to produce a specified number of zeros at the beginning of the solution. In this case, bitcoin uses SHA-256, then the latest generation of SHA with a hashing value of 256 bits, created by the U.S. National Security Agency. Satoshi knew it would require a lot of computing power to get the solution to create a block,[28] which is one of the major criticisms of bitcoin production. More computing power requires more energy. More energy puts a strain on energy supplies and contributes to global warming. More about that later in a later chapter.

Other cryptocurrencies that use PoW to create coins use other hashing systems that prove transactions in seconds. For example, when Ethereum used PoW to verify blocks, the hashing system it used, Keccak-256, was able to create blocks every 10 to 20 seconds.[29]

For our purposes, we will focus on bitcoin as it is the most widely known cryptocurrency.

To find the predetermined solution, six elements in what is called the blockchain header are combined producing a 256-bit string of zeros and ones. In order to complete the block, the program has to generate the correct number of zeros at the beginning of the solution. Those elements in the header, which is used to identify a block, contains the timestamp, the blockchain version (there are four), the Merkle root (a hash of all the transactions in that block), the previous block hash, the difficulty target (how hard will bitcoin make it calculate a block in 10 minutes), and a nonce (number used once), an arbitrary string of numbers miners use to find the correct algorithm.[30] Finding the correct nonce is like finding that unknown variable in an algebra problem necessary to solve an equation.

BLOCK
Components

GENESIS BLOCK

Block header

The program creates a new nonce until the right combination is found. It goes through endless calculations in seconds, so computations need much computing power.

Imagine if you had to find a string of 256 numbers—zeros and ones, with a solution requiring the first 32 digits to be zeros. You do so by flipping a coin where heads are zeros and tails are ones. It might take you a while. Imagine you were in a race with thousands of others and had to come up with the right combination in 10 minutes. This is where computing power comes in. Even a warehouse of computers created to mine bitcoin is no guarantee that any of those nodes will find the correct calculation.

Satoshi calculated each block should take 10 minutes in order to control the number of bitcoins created. This, of course, is an average time. Sometimes it takes longer, and sometimes it takes even less time. The algorithmic solution is assessed every 14 days (2016 blocks) to ensure blocks are not created too quickly or too slowly. If it gets easy, more zeros are required at the beginning of the string. Fewer zeros are needed if the solution proves more difficult, threatening the time limit.

As mentioned, PoW solves the problem of consensus. In the absence of a centralized authority (such as a bank), the job of nodes is to verify the integrity of the block before sending it to additional nodes[31] for further verification. This network ensures the integrity of the data transmitted.[32] Miners that create a verifiable block are rewarded with cryptocurrency and transaction fees.[33] Satoshi reasoned that these fees were necessary to incentivize honest work. The transaction fees are a fraction of transaction fees charged by financial institutions. Based on the computing power of the day, he reasoned it would be cheaper for miners to be paid well and work within the system rather than spending a lot more money buying computer power to cheat it. The odds rested with the honest nodes.

Bitcoin miners were initially rewarded with 50 bitcoins when they created blocks. Given the ease required to mine bitcoins and the fact that only 21 million bitcoins were created, a code was written into the program to reduce the reward, cutting it in half when 210,000 blocks were created. This promoted scarcity and offset inflation.[34] The halving process occurs every four years, as that is how long it takes to create 210,000 blocks. There have been four halvings. The last halving occurred on May 11, 2020,[35] when the reward was reduced from 12.5 bitcoins to 6.25 bitcoins. The next halving is scheduled for April 2024 when the reward will be reduced to 3.125 bitcoins. Of the 21 million bitcoins created, just over 19 million have been mined. The last halving will coincide when the last bitcoin is mined in 2040.

Consensus

There's an old saying that "honesty is the best policy." It was an idea taught to children to encourage them to do the right thing. Satoshi wasn't so naïve. In the absence of a third party, such as a bank, to sort out a

---

[31] *Simply Explained, How a blockchain works.* www.youtube.com/watch?v=SSo_EIwHSd4&t=4s&ab_channel=SimplyExplained.

[32] Geroni. *Blockchain Nodes.* https://101blockchains.com/blockchain-nodes/.

[33] Hooper. *Transaction Fees Explained.* https://cointelegraph.com/explained/transaction-fees-explained.

[34] Whittaker. *Bitcoin Halving.* www.forbes.com/advisor/investing/cryptocurrency/bitcoinhalving/#:~:text=The%20Bitcoin%20halving%20is%20when, counteract%20inflation%20by%20maintaining%20scarcity.

[35] Conway. *What Is Bitcoin Halving.* www.investopedia.com/bitcoin-halving-4843769#:~:text=Bitcoin%20last%20halved%20on%20May,maximum%20supply%20of%2021%20million.

transaction, blockchain would need to create a network where the goal is to earn money by embracing the PoW model.

But having just one person verify a claim doesn't necessarily make it so. This is why, he suggested a network of nodes to verify the work done to create the block, which requires them to verify the hash created by the successful miner. Still, that wasn't enough. Someone could come along and tamper with the blocks by creating a new hash and starting a new chain (fork) with corrupted data. The block was going in one direction, while someone could take control of a particular block and create a new blockchain, beginning with the hijacked block. Recall the example of Jack's doctored photos from the last chapter.

To avoid this problem, Satoshi advocated for creating consensus, or as you know it, majority rule.

How would you define a majority? Everyone? Ninety percent? What number would be the best representative of a majority? Satoshi chose 51 percent, which makes sense given the number of miners, time constraints, and size.

Miners pick up transactions to form blocks verified repeatedly by other nodes, who then make their own copies of the blockchain. Over time, some block branches grow longer, which Satoshi assumed would result in some nodes leaving the blockchain branch they were on and moving to the longer chain, believing it to be the correct one.[36]

The more people working on one blockchain branch, the more agreement there is that the blocks are correct, making it harder for someone to hijack it.

Once the block is created, others in the network validate it by comparing the new hash to the previous hash block.

Bitcoin transactions must be confirmed between three and six times, depending on the amount sent.[37] Some exchanges only require three confirmations, while others only need one.[38]

---

[36] Satoshi. *Bitcoin White Paper*. https://nakamotoinstitute.org/bitcoin/.

[37] Tuwiner. *Bitcoin Confirmations*. https://buybitcoinworldwide.com/confirmations/.

[38] GoCardless. *Validating Bitcoin Transactions*. https://gocardless.com/en-us/guides/posts/bitcoin-transaction-verification/#:~:text=Some%20exchanges%20will%20process%20a,confirmed%20at%20least%20three%20times.

As mentioned earlier and later in this book, PoW requires a great deal of computational power, especially to mine bitcoins. To speed up the process and greatly reduce energy consumption, many blockchains use a consensus method known as proof of stake (PoS). The Ethereum blockchain, which used PoW, conducted a *hard fork* and switched to PoS on September 15, 2022, ending mining. Another energy-saving alternative is called proof of authority (PoA).

PoS

PoS is a consensus mechanism where cryptocurrency holders put up or stake a set amount of their currency for the right to validate blocks.[39] Anyone wishing to become a validator on the Ethereum blockchain must stake a minimum of 32 ETH.[40] On September 21, 2023, one ETH was worth U.S.$1,619.94.

The job of these validators also includes keeping records.[41]

Unlike miners who compete to find the right computation, these validators are chosen at random. So, the more coins one puts up, the greater the chance of being selected. Some pool their money with other validators, increasing their opportunity to create blocks and earn rewards.[42]

A validator checks the transactions in the block to make sure they are accurate. The Ethereum model creates groups of 128 validators, of which one creates the block, while others validate it. Like PoW, PoS requires 51 percent consensus, which makes attacks difficult as so much money would be necessary for bad actors to take control of a blockchain.

---

[39] Daly. *What Is Proof of Stake.* www.fool.com/investing/stock-market/market-sectors/financials/cryptocurrency-stocks/proof-of-stake/.

[40] Frankenfield. *What Proof-of-Stake Means.* www.investopedia.com/terms/p/proof-stake-pos.asp.

[41] Ibid.

[42] Daly. *What Is Proof of Stake.* www.fool.com/investing/stock-market/market-sectors/financials/cryptocurrency-stocks/proof-of-stake/.

Validators are rewarded if the block's information is correct[43] but risk financial penalties if they produce bad or fraudulent transactions.[44]

Unlike PoW, PoS requires a fraction of the energy as there are no algorithms to process. In 2022, Ethereum mining used between 46.31 terawatt hours (TWh) and 93.98 TWh per year. After the blockchain switched to PoS, energy consumption related to Ethereum dropped 99.99 percent.[45]

Concerns about PoS include fears those with larger stakes can have an undue influence to validate transactions.[46]

PoA

A term coined in 2017 by Gavin Wood, a co-founder of Ethereum, PoA is another consensus algorithm whereby validators, who have undergone a rigorous background check, earn the right to validate transactions and create blocks using a software program.[47] It's an automated process, so the validators don't need to constantly monitor their computers.[48]

One benefit to PoA is that the program's hardware doesn't have to be expensive, as the calculations are not as difficult as PoW.[49] Because the system is automated, blocks are produced at regular intervals and are programmed to protect against a 51 percent attack.[50]

While PoA can be used for public blockchains, it is more likely to be used for private blockchains and therefore requires permission to access.[51]

---

[43] Ibid.

[44] Napoletano and Curry. *Proof of Stake Explained.* www.forbes.com/advisor/investing/cryptocurrency/proof-of-stake/.

[45] Sarkar. *Ethereum's Merge Reduces Power Consumption.* https://cointelegraph.com/news/the-merge-brings-down-ethereum-s-network-power-consumption-by-over-99-9.

[46] Daly. *What Is Proof of Stake.* www.fool.com/investing/stock-market/market-sectors/financials/cryptocurrency-stocks/proof-of-stake/.

[47] Antolin. *What Is Proof-of-Authority.* www.coindesk.com/learn/what-is-proof-of-authority/.

[48] Ibid.

[49] "Apla Blockchain Platform Guide." *Proof-of-Authority Consensus.* https://apla.readthedocs.io/en/latest/concepts/consensus.html.

[50] Ibid.

[51] Rousey. *Proof of Authority Guide.* https://changelly.com/blog/what-is-proof-of-authority-poa/.

Storage

The rules of blockchain require that information about transactions be stored in perpetuity. That's a lot of information that has to be stored somewhere. It was an issue Satoshi addressed in his white paper, which the thousand or so other blockchains address in their own way.

Transactions themselves don't take up a lot of space. Using tools like Merkle trees, Merkle roots, and a process called *sharding*, transaction information can be easily broken down into smaller, specific pieces and stored worldwide while taking little space.

A Merkle tree is a *tree* where each *leaf* is the cryptographic hash of a data block.[52] A Merkle root is the hash of all the transactions that are part of a block.[53]

Satoshi suggested that nodes use a Merkle tree to list transactions, pare down repetitive information to the basic information necessary to identify the transaction, and then hash that information to create the root.[54] Some blockchains, including bitcoin, use it today. Others use sharding, basically breaking up large blocks of data or platforms into smaller, more manageable ones.[55] As blockchains have grown in purpose, there was a recognition there would need to be a means for improving performance. Sharding can enhance scalability. Blockchain was designed for nodes to be responsible for maintaining records on their network, which causes the network to slow down.[56] Sharding reduces the amount of information they are required to oversee while helping to speed up the network.[57]

---

[52] Simplilearn. *Merkle Tree in Blockchain.* www.simplilearn.com/tutorials/blockchain-tutorial/merkle-tree-in-blockchain#:~:text=It's%20a%20mathematical%20data%20structure,and%20content%20of%20the%20data.

[53] Frankenfield. *What Is a Merkle Root.* www.investopedia.com/terms/m/merkle-root-cryptocurrency.asp.

[54] Satoshi. *Bitcoin White Paper.* https://nakamotoinstitute.org/bitcoin/.

[55] Howell. *Blockchain Sharding.* https://101blockchains.com/what-is-blockchain-sharding/#:~:text=In%20the%20case%20of%20sharding,latency%20and%20prevent%20data%20overload.

[56] Fuentes. *What Is Sharding.* www.rootstrap.com/blog/what-is-sharding-and-how-is-it-helping-blockchain-protocols/#:~:text=The%20most%20important%20advantage%20of,significantly%20slowing%20down%20transaction%20times.

[57] Ibid.

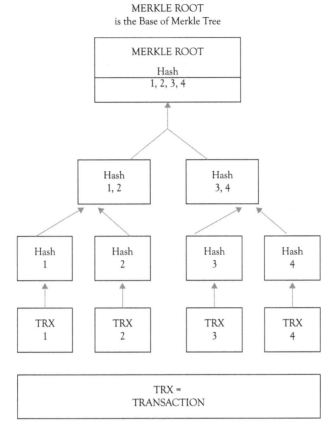

Merkle tree

There is an issue regarding security. With each node recording its own data, there is a concern that a hacker could infiltrate the shard and corrupt or take it over.[58]

As of June 2023, there were about 1,000 blockchains,[59] each containing thousands of blocks. The average size of a bitcoin block is 1 MB, although realistically, it could hold 2 MB. Still, some argue one bitcoin block could hold up to 4 MB.[60]

[58] Frankenfield. *What Is Sharding.* www.investopedia.com/terms/s/sharding.asp.

[59] McGovern. *Number of Blockchains in 2023.* https://earthweb.com/how-many-blockchains-are-there/.

[60] Bitcoin Magazine. *Bitcoin Blocksize Limit.* https://bitcoinmagazine.com/guides/what-is-the-bitcoin-block-size-limit.

The bitcoin blockchain occupied less than 1 GB up to February 2009 and continued a slow and steady growth rate until 2014, when it began to expand by as much as 1 GB every few days.[61] As of August 21, 2023, bitcoin blockchain size reached 493.28. GB.[62]

An Alternative or the Future?

Blockchain offers an alternative method for sending and receiving data while giving control back to users, not corporations. The success of blockchain, which faces hurdles, is central to driving the next generation of the World Wide Web, referred to as Web3.

As you will read in the following chapters, a cross-section of businesses, industries, services, and governments worldwide are betting on this technology. They are using blockchain to store land records, vote, share medical records, purchase property, and buy stock, to name a few.

Others aren't so sure, pointing to many problems based on today's computer architecture.

For one, there's the matter of scale. Take bitcoin transactions, for example. Today, bitcoin can handle 4.6 transactions per second. Visa, on the other hand, averages some 1,700 transactions per second.[63] Visa transactions require a 14-step process involving at least six different commercial entities.[64]

One of the most significant issues blockchain faces is the large amounts of energy required for PoW, a topic to be discussed in more depth in the next chapter. The blockchain ecosystem is mindful of this and moving to reduce energy consumption.

There is also the issue of regulation. Today, governments are looking at ensuring blockchain technology won't be used for nefarious purposes

---

[61] de Best. *Size of Bitcoin Blockchain From 2009–2022*. www.statista.com/statistics/647523/worldwide-bitcoin-blockchain-size/.

[62] Ibid.

[63] L. Kenny. *Blockchain Scalability Problem*. https://towardsdatascience.com/the-blockchain-scalability-problem-the-race-for-visa-like-transaction-speed-5cce48f9d44.

[64] Blocknative. *Liquidity 2020*. www.youtube.com/watch?v=aZPx7K8XI68&t=932s&ab_channel=Blocknative.

such as tax evasion, funding terrorism, and shielding assets garnered in drug, slave, or sex trafficking.

The goals set by proponents of blockchain technology are revolutionary, promising to change the technological landscape for the foreseeable future. Meeting those goals while answering the questions that, in effect, challenge the notion of privacy that led to its creation will take time to sort out.

PoW's Dirty Reputation

One of the biggest criticisms facing blockchain is that mining coins or tokens using PoW requires a lot of energy—some of it is dirty energy that contributes to the rising levels of carbon dioxide that help feed global warming.

As of this writing, 2,422 coins, including bitcoin, require PoW to validate transactions.[1]

Some government concerns are so dire that in October 2022, the European Union released draft proposals to label cryptocurrencies based on energy consumption. The EU favors energy-efficient validation such as PoS.[2]

In the case of bitcoin, the high use of energy is by design. In his whitepaper, Satoshi argued that the more computer power the network controlled to create unique hashes, the less likely hackers would be able to hijack the blocks. If a hacker altered one block, they would have to redo the PoW for every block created on that blockchain that preceded the one hijacked. Members of the network would notice the change as they could easily compare it to their copies.[3]

There is no question that high amounts of energy are required. Others who also study the issue, however, disagree on the reported energy levels and the reported levels of carbon emissions.

Energy Consumption

Studies point specifically to bitcoin mining, the most recognized blockchain, as the culprit. Several studies and reports have been made on the energy required to mine coins. Those studies put that energy consumption between 45 terawatts (TWh) and over 100 TWh annually.

---

[1] Cryptoslate. *Proof of Work.* https://cryptoslate.com/cryptos/proof-of-work/.
[2] Keller. *EU Targets Bitcoin Energy Efficiency.* https://forkast.news/eu-bitcoin-energy-efficiency-labelling-crypto/.
[3] Satoshi. *Bitcoin White Paper.* https://nakamotoinstitute.org/bitcoin/.

The world reportedly used 25,530 TWh of electricity in 2022, according to Statista.com.

Two other crucial blockchain elements are communication between nodes and storage, both of which require much less energy.

On the high end, a study by the Swiss Federal Office of Energy focused on the bitcoin blockchain found it required more than 100 TWh per year.[4] At the same time, bitcoin storage used between 33 megawatts (MWh) and 3 gigawatts (GWh) annually. Communication between nodes only required 6 MWh.[5] (There were an estimated 12,000 full nodes in 2021, according to the study.)[6] A full node records blockchain transactions and stores the ledger.

The Swiss study concluded that PoW blockchains should be discouraged in favor of consensus methods that use less energy.[7]

Other studies and news reports offer different findings. One study put the amount at half of 1 percent of all the energy consumed in the world,[8] while another put the amount greater than what is used in Norway,[9] which consumed 123 TWh in 2020.[10]

On the other end, a review by the International Energy Agency[11] determined bitcoin miners used 45 TWh in 2018, a figure corroborated by an independent peer review[12] that found that bitcoin miners used 45.6 TWh that year. That amount is less than Venezuela, which reportedly

---

[4] Swiss Federal Office of Energy. *Blockchain Energy Consumption.* www.vs.inf .ethz.ch/publ/papers/Coroama2021_BlockchainEnergy.pdf.

[5] Ibid.

[6] Ibid.

[7] Ibid.

[8] Huang, O'Neill, and Tabuchi. *Bitcoin's Excessive Energy Demands.* www.nytimes .com/interactive/2021/09/03/climate/bitcoin-carbon-footprint-electricity.html.

[9] Schmidt. *Why Bitcoin Uses so Much Energy.* www.forbes.com/advisor/investing/ cryptocurrency/bitcoins-energy-usage-explained/#:~:text=It's%20estimated%20 that%20Bitcoin%20consumes,annual%20electricity%20consumption%20 of%20Norway.

[10] Enerdata. *Norway Energy Information.* www.enerdata.net/estore/energy-market/norway/.

[11] G. Kamiya. *Bitcoin Energy Use.* www.iea.org/commentaries/bitcoin-energy-use-mined-the-gap.

[12] Stoll, Klaaßen, and Gallersdörfer. *Bitcoin's Carbon Footprint.* www.cell.com/joule/ fulltext/S2542-4351(19)30255-7?_returnURL=https%3A%2F%2Flinkinghub .elsevier.com%2Fretrieve%2Fpii%2FS2542435119302557%3Fshowall%3Dtrue.

consumed 56 TWh a year later.[13] The IEA found that bitcoin miners used 29 TWh during the first six months of 2019.[14] And yet another study cited in the IEA report put mining usage at 35 TWh in 2018 and 41 TWh in 2019.[15]

A 2020 study, *The Energy Consumption of Blockchain: Beyond Myth*, determined that while there could be no doubt that mining used a lot of energy, a true measurement is hard to determine, given unknowns such as the number of miners, the hardware being used, and the amount of work being put in to arrive at solutions, so their focus turned to extremes— high- and low-end energy demand, depending on the coin being mined.[16] Bitcoin requires more energy because of the difficulty necessary to solve its algorithm. It is also a fact that energy costs in some countries are far cheaper than in others. The 2020 study determined more work needed to be done to determine actual usage.

Carbon Emissions

Regarding greenhouse gas emissions, two studies concluded mining Bitcoin could raise temperature levels by as much as 2°C within 30 years, if not sooner.[17]

One study in *Nature Climate Change* published in October 2018 examined the rate of electricity paid per kilowatt hour (KWh) and the carbon equivalent. Based on its growth rate, following similar growth patterns of other generally accepted technologies in the early stages, it could create an electricity demand that could raise carbon emissions by 2°C within three decades, if not sooner.[18] The study stated that reducing bitcoin's carbon footprint "should not rest only on some yet-to-be-developed

---

[13] Wikipedia. *Electric Energy Consumption*. https://en.wikipedia.org/wiki/Electric_energy_consumption.

[14] Kamiya. *Bitcoin Energy Use*. www.iea.org/commentaries/bitcoin-energy-use-mined-the-gap.

[15] Ibid.

[16] Sedlmeir, Buhl, Fridgen, and Keller. *Blockchain Energy Consumption*. https://link.springer.com/article/10.1007/s12599-020-00656-x#Sec9.

[17] Mora, Rollins, Taladay, Kantar, Chock, Shamada, and Franklin. *Bitcoin Emissions Could Push Global Warming*. www.researchgate.net/publication/328581842_Bitcoin_emissions_alone_could_push_global_warming_above_2C.

[18] Ibid.

hardware," but rather by using simple measures such as increasing the number of transactions per block[19] (now at 2,000), an idea some agree is possible. Another suggestion was to reduce the difficulty level needed to find the correct algorithm to create a block.[20]

The paper was immediately criticized as "dangerous, irresponsible, and misleading."[21] Following the paper's release, *ThinkProgress* contracted experts who roundly challenged the paper's assumptions that, for instance, technology would remain unchanged and bitcoin's energy demands would remain unchanged for the foreseeable future, even though steps were already taking place in blockchains to improve efficiency.[22]

One critic noted that when the paper was published, bitcoin's electricity use only constituted one-tenth of one percent of global electricity usage.[23] That's a drop in the bucket compared to the amount of greenhouse gasses produced by the transportation sector and industry.[24] In 2022, global carbon emissions from fossil fuels and industry were estimated at 37.5 gigatons of carbon dioxide ($GtCO_2$), according to Statista .com. One gigaton is equivalent to one billion metric tons, of 10,000 fully-loaded U.S. aircraft carriers, according to the National Aeronautics and Space Administration (NASA).

Another study focused on blockchain operations in China, drawing conclusions based on the *theory of carbon footprint* for creating a theoretical model to determine their findings.

China banned bitcoin mining in 2021. Despite the crackdown, bitcoin mining went underground and continues in earnest. China now ranks second in the world in bitcoin mining.[25]

The findings of this study on bitcoin mining in China are based on the lucrative nature of bitcoin mining, which requires greater computer power

---

[19] Ibid.

[20] Ibid.

[21] Romm. *Experts Debunk Study.* https://thinkprogress.org/experts-debunk-dangerous-and-misleading-study-hyping-bitcoin-energy-use-8f8744672611/.

[22] Ibid.

[23] Ibid.

[24] Ibid.

[25] Shen. *China Banned Bitcoin Mining but No.2 in Bitcoin Mining.* https://forkast.news/china-banned-bitcoin-mining-became-no-2-bitcoin-miner/.

and energy, creating more emissions.[26] Their model looked at Bitcoin miners in coal and hydroelectric regions to draw a complete picture.

As energy prices increase and the reward for solving the bitcoin algorithm decreases when the reward for it is again halved, these researchers believe miners will stop mining in China. They deduce that energy consumption for bitcoin miners will peak in 2024 at 296.59 TWh, equivalent to the combined power consumption of Italy and Saudi Arabia in 2016. This peak will result in peaking greenhouse emissions of 130.5 million metric tons attributed to mining, greater than the Czech Republic and Qatar's combined emissions reported in 2016.[27]

The criticism surrounding bitcoin mining energy use has sparked many dire headlines over the years. *Newsweek* famously wrote in December 2017 that, based on estimates, bitcoin mining would consume all available electricity by 2020.[28]

Computer technology, in general, is no stranger to criticism. In an article in *Forbes* published in 1999, the author predicted that the demand for electricity to power computers was outstripping the computer industry's efforts to improve efficiencies. This, the writer contended, could dramatically impact energy supplies.[29] The gist of that article was that despite improvements made to personal computers, their peripherals, and the Internet, the digital age was taxing the energy grid and would dramatically drive up energy demands.[30] Large websites, the author wrote, consumed the same amount of electricity as a small village.[31]

At this time, determining the amount of energy consumed by blockchain technology presents challenges that have yet to be resolved.[32]

---

[26] Jiang, Li, Lu, Hong, Guan, Xiong, and Wang. *Carbon Emissions Policy Assessment in China.* www.nature.com/articles/s41467-021-22256-3.

[27] Ibid.

[28] Cuthbertson. *Bitcoin Mining to Consume All Electricity by 2020.* www.newsweek.com/bitcoin-mining-track-consume-worlds-energy-2020-744036.

[29] Forbes. *Dig More Coal—PCs Coming.* www.forbes.com/forbes/1999/0531/6311070a.html?sh=697e414a2580.

[30] Ibid.

[31] Ibid.

[32] Sedlmier, Buhl, Fridgen, and Keller. *Blockchain Energy Consumption.* https://link.springer.com/article/10.1007/s12599-020-00656-x#Sec9.

Even so, blockchain developers and their supporters are aware of the criticism and are working to improve efficiencies to reduce the carbon footprint created by this technology.

Now that we have defined blockchain, how it works, and concerns raised about energy consumption, the remainder of this section will focus on how blockchain technology is used in the public and private sectors.

Blockchain and the Supply Chain

A growing segment of consumers is obsessed with food quality. Wanting healthy food and concerned about the use of pesticides, additives, and harvesting conditions, health-conscious consumers are flocking to food labels claiming the contents are *organic*.

Organic food sales have steadily increased since 2000, with huge spikes during the global pandemic when global sales of organic food jumped from U.S.$106 billion in 2019 to U.S.$120.65 billion in 2020.[1]

The rise in sales has attracted fraudsters looking to cash in on the growing trend. Food fraud globally costs consumers between U.S.$40 and U.S.$50 billion annually compared to U.S.$10 and U.S.$15 billion the decade before.[2]

Business concerns looking to get a handle on food fraud and other supply chain issues are turning to blockchain technology for solutions.

Blockchain technology allows users to record prices and determine the place of origin, quantity, quality, and delivery, all in real time.[3] It provides each supply participant involved in the product production with a copy of the production data.[4]

Blockchain technology allows participants to verify the legitimacy of a product, whether it be a pair of jeans, pharmaceutical drugs, or a bushel of corn, all based on the product's paperwork.[5] With the transparent ledger, the creation of those products can be tracked from start to finish.

---

[1] Shahbandeh. *Worldwide Organic Food Sales 1999–2020.* www.statista.com/statistics/273090/worldwide-sales-of-organic-foods-since-1999/.

[2] FreshByte Software. *Food Fraud Costs Billions.* www.freshbyte.com/blog/food-fraud-costs-billions-each-year.

[3] Pahulje. *Supply Chain Transparency With Blockchain.* https://blog.flexis.com/achieving-supply-chain-transparency-through-blockchain.

[4] Ibid.

[5] Gaur and Gaiha. *Transparent Supply Chain.* https://hbr.org/2020/05/building-a-transparent-supply-chain.

Producers and retailers are keenly aware that consumers are paying close attention to how foreign products are produced, under what conditions they are made, and whether the materials used are genuine or counterfeit.

Blockchain is also being used today in a handful of industries to verify how and where products are produced, that they are produced in locations that provide safe working conditions, and that their employees are paid competitive wages.[6] Blockchain technology also guards against substandard and counterfeit products.[7]

This transparent audit allows parties to review the process, catch errors, verify that supply and manufacturing standards have been met, and hold parties accountable if those standards are not met. Because blockchain information cannot be altered, there is no way for a supplier or manufacturer to cheat and change the report to reflect otherwise.[8]

Globalization has brought food production into sharp focus. With manufacturers scrambling to reassure customers that their products are produced ethically and made with pure ingredients, putting that information on a blockchain adds one more layer of legitimacy to help alleviate consumers' concerns.

Tracking the Food Supply

Consumers and producers are already benefiting from blockchain technology. In partnership with IBM, Walmart began a tracking program with two other entities in 2016 to follow pork and pork products coming out of China.[9]

Alibaba, China's leading online retailer, launched a trial program in 2018 that allows shoppers to verify the authenticity of food bought

[6] Mehra and Dale. *How Blockchain Can Deliver Fair Labor in Supply Chains*. https://reliefweb.int/report/world/how-humanitarian-blockchain-can-deliver-fair-labor-global-supply-chains.

[7] Deloitte. *Blockchain and Supply Chain Transparency*. www2.deloitte.com/us/en/pages/operations/articles/blockchain-supply-chain-innovation.html.

[8] Emergen Research. *Top Companies in Blockchain Supply Chain*. www.emergen-research.com/blog/top-7-leading-companies-in-the-blockchain-supply-chain-industry.

[9] Sristy. *Blockchain in Food Supply Chain*. https://one.walmart.com/content/globaltechindia/en_in/Tech-insights/blog/Blockchain-in-the-food-supply-chain.html.

online by scanning a code on the packaging using their mobile device. The program was implemented to combat fake food products from New Zealand and Australia.[10]

When Anheuser-Busch InBev launched a beer brand in Zambia in 2015 using cassava (a nutty-flavored, starchy root vegetable) instead of barley, working with small farmers proved difficult. The company had to deal with poor recordkeeping coupled with payment issues because those farmers didn't have access to banks. Using blockchain technology, they could track the quality of cassava from farmers while simultaneously providing them with electronic payments for their crops.[11]

Coffee growers in Kenya, women, in particular, are benefiting from the blockchain. Historically, earnings for Kenyan coffee growers weren't enough to bring them above the poverty level. Kenyan women, who only own 1 percent of land but do 90 percent of the work, largely go uncompensated.[12] Kahawa (1893), founded by Kenyan Margaret Nyamumbo, a third-generation coffee grower with a business degree from Harvard University, partnered with technology company Bext360 to provide a blockchain solution.[13] This technology company utilizes blockchain to streamline supply chains to cut out the middleman. As a result of this partnership, farmers are now getting their fair share of the coffee beans they produce. Furthermore, Nyamumbo is dedicating 25 percent of company profits to providing women credit so that they can participate in the coffee trade.[14] In addition, consumers can use the blockchain to tip farmers simply by scanning a QR code on the packaging.[15]

---

[10] Millward. *Alibaba Rolls Out Blockchain Pilot.* www.techinasia.com/alibaba-fake-food-blockchain-pilot.

[11] Knapp. *AB InBev Banking on African Farmers.* www.forbes.com/sites/alexknapp/2019/04/16/this-buds-for-blockchain/?sh=62d944845966.

[12] McCormick. *Blockchain Solution That Deserves the Buzz.* www.forbes.com/sites/meghanmccormick/2019/08/30/finally-one-blockchain-solution-that-deserves-the-buzz/?sh=496bf5684f9b.

[13] Morpheus Labs. *Bridging Supply Chain With Blockchain.* www.morpheuslabs.io/bridging-supply-chain-and-its-future-with-blockchain/.

[14] McCormick. *Blockchain Solution That Deserves the Buzz.* www.forbes.com/sites/meghanmccormick/2019/08/30/finally-one-blockchain-solution-that-deserves-the-buzz/?sh=496bf5684f9b.

[15] Ibid.

Monitoring Quality and Working Conditions

The fashion world uses blockchain to protect its brand against a global counterfeit market worth billions of dollars. Additionally, the industry is well aware of consumers' environmental concerns, preferring that products be produced ecofriendly. Media reports have also heightened awareness regarding the treatment of workers.[16]

London-based fashion designer Martine Jarlgaard was the first, teaming up with technology company Provenance in 2017 to launch a pilot blockchain project to track the creation of clothing from start to finish. Each garment was assigned a unique digital token (more about tokens later), so Provenance could track its movement, allowing for full transparency and traceability of each item.[17]

The industrywide movement to incorporate blockchain would allow consumers to support legitimate fashion labels while weeding out the bad actors.

Concerned about working conditions and the political climate in which diamonds are produced, London-based De Beers, the leading manufacturer of diamonds, launched a pilot blockchain program in 2020 that successfully tracked 100 high-value diamonds from the mine to the diamond cutter, polisher, to the jewelry store.[18]

Blockchain can ferret out counterfeit drugs and remove them from the supply chain. The counterfeit drug business, which poses a grave health risk to consumers, was worth U.S.$200 billion in 2020.[19] Blockchain could stop that, ensuring consumers received genuine pharmaceuticals that did not negatively impact their health.

---

[16] Everledger. *Fashion Brands and Blockchain.* https://everledger.io/how-fashion-brands-are-taking-advantage-of-blockchain-apparel/.

[17] Arthur. *Blockchain Is Aiding This Fashion Collection With Transparency.* www.forbes.com/sites/rachelarthur/2017/05/10/garment-blockchain-fashion-transparency/?sh=3fee631974f3.

[18] Henderson. *De Beers Tracks Diamonds Using Blockchain.* https://supplychaindigital.com/technology/de-beers-tracks-100-diamonds-through-supply-chain-using-blockchain.

[19] Mikulic. *U.S. Economic Loss From Counterfeit Drugs 2020.* www.statista.com/statistics/1181283/us-cost-due-to-counterfeit-drugs-by-scenario/#:~:text=Based%20on%20estimates%20saying%20the,revenues%20in%20the%20United%20States.

The Drug Chain Supply Chain Security Act (DSCSA) was enacted by the U.S. Congress on November 27, 2013, to create an interoperable system to identify and trace certain prescription drugs distributed in the United States.[20]

An interoperable system is defined as the ability of one computer system to share data with another.

The law set incremental dates for enactment, with 2023 being the year the interoperable system was to be operational. To meet the challenge, Chronicled, a San Francisco-based tech company, and The LinkLab LLC, also of San Francisco, announced in 2017, they would use the MediLedger Network, a blockchain program it administers for the life sciences and health care industries, to tackle counterfeit drugs.[21] The blockchain would track and trace pharmaceutical drugs and prevent counterfeit medicines from entering the supply chain.[22]

This program, and others like it, could trace the source of counterfeit drugs and accelerate investigations and recalls, providing consumers with safely produced drugs.[23]

Energy

In 2018, the Abu Dhabi National Oil Company announced a partnership with IBM to set up a pilot blockchain project to *track, validate and execute* transactions from the well to the customer.[24]

---

[20] U.S. Food and Drug Administration. *Drug Supply Chain Security Act.* www.fda.gov/drugs/drug-supply-chain-integrity/drug-supply-chain-security-act-dscsa#:~:text=The%20Drug%20Quality%20and%20Security,distributed%20in%20the%20United%20States.

[21] Chronicled. *Blockchain Project to Safeguard Pharmaceuticals Announced.* www.prnewswire.com/news-releases/chronicled-and-the-linklab-announce-the-mediledger-project-a-revolutionary-blockchain-backed-system-to-safeguard-the-pharmaceutical-industry-300522426.html.

[22] Brett. *MediLedger and Blockchain.* www.enterprisetimes.co.uk/2018/05/08/mediledger-chronicled-and-blockchain/.

[23] Ibid.

[24] Ledger Insights. *Abu Dhabi Oil, IBM Blockchain Supply Chain Pilot.* www.ledgerinsights.com/abu-dhabi-oil-ibm-blockchain/.

Power companies and utilities are also looking at incorporating blockchain to improve efficiency and cut costs.[25]

In 2018, WePower, a green energy trading company matching energy producers with wholesale buyers,[26] teamed up to tokenize energy data related to Estonia's power grid consumption and production. The data were uploaded onto the Ethereum blockchain, which converted the information into blocks.[27] Hourly data were gathered from 700,000 households and converted into energy tokens. Each token represents one KWh of power that can be sold on the wholesale energy market.[28]

WePower uploaded 26,000 hours and 24 TWh of energy consumption data to the Ethereum blockchain and subsequently created 39 billion energy tokens,[29] each representing one KWh of power, that can be sold on the wholesale energy market.[30]

In Australia, blockchain startup Power Ledger came together with developer Nicheliving to create a microgrid trading platform where residents on 100 of their properties can sell excess energy to neighbors, using blockchain to make trades.[31]

In Spain, Acciona Energy and Iberdrola, two of the country's largest energy companies, have turned to blockchain technology to prove the renewable power they supply is 100 percent renewable. Acciona incorporated blockchain technology into two of its renewable storage facilities—a wind storage facility and a solar energy facility, to guarantee the energy it

---

[25] Khodaei. *Utilities Assess Decentralizing Power Grid With Blockchain.* https://utilityanalytics.com/2021/09/utilities-assess-benefits-and-challenges-of-decentralizing-the-power-grid-through-blockchain-technology/.

[26] Moskvitch. *Estonia Looks at Blockchain.* www.wired.co.uk/article/blockchain-energy-renewables-estonia-tokenisation.

[27] J. Deign. *WePower Tokenizes Grid.* www.greentechmedia.com/articles/read/wepower-is-the-first-blockchain-firm-to-tokenize-an-entire-grid.

[28] Ibid.

[29] Moskvitch. *Estonia Looks at Blockchain.* www.wired.co.uk/article/blockchain-energy-renewables-estonia-tokenisation.

[30] J. Deign. *WePower Tokenizes Grid.* www.greentechmedia.com/articles/read/wepower-is-the-first-blockchain-firm-to-tokenize-an-entire-grid.

[31] Heasman. *Blockchain-Based Microgrid in Australia.* https://decrypt.co/26478/power-ledger-rolls-out-blockchain-based-microgrid-in-australia.

produces is 100 percent from renewable sources.[32] For its part, Iberdrola, which provides power to 100 million customers, uses blockchain technology to provide information about the energy created at its wind farms and hydroelectric plant.[33]

Two other projects, one in the United States and one in South Africa, allow consumers to trade energy tokens with others. The Brooklyn (NY) Microgrid program allows grid members to buy, sell, and trade excess energy captured from their solar panels with the excess energy stored on their grid. The Sun Exchange program in South Africa involves private investors who erect solar panels in areas of the country where solar power is the most efficient, then lease those panels to schools and businesses.[34]

Blockchain technology is also being used as a conduit for charging electric vehicles. Share&Charge Foundation, based in Essen, Germany, connects open peer-to-peer (P2P) charging stations with electric vehicle owners.[35] Owners of charging poles who join the network can set their price for a charge. Owners of electric vehicles use an app to locate a charging pole and pay using the blockchain.[36]

Chargemap, a French-based company, offers similar services, ensuring users that the electricity they use to charge their vehicles comes from 100 percent renewable energy sources.[37]

[32] Power Technology. *Blockchain Technology at Two Spanish Storage Facilities.* www.power-technology.com/news/acciona-uses-blockchain-technology-two-storage-facilities-spain/.

[33] Ledger Insights. *Spain's Iberdrola Adopts Blockchain.* www.ledgerinsights.com/iberdrola-blockchain-renewable-energy-proof/.

[34] Ellsmoor. *Companies Spearheading Blockchain for Renewable Energy.* www.forbes.com/sites/jamesellsmoor/2019/04/27/meet-5-companies-spearheading-blockchain-for-renewable-energy/?sh=5c5f37d9f2ae.

[35] Lei, Masanet, and Koomey. *Analyzing Direct Energy Use on Blockchain.* www.sciencedirect.com/science/article/pii/S0301421521002925.

[36] Share&Charge Foundation. *Share and Charge.* www.youtube.com/watch?v=7TBR1nq83tE&ab_channel=Share%26ChargeFoundation.

[37] Lei, Masanet, and Koomey. *Analyzing Direct Energy Use on Blockchain.* www.sciencedirect.com/science/article/pii/S0301421521002925.

Shipping

Goods travel the globe the way they have always done. They are packed in cartons, put into crates and shipping containers, then sent out by air, rail, or sea. Not much has changed. Large barges pull into port and are offloaded by dockworkers to await transportation to their next or final destination. The paperwork is the same. Aside from using barcodes to track items, the paper trail still relies on physical paper being passed along, which is how it was done 100 years ago. Startups have attempted to modernize the process, meeting with limited success.[38]

As with other assets, the paperwork could be tokenized and shared on the blockchain providing an open account of each item shipped from start to finish while reducing paperwork and the possibility for errors.[39]

Blockchain offers the kind of transparency consumers are looking for to ensure the products they buy are safe and produced in a way that mirrors the high standards they expect.

---

[38] Consensys. *Blockchain for Global Trade and Commerce.* https://consensys.net/blockchain-use-cases/global-trade-and-commerce/.

[39] Ibid.

Blockchain and Health Care

Keeping up with your medical records can be daunting, especially if you suffer from a chronic illness. Bouncing from one specialist to the next, a folder full of medical information (history, tests, medications, CT scans, and X-rays), you find yourself explaining and re-explaining every ailment and symptom you have experienced, what treatment you received or are currently receiving, and what drugs you are taking. Each office only has its own set of records for the treatment it provides you, so you have to provide that information to your other doctors so they can amend your file.

Having to go to the emergency room can be a frightening experience. Whether it's you or your family member, you find yourself not only trying to tell the attendant what's wrong, but you have to remember what medicines you or your family member are taking and are allergic to, if any. What they know about you is reduced to lines of notes on a clipboard taken when you enter the hospital.

Medical information is no longer just paper. A number of apps available from your app store, some of which connect to wearable monitors, allow you to keep tabs on your blood pressure, heart rate, glucose, and so on, providing ease of use and convenience. On the other hand, if that information found its way to your health insurance company, it could be used against you.[1]

Blockchain addresses these issues by allowing you to keep your medical records encrypted in one place that can be quickly and effortlessly shared with anyone who needs them.

Recordkeeping

Estonia, located in the Baltic region north of Europe, is considered one of the most digitally progressive countries in the world. They launched a

---

[1] Robeznieks. *Insurers Want Patients to Use Wearables.* www.ama-assn.org/practice-management/digital/insurers-want-patients-use-wearables-could-be-problem.

blockchain program in 2016 to digitize and encrypt medical records for 1.3 million residents.[2] Estonians are issued *smart cards* that provide access to those records, stored on a cloud, and accessible at 1,000 government portals. The records are timestamped and cannot be altered.[3]

On the one hand, Estonia's example of blockchain's capabilities in storing immutable encrypted records is to be applauded, demonstrating that such an undertaking is possible. On the other hand, the government is in charge of maintaining those records. In the blockchain ecosystem, individuals manage those records, not a third party, much less the government.

Patientory, Atlanta, GA, first built a platform on the blockchain for electronic medical records so that they could be shared by patients seamlessly with doctors and other caregivers.[4] The platform then created an app, allowing users to create and store their medical records and instructions and track doctor's appointments and medical bills.[5]

Coral Health, Boston, MA, offers an app compliant with the Health Insurance Portability and Accountability Act of 1996 (HIPPA). The app, created in 2018, incentivizes individuals to collect all their medical information in one place, which they then control and share on a blockchain.[6]

Others working to consolidate and preserve medical records on the blockchain include Iryo of Slovenia, which created an open-source distributed health care network platform where patients' health records can

[2] Chauhan, Malhotra, Chandak, and students of the International Institute of health Management Research. *Blockchain and Healthcare in Estonia.* https://innohealthmagazine.com/2021/in-focus/what-is-estonia-doing-with-blockchain-in-providing-healthcare-to-its-citizens/.

[3] Ibid.

[4] Волков. *Patientory.* https://medium.com/@BtcetHmaker/patientory-how-it-work-f3e22fad50f0.

[5] Patientory Inc. *Patientory Introduction.* www.youtube.com/watch?v=a464 XQSGmDQ&ab_channel=PatientoryInc.

[6] Batista. *Healthcare Blockchain Startup Announces Healthcare App and Token Sale.* www.medgadget.com/2018/08/healthcare-blockchain-startup-coral-health-announces-health-records-app-and-upcoming-token-sale-interview.html#:~:text=Categories-,Healthcare%20Blockchain%20Startup%20Coral%20Health%20Announces%20Health,and%20Upcoming%20Token%20Sale%20(Interview)&text=Once%20using%20the%20app%2C%20patients,%2C%20healthcare%20organizations%2C%20and%20researchers.

be stored in one uniform system.[7] The consolidated records are immutable and controlled by the patient.[8]

London-based Medichain offers a blockchain platform that allows patients to communicate directly with their doctors for online consultations that are then added to the patient's digital records.[9] Patients can provide their doctors quick access to their records through mobile devices.[10]

These companies represent a handful of startups looking to use blockchain technology to create a model to empower people to manage and control their medical records.

Patients as Medical Collaborators

Blockchain not only makes it possible to share patient records, but it also offers platforms for patients to share their medical conditions, or the medical needs of family members, with medical researchers who use that data to look for breakthroughs. One such company, doc.ai of Palo Alto, CA, is an AI platform that enables machine learning to evaluate medical information to *develop personal health insights and predictive models* through its mobile device app.[11]

Those wishing to participate put their medical information onto the doc.ai app, which *uses deep learning models to form a range of health-related issues.*[12]

Interested parties can also apply to participate in research-sponsored trials for parent groups, pharmaceutical companies, and health care

---

[7] Iryo. *Iryo to Disrupt Medical Data Ownership*. www.prnewswire.com/in/news-releases/healthcare-blockchain-startup-iryo-aims-to-disrupt-medical-data-ownership-by-giving-full-control-to-the-patient-676361703.html.

[8] Iryo. *Iryo Bringing Medical Records to Patients*. www.youtube.com/watch?v=6irGhqNZj68&ab_channel=Iryo

[9] Medichain. *Own Your Health*. https://medicalchain.com/en/.

[10] Medichain. *Medichain Showcase Video*. www.youtube.com/watch?v=cO-prfZBmyw&ab_channel=Medicalchain.

[11] Google Cloud. *doc.ai: Mobile AI App for Medical Research*. https://cloud.google.com/customers/doc-ai.

[12] Ibid.

providers.[13] Research trials currently underway include a study of Crohn's Disease, allergies,[14] and children's seizures.[15]

Those looking to participate in medical trials can do so through New York City-based Embleema, a HIPPA-compliant medical blockchain that allows individuals to share their medical information for trials and be compensated for it. The platform ensures the patient's data remain in the patient's control and cannot be sold or shared without the person's consent.[16] Embleema also allows real-time patient data sharing between hospitals, doctors, and pharmacists.[17]

Taking it a step further, a handful of blockchain startups have created platforms where willing participants can sell their DNA samples directly to research groups and pharmaceutical companies that need samples to create *new drugs, therapies, and diagnostic tests.*[18]

Big pharma and other research groups have gotten DNA samples from companies like 23andMe, which sell home genetic test kits used to track one's ancestry.[19] Recognizing it was not theirs to sell, a handful of blockchain startups are looking to empower consumers and allow them to sell their DNA samples directly if they choose. 23andMe states on hits website it will not provide genetic material to any third party without the customer's explicit consent.

EncrypGen of Coral Springs, FL, set up a data file where individuals looking to sell their DNA can create a profile. The company strips away any identifiable information such as name, e-mail address, and other sensitive information, so when researchers search their database, all they find is a *raw DNA data file.* Researchers go through the database and purchase access to the seller's DNA data with EncrypGen's $DNA tokens if they

---

[13] Ibid.

[14] Ibid.

[15] Doc.ai: a Sharecare company. *doc.ai for Patients and Consumers.* www.youtube.com/watch?v=nWMfRnqr_cA&ab_channel=doc.ai%3AaSharecarecompany.

[16] Spanu. *New Platform Empowers Patients to Own & Share Medical Data.* https://healthcareweekly.com/embleema-blockchain-healthcare/.

[17] Ibid.

[18] Ahmed and Shabani. *DNA Marketplace: An Analysis of Ethical Concerns.* www.frontiersin.org/articles/10.3389/fgene.2019.01107/full#B3.

[19] Zhang. *Big Pharma Would Like Your DNA.* www.theatlantic.com/science/archive/2018/07/big-pharma-dna/566240/.

find a sample they want. Once a sample is selected, the donor is notified and can accept or reject the offer. Another caveat to the company is that donors can remove their files anytime.[20]

LunaDNA, of San Diego, CA, accepts participants if they provide broad consent for studies for which they receive Luna Coin. If a third party, such as an academic researcher or pharmaceutical company, wants to use that sample in clinical trials, LunaDNA facilitates the meeting between the two parties. If the meeting is successful and that company is given permission by the donor to buy the DNA file, the seller gets Luna Coin.[21]

How Blockchain Serves the Medical Community

Blockchain technology is not only empowering the patient, but primary and secondary caregivers are also using it to simplify and manage their records.

Physicians can use blockchain to consolidate their medical certifications, professional references, admitting privileges, work history, and education, to name a few.[22] Keeping up with all that paperwork, which can be stored in multiple places as doctors may serve several hospitals, takes a lot of manual labor to manage. Professional Credentials Exchange, Grand Rapids, MI, was created to consolidate those records on a blockchain and make them available to member health care organizations.

Looking to get a better handle on their bottom lines, some of the leading health care insurers in the United States pooled their resources to form a consortium. They partnered with IBM and PNC Financial Services to create Avaneer Health to track and monitor insurance claims

---

[20] Hereward and Curtis. *DNA Could Become Next Cryptocurrency.* www.weforum .org/agenda/2018/02/new-cryptocurrencies-could-let-you-control-and-sell-access-to-your-dna-data.

[21] Ibid.

[22] Credentialing Provider Management. *What Is Physician Credentialing.* https:// verisys.com/what-is-physician-credentialing/#:~:text=In%20healthcare%2C%20 physician%20credentialing%20is,%2C%20work%20history%2C%20and%20 more.

and medical procedures.[23] The group's initial aim is to oversee claims and payment processing, health data exchanges, and provider directories.[24]

Say someone is scheduled for a specific medical procedure. The doctor or hospital first must check with the insurer to see if that procedure is covered in the patient's policy. This can take one or two weeks. Putting approval codes for those procedures on the blockchain speeds up the process.[25]

Keeping up with patients' health, doctor's credentials, and medical costs can be daunting for any medical office or hospital. Try keeping up with the health of a nation. In the United States, that job falls to the Centers for Disease Control and Prevention (CDC), which is charged with protecting the American public from health threats.

Working with health care professionals and health departments around the country, the CDC gathers and disseminates data on reported public health threats, then offers guidance on how to combat them. With so much information flowing in and so many participants providing information, the CDC and IBM built a blockchain-based system in 2017 that closely monitors who has access to information and how that information flows to the organization.[26] It could also be used to track national health trends and issues, such as the opioid crisis, CDC officials said in an interview with NextGov.[27]

Supply Chain

As noted in the previous chapter, counterfeit drugs are a multibillion-dollar business. Several startups are working to combat those drugs, which can cause patients great harm. A number of companies, such as Blockpharma of Paris, France, are working to battle the counterfeit drug market. Blockpharma, which tracks the shipment of drugs, has an app

---

[23] Ledger Insights. *Blockchain Utility Avaneer Health Launched.* www.ledgerinsights.com/leading-healthcare-firms-launch-blockchain-utility-avaneer-health/.
[24] Ibid.
[25] Ibid.
[26] Corrigan. *CDC Is Testing Blockchain.* www.nextgov.com/emerging-tech/2018/11/cdc-testing-blockchain-monitor-countrys-health-real-time/152622/.
[27] Ibid.

that alerts patients if they are taking *false* drugs. The company boasts it weeds out 15 percent of all counterfeit drugs.[28]

Combatting Medical Fraud

Medical fraud, which includes Medicare and Medicaid fraud, costs insurers and taxpayers in the United States somewhere between U.S.$70 billion to U.S.$234 billion annually, according to one report.[29] A more conservative estimate proffered by the National Health Care Anti-Fraud Association puts the cost at U.S.$68 billion annually, or 3 percent of the nation's U.S.$2.26 trillion spent on health care, while recognizing that others put the estimate at 10 percent of spending or U.S.$230 billion annually.

It's a lot of money, regardless of which end of the spectrum it falls. Medical fraud hurts everyone.

Blockchain technology used to combat fraud in other sectors of economies could be adapted to root out the problem. One report suggests medical fraud begins when people manipulate or destroy data. As information on a blockchain is timestamped and immutable, it is a perfect tool for reducing or preventing medical fraud.[30] That same report noted that some Canadian banks use blockchain technology for identity verification. The same or similar program could be used to combat identity fraud.[31]

Embracing Change

Although the medical establishment is making strides to improve efficiencies related to patient care, that same community itself is slow to embrace it.

---

[28] Built In. *Hi, We're Blockpharma.* https://builtin.com/company/blockpharma.

[29] NCSL. *Combatting Health Care Fraud, Waste and Abuse.* www.ncsl.org/research/health/combating-health-care-fraud-and-abuse.aspx#:~:text=%22%20Health%20Care%20Fraud%20Is%20Costly,harming%20both%20patients%20and%20taxpayers.

[30] Matthews. *Preventing Medical Fraud With Blockchain Technology.* https://hitconsultant.net/2018/07/10/blockchain-technology-medical-fraud/.

[31] Ibid.

Maxim Scherbina, cofounder and chief financial officer for Blaize, a company that builds AI platforms, voiced his frustration at the lack of change despite industrywide enthusiasm for the technology.[32] He cited an IBM survey of 200 health care executives in 2017, in which 58 percent of the respondents said they planned to adopt blockchain technology between 2018 and 2019. That didn't happen, he said, recognizing that the health care industry is one of the most conservative institutions and slow to embrace change. Many, he noted, still use paper records.[33]

Others share his opinion.

Several studies have concluded that medical recordkeeping needs modernization. While many medical offices use computers, recordkeeping is another issue. One British review noted that while 90 percent of American doctors use computers, they are not interoperable. That is, their computers cannot communicate with other computer systems, thereby hampering efforts to share information.[34] The review found that the interoperability problem wasn't just among general practitioners but extended to specialists who may use noncompatible systems. This restricts doctors from obtaining all the necessary information to treat a patient adequately.[35]

Another issue is medical mistakes due to poor recordkeeping. This can lead to errors if records are not updated when sent out to other physicians working on the same case.[36]

Then there is the matter of cost in terms of finance and security. Copying patient records can get expensive. On average, patients in the United States pay U.S.$1 per page for the first 20 pages of copied records and between 10 and 80 cents for each additional page, plus postage.[37] The cost

---

[32] Sherbina. *Opportunities and Risks With Blockchain Technology.* https://blaize .tech/article-type/blockchain-in-healthcare-opportunities-and-risks-of-using-blockchain-technology/.

[33] Ibid.

[34] Vazirani, O'Donoghue, Brindley, and Meinert. *Implementing Blockchains for Efficient Healthcare.* www.ncbi.nlm.nih.gov/pmc/articles/PMC6390185/#ref27.

[35] Ibid.

[36] Ibid.

[37] Torrey. *Medical Records Copy Costs.* www.verywellhealth.com/cost-of-getting-copies-of-your-medical-records-2615313.

for nonpaper items like X-rays and biopsy slides varies. Copies of biopsy slides can cost anywhere between U.S.$10 and U.S.$120.[38]

Transferring records promptly and safely is another issue facing today's health care professionals. If records are unavailable when needed, then the tests or the imaging have to be replicated, costing time and money, while sending records by e-mail is not considered secure.[39]

While some may see the medical establishment as stodgy and slow to change, others point out significant issues with blockchain technology that give them pause. These concerns include the complexity of initiating blockchain transactions, keeping up with key pairs needed to encrypt and decrypt information, the limited number of transactions occurring on the blockchain at any given time, and access.[40]

A Deloitte study found more than 6,500 blockchain programs that use "diverse platforms with multiple coding languages, protocols, consensus mechanisms, and privacy measures."[41] The study said standardization would greatly enhance integration, allowing multiple users to conduct cross-blockchain transactions.[42]

The UK review determined that blockchain could be the solution for securely maintaining and distributing patient records but not in its current form.[43]

To access a blockchain today, one needs both private and public keys. If there is only one key and it is lost, then access is denied. If that private key was stolen, the holder could access the entire block of patient

---

[38] Ibid.

[39] Vazirani, O'Donoghue, Brindley, and Meinert. *Implementing Blockchains for Efficient Healthcare.* www.ncbi.nlm.nih.gov/pmc/articles/PMC6390185/ https://jmir.org/2019/2/e12439/.

[40] COE-EDP. *Blockchain in Healthcare.* www.devdiscourse.com/article/technology/1553504-blockchain-in-healthcare-opportunities-and-challenges.

[41] Schatsky, Arora, and Dongre. *Blockchain: Five Vectors of Progress.* www2.deloitte.com/us/en/insights/focus/signals-for-strategists/value-of-blockchain-applications-interoperability.html.

[42] Ibid.

[43] Vazirani, O'Donoghue, Brindley, and Meinert. *Implementing Blockchains for Efficient Healthcare.* www.ncbi.nlm.nih.gov/pmc/articles/PMC6390185/#ref27.

information. On the other hand, the Deloitte study found that keeping up and using individual keys is not practical.[44]

The UK review agreed, noting that storing copies of blockchain records on a myriad of computers created as a result of verification was impractical. Their solution suggests a *data lake* where patient information is stored on a cloud with blockchain access for patients, providers, and research labs.[45] This type of system, which would have to comply with patient privacy laws, could also solve the issue of patient confidentiality, as now required by law in most parts of the world, where approval is provided in a smart contract.[46]

The Deloitte study reported that some 17 states had passed dozens of bills relating to blockchain, including those addressing smart contracts and cryptographic signatures. Still, the study concluded that more needs to be done.[47] While U.S. states are moving forward, the federal government is only now grappling with how to regulate cryptocurrency,[48] not to mention social media platforms.

The overall consensus is that blockchain technology could solve a number of issues facing the health care industry today. The question is how it can be adapted to fit industry needs while supporting privacy rights.[49]

---

[44] Schatsky, Arora, and Dongre. *Blockchain: Five Vectors of Progress.* www2 .deloitte.com/us/en/insights/focus/signals-for-strategists/value-of-blockchain-applications-interoperability.html.

[45] Vazirani, O'Donoghue, Brindley, and Meinert. *Implementing Blockchains for Efficient Healthcare.* www.ncbi.nlm.nih.gov/pmc/articles/PMC6390185/#ref27.

[46] Ibid.

[47] Ibid

[48] G.H. You. *Congress Should Regulate Cryptocurrency.* https://foreignpolicy .com/2021/12/07/cryptocurrency-regulation-congress-hearing-stablecoin-digital-currency/.

[49] Avidor. *Is Blockchain HIPPA Compliant.* https://masur.com/lawtalk/is-blockchain-hipaa-compliant/.

Blockchain and Identity

Identity today rests on showing your papers—a driver's license, identity card, or passport, each recorded on centralized databases and verified by a pair of eyes at the airport, voting booth, or traffic stop. It requires providing a PIN or matching signature after swiping or scanning your credit or debit card at a restaurant, grocery store, or retail outlet.

In this new world of blockchain, there are no third parties to confirm that you are the one who booked that hotel reservation, bought that coat at the international store, or boarded that airplane. Instead, your identity is encapsulated in an encrypted string of data containing identifiable information about you, which can be seamlessly passed from your mobile device to the recipient's platform using a digital signature. With blockchain technology, that platform is programmed to confirm that information while ignoring any contrary information from other sources.

Unlike the forms of identity widely used today, which are under the control of public and private data banks, blockchain technology will allow you to create, collect, and control your digital identity. You are the one who decides with whom to share your information and how much you want or need to share. You don't need to trust others to keep that information safe. It's under your control. And you will no longer need multiple forms of identification to prove who you are. The database you create on your app will do that for you.

So, what is our identity? We know who we are, but how do we prove it? It appears obvious, but it's more complicated than that.

Identity

Overwhelmed by obstacles and a potential scandal, our protagonist, George Bailey (*It's A Wonderful Life*), got his wish and, for a time, existed without an identity. He had no *papers*, as Clarence, his guardian angel, pointed out when George feverishly looked through his wallet to identify himself. No matter how hard he tried to convince his family and friends who he was, they thought he was mad, arguing they had never seen him before. Even his personal anecdotes about their lives failed to persuade them. It was a frightening, surreal moment George never fully grasped until he was granted his second wish and got his life back.

While the inspirational holiday classic has a happy ending, the lack of personal identity is a fact of life for some 1.1 billion people across the globe.[1] For them, there is no joyful resolution. They have no papers, which means they have no way of proving who they are, prohibiting them from opening a bank account, voting, getting an education, or participating in what much of the world enjoys by virtue of having an identity.[2] These numbers include refugee children whose records have been lost or not created due to war.[3]

The creation of one's identity begins at birth with a convergence of old information about the parents coupled with new data about this new baby, which is etched onto a hospital form. That paperwork is typically transcribed and shared with the state, which creates an official birth certificate. It includes a name, date of birth, city, state, nationality, race, and parents—facts that bind these newborns to their families and society at large. It is the first of many legal documents necessary to be able to participate in daily life.

For Americans, the next single-most-important legal document is a Social Security card, now available for newborns. This nine-digit number is required for just about everything. The Social Security Act of 1935, signed into law by President Franklin D. Roosevelt (March 4, 1933– April 12, 1945), was established solely to provide a retirement fund for those 65 years of age and older. The Social Security number, created in 1936, was used to track recipients' earnings to determine federal benefits, later including government benefits like Medicare and Medicaid coverage created 30 years later.[4]

---

[1] Consensys. *Blockchain Digital Identity*. https://consensys.net/blockchain-use-cases/digital-identity/ (accessed February 22, 2022).

[2] Ibid.

[3] Kunz. *Identity a Human Right*. www.ted.com/talks/dominique_kunz_why_identity_is_a_human_right.

[4] Puckett. *The Social Security Number*. www.ssa.gov/policy/docs/ssb/v69n2/v69 n2p55.html#:~:text=The%20Social%20Security%20number%20(%20SSN%20) %20was%20created%20in%201936%20for,the%20SSN%20has%20expanded %20substantially.

The use of that number has since expanded beyond what it was designed to do. It serves as another identity card. You need it to get a job, pay taxes, open a bank account, get a loan or line of credit, credit card, student loan, mortgage, driver's license, and passport.[5]

Colleges, hospitals, charities, schools, summer camps, retailers, and service providers, to name a few, also require it as part of the profile they keep about you and your children.[6]

But even the use of Social Security numbers is not infallible. According to a *CBS* news report, some 20 million Americans have more than one Social Security number.[7] Fraud accounts for 15 to 20 percent of that number. However, a significant percentage of second numbers are created through human error. For example, a new number can inadvertently be created if a digit from the original number on a credit card application is incorrectly entered. That clerical error creates a second number that stays with the applicant, causing problems later.[8]

Social Security numbers are also a prime target for identity thieves who can use that number to create an alternate lifestyle, leaving victims to pay the bill.

Online Identity

The digital age provides users with greater portability. Rather than going to a bank to make a deposit or a payment, bank customers can use their bank's online platform. All they need for access is a username and password that is *securely* stored on the bank's central computer server.

You can use a debit, credit card, or pay app on your mobile device when you go shopping, allowing you to scan and go or, in some cases, provide a PIN or signature.

---

5 Robyn. *Who Needs Your Social Security Number.* https://moneycarevt.com/who-needs-your-social-security-number-and-when-to-refuse-to-give-it-out/#:~:text=You%20do%20need%20to%20give,Security%20number%20(SSN)%20to%3A&text=The%20three%20main%20credit%20reporting,Medicaid%2C%20and%20other%20aid%20programs%60.

6 Ibid.

7 Cooper. *20 Million Americans Have Extra SSN.* www.cbsnews.com/news/for-20-million-americans-one-social-security-numbers-not-enough/.

8 Ibid.

Using these platforms also carries a risk. Thieves and hackers can cause harmful mischief and financial calamity if they are able to steal banking or credit information from you, your device, or that third-party platform that stores that information. For example, card skimming—the illegal use of electronic devices to secretly record card transactions, today costs consumers and financial institutions in the United States more than $1 billion annually, according to the Federal Bureau of Investigation.[9] Thieves place a device called a skimmer, which looks like a card reader, over the actual card reader, which skims the data off the card and stores it on an electronic device. A hidden camera, or, more recently, a keypad overlay, is used to record the PIN.[10] They can be placed on automated teller machines (ATMs), point of sale (POS) terminals, and fuel pumps that allow customers to pay at the pump rather than go inside.[11]

The Online World

If you want to buy a pair of shoes or a laptop, you no longer have to go into a store. You register with a retail platform, create a username and password, provide a street address and a credit card, and are ready to shop. Again, that username, password, and other personal and financial information are stored on that platform's central computer.

To join a social media site, you create your online presence with your name, or a screen name, and password. What happens if your account gets hacked? There are plenty of stories about hackers who stole passwords and attempted to steal the account holder's identity. In some cases, it was easy to prove the account was hacked; in other cases, it may have taken weeks or months to resolve.

The Web is the gateway to a digital world, easily accessed with a username and password. By the same token, the more sites you join, the more passwords you accumulate. Maybe you use just one or two passwords for all of your sites. Perhaps you use separate passwords stored on

---

[9] Federal Bureau of Investigation. *Skimming*. www.fbi.gov/how-we-can-help-you/safety-resources/scams-and-safety/common-scams-and-crimes/skimming#:~:text=Criminals%20use%20the%20data%20to,than%20%241%20billion%20each%20year (accessed October 7, 2022).

[10] Ibid.

[11] Ibid.

your computer and mobile devices. Maybe not. Maybe they are so simple hackers can easily figure them out. Maybe not. Convenience steps in when you forget your password, taking comfort that you can always request to reset it. If your media account is hacked, you can change the password. If your financial information is hacked, you could spend a lot of time and energy to reclaim your credit.

What cannot be reset is your digital history used to make online platforms billions of dollars or financial ruin caused by a security breach.

Relying on trusted third-party platforms, large or small, requires accepting the loss of privacy and the risk that the information about you could be compromised by hackers eager to cripple the network or capitalize on stolen data.

In response to security, many platforms are adopting two-step verification. After entering your password, you are sent an e-mail or SMS text with typically a six-digit number you must insert to gain access. If the platform sends an SMS, then you have to be sure to have your smartphone handy. Some use an authenticator, which also requires you to have a device handy if you are working on a personal computer. Checking one's bank account balance can be taxing.

Identity Reboot

The rise of mainstream platforms has hastened the push to take back control of personal identity by creating a decentralized system whereby the individual decides who, where, and when to share personal information.

Decentralized Identity

A decentralized identity based on blockchain technology boils down to a simple idea: Reducing the sum of who you are on paper into a string of verified encrypted computer code stored on a blockchain. This data serves as one's credentials, or what some call *verifiable claims* or *decentralized identifiers* (DIDs), to support their claim of facts pertaining to one's identity.[12]

---

[12] Hanson. *Keys to Decentralized Identity*. www.youtube.com/watch?v=gWfAIYXcyH4&t=1369s&ab_channcl=Okta.

In short, decentralized identity allows individuals to establish their identity using *identifiers* to maintain control over their personal information, protect it, and use it wherever they like.[13]

So, what is an identifier? What are the attributes necessary to prove digital identity? The World Wide Web Consortium (W3C) defines DID as "a globally unique identifier that does not require a centralized registration authority because it is registered with distributed ledger technology or other forms of decentralized network."[14] In layman's terms, an individual registers unique information about themselves on a blockchain that says, "Hey, it's me."

This information could include one's birth certificate, Social Security number, education, citizenship, driver's license, passport, credit information, vaccination certificates, and biometrics—"the measurement and statistical analysis of one's unique physical and behavioral characteristics."[15] These include fingerprints, voice recognition, and retina scans, to name a few.

In this new paradigm, passwords are no longer necessary. Instead, consumers use an app—a digital *wallet* (some refer to as an identity wallet) that contains *unphishable cryptographic keys* solely controlled by the users to authenticate their identity.[16]

When you share your identity from a digital wallet, you no longer have to provide your information to countless platforms each time you purchase goods and services, putting your data in harm's way.[17] Instead, you present your identity wallet, which initiates the transaction with a digital signature. The transaction is completed after accessing a public key from your ledger holding the information related to your transaction. If you are buying lunch, the restaurant will access the public key connected

---

[13] Dragonchain. *Self-Sovereign Identity & DecentralizedIdentity.* https://dragonchain.com/blog/decentralized-identity-self-sovereign-identity-explained.

[14] Metadium. *Decentralized Identifiers.* https://medium.com/metadium/decentralized-identifiers-the-easy-guide-fb96429e8b24.

[15] Gillis. *Biometrics.* www.techtarget.com/searchsecurity/definition/biometrics (accessed October 7, 2022).

[16] Shou. *Decentralized Identity Is Reshaping Privacy.* www.forbes.com/sites/forbestechcouncil/2021/12/10/how-decentralized-identity-is-reshaping-privacy-for-digital-identities/?sh=3819ba0e3226.

[17] Ibid.

to your banking information. If you are flying abroad, you can use it by presenting your wallet at the airport. All the check-in desk needs to do is access a public key attached to your passport.[18]

Decentralized identifiers (DIDs)

One program being developed for air travelers, the *Known Traveler Digital Identity*, is envisioned as a program that protects personal identity while safeguarding national security. Travelers would be able to download an app onto their digital devices, create a profile, and then add information using verifiable information such as their passport or digital

---

[18] Hanson. *Keys to Decentralized Identity.* www.youtube.com/watch?v= gWfAIYXcyH4&t=1369s&ab_channel=Okta.

passport and other verifiable information to be shared with airlines and the hotel where the traveler is staying.[19]

The program is made possible using the blockchain distributed ledger, cryptography, and biometrics.[20] The traveler could then move quickly and effortlessly through an airport and check into a hotel without complication. The more travels one takes, the greater their profile and the greater the trust developed between all parties concerned.[21]

While this program has not been rolled out, a number of pilot programs are already underway to provide digital identity solutions for a broad spectrum of uses, including the Illinois Blockchain Initiative. Launched in 2017, the consortium of state and county offices teamed up with Evermym, a self-sovereign identity solutions firm, to place birth certificates on a blockchain.[22] The information is only available to the owner of the information or other individuals granted access to it.[23] Other countries are also interested in the idea.[24]

In addition, several countries have, or are planning to develop, digital identity programs to provide individuals with a universal identity.[25] Success would mean 1.1 billion people could get their lives back.

What Problems Will Decentralized Identities Solve?

The use of decentralized identity solves three issues. The first is privacy and the ability to keep vital information to oneself.[26] This effort echoes

---

[19] Accenture Technology. *Traveller Digital Identity.* www.youtube.com/watch?v=cnUAQKKnEAU&ab_channel=AccentureTechnology.

[20] Ibid.

[21] Ibid.

[22] Okta. *Blockchain and Identity.* www.okta.com/resources/whitepaper/practical-thoughts-on-blockchain-and-identity/ (accessed March 2, 2022).

[23] Leary. *Illinois, Blockchains and Physical BirthCertificates.* https://futurism.com/illinois-is-experimenting-with-blockchains-to-replace-physical-birth-certificates.

[24] Ibid.

[25] Thales. *Digital Identity Trends.* www.thalesgroup.com/en/markets/digital-identity-and-security/government/identity/digital-identity-services/trends#:~:text=Usually%20issued%20or%20regulated%20by,as%20defined%20by%20national%20law.

[26] Hanson. *Keys to Decentralized Identity.* www.youtube.com/watch?v=gWfAIYXcyH4&t=1369s&ab_channel=Okta.

the establishment of privacy laws by governments worldwide, such as the General Data Protection Regulation passed by the European Union in December 2021, requiring organizations to uphold the privacy rights of anyone living within EU territory.[27]

The second is for security. Centralized platforms holding personal information have been the target of hackers, some of whom have been successful.[28] These attacks can come in the form of phishing, malware, and ransomware, all with devastating consequences.[29] In 2005, the first year marking the rise of large-scale attacks, there were 136 data breaches reported.[30]

The third reason is mobility. More and more consumers are turning to apps that allow them to pay at the checkout lines with a payment app that will automatically complete the transaction.[31]

Identity wallets could help protect data, secure personal and financial information, and guard against data breaches.

Issues Facing Decentralized Identity

The move toward decentralized identification is still a work in progress. Decentralized identity challenges include adopting a standard that any organization or institution would recognize.[32]

There's the issue of interoperability. Different types of distributed ledgers will need to communicate with one another so that the user can easily navigate a broad spectrum of decentralized platforms without the need to create separate identifiers for each platform.[33]

---

[27] Usercentrics. *The EU's General Data Protection Regulation.* https://usercentrics .com/knowledge-hub/the-eu-general-data-protection-regulation/#:~:text= What%20is%20the%20General%20Data,has%20been%20collected%20 or%20processed.

[28] Hanson. *Keys to Decentralized Identity.* www.youtube.com/watch?v= gWfAIYXcyH4&t=1369s&ab_channel=Okta.

[29] J. De Groot. *History of Data Breeches.* https://digitalguardian.com/blog/ history-data-breaches.

[30] Ibid.

[31] Hanson. *Keys to Decentralized Identity.* www.youtube.com/watch?v= gWfAIYXcyH4&t=1369s&ab_channel=Okta.

[32] Fractal. *Decentralized Identity Challenges.* https://medium.com/frctls/ decentralized-identity-challenges-how-to-tackle-them-7bf1f36e5f2c.

[33] Ibid.

Both issues have been recognized and are being addressed.

However it plays out, ease of use is essential from creating the wallet, correctly importing identifiers, and finally, navigating check points. No one will want to use it if it's too complicated, regardless of the security or convenience it provides.

Blockchain and Government

Blockchain is all about trust, having faith that this trustless ecosystem offers a viable alternative to centralized authorities. Mention *trust* and *government* in the same sentence, and you most likely get dirty looks and an earful of complaints.

Who trusts the government? A recent poll found that trust in the American government stood at 20 percent but ranked higher when asked about the government's response to specific areas.[1] In other words, if citizens believe the government is meeting their needs, they love it. If not, then not so much.

Looking to increase trust, lower costs, and secure their data, governments worldwide have implemented, plan to implement, or are studying the implementation of blockchain technology.

Government for the People

When one visits any local, state, or federal government office in the United States, most likely, one will be met with a tsunami of paperwork.

If they are looking for specific documents, they will find volumes of bounded paper dated, categorized, and alphabetized to peruse. The contents of those bound volumes are indexed in another bound book or electronically stored. If someone wants a copy of the document searched for, there's a copier machine ready to use. Just pay the copy fee.

This barrage of paperwork comes from various sources, mainly from lawyers filing complaints, deeds, or other records or answering on behalf of their clients. Specified offices provide applications for marriage licenses, voter registration, permits, and incorporation, to name a few. Then there are the lawsuits and court actions. Those documents create a

---

[1] Pew Research Center. *Americans' Views of Government.* www.pewresearch.org/politics/2020/09/14/americans-views-of-government-low-trust-but-some-positive-performance-ratings/.

mound of paper sent daily to and from thousands of government offices across the country.

Then there is the myriad of board meetings that agencies host. Each public meeting requires collecting, copying, and collating information packets related to that meeting for all board members, including a copy of the minutes from the previous session.

Keeping files organized while managing slews of incoming documents is time-consuming, laborious, and monotonous work that must be done to keep the government humming.

What does that have to do with blockchain? Like the private sector, governments are looking at blockchain technology to keep accurate paperwork accounting while reducing costs. Let's look at two significant areas of government responsibility and how blockchain can improve them—voting and property registration.

Voting

The voting process itself isn't complicated. In the United States, a registered voter checks in with a poll worker, then takes a paper ballot, and checks or punches holes in the boxes next to the candidate's name of their choice or votes on an electronic voting machine. In some cases, registered voters can vote online or by absentee ballot, which can be a paper ballot or an online ballot. Some states require absentee paper ballots to be notarized, which can be difficult to obtain for overseas residents. Voters these days are typically required to show some proof of identity when they show up to vote. If they are denied a ballot due to a questionable ID, they can file a provisional ballot that officials will examine later to determine whether that vote should be counted.

The ballots are dropped into a box, or recorded on a voting machine, to be tabulated at the end of the day. They are taken to specific locations where they are tallied by poll workers who volunteer or are paid to count the votes collected that day and the absentee ballots mailed in. Once all the votes are tabulated, they are certified by the secretary of state. In most cases, the results are available hours after polls close. In other cases, determining the winner can take days or weeks.

Before 2020, only ballots cast in countries run by despots and autocrats were suspect. Who gets 99 percent of the vote? Many of these countries allowed election monitors outside their borders to observe the proceedings and give the world a sense of legitimacy. All these monitors can do, however, is watch the proceedings. Their reports have no bearing on the outcome. Of course, the losers and their followers often cry foul if they fall short, claiming voter irregularities, but that's to be expected. That tactic made its way to American shores when President Donald Trump planted the seeds of voter fraud as a candidate seeking re-election, suggesting the that if he lost the 2020 presidential election, it would be due to voter fraud. Trump, trailing in the polls early on in his re-election bid, reiterated his claims. He never let up on his claims after Joe Biden was declared the winner.

The debate led by Republican voters was so contentious that the polls taken in 2021 indicated that one-third of voters believed the 2020 presidential election had been stolen.[2]

Similar claims were echoed in America's 2022 midterm elections. Like 2020, there were claims of voter irregularities but to a lesser degree. Despite the hysteria, no cases of widespread fraud were uncovered.

In countries where democracy is just a word, these claims may or may not have merit. In a historic democracy like the United States, such unfounded claims can undermine one of the fundamental pillars on which the country was founded.

Voting machines, often at the center of the debate, are widely used across the United States. They vary from state to state and county to county. The specter of hacking voting machines is typically revisited with each election through news reports and commentaries. And after each election, no such evidence can be found. Despite safeguards, voters remain concerned that their votes can be altered or disappear, even though 27 states require a paper trail for election audits.[3]

The solution to quell anxiety and dampen conspiracy theories could rest with blockchain technology, the decentralized public ledger that is timestamped and immutable. Many blockchain startups are working on voting systems they say will protect the vote.

---

[2] Greenwood. *One-third of Americans Believe Biden Won With Voter Fraud.* https://thehill.com/homenews/campaign/559402-one-third-of-americans-believe-biden-won-because-of-voter-fraud-poll/.

[3] Wikipedia. *Voter-Verified Paper Audit Trail.* https://en.wikipedia.org/wiki/Voter-verified_paper_audit_trail#:~:text=In%20the%20United%20States%2C%2027, statewide%20or%20in%20local%20jurisdictions.

Horizon State, Wellington, New Zealand, developed a digital ballot box in 2017 for MiVote, a democracy startup in Australia. MiVote uses the Internet to allow its members to vote on communal issues that concern their members. Votes were placed on Horizon State's decentralized ledger and verified by nodes while maintaining voter anonymity.[4]

Horizon State Chief Product Officer Jamie Skella told *Forbes* magazine in a 2017 interview his company had contacted non-governmental organizations (NGOs) in both local and national governments worldwide that showed interest in the technology.[5] One organization, New Zealand's Opportunity Party, successfully used Horizon State's system for its leadership election in 2018.[6] The following year, the South Australian Government used the blockchain to hold a public election for the Recreation Fishing Advisory Council.[7]

It looked like Horizon State was on the cusp of a breakout when it suddenly closed its doors in late 2019. The company was hit with a lawsuit filed by its founder and former chief executive officer for "an alleged breach of terms and conditions by Horizon State under Fair Work."[8] With insurmountable legal costs needed to defend themselves, the startup abruptly shut down.[9]

The city of Zug, Switzerland, held a test election using blockchain in June 2018, built on a digital ID app the city rolled out eight months earlier. Rather than using a centralized computer to store votes, the city used blockchain technology. Of the 240 participants with access to the voting app, 72 participated. Of that number, all but three reported ease of use.[10] The test was hailed a success.[11]

---

[4] Mavadiya. *Blockchain Ballot Boxes and Blockchain.* www.forbes.com/sites/madhvimavadiya/2017/10/13/blockchain-ballot-boxes/?sh=48aa64e9140d.

[5] Ibid.

[6] Micky News. *Blockchain Voting in New Zealand.* https://micky.com.au/blockchain-voting-to-be-used-in-new-zealand-politics/.

[7] Campbell. *Horizon State Shuts Down After Lawsuit.* https://finance.yahoo.com/news/blockchain-voting-platform-horizon-state-140552054.html?guccounter=1.

[8] Munro. *Horizon State collapses.* www.finder.com.au/australian-cryptocurrency-horizon-state-collapses-under-lawsuit-from-founder-oren-alazraki.

[9] Ibid.

[10] Swissinfo.ch. *Switzerland's Blockchain Vote Successful.* www.swissinfo.ch/eng/business/crypto-valley-_-switzerland-s-first-municipal-blockchain-vote-hailed-a-success/44230928.

[11] Ibid.

Later that year, Tsubuka, Japan, held its first blockchain election for social projects. The platform was built around Japan's *My Number* 12-digit digital identification program. Like the vote in Zug, the vote was conducted using blockchain technology.[12] While Tsukuba Mayor Tatsuo Igarashi found it easy to use, some voters reported they were unsure if their vote was counted. This system required voters first to scan their My Number card for identification with blockchain added as a safeguard.[13]

A few American states have also initiated pilot projects using Voatz, a mobile voting application that uses blockchain architecture and allows registered voters to vote from their mobile devices. Based in Boston, MA, the company has shown promising results, despite concerns from experts that votes could be compromised.

The use of the app is relatively simple. According to company literature, it works like this:

Once a voter submits a ballot, three distinct records are created that allow a voter to verify their vote is recorded and counted as they intended.

1. Ballot Receipt: Soon after voting, voters receive an encrypted, anonymized receipt to verify their selections. This receipt is password protected and signed with an anonymous ID (only the voter knows this password and anonymous ID).
2. Paper Ballot: A paper ballot is generated and printed at the jurisdiction for tabulation.

   This paper ballot is signed with the same anonymous ID, and this paper ballot constitutes the record being counted.
3. Blockchain Record: All ballot selections pass through multiple distributed nodes on a Public-permissioned blockchain network. If the votes pass all checks, they are stored as a Tanper-resistant record alongside all other votes.[14]

---

[12] Berman. *Japanese City Votes Using Blockchain.* https://cointelegraph.com/news/japanese-city-tsukuba-trials-blockchain-based-voting-system.

[13] O'Brien. *Japanese City Uses Blockchain-Based Voting System.* https://bitcoinist.com/japanese-city-introduces-blockchain-based-voting-system/.

[14] Voatz. *How Voatz Works.* https://voatz.com/type/5-how-voatz-works/.

West Virginia became the first state in the United States to experiment with blockchain voting using the Voatz system. In that trial, 144 people from 31 counties in the state successfully voted in the 2018 midterm election. Despite the claims of success, the company was criticized for failing to share information to evaluate just how successful it had been.[15]

Regardless, the state moved forward to contract with Voatz to provide its services in the November 2020 election. Two worrisome studies from the Massachusetts Institute of Technology (MIT), Cambridge, MA, and the U.S. Department of Homeland Security claimed to find vulnerabilities, so the contract was canceled.[16]

Although West Virginia ended its experiment, Denver, CO, elected to try the Voatz app for the 2018 midterm elections. The city worked alongside the National Cyber Security Center, which monitored the app given to the city's military citizens stationed abroad and civilians who lived overseas.[17] A follow-up study by the Cyber Security Center concluded it was an overall success despite some initial concerns. These concerns were over device security, voter identity, the integrity of the cast ballot, and the ability to audit those ballots to ensure they match the reported tallies. The study concluded the company had effectively addressed those issues.[18]

Oregon followed suit in a special election in November 2019, testing a smartphone app created by Tusk Philanthropies using the Voatz mobile election platform. Again, this voting app was only made available to registered voters from two counties in the state living overseas. Military personnel and their dependents were also given the app.[19]

---

[15] Grauer. *West Virginia's Blockchain Voting Experiment.* https://slate.com/technology/2019/07/west-virginia-blockchain-voting-voatz.html.

[16] Sinclair. *West Virginia Ditches Blockchain Voting App.* www.coindesk.com/policy/2020/03/02/west-virginia-ditches-blockchain-voting-app-provider-voatz/.

[17] Kenney. *Denver Offers Blockchain Voting to Military, Overseas Voters.* www.govtech.com/dc/denver-offers-blockchain-voting-to-military-overseas-voters.html.

[18] Senti. *Denver Mobile Voting Pilot Report.* https://cyber-center.org/wp-content/uploads/2019/08/Mobile-Voting-Audit-Report-on-the-Denver-County-Pilots-FINAL.pdf.

[19] Cant. *Two US Jurisdictions Use Blockchain Mobile Voting.* https://cointelegraph.com/news/two-more-us-jurisdictions-launch-blockchain-based-mobile-voting.

The Voatz system was used in 2019 for special party elections by Democrats and Republics in Arizona, South Dakota, and Michigan.[20]

Then in 2020, a Utah voter became the first in the nation to cast a ballot in the Presidential Election using the Voatz app[21] despite repeated objections from MIT researchers.[22]

On November 11, 2022, Voatz released a statement on its website[23] that it had successfully participated in the 2022 elections in Boston, MA, and North Bay, Ontario. The statement also stated that up to that date, Voatz had successfully participated in 115 elections globally, enabling more than 2.1 million people to vote using their app. No information for 2023 was available at this writing.

Blockchain technology is widely used today to transfer trillions of dollars worldwide and protect food chains and health records. Voting is considered sacrosanct, requiring any alteration to meet even higher standards. As the technology evolves, expect those standards to meet the challenge and, over time, become accepted to restore voter confidence. Neither can there be any doubt that concerns will follow.

Property

In 2018, global real estate transactions totaled U.S.$1.75 trillion, up 4 percent from the previous year.[24] Land transactions include a paper trail that is far from uniform.[25] Now imagine if someone doesn't have a title to a property or the property the person wishes to buy isn't registered due to

---

[20] Anzalone. *Republican and Democrats Use Voatz.* www.forbes.com/sites/ robertanzalone/2020/09/30/blockchain-voting-can-work-both-republican-and-democrats-use-voatz/?sh=2b8a4964ee9e.

[21] Pressgrove. *Utah County Makes History With Presidential Blockchain Vote.* www .govtech.com/products/utah-county-makes-history-with-presidential-block-chain-vote.html.

[22] Abazorius. *MIT Researchers Identify Vulnerabilities in Voting App.* https://news .mit.edu/2020/voting-voatz-app-hack-issues-0213.

[23] Voatz. *2022 Election in U.S. and Canada.* https://voatz.com/2022/11/11/ 2022-elections-in-the-us-canada-successfully-completed/.

[24] CoreLedger. *Land Registry on Blockchain.* https://medium.com/coreledger/ land-registry-on-blockchain-a0da4dd25ea6.

[25] Ibid.

a lack of paperwork. That's true for 70 percent of the world's population who lack a *legally registered* title to the land they own.[26] With land and property serving as the agreed-upon cornerstone for economic growth, this lack can impede future development. Without a means to register land, landowners without proper documentation fear that their land can be taken away.[27]

The causes for the lack of records include war, natural disasters, fraud, and corrupt government officials. Resolving ownership can be an uphill battle, especially for those with limited means. Land disputes can wind up in court, take years to resolve, or result in violent death. In 2019, 212 people were killed in land disputes, according to a report filed by *Global Witness*. The report found that more than half of those killings occurred in Colombia and the Philippines.[28]

Most land disputes wind up in court, which takes time and money. In India alone, a property challenge takes an average of 20 years—one generation, to resolve.[29]

Several countries have taken on blockchain programs to solve titling problems. They include Ghana,[30] the Republic of Georgia, Brazil, the United Arab Emirates, Ukraine, the Republic of Honduras,[31] the United Kingdom,[32] India,[33] and Sweden.[34] Projects like the ones in Ghana,

---

[26] Shang and Price. *Blockchain-Based Land Titling Project in the Republic of Georgia.* https://direct.mit.edu/itgg/article/12/3-4/72/9852/A-Blockchain-Based-Land-Titling-Project-in-the.

[27] Ibid.

[28] Chandran. *Deadly Land Conflicts Rising.* www.reuters.com/article/us-global-landrights-violence-idUSKCN24U005.

[29] Singh. *Role of Blockchain Technology in Indian Scenario.* https://iopscience.iop.org/article/10.1088/1755-1315/614/1/012055/pdf#:~:text=Blockchain%20in%20the%20land%20registry,buyer%20through%20an%20application%20form.

[30] GovChain. *Ghana.* https://govchain.world/ghana/.

[31] Shang and Price. *Blockchain-Based Land Titling Project in the Republic of Georgia.* https://direct.mit.edu/itgg/article/12/3-4/72/9852/A-Blockchain-Based-Land-Titling-Project-in-the.

[32] Sharma. *Blockchain Land Registries Worldwide.* www.blockchain-council.org/blockchain/blockchain-land-registeries-across-the-globe/.

[33] Bhattacharya. *Blockchain Helping Build Indian City.* https://qz.com/india/1325423/indias-andhra-state-is-using-blockchain-to-build-capital-amaravati.

[34] Kim. *Sweden's Blockchain Land Registry Demos.* www.coindesk.com/markets/2018/06/15/swedens-land-registry-demos-live-transaction-on-a-blockchain/.

Georgia, and India are a recognition by these governments that something must be done to protect people's land rights and reduce violence and government corruption.[35]

The Republic of Georgia

Like many nations, the Republic of Georgia has had a history of corruption. The Bureau of Technical Inventory and the Department of Land Management oversaw land registration through the mid-2000s. However, these agencies lacked transparency, which allowed corrupt public officials to change land records to benefit themselves.[36] President Mikheil Saakashvili's administration introduced reforms to cut down on bureaucracy. These reforms included the creation of the National Agency of Public Registry in 2004, which simplified land registration and digitized land records. Still, people were mistrustful. To ensure trust, the government in 2016 partnered with Bitfury, a blockchain technology company headquartered in Amsterdam, to create a pilot program to move the country's land registry to a blockchain platform.[37]

Following the implementation of the first phase, the time it took to register land in the country was reduced to one day. It was recently ranked third of 189 countries in property registration, ahead of countries like the United States, which takes an average of 15.2 days, and Germany, which takes 39 days.[38] Registration costs were significantly reduced as well, down to 0.1 percent of the total property value. The improvements earned the country recognition from the World Bank.[39] The government

---

[35] Daniel and Speranza. *Role of Blockchain Documenting Land Users' Rights.* www.frontiersin.org/articles/10.3389/fbloc.2020.00019/full#:~:text=Land%20 Administration%20Context-,Blockchain%20technology%20is%20a%20 peer%2Dto%2Dpeer%20protocol%20that%20can,the%20management%20 of%20land%20rights.

[36] Shang and Price. *Blockchain-Based Land Titling Project in the Republic of Georgia.* https://direct.mit.edu/itgg/article/12/3-4/72/9852/A-Blockchain-Based-Land-Titling-Project-in-the.

[37] Ibid.

[38] Ibid.

[39] Ibid.

of Georgia was so impressed with the program that it initiated the second phase in 2017 to expand the program.[40]

To keep sensitive data private, as part of Phase 2, Bitfury proposed the creation of a hybrid blockchain, a mix of public and private blockchains.[41] A public blockchain is decentralized and open to all. By contrast, a private blockchain is only open to invited people. Typically, these members comprise a single entity or a consortium of businesses or organizations. As the amount of data in a transaction is limited on a public blockchain, Bitfury proposed storing the hash with the bulk of the paperwork on the private blockchain.[42]

The titling program is well underway today, helping to facilitate government services.[43] Landowners can quickly check their titles using their smartphones, which reduces the possibility of fraud.[44]

India

The government of the Indian state of Andhra Pradesh, created in 2013, needed land to build its capital. They approached more than 24,000 farmers in 22 villages, asking for the 53,000 acres needed to build it.[45] Farmers were offered plots of land designated for residential and commercial development in exchange for the acreage, which would be registered on a blockchain.[46]

These farmers lacked trust in the government and didn't understand blockchain. But when presented with a sample blockchain certificate and plot map, they quickly realized their rights to their land would be protected.[47]

---

[40] Ibid.

[41] Ibid.

[42] Ibid.

[43] New America. *Restoring Trust in Public Land Registries.* www.newamerica.org/digital-impact-governance-initiative/digital-impact-and-governance-initiative/digi-blogs/project-capsule-georgia-land-titling-system/.

[44] Ibid.

[45] Bhattacharya. *Blockchain Helping Build Indian City.* https://qz.com/india/1325423/indias-andhra-state-is-using-blockchain-to-build-capital-amaravati/.

[46] Ibid.

[47] Ibid.

Like other countries, land records in India are paper records that can be incomplete, lost, destroyed, or forged, resulting in lengthy disputes against the government and between landowners. The tumult can lead to violence and even death.[48] Even digitized documents are suspect as they can be altered or contain incorrect information.[49]

While there are holdouts mistrustful of the government, most farmers are participating in the blockchain registration program, which began in 2017. Recording titles, which are time-consuming and can cost 5,000 rupees (or around U.S.$67), now only takes a few hours to complete, costing 5 rupees (U.S.$0.07) to register.[50]

The issue for farmers isn't the public blockchain. The problem is that the program, like the Republic of Georgia, is a hybrid blockchain with the government in charge of the private blockchain. Farmers have reported being pressured and threatened by government officials to surrender their land. Some report that government officials have gone so far as to cut off water and electricity to those who refused to buckle. Another issue is that while plots are posted on maps, farmers say they haven't been shown the land they were given. Some claim that some plots are better positioned than others.[51]

Despite the controversies, the project is moving forward. While blockchain won't end land disputes, it does offer a measure of accountability.[52]

The United States

Unlike some countries, there are several legal hurdles to overcome if a blockchain system were to be implemented in the United States. One of the primary tenants of using a public blockchain is that it is an open, decentralized ledger independent of third parties, including the government. Removing government is contrary to government offices across the United States, which see their role of record keeping

[48] Ibid.
[49] Ibid.
[50] Ibid.
[51] Ibid.
[52] Ibid.

as a cornerstone of citizens' trust in government. That trust ensures the government is accountable to its citizens.[53] A hybrid blockchain could alleviate those issues.

With great fanfare, the city of South Burlington, VT, partnered in 2018 with Propy to bring blockchain titling to the state. Propy is a private company supported by Silicon Valley and the National Association of Realtors, which sells properties online using blockchain.

The Vermont State Legislature wanted to be a pioneer in this area, and South Burlington had a resident wanting to register property on the blockchain, South Burlington City Clerk Donna Kinville said in an e-mail exchange.

The process of registering the property was simple. The deed itself is the same as any deed but includes a digital signature or hash and a QR code at the end of the document. Scan the code, and one is taken to the deed's location on the blockchain,[54] where the property is registered instead of the city's recording system.[55]

The city provided Propy with additional information so the company could build a database, but the pilot phase ended before any more properties could be added, and the city chose not to continue, Kinville said. This one property is the only property from South Burlington listed on the blockchain.

While state lawmakers were ready to move forward, the Vermont Secretary of State's office, joned by the Vermont League of Cities and Towns and the Clerk's Association, disagreed. Following a lengthy review, they voiced their concerns in a white paper released in January 2019.[56] While recognizing the value of blockchain, the white paper outlined several hurdles that, in their estimation, required more diligent

---

[53] Office of Vermont Secretary of State. *Blockchains for Public Recordkeeping White Paper.* https://sos.vermont.gov/media/r3jh24ig/vsara_blockchains_for_public_recordkeeping_white_paper_v1.pdf.

[54] Miller. *Blockchain Property Deed.* www.govtech.com/biz/heres-what-a-blockchain-property-deed-looks-like.html.

[55] Ibid.

[56] Office of Vermont Secretary of State. *White Paper.* https://sos.vermont.gov/media/r3jh24ig/vsara_blockchains_for_public_recordkeeping_white_paper_v1.pdf.

study. For example, specific steps for recording property in the United States are set by state statute. The law requires that government offices record, maintain, and securely store those records.[57] State law related to the land registry would need to be changed to accommodate the new technology.

Regarding the blockchain, the white paper's authors noted that public blockchains are not nimble. Aside from storing records, these public documents must be made available and transferable at a moment's notice. The machinations involved in transferring that data to other local, county, and state offices and courtrooms quickly and cost-effectively pose significant challenges.[58] Records today already employ recognized verification through a *chain of custody* that verifies the integrity of documents as they are passed from one office or department to the next.[59]

Another concern is storage. Under the law, records must be, in many cases, held in perpetuity.

The study recognized that blockchain is a relatively new technology that relies on third-party nodes on a decentralized system but are not within the purview of government offices. What happens over time if this independent network grows smaller or is successfully hacked? And there's the question about the future of blockchain. It is here today, but what about the future? What happens to those records if the blockchain collapses or changes over time? If the plan was to begin with new properties, the white paper questions how blockchain and today's recording system could easily be bridged.

The study concluded that all blockchain could do would be to provide another unnecessary layer of technology that would require much money, time, and education to implement. On the other hand, putting more money into strengthening its existing digital system would accomplish the same results without adding new technology and training.[60]

---

[57] Ibid.
[58] Ibid.
[59] Ibid.
[60] Ibid.

Looking Ahead

Each country has its laws regarding the titling of property. Still, experts agree that with so much at stake, something needs to be done to ensure that property is properly recorded and registered to provide transparency and is immutable to protect landowners. Although the blockchain cannot store all the information associated with property ownership, there's enough that can be used to prove ownership while preventing fraud. Ultimately, it comes down to creating a system people can trust.

Blockchain, Banks, and Financial Institutions

Blockchain technology is expected to significantly disrupt banks and financial institution cutting into their bottom line.[1] Today, most bank customers—consumers and businesses, use their accounts to deposit earnings, pay bills, and save money, despite earning little interest. As of September 2023, savings account rates paid 0.56 percent while high yield deposits paid an average of 5 percent.[2] Banks, otherwise, use money deposited to make loans at higher interest rates. They also earn large sums of money from banking fees and overdraft charges, which account for 40 percent of their revenue stream.[3]

Recognizing the impact blockchain technology and the growing use of cryptocurrency is having, several banks are looking to this technology to streamline their business and reduce overhead. By one estimate, banking overhead could be reduced by as much as 30 percent (U.S.$10 billion) annually.[4]

Investment banks looking to incorporate blockchain technology include JPMorgan Chase, Citigroup, and Goldman Sachs.[5]

Traditional banking is in for a challenge as they face competition from less traditional banking and financing startups that don't need a central office or branches to conduct business. With less overhead, they can focus

---

[1] Andrews. *Cryptocurrencies Threaten Banking's Moneymaker.* www.gsb.stanford.edu/insights/cryptocurrencies-could-eliminate-bankings-easiest-moneymaker.

[2] Bond. *Average Interest Rate for Savings.* https://smartasset.com/checking-account/average-savings-account-interest.

[3] Pisani. *Growth of Bank Fees.* www.cnbc.com/2017/07/21/the-crazy-growth-of-bank-fees.html.

[4] Tuwiner. *Blockchain Statistics, Facts, and Trends.* https://buybitcoinworldwide.com/blockchain-statistics/.

[5] CB Insights Research Briefs. *Banking Is the Beginning.* www.cbinsights.com/research/industries-disrupted-blockchain/.

on creating networks that allow consumers ready access to their money without traditional delays.

In 2021, venture capitalists put up U.S.$132 billion for financial technology (FinTech) startups offering to create services on the blockchain. Of that amount, U.S.$63 billion was designated for startups in the United States.[6] By the end of 2021, there were 10,755 startups in the Americas and 9,323 in Europe, the Middle East, and Africa.[7]

With blockchain technology, funds can be transferred spontaneously and effortlessly at a fraction of the cost of conventional financial institutions and pay platforms that charge high transaction fees.[8]

Let's say you have a child away at university. They need money now as they are short on funds and need to cover expenses immediately. Traditional methods take time and additional money. You could put a check in the mail, but short of a next-day delivery, which can be expensive, standard first-class service takes several days. Foreign banks may not recognize your check for those living out abroad. If they do, it will take time to process.

Wiring money from a bank is also labor-intensive if the amount to be sent exceeds a specified amount. You must go to your bank, sit with a representative, and explain what you are doing with your money, especially if a significant amount is going overseas. Transfers can take several hours to complete, especially if it is an overseas transaction.

On the other hand, depending on delivery and the method of payment used, Western Union typically provides money in minutes, or in just a few working days.[9]

Payment platforms like PayPal are more convenient as you can sit in front of your computer, log on, and send your payment. But wait! There's

---

[6] Leimer. *Web3, DeFI, and Banking*. https://internationalbanker.com/banking/web3-defi-and-the-atonement-of-purpose-is-banking-ready-to-answer-tomorrows-questions/.

[7] Ibid.

[8] Dquindia Online. *Blockchain Uses in Banking*. www.dqindia.com/top-5-uses-blockchain-banking/.

[9] Western Union. *How Long Does It Take to Rreceive Money*. https://wucare.westernunion.com/s/article/When-can-the-receiver-pick-up-the-money-I-sent?language=en_US#:~:text=Money%20in%20Minutes%20service%20for,could%20vary%2C%20depending%20on%20country.

no money on your PayPal account. So, first, you must transfer money from your bank to your account before sending it to your child. Time is running. Let's say there is money in the account. Fine, but there is a limit to how much you can send at one time. There are fees, and you must realize it can take up to five business days for the money to be transferred.

If you have a cryptocurrency account, transferring crypto is immediate, taking as little as a few hours for the money to be deposited into the receiver's wallet at a fraction of the cost banks and platforms charge for such transfers. Once the cryptocurrency is in the receiver's account, they can immediately sell it with the proceeds sent directly to their bank account.

Cryptocurrency payments could also provide same-day payments to creditors and service providers, especially when time is of the essence by bypassing banks which require several business days to process those transactions.

Businesses, small businesses in particular, face similar challenges when transferring money abroad. Transactions can take up to two days.[10] Such transfers are lucrative for banks, which were expected to reach U.S.$35 trillion in 2022 in business-to-business cross-border transfers.[11]

Recognizing the challenges facing them from blockchain platforms, a number of international banks are partnering with the Ripple Network. This blockchain-based payment platform uses its own cryptocurrency (XRP)[12] to make those transfers. Transactions take seconds to confirm, not days, at a fraction of the cost.[13]

Blockchain's cost for business-to-business cross-border transfers was U.S.$122 million in 2020 but is expected to rise to U.S.$1.8 billion by 2025.[14]

Some start-ups include Congi and Fiat24.

---

[10] Arvelaiz. *International Banks Use Ripple.* https://bitcoinist.com/why-top-international-banks-partnered-to-use-ripple/.

[11] CB Insights Research Briefs. *Industries Blockchain Could Transform.* www.cbinsights.com/research/industries-disrupted-blockchain/.

[12] Frankenfield. *Ripple.* www.investopedia.com/terms/r/ripple-cryptocurrency.asp#:~:text=Ripple%20is%20a%20blockchain%2Dbased,owned%20servers%2C%20to%20confirm%20transactions.

[13] Arvelaiz. *International Banks Join to Use Ripple.* https://bitcoinist.com/why-top-international-banks-partnered-to-use-ripple/.

[14] CB Insights Research Briefs. *Industries Blockchain Could Transform.* www.cbinsights.com/research/industries-disrupted-blockchain/.

Congi is an online banking platform with no minimum deposit and charges no bank or overdraft fees. The accounts are protected with multifactor identification and offer access to 55,000 no-fee ATMs worldwide.[15] The platform, built on Web 2.0 and Web 3.0 technology, offers traditional services and blockchain offerings such as NFTS. The platform rolled out a digital wallet in 2023 allowing customer to buy and sell cryptocurrency.[16]

Fiat24 is a banking platform built entirely on a blockchain. The platform, which charges no bank fees, uses smart contracts and P2P confirmation to send and confirm transactions. Users create a unique nonfungible token (NFT) when they sign up, which is used to prove their identity.[17]

Loans

Traditional lending practices require a mountain of forms, credit scores that may or may not be reliable, and lending and processing fees. A decision is then rendered after several days, a week, or longer, depending on the type of loan one is seeking. Approval for a mortgage, for example, takes about a week, although it could be longer, according to published industry averages. Smaller loans typically take three to seven days.

Blockchain and related technologies could reduce the waiting time and fees paid to third parties for their services. Blockchain would allow more lenders to compete for business with its worldwide reach.

Once a lender has been selected, they could implement an agreement using a smart contract.

Say you were looking to buy a home. Typically, you would need to fill out a lengthy application and then retrieve information, such as your credit scores, income history, and so on, held by third parties.

That information could be encrypted and stored on the blockchain, which can then be shared with a larger pool of lenders. Once your loan is approved, a smart contract could be initiated to approve the sale, set up a home loan account, and register the property.[18]

---

[15] Congi. *Congi App.* https://getcogni.com/.

[16] Strack. *Regulation at Congi Bank.* https://blockworks.co/new-web3-head-at-digital-bank-cogni-braces-for-more-regulation/.

[17] Cassiopeia Services. *Web3 Banking.* https://cassiopeiaservicesltd.medium .com/web3-banking-has-arrived-meet-fiat24-3ff07592036e.

[18] Home Loan Experts. *Blockchain Mortgage.* www.homeloanexperts.com.au/home-loan-articles/blockchain-mortgage/.

There are two types of blockchain lenders. There are centralized lenders (CeFI), which take control of one's cryptocurrency account during loan repayment, and decentralized lenders (DeFI), which utilize smart contracts and typical repayment methods. Borrowers keep control of their cryptocurrency but can lose it if they default on their loan.[19]

Portability is the name of the game. Whether you are on the go, mistrustful of traditional financial institutions, or lack the necessary capital to have an account, FinTech startups offer growing services to meet your needs.

Startups include Compound, an open, decentralized finance (DeFi) platform built on the Ethereum blockchain that brings borrowers and lenders together without a third party. Lenders deposit cryptocurrency into a pool that borrowers can access.

Lenders and borrowers earn interest on deposits based on an algorithm that sets a rate based on the supply and demand of the tokens deposited. After depositing their cryptocurrency, they can borrow against that amount for less interest. As their reward, borrowers are issued *cTokens* representing whatever cryptocurrency they can use on the Ethereum blockchain, or they can cash out.[20]

Borrowers must provide collateral greater than the amount they need to protect investor interests.[21]

We'll discuss this topic again in the NFTs section.

Raising Capital

Blockchain can also help raise capital. Companies using blockchain can raise venture capital using initial exchange offerings (IEOs), equity token offerings (ETOs), and security token offerings (STOs).

IEOs are a "variant of initial coin offerings (ICOs), operated directly by cryptocurrency exchanges."[22] An ICO is when coins are offered to

---

[19] Daley. *Crypto Loan Companies Using Blockchain.* https://builtin.com/blockchain/lending-loans-borrowing-mortgages.

[20] Ivy. *What Is Compound Finance.* https://thedefiant.io/what-is-compound-crypto.

[21] Ibid.

[22] Wikipedia. *Initial Exchange Offering.* https://en.wikipedia.org/wiki/Initial_exchange_offering#:~:text=Initial%20exchange%20offering%20(IEO)%20is,its%20reserve%20for%20Tether%20tokens.

investors in exchange for their investment.[23] The two are similar, but in the case of an IEO, the coins or tokens are offered to partnering exchanges rather than ICOs, which are offered directly to investors.[24]

An STO is like an ICO, but an STO token represents an investment contract for an underlying security asset like stocks, bonds, or real estate.[25]

Securities

Buying and selling securities today is mired in the past. Although today's apps allow one to click and buy or sell on their computer, tablet, or smartphone, the paperwork behind those transactions hasn't changed. The model is still built on *paper ownership*, which requires the transaction to navigate through clearinghouses, brokers, depositories, and custodial banks to keep up with who owns what.[26] In other words, when one buys or sells assets, the paperwork must go through several third parties, which adds to costs. Sorting out all the paperwork and finalizing it can take one to three business days.[27]

Blockchain clarifies ownership and speeds up transactions while reducing costs. One can quickly transfer the asset as digital tokens using a distributed ledger.

As you can see from this small sampling, blockchain can revolutionize finance, offering speed, transparency, and security while reducing overhead. Building efficient and effective platforms for industry providers will take time. Still, as you have seen from just a handful of pilot projects and startups, there is an awareness that this new technology can play a significant role in business and commerce.

---

[23] Frankenfield. *Initial Coin Offering.* www.investopedia.com/terms/i/initial-coin-offering-ico.asp#:~:text=Initial%20coin%20offerings%20(ICOs)%20are, have%20yielded%20returns%20for%20investors.

[24] Beedham. *Difference Between ICOs and IEOs.* https://thenextweb.com/news/initial-exchange-offering-ieo-ico.

[25] Pauw. *What Is an STO.* https://cointelegraph.com/explained/what-is-an-sto-explained.

[26] CB Insights Research Briefs. *How Blockchain Could Disrupt Banking.* www.cbinsights.com/research/blockchain-disrupting-banking/.

[27] Ibid.

Blockchain and Real Estate

One of the bedrocks of personal financial security anywhere globally is homeownership. Unlike other tangible assets, houses can increase in value, producing more cash if the house is sold at a later date. Otherwise, homeowners can borrow money to cover expenses using the value accrued by their homes over time.

Finding a home can be challenging, especially in times of heavy demand. Demand is driven by economic growth, high incomes, and low interest rates, to name a few,[1] resulting in escalating prices.

Over the past two decades, this coveted investment outperformed the stock market, providing returns of between 9.5 and 11.8 percent, depending on the property, compared to the stock market, where investors earned an average of 8.8 percent.[2]

In 2021, the average home in the United States sold for U.S.$453,700, up from U.S.$391,900 a year earlier.[3] There were 6.12 million homes sold in the United States in 2021, up from 5.64 million in 2020.[4] Factor in that the average real estate commission is between 5 and 6 percent, with the sales representatives for the buyer and seller splitting that commission equally.[5]

---

[1] PVS_admin. *Economic Factors Affecting Housing Market.* https://pvsbuilders.com/economic-factors-affecting-housing-market/.

[2] VAVE. *Real Estate Tokenization Overview.* https://vave.io/blog/real-estate-tokenization/real-estate-tokenization-an-overview-of-the-new-investment-trend/.

[3] Statista Research Department. *Average Sales Price of New Homes Sold in U.S. 1965–2021.* www.statista.com/statistics/240991/average-sales-prices-of-new-homes-sold-in-the-us/.

[4] Statista Research Department. *Existing Homes Sold in U.S. 2005 to 2023.* www.statista.com/statistics/226144/us-existing-home-sales/.

[5] Redfin. *Real Estate Commissions.* www.redfin.com/guides/how-much-is-real-estate-agent-commission-buyer-seller.

Other closing costs can include pro-rata taxes, home association dues, attorney's fees, and title fees, to name a few.[6]

Tokenization

Now imagine the ability to reduce those closing costs significantly. Blockchain makes that possible. How? By tokenizing the home and putting it on a blockchain where one or more buyers can buy it with cryptocurrency.

So, what does it mean to tokenize a home? The value of the home or property is transferred to a digital token that is then placed on the blockchain where it can be put up for sale.[7] Token value can also be broken down into shares allowing multiple parties to become stakeholders.[8]

Blockchain technology allows buyers and sellers to connect with one another without the need for an intermediary, which helps lower the cost of buying or selling property. The technology also allows property to be sold quickly and safely while reducing the risk of fraud.[9] Several sales platforms, including some offered by traditional realtors, are using blockchain today to do just that.

No sale caught more attention than the U.S.$22.5 million purchase of a Miami Beach penthouse sold on the Ethereum blockchain in 2021, making it the most expensive property bought using cryptocurrency.[10] Commission alone could have added U.S.$1.35 million to the cost using traditional methods.

---

[6] Ayers. *Closing Costs*. https://listwithclever.com/real-estate-blog/do-closing-costs-include-realtor-fees/.

[7] X. Charles. *Real Estate Tokenization*. www.finextra.com/blogposting/21252/upgrading-real-estate-tokenization-to-the-next-level#:~:text=The%20process%20of%20real%20estate,raise%20capital%20for%20investment%20development.

[8] Geroni. *Tokenization Explained*. https://101blockchains.com/tokenization-blockchain/.

[9] Redolfi. *Blockchain Real Estate Transactions*. www.forbes.com/sites/forbesbizcouncil/2021/10/27/the-future-of-real-estate-transactions-on-the-blockchain/?sh=362a55b49387.

[10] Mafi. *Expensive Miami Beach Home Bought With Cryptocurrency*. www.architecturaldigest.com/story/miami-beach-home-most-expensive-bought-cryptocurrency.

Liquidity

The ability to place properties on the blockchain can help alleviate liquidity issues. Tokens can be exchanged quickly and converted into cash.[11] Homeowners can bypass traditional methods and put their property on a public blockchain, making it available to a broader audience. The wider the audience, the better the opportunity to sell.[12]

The owners of commercial properties can also benefit. Rather than waiting for one investor to come through with a deal, commercial property can be divided into tiny units (square feet/square meters), tokenized, and sold to investors. Tokenization provides the needed cash while offering an investment opportunity to those who could not otherwise afford such a hefty investment.[13]

Property transactions could be significantly simplified using blockchain. Buyers, sellers, lessors, and lessees could deal directly without an intermediary. ATLANT, for example, uses blockchain to offer tokenized ownership and P2P rentals.[14]

The tokenization of real estate will make it easier to enter the market. Tokens offer liquidity, while the ledger offers transparency.[15]

Placing property on a distributed ledger streamlines the process by eliminating the need to cull through public records and validating titles to ascertain property history, ultimately lowering costs. A review by Goldman Sachs estimates blockchain-driven property records could save consumers up to U.S.$4 billion.[16]

We'll discuss property and real estate further in the chapter on NFTs.

---

[11] SC& SCAND. *Blockchain Real Estate Transactions*. https://scand.com/company/blog/the-future-of-real-estate-transactions-on-the-blockchain/#:~:text=But%20why%20do%20more%20and,property%20history%20and%20its%20status.

[12] Kaur. *Blockchain Disrupting Real Estate Market*. https://medium.datadriveninvestor.com/blockchain-in-real-estate-how-this-disrupts-the-market-394ea2a230ac.

[13] J. Liebkind. *Blockchain Changing Real Estate*. www.investopedia.com/news/how-blockchain-technology-changing-real-estate/.

[14] Newsbtc. *ATLANT Using Blockchain*. www.newsbtc.com/news/atlant-blockchain-real-estate-ecosystem/#:~:text=ATLANT's%20blockchain%20platform%20is%20designed,property%20on%20a%20distributed%20ledger.

[15] Ibid.

[16] Ibid.

What's Ahead

In the future, buyers will be able to check the history of a property and view inspection reports on a blockchain. Blockchain technology will allow potential buyers to determine if there are any issues beforehand.[17] It will take time as there are questions if smart contracts can handle intricate details needed to execute a sale correctly; how to integrate the technology into recording services in countries like the United States where recording and maintaining land titles is constitutionally prescribed; and how it will affect today's legal community.[18]

---

[17] Kaur. *Blockchain in Real Estate.* https://medium.datadriveninvestor.com/blockchain-in-real-estate-how-this-disrupts-the-market-394ea2a230ac.
[18] Aufrichtig. *The Blockchain Easement.* https://cardozoaelj.com/2021/10/25/the-blockchain-easement-benefits-and-drawbacks-of-blockchain-technology-in-real-estate/.

Blockchain and Print Media

Print journalism, as we know it, is in trouble. Declining readership and competition from alternative sources, particularly from Internet sources, are forcing many to scale down their operations, merge, or close their doors.

Once the primary sources of information and influence, newspapers have taken a beating over the past decade trying to compete with the Internet. Newspapers, which earn money with advertising, initially created their own websites, which were free to the public, offering extras like news updates and alerts to attract *hits*, proving to advertisers they still held sway. Some quickly learned they needed to charge for access to protect their subscriptions. Why pay if the content is free? So, they set up paywalls. Visitors, who did not have subscriptions, were granted access to a handful of articles each month with hopes this would entice them to sign up.

Advertising rates are based on the number of paid subscriptions. The larger the subscription base, the more they can charge advertisers. When subscriptions decline, advertising revenues drop, forcing layoffs and, in many cases, mergers or closures.

Advertising revenue in the United States went from U.S.$46.2 billion in 2002 to U.S.$22.1 billion in 2022, as daily readership went from 55.8 million in 2000 to 24.2 million in 2020.[1]

The number of daily newspapers in the country dropped from 1,472 in 2004 to 1,230 in 2022. This includes 100 dailies that were converted to weekly newspapers.[2] The number of weekly newspapers that either merged or went out of business totaled 2,514 between 2004 and 2022,

---

[1] Grundy. *Decline in Print Publishing Revenue Survey.* www.census.gov/library/stories/2022/06/internet-crushes-traditional-media.html.

[2] Watson. *"Local Newspaper Losses in U.S. 2004–2022.* www.statista.com/statistics/944134/number-closed-merged-newspapers/#:~:text=A%20report%20on%20local%20news,to%201%2C500%20to%20under%201%2C250.

while the number of nondailies (those that publish one to three times per week) dropped from 7,419 in 2004 to 5,147 in 2022.[3]

One growing trend has been the creation of nonprofit news organizations. The biggest impact has been on coverage of the statehouse. Some 80 nonprofit news organizations across the United States accounted for 20 percent of news organizations covering state capitols in 2022, up from 6 percent in 2014.[4] Aside from government, nonprofits focus on the environment, education, and social justice and inequality.[5]

These nonprofits include *ProPublica, The Intercept, The Texas Tribune, Mississippi Center for Investigative Reporting, Mississippi Today, Global Reporting Center*, and the magazine *Mother Jones*.

These news organizations, which numbered 172 in 2012,[6] are among 1.5 million nonprofits in the United States alone[7] competing for donations. While primary funding comes from foundations, many raise money through membership programs, reaching out to consumers already inundated with requests.

While circulations decline, the age of readers continues to increase, a trend that began well before the digital age. A 2017 nationwide survey conducted by Neilsen Scarborough of more than 204,000 residents across the United States found the median age of those who read the print editions of daily newspapers was 53.5 years, while those who read online

---

[3] Ibid.

[4] Forman-Katz, Shearer, and Masta. *Nonprofit News in Statehouse Coverage.* www.pewresearch.org/fact-tank/2022/04/29/nonprofit-news-outlets-are-playing-a-growing-role-in-statehouse-coverage/#:~:text=Pew%20Research%20Center's%20accounting%20of,outlets%20that%20cover%20U.S.%20statehouses.

[5] Ibrisevic. *Nonprofit Journalism.* https://donorbox.org/nonprofit-blog/nonprofit-journalism-funding#:~:text=Nonprofit%20news%20organizations%20focus%20on,media%20organizations%20are%20decades%2Dold.

[6] Forman-Katz, Shearer, and Masta. *Nonprofit News in Statehouse Coverage.* www.pewresearch.org/fact-tank/2022/04/29/nonprofit-news-outlets-are-playing-a-growing-role-in-statehouse-coverage/#:~:text=Pew%20Research%20Center's%20accounting%20of,outlets%20that%20cover%20U.S.%20statehouses.

[7] Ariella. *Number of Nonprofits 2022.* www.zippia.com/advice/nonprofit-statistics/#:~:text=There%20are%20over%201.5%20million,around%2010%20million%20nonprofits%20worldwide.

editions on their personal computers was 41.4 years. Those who viewed newspapers on their mobile devices were 38.6 years.[8]

Newspapers aren't the only ones suffering. Magazines have also been hit by readers who prefer digital formats over print, forcing the industry to make dramatic changes. Many magazines, like newspapers, offer customers the option of print or online editions, or both. Some magazines, like a handful of newly constituted newspapers, offer digital-only editions.

There's no paper or ink to buy, but digital editions still cost money, so publishers must find ways to attract advertisers. Some invite advertisers to post ads directly or use popups, which readers can find annoying. Readers have fought back using ad blockers only to be countered by websites that remind consumers it costs money to operate the site, and so would they kindly pause their ad blocker. Failing to do so can result in a lack of access.

Worldwide, nearly 43 percent of internet users use ad blockers. Indonesia ranks highest, with almost 60 percent using ad blockers, while Mexico ranked lowest with just over 17 percent. In the United States, nearly 39 percent use ad blockers.[9]

Another way to keep up with site visitors is through cookies, which identify the computer and its user. They were initially designed to improve the user's experience by remembering information like usernames and passwords. Today, they track users' movements, interests, and purchases, information the site holds onto for the next time the user visits. They can also spy on users and share their browsing history.[10] Of course, the site asks permission. Typically, most visitors don't think twice about it and agree. After all, visitors can clean their cookies later.

Popup ads and cookies may be necessary for online platforms to earn money, but they don't inspire confidence among users. A Pew study

---

[8] Conaghan. *All Ages Read Newspapers.* www.newsmediaalliance.org/age-newspaper-readers-platforms/.

[9] Dean. *Ad Blocker Usage.* https://backlinko.com/ad-blockers-users.

[10] Stewart. *Cookies.* www.vox.com/recode/2019/12/10/18656519/what-are-cookies-website-tracking-gdpr-privacy.

found that 68 percent of adults have a negative view of targeted ads, with 59 percent reporting they were aware they were being targeted.[11]

Online users aren't the only ones troubled. It's been estimated that publishers and content providers lost between U.S.$16 billion and U.S.$78 billion in ad revenue in 2020 due to ad blockers.[12] To counter the losses, some publishers are turning to subscriptions to build a following, which has garnered mixed results.[13]

It boils down to this. Readers need to feel their private information and viewings are private. Publishers need to make money to provide information to build a following and grow. Advertisers need to know that the money they spend on advertising is worth the expense. So, what's the solution?

A Token Solution

Recognizing that online advertising was *broken*, Brave Software, an online startup, developed a browser they believe can satisfy all three interested parties.[14] The Brave Browser, an open-source browser, blocks ads and trackers, replacing advertising with their advertisers. Users who agree to view ads receive basic attention tokens (BATs), which they can then pass on to publishers and individual content providers to support their sites.[15]

---

[11] Sullivan. *Pew Survey: Targeted Ads Unacceptable.* https://martech.org/pew-survey-targeted-ads-negatively/?utm_campaign=tweet&utm_source=socialflow&utm_medium=twitter.

[12] Jatain. *Countering Revenue Loss From Ad Blockers.* https://digitalcontentnext.org/blog/2020/08/12/countering-the-revenue-loss-caused-by-ad-blockers/.

[13] Setupad. *Ad Blocker Trends 2022.* https://setupad.com/blog/ad-blockers-trends-tips/.

[14] Brave Software. *Basic Attention Tokens in Advertising.* https://basicattentionto-ken.org/static-assets/documents/BasicAttentionTokenWhitePaper-4.pdf.

[15] Keiser. *Brave Browser Basics.* www.computerworld.com/article/3292619/the-brave-browser-basics-what-it-does-how-it-differs-from-rivals.html#:~:text=The%20web%20browser%20from%20Brave,money%20to%20sites%20they%20like.&text=Boutique%20browsers%20try%20to%20scratch,underserved%20by%20the%20usual%20suspects.

BATs are utility tokens, which are tokens that are issued by platforms to raise capital. They can be redeemed for goods or services on that platform. We will discuss utility token in greater detail in the section on cryptocurrency.

The Brave browser uses a ledger system that measures users' attention and rewards the publishers based on that information.[16]

Users' private information is not collected, allowing them to surf the Web anonymously.[17]

It is seen as a win–win for everyone. Users get tailored ads, publishers, and individual content providers earn needed revenue, while advertisers can focus their ads on what users are interested in.[18]

As of August 2022, the Brave browser reportedly attracted 57.42 million monthly active users and 19.3 million daily users.[19] Compare that to Google's Chrome browser, which reported between 2.65 billion[20] and 3.3 billion users.[21] Safari came in second, in that report with around 945 million users.[22] Firefox was next with 181 million, followed by Microsoft Edge with 171 million. Samsung Internet garnered 167 million users, followed by Opera with 112 million users.[23] Combined, these companies represent about five billion browsers that, with the exception of Opera, consume users' private data for the privilege of browsing.

The Brave browser is a start that protects everyone's interests—users, advertisers, and publishers who can funnel their profits back into newspapers, allowing them to do what they do best: report the news.

---

[16] Brave Software. *Basic Attention Tokens in Advertising.* https://basicattentiontoken.org/static-assets/documents/BasicAttentionTokenWhitePaper-4.pdf.

[17] Hayes. *What Is Basic Attention Token.* www.investopedia.com/terms/b/basic-attention-token.asp.

[18] Brave Software. *Basic Attention Tokens in Advertising.* https://basicattentiontoken.org/static-assets/documents/BasicAttentionTokenWhitePaper-4.pdf.

[19] Wikipedia. *Brave Browser.* https://en.wikipedia.org/wiki/Brave_(webbrowser).

[20] Dean. *Google Chrome Statistics for 2022.* https://backlinko.com/chrome-users.

[21] K. Balakumar. *3 Billion Use Google Chrome.* www.techradar.com/news/google-chrome-browser-now-has-more-than-3-billion-users.

[22] Ibid.

[23] Ibid.

Blockchain and the Practice of Law

The practice of law has seen its highs and lows through the centuries. Beginning in ancient Greece and Rome, individuals were expected to argue their cases. Still, they would ask another to argue on their behalf. Over time, these representatives evolved into advocates trained in rhetoric, not law. By the start of the Byzantine Empire, 395 BC, the legal profession had become "well-established, highly regulated, and highly stratified."[1]

The profession collapsed following the fall of the Roman Empire up through the early period known as the Dark Ages (AD 476–1000). Beginning in 1150, the legal profession saw a revival as a small group of Catholic priests who became experts in canon law. However, their vocation remained the priesthood. Between 1190 and 1230, there was a shift as some chose to focus on canon law as their profession.[2]

Common law, based on "court-established legal precedents rather than statutes,"[3] was established in England following the Norman Conquest of 1066. Judges and juries rendered verdicts.[4] Civil law, which is based on law passed by legislation,[5] has its roots in the 6th century, flourishing in Europe beginning in the 11th century.[6]

Modern law is set by legislative action as well as legal precedents, the latter able to overturn the former. Practicing law today requires more attention from attorneys who find themselves juggling more and more

---

[1] Wikipedia. *History of Legal Profession.* https://en.wikipedia.org/wiki/History_of_the_legal_profession.

[2] Ibid.

[3] Vuleta. *What Is Common Law.* https://legaljobs.io/blog/what-is-common-law/.

[4] Ibid.

[5] Ibid.

[6] Berkley Law. *Common Law and Civil Law Traditions, Berkeley Law.* www.law.berkeley.edu/wp-content/uploads/2017/11/CommonLawCivilLawTraditions.pdf.

responsibilities at once as well as more and more time managing their paperwork. A study in 2018 found that lawyers spend 48 percent of their time on such things as moving information on software and updating client trust ledgers.[7]

Information gathered for a survey conducted in the United States, the United Kingdom, France, Germany, Australia, and Japan found that attorneys spend an average of 11.2 hours per week "creating, editing, reviewing and/or approving electronic documents," of which six hours were wasted, according to the report.[8]

The survey found this loss in productivity costs legal firms an average of U.S.$9,071 per attorney or a loss of 9.8 percent in total productivity. The study said that a firm with 100 lawyers comes to more than U.S.$900,000 annually.[9]

Another troubling discovery was that a significant number of documents collected by attorneys they were supposed to have filed were missing from their firm's centralized file system. That's because lawyers are not as diligent about following the steps necessary to file those documents, according to the survey. It found that *typical* law firms are missing around 50 percent of their information.[10]

Also, the survey found that 80 percent of intellectual property in firms is stored or shared via e-mail. However, their document management systems, developed in the 1980s "before the Internet and mobile computing," do not "automatically include e-mails as part of their document collection process," according to the survey findings.[11]

Seeking solutions, the legal profession is moving to blockchain technology, which "can streamline, re-engineer, automate, disintermediate, and secure many processes without losing any of the judicial authority. Optimizing various industry features will make the legal and financial sectors more efficient and productive while lowering friction and costs."[12]

---

[7] Consensys. *Blockchain Law.* https://consensys.net/blockchain-use-cases/law/.
[8] MetaJure Team. *Lawyers Lost Time.* https://metajure.com/lawyers-waste-six-hours-a-week-on-document-management-issues-2/.
[9] Ibid.
[10] Ibid.
[11] Ibid.
[12] Ibid.

The legal profession expects blockchain to positively impact real estate law, estate planning, and intellectual property rights.[13]

A 2017 survey of PwC law firms found that 70 percent of law firms surveyed would use smart contracts for *transactional legal services*, while 41 percent would use blockchain for the same purpose. Another 31 percent said they would use blockchain for providing high-value legal services, and 21 percent said they would use it for business support.[14]

These tools can be instrumental in aiding attorneys to improve efficiency and reduce their time spent on paperwork. Blockchain could help them draft contracts, record commercial transactions, and be used to help verify legal documents.[15] Two such programs now available are OpenLaw and Integra Ledger.[16]

OpenLaw is a blockchain program on Ethereum that allows lawyers to create and execute contracts.[17] Integra Ledger offers a program that enables blockchain technology to be integrated into existing programs without the need to build a program from the bottom up.[18]

Smart Contracts

Smart contracts are a crucial blockchain tool expected to play an integral role in contract preparation. A smart contract, embedded in a transaction, is a self-executing contract activated when the terms and conditions initially agreed upon between two parties are realized.[19]

---

[13] Practice Panther in Security. *Blockchain in Law Firms*. www.practicepanther .com/blog/how-blockchain-technology-will-drive-clients-to-your-law-firm/.

[14] ABC Legal Services. *Blockchain and the Legal Profession*. www.abclegal.com/ blog/legal-tech-blockchain.

[15] Y. Han. February 20, 2018. *How Blockchain Technology Is Transforming the Legal Industry, Bloomberg Law*. https://news.bloomberglaw.com/tech-and-telecom-law/ how-blockchain-technology-is-transforming-the-legal-industry.

[16] Ibid.

[17] ConcenSys Media. *Introducing OpenLaw*. https://media.consensys.net/ introducing-openlaw-7a2ea410138b.

[18] Artificial Lawyer. *Integra Ledgers' Tools*. www.artificiallawyer.com/2018/10/16/ integra-ledger-launches-tools-to-add-blockchain-tech-to-all-legal-software/.

[19] Frankenfield. *What Are Smart Contracts*. www.investopedia.com/terms/s/ smart-contracts.asp Contracts on the.

The term *smart contract* was coined in 1996 by Nick Szabo, the legal scholar, computer programmer, and cryptography. He defined *smart contracts* as "computerized transaction protocols that execute the terms of a contract."[20]

Smart contracts are not contracts in the legal sense of the word but are used to activate agreements. They are simply a string of code that, for example, allows assets or services to be passed from one person to the next if certain conditions are met. The transfer is made without the need for an intermediary. Smart contracts are also used for automatic payments, escrow arrangements, insurance settlements, automatic ordering, royalty payment management and distribution, and payments for goods on delivery.[21]

If smart contracts include the elements of a legal contract, some argue they should be treated as such.[22]

Most legislative initiatives to codify the use of smart contracts do so with a narrow focus on what they are, the recognition of signatures, and whether they can be admitted into evidence in court cases.[23]

Another issue is that smart contracts cannot be amended.[24]

Regulatory guidance is needed, some say.[25] Otherwise, the laws supporting smart contracts could find that they may not be applicable in all states. The lack of uniformity could result in a hodgepodge of state laws that don't apply outside their borders, leading to further confusion at the federal level.[26]

The same debate is being voiced worldwide, with most countries accepting smart contracts as long as they are legal. If so, they should not cause problems in existing legal frameworks. The UK's Law Commission

---

[20] Ibid.

[21] Bowles. *Smart Contracts and Enforcement.* https://emlaw.co.uk/smart-contracts-legally-enforceable/.

[22] Ibid.

[23] Ferreira. *Smart Contracts and Legal Challenges.* https://cointelegraph.com/news/smart-contracts-and-the-law-tech-developments-challenge-legal-community.

[24] Ibid.

[25] Ibid.

[26] Ibid.

published a report at the end of 2021, concluding that "the law of England and Wales can facilitate and support smart legal contracts without the need for reform."[27] Some argue otherwise, recognizing that smart contracts are relatively new instruments, so it is too early to tell what impact they might have on existing law.[28]

While some recognize the limitations of smart contracts as they now stand, the legal establishment largely seems comfortable that these are issues that can and will be addressed, allowing them to proceed with their plans to implement this technology.

Some say change is slow in the legal community, so it will take time before the profession fully embraces the technology. In the end, experts believe that blockchain technology will become an integrated tool that enhances their work rather than taking away from it.[29]

---

[27] Artificial Lawyer. *UK Law Commission OKs Smart Contracts*. www.artificiallawyer.com/2021/11/25/uk-law-commission-gives-smart-contracts-the-green-light/.
[28] Chandler. *Smart Contracts as Legal Contracts*. https://cointelegraph.com/news/smart-contracts-are-no-problem-for-the-worlds-legal-systems-so-long-as-they-behave-like-legal-contracts.
[29] W. Sean. *Improving Law Offices With Blockchain*. www.theracetothebottom.org/rttb/2020/4/1/blockchain-technology-improving-law-offices-or-decreasing-the-need-for-lawyers.

Blockchain

Travel and Entertainment

We all love our free time, whether it's eating out at a restaurant, taking in a show, going to a concert, or packing up the bags for that long-anticipated getaway. It's our free time, and with the demands of our ever-encroaching jobs, it's essential to make sure our plans are affordable and secure.

Several companies specializing in travel and entertainment are turning to blockchain technology to give consumers control over their wallets and personal information.

Leisure travel and entertainment is a multitrillion-dollar business. Between 2000 and 2020, global travelers spent just under U.S.$65 trillion on leisure and tourism, or an average of U.S.$3.1 trillion per year.[1] The COVID-19 pandemic significantly reduced travel in 2020, cutting that year's projected total by 49.3 percent to U.S.$2.37 trillion, a level not seen since 2003.[2]

This staggering amount spent on travel and entertainment in 2019 accounted for 10.94 percent of the global gross domestic product (GDP) but only 5.5 percent of the GDP in 2020 due to pandemic-related travel restrictions.[3]

Regarding overall expenditures, China was ranked first in 2017, with U.S.$257.7 billion spent on traveling, followed by the United States, whose citizens spent U.S.$173.9 billion. Germany ranked third, with U.S.$97.6 billion, and the UK came in fourth, with U.S.$71.7 billion.[4]

---

[1] Statista Research Department. *Tourism spending Worldwide 2019–2021*. www .statista.com/statistics/1093335/leisure-travel-spending-worldwide/.

[2] Ibid.

[3] World Travel Tourism Council. *Economic Impact Reports 2022*. https://wttc .org/research/economic-impact.

[4] Index Mundi. *International Tourism Expenditures Rankings*. www.indexmundi .com/facts/indicators/ST.INT.XPND.CD/rankings.

According to one statistic, Americans spend an average of U.S.$1,145 per person on a summer vacation or U.S.$4,580 for a family of four.[5] Included in that total were various fees and surcharges collected by third parties.

Rental Property

One of the most significant expenditures is lodging. In response to escalating hotel prices, which cost an average of U.S.$141 per night,[6] consumers are embracing rental properties that provide the holiday experience with all the comforts of home for less.

Several blockchain startups are looking to offer travelers an alternative method of booking lodging and entertainment packages they say will cut reservation costs and fees even more by removing the middleman, all while protecting personal information.[7] Today, large corporations hold personal information that can be used, bought, sold, or shared with others. Blockchain technology uses decentralized servers to keep customer information in the customer's hands.[8]

How effective can blockchain be in cutting costs? Airbnb, which burst onto the scene in August 2008, now controls 20 percent of the rental property market.[9] For its services, Airbnb collects a whopping 20 percent fee.[10] By comparison, a blockchain alternative like Dtravel, a community owned and governed by its users,[11] charges between 5 and 10 percent.[12]

---

[5] M. Yaqub. *Average Vacations Costs*. www.renolon.com/average-vacations-cost-and-spending-statistics/.

[6] Price. *Average Vacation Cost*. www.valuepenguin.com/average-cost-vacation.

[7] Magyar. *Vacation Rentals and Blockchain*. https://rentalsunited.com/blog/blockchain-vacation-rentals/.

[8] Ibid.

[9] Clifford. *Competitors for Airbnb*. https://hospitable.com/competitors-for-airbnb/#:~:text=Airbnb%20market%20share&text=Statistics%20from%202019%20estimate%20that,the%20realms%20of%20%20%2420Billion.

[10] Cassell. *Blockchain Startups in Travel Industry*. https://investorplace.com/newdigitalworld/2022/03/3-blockchain-startups-to-watch-in-the-travel-industry-as-vacations-make-a-comeback/.

[11] Rentalz. *Dtravel Blockchain Booking*. https://shorttermrentalz.com/news/dtravel-first-travel-booking-blockchain/.

[12] Cassell. *Blockchain Startups in Travel Industry*. https://investorplace.com/newdigitalworld/2022/03/3-blockchain-startups-to-watch-in-the-travel-industry-as-vacations-make-a-comeback/.

Let's look at a few other examples.

EzyStayz, based in the Asia-Pacific region, is a smart contract platform that offers P2P connections between travelers and hosts worldwide, saving travelers money. Payments are made using the Ezy token, the company's cryptocurrency. Property owners list their properties for a low fee. Using this platform gives them another platform to earn revenue with their property.[13]

Travala, a blockchain-based site from the UK, offers short-term rental properties worldwide, allowing customers to pay using one of 30 different types of cryptocurrencies, including its own AVA token, along with traditional payment methods. The site boasts it can reduce fees by 15 percent.[14]

Webjet of Australia is a traditional travel site for Australia and New Zealand. To improve customer experience, the agency added blockchain technology to answer questions about inaccurate or lost hotel bookings. Using blockchain to post problems such as incorrect bookings, the company can provide real-time information that it can quickly share with customers, agents, and hotels.[15] In addition, travelers can save money with lower booking fees.[16]

Nothing is more frustrating than landing at an airport, going to the baggage claim and discovering your luggage didn't arrive. Blockchain technology allows customers and airlines to track luggage from check-in to the end of the flight.[17] In 2017, Air New Zealand came together with Winding Tree, a Swiss travel startup built as a decentralized marketplace

---

[13] Victor. *Holiday Rental Using Blockchain.* https://medium.com/@Mexite3yo/ ezystayz-unleashing-the-full-potentials-of-global-holiday-rental-using-block-chain-technology-e9775f6e4432.

[14] Cryptonews.com. *Travala.com.* https://cryptonews.com/coins/travala/#:~:text= Travala%20promises%20to%20combat%20high,as%20Expedia%20or%20 Booking.com.

[15] Liebkind. *Blockchain to Change Travel.* www.investopedia.com/news/ 6-companies-using-blockchain-change-travel-0/.

[16] Ibid.

[17] EAS Intelligence. *Blockchain in Aviation Sector.* www.eos-intelligence .com/perspectives/transportation/blockchain-likely-to-make-a-safe-landing-in-aviation-sector/.

on the Ethereum blockchain, to look at blockchain solutions to track luggage and improve security and boarding.[18]

As more and more people go online to plan their getaways, blockchain could be a supportive tool that helps them save money while offering security and safety.

Concerts and Events

Scalpers can ruin any event before it gets started. It's inevitable that when big names announce tours, scalpers lie in wait to grab as many tickets as they can, then sell those tickets at inflated prices. Efforts have been made to limit ticket sales to individuals, but scalpers find ways to get around the rules. Blockchain technology would allow promoters to sell directly to individuals, bypassing the middleman.[19] The technology could also enable concert-goers at music festivals to choose specific performances they want to see.[20]

Theme Parks

Blockchain technology could help vacationers plan their next trip to their favorite amusement park. They could use blockchain to book in advance, ensuring their bookings are secure.

Because the information is transparent and immutable, scalpers cannot forge or sell tickets for a higher price.[21] Park visitors also could rest assured their tickets can't be lost or stolen.

---

[18] Chavez-Dreyfuss. *Winding Tree Travel and Blockchain.* www.reuters.com/article/us-blockchain-travel-airnewzealand-idUSKBN1DM2KQ.

[19] Treehouse Technology Group. *Blockchain and Concerts.* https://treehousetech-group.com/blockchain-and-concert-experience/#:~:text=Blockchain-based%20ticketing%20platforms%20can,with%20ticketing%20sites%20like%20TicketMaster.

[20] Ibid.

[21] VeriDoc Global. *Blockchain and Theme Park Tickets.* https://veridocglobal .medium.com/theme-park-tickets-and-veridoc-globals-blockchain-solution-a-winning-combination-c731f8befbd0.

One exciting possibility is creating a blockchain-based theme park currency that could be traded for goods and services.[22]

The use of blockchain technology in the world of entertainment is endless.

What's Possible?

In the age of apps, QR codes, and digital wallets controlled by consumers who expect immediacy, the travel and tourism industry (looking to reinvent itself for the next generation of consumers) is turning to technology for help. If it can be tokenized and activated by a smart contract, it can become a valuable tool to meet the demand of the *click it* world.

---

[22] Pitchforth. *Blockchain and Theme Parks.* www.coindesk.com/tech/2017/05/16/5-ways-theme-parks-could-embrace-blockchain-and-why-they-should/.

What's Ahead for Blockchain?

Blockchain, built on the idea of privacy and transparency, allows two parties to transact with one another, without the need for a third party to oversee that transaction.

Transactions are stored on decentralized public ledgers in blocks as pieces of encrypted code, including senders, receivers, and their addresses. Transactions include smart contracts, which activate if all conditions are met. Once transactions are made, they cannot be altered or erased. They are immutable.

This book only scratches the surface of blockchain's potential, touching on obvious samples of how blockchain is currently being used and how it is envisioned to be used.

Blockchain technology has been embraced by those who believe the online world, controlled by large third-party centralized platforms, is too intrusive. At the same time, it is being adopted by those same institutions that think it will reduce paperwork and streamline their operations, all while saving money.

The reality is that blockchain is still a work in progress. The amount of data stored on individual blocks are currently limited, requiring other considerations, such as a hybrid blockchain—a mix of public and private spaces—to store data. There are also issues regarding long-term storage that need to be addressed. There are also oversight issues to be addressed as governments worldwide look at how this technology is being used while considering what steps need to be taken to provide oversight. There are legal issues to be solved regarding smart contracts in a landscape where case law is, for the moment, scare, if not nonexistent.

Like any new technology, we are at the starting gate. What's envisioned today will certainly be modified or changed radically to fit what is needed. What is certain is that the Web and how it is being used today are changing.

Cryptocurrency

Introduction

On All Hallows' Eve, October 31, 1517, German Catholic monk and scholar Martin Luther posted his *95 Theses* to the door of the Castle Church in Wittenberg, Germany, attacking the church, in particular for the practice of selling indulgences—forgiveness of one's sins. His heretical challenge of church authority launched the Protestant Reformation.

On October 31, 2008, 491 years after Luther's revolutionary post, the mysterious Satoshi Nakamoto posted his infamous white paper, *Bitcoin: A Peer-to-Peer Electronic Cash System*, on the Internet, attacking financial institutions for their one-sided control over Internet commerce. His solution was a P2P electronic payment system he called *Bitcoin* using a public open ledger called *blockchain* that allows two people to transact business anonymously with the aid of a *trustless* network of decentralized computer operators. The paper sparked the cryptocurrency revolution, ushering in a new age of commerce designed to loosen, if not eliminate, the grip of private institutions over the Internet and commerce while restoring personal privacy.

Since the launch of the first bitcoin in January 2009, the cryptocurrency market has exploded, setting off a 21st-century gold rush similar to the California Gold Rush of the mid-19th century. The noble cause championed by Satoshi would be eclipsed by the prospect of riches found in *mining* and holding bitcoin, although its inflated value would take several years to be realized. Financial investors, anxious to get in on crypto fever, rushed in, creating exchanges and demand, overshadowing the tech creators who joined in and used cryptocurrency to raise capital for their projects. In 2023, there were more than 10,000 coins and tokens in circulation.[1] Many become worthless, while others have enjoyed a meteoric ride; many based on hype.

---

[1] Howarth. *Cryptocurrencies in 2024.* https://explodingtopics.com/blog/number-of-cryptocurrencies.

The rush to crypto and the rags-to-riches-to-rags stories that followed have tainted the movement, overlooking the utility of its key component—the blockchain. The blockchain delivers incorruptible data that cannot be altered or challenged by being outfitted with components like an immutable timestamp, smart contracts, and cryptography.

Aside from cryptocurrency, blockchain technology is used to transmit information about business, finance, medicine, law, and real estate, to name a few. As you read in the previous section, it's being used today to combat counterfeit foods and fasion, and slave labor. Governments are employing blockchain to register property, while realtors are embracing it to sell residential and commercial properties. Why? Because blockchain cuts out the middleman, saving both time and money. Blockchain technology is also being employed by some governments, including the United States, as a tool for voting.

It all started with cryptocurrency—virtual money created to conduct transactions.

This section will introduce you to the basics of cryptocurrency—what it is, the tools needed to wield it, and how it is being used today.

Money: Everyone's Favorite Topic

When we use the term *cryptocurrency*, most people immediately think of *bitcoin*, the premier virtual form of currency. Bitcoin was launched in January 2009, following the release of Satoshi's whitepaper a few months earlier. He pondered the idea of a "peer-to-peer electronic cash system"[2] without needing a centralized third-party platform such as a bank to complete transactions. Instead, he suggested assets could be transferred using an existing, yet unused, software protocol created over a decade earlier called a *blockchain*.

Bitcoin is a virtual currency. It has no physical form. Like fiat money (money issued by a central authority), virtual currency represents value. However, unlike fiat money, virtual money is not legal tender. That is, it does not have central authority (government) backing. Instead,

---

[2] N. Satoshi. *White Paper.* https://nakamotoinstitute.org/https://nakamotoinstitute .org/bitcoin/.

cryptocurrency is created by private developers[3] and derives its value from expectations.

As you recall from the last section, transactions are placed in a pro-tected layer of coding referred to as a *block* containing the names of the sender, receiver, addresses, and contents. An unalterable timestamp records the time and date of the transaction. The block also has a unique cryptographic fingerprint, called a *hash*, that identifies the block and its contents. The block contains a smart contract that executes the trans-action if all conditions are met. While the contents are known only to the sender and receiver, the block and its encrypted contents are moni-tored by a worldwide, decentralized network that verifies all transactions and ensures the block is not tampered with or changed. Blocks are added through a verification process. Once verified, they are added to those that preceded it, forming a blockchain. Once created, blockchains can never be altered or deleted. They will exist in perpetuity.

Since the launch of bitcoin, which has skyrocketed in value, the tech world has seen a proliferation of cryptocurrency coins and tokens eager to follow the trajectory of bitcoin.

Where Does Cryptocurrency Get Its Value?

The value of virtual currency is based on speculation, utility, and con-vergence.[4] Investors see it as an investment that can make themselves rich. Others view virtual currency as an alternative to buying and trading goods and services with fiat currency. A study published in the *Journal of Money, Credit and Banking* in 2019 found that speculators favorably react if they suspect a virtual currency will be successful.[5] The high volatility, which has followed bitcoin and other virtual currencies, is the result of *growing pains*, the study found.

---

[3] Frankenfield. *Virtual Currency*. www.investopedia.com/terms/v/virtual-currency .asp#:~:text=Virtual%20currencies%20are%20a%20form,physical%20 incarnation%20like%20paper%20money.

[4] van Oordt and Bolt. *Virtual Currency Speculation*. https://cepr.org/voxeu/ columns/speculation-and-price-virtual-currency.

[5] Bolt and van Oordt. *Virtual Currency Values*. https://onlinelibrary.wiley.com/ doi/full/10.1111/jmcb.12619.

The study, conducted by Wilko Bolt and Maarten R. C. van Oordt, found investors did better to hold cryptocurrency to see it rise in value rather than spend it. This idea, the authors said, echoed the writings of Irving Fisher, an American economist (1867–1947). Fisher argued in writings in 1911 that speculators could effectively control the money supply by withdrawing currency, hoping its future value would increase over time. He based this on the fact that on the run-up to the U.S. government's promise to redeem the greenback (officially known as U.S. Notes), some of the currency was withdrawn, waiting for the rise.[6]

These notes were called greenbacks because they were printed on green paper. This paper currency was first issued in 1862 to help pay for the American Civil War (April 12, 1861–April 9, 1865). More than U.S.$400 million in legal tender were printed.[7] The value of this legal tender was pegged to gold. Looking to get away from paper money, the U.S. Congress in 1875 passed the Redemption Act, which provided that the paper currency could be redeemed for gold. The goal was to reduce the number of greenbacks in circulation to U.S.$382 million.[8] Congress set January 1, 1879, as the start date.[9] Due to stiff opposition, the 45th Congress (1877–1879) amended the law to expand paper currency and continue to mint a limited number of silver dollars.[10]

The plan to reduce paper money, however, had the opposite effect. After U.S. Treasury Secretary John Sherman secured enough gold to purchase the paper, people realized their paper money was *good as gold* and found it unnecessary to redeem right away, allowing the paper money's acceptance to grow.[11]

---

[6] Ibid.

[7] Chen. *Greenback*. www.investopedia.com/terms/g/greenback.asp#:~:text=A%20 greenback%20is%20a%20slang,help%20finance%20the%20civil%20war.

[8] Wikipedia. *Greenback*. https://en.wikipedia.org/wiki/Greenback_(1860s_money).

[9] The Editors of Encyclopedia Britanica. *Greenback Movement*. www.britannica .com/event/Greenback-movement.

[10] Ibid.

[11] The Editors of Encyclopedia Britannica. 2022. "Resumption Act of 1875," *Encyclopedia Britannica*. www.britannica.com/topic/Resumption-Act-of-1875 (accessed October 13, 2022).

The best-known virtual coin known for volatility is bitcoin. It sold for nine cents in 2010 but skyrocketed in value to under U.S.$1,238 in 2013 before dropping to U.S.$687 that year.[12] Between 2016 and 2020, the price leaped from just over U.S.$900 to just over U.S.$19,346 in 2020.[13] Between 2021 and September 2022, holding bitcoin was like riding a rollercoaster. Prices surged from a high of just under U.S.$69,000 in November 2021 to a low of U.S.$28,000 in May 2022.[14] By mid-October 2022, the price for one coin was down to just over U.S.$19,000.[15]

Aside from speculation, two other factors influence price fluctuations, according to the study published in the *Journal of Money, Credit and Banking*. One is utility. Consumers must be willing to use virtual currency to make payments. Then that willingness to use it must be able to drive merchants to accept it and be willing to pay for the transactions as they do for credit and debit cards, but potentially at a lower cost.[16]

Simply put, the researchers surmised that as consumers embrace virtual currency, use it regularly, and put more virtual currency in circulation, speculation will decline and thereby reduce price volatility.[17]

The researchers also recognized their study constituted a *first step*, and more studies are needed to explain the virtual economy.[18]

Bitcoin found its way into the retail sector because developers and holders of bitcoin knew they had to be spent if the coins were to have utility.

Satoshi mined the very first bitcoin on January 3, 2009.[19] It would be just over 17 months before the first bitcoin was spent. That happened on May 22, 2010. On that day, Florida-based crypto developer Laszlo Hanyecz paid 10,000 bitcoins, then worth approximately U.S.$41,

[12] J. Edwards. *Bitcoin's Price History*. www.investopedia.com/articles/forex/121815/bitcoins-price-history.asp.

[13] Ibid.

[14] Ibid.

[15] YCharts. *Bitcoin Price*. https://ycharts.com/indicators/bitcoin_price.

[16] van Oordt and Bolt. *Virtual Currency Speculation*. https://cepr.org/voxeu/columns/speculation-and-price-virtual-currency.

[17] Ibid.

[18] Ibid.

[19] Wikipedia. *Bitcoin*. https://en.wikipedia.org/wiki/Bitcoin.

for two Papa John's pizzas.[20] In December 2021, that equated to more than U.S.$5.71 billion! No, that's not a typo. The value was U.S.$5.71 billion. Of course, it's easy to look back in hindsight and then gasp in disbelief. But remember, in those days, cryptocurrency was an untested novelty. Who knew, right? Look at comic books, for example. Do you think your mom would have thrown out your prized stack had she known how much they would have appreciated in value in today's market? On the other hand, had she left them alone, maybe that value wouldn't be as dramatic.

Although it wouldn't be surprising if there were days when Hanyecz regretted his decision, without his selfless contribution, the utility of bitcoin might have remained an untested novelty.

Hanyecz's actions did not go unnoticed. The crypto ecosystem marks May 22 as *Pizza Day* in honor of his legendary purchase.[21]

---

[20] DeCambre. *Bitcoin Pizza Day.* www.marketwatch.com/story/bitcoin-pizza-day-laszlo-hanyecz-spent-3-8-billion-on-pizzas-in-the-summer-of-2010-using-the-novel-crypto-11621714395.

[21] Ibid.

From Cows to Crypto

The Evolution of the Swap

Money, or the concept of money in all its forms, has been around since the dawn of civilization. What began as P2P transactions (I'll swap two chickens for your cow) has evolved into a centralized financial system controlled by well-staked financial institutions that have dominated global commerce for over two centuries. In a significant pushback, backers of cryptocurrency, fueled by Satoshi's pioneering thinking, are challenging the idea that banks are necessary for basic financial transactions. Instead of writing a check or sending money over PayPal, each involving a bank or payment platform that can take several days to process, cryptocurrency holders send virtual money that is received instantaneously without needing a third party.

To understand the future, it's a good idea to look at the past. Technology changes over time, but in the end, transactions between two people have always remained the same: I give you something of value for something of value in return.

Before we exchanged money for food, our ancestors bartered—a system of trading goods and services for something of like value. Cows were reportedly a favorite animal to trade for, say, grain. That was then. If you are of a certain age, you probably swapped baseball cards. For the younger generation, it's *Pokémon* cards. Or perhaps you needed something someone else had but were short on cash, so you traded your time, energy, or skills for it. For example, Dennis is a college student who needs a place to live while studying. He has a part-time job, but it isn't enough to pay for an apartment. He finds a comfortable garage apartment belonging to the Wilsons, a retired couple who need help maintaining their property. Mrs. Wilson often complains that her husband is too old to climb ladders and lift heavy boxes, a charge he rebuffs. Anyway, the couple strikes a deal with young Dennis. He can live in the apartment while he's in school in exchange for helping around the house. Dennis agrees. No cash exchanges hands, but the value is transferred through the bartering process.

Swapping favors is another form of barter that works well if both sides keep up their end of the bargain. Mark says, "Hey, David. I'll pick up our lunch if you look after the office for me." David agrees. Now then, two outcomes are possible. In one, Mark returns to the office with lunch and finds David on the phone handling a call that would have otherwise been missed.

On the other hand, when Mark returns with lunch in hand, he finds the office empty, with phones ringing off the hook and David nowhere to be found. Mark says to himself, "I knew better than to trust that guy." In either case, no money changes hands—only a met or unmet promise.

Some favors boil down to a request with an implied promise to repay the debt. Barbara is at her desk when Sam comes up to ask, "Hey Barbara, do me a favor and loan me $20. I'll get it back to you next week." Barbara must consider her options. Aside from whether she has the cash or can afford to lend it, she must decide if she can trust Sam to repay her. She has the promise of repayment but no guarantee.

The use of blockchain takes out the guesswork.

Swapping Salt for Gold

The practice of bartering can be traced back to tribes in ancient Mesopotamia (6000 BC),[1] which was then adopted by the Phoenicians, who found it useful when traveling across oceans to other lands. The Babylonians picked up the practice and improved it, trading such things as food, weapons, tea, human skulls, and spices.[2] Salt, also popular in those times, served as pay for Roman soldiers.[3]

Finding the need for portability, people began trading tokens—vouchers that could be exchanged for goods and services. Valuable tokens included seashells, stones, and other items thought unique. Colorful

---

[1] Mintlife. *Barter System*. https://mint.intuit.com/blog/personal-finance/guide-to-the-barter-economy-the-barter-system-history/.

[2] Ibid.

[3] Ibid.

seashells, for example, were formed into shapes or fashioned into beads and made into prized jewelry readily accepted as currency.[4]

Coins were first recorded in 600 BC in the kingdom of Lydia (located in what is now modern-day Turkey).[5] These first coins, made of electrum, an alloy of gold and silver, were minted by merchants who used them to pay transactions.[6]

Before they found their way into coins, gold and silver enjoyed popularity among those with means. Gold, dating back to the fourth century BC, when copper and other metals were mined,[7] was acquired by wealthy Egyptians in the third century BC. Artisans fashioned gold into jewelry and other ornaments.[8] While popular among the living, it was also used to create death masks and other ornate pieces for the tombs of the pharaohs.[9] Historians point to two specific reasons for gold's popularity there. First, Egyptians believed gold to be the flesh of Ra, their sun god.[10] Second, gold was plentiful in the region, even though difficult and expensive to extract and transport.[11]

Solid gold coins were first minted in China between 221 and 207 BC.[12]

Like gold, silver also found great appeal among ancient civilizations. A soft, aesthetically pleasing metal when polished, it was used as tableware, ornaments, or as *hacksilver* (fragments of silver) used for trade.[13] Silver coins first appeared in 550 BC in the Eastern Mediterranean.[14]

---

[4] Wikipedia. *Shell Money.* https://en.m.wikipedia.org/wiki/Shell_money.

[5] Whipps. *Coin History.* www.livescience.com/2058-profound-history-coins.html.

[6] van der Crabben. *Coinage.* www.worldhistory.org/coinage/.

[7] Altaweel, Sandvick, and Lambrecht. *Gold in Ancient Civilizations 2022.* https://dailyhistory.org/How_Did_Gold_Become_Desired_by_Ancient_Civilizations.

[8] Ibid.

[9] Providentmetals.com. *Precious Metals in Ancient Egypt.* https://blog.providentmetals.com/how-precious-metals-were-used-in-ancient-egypt.htm#.Y2-sTXaZND9.

[10] Altaweel, Sandvick, and Lambrecht. *Gold in Ancient Civilizations.* https://dailyhistory.org/How_Did_Gold_Become_Desired_by_Ancient_Civilizations.

[11] Ibid.

[12] Ibid.

[13] Cartwright. *Silver in Antiquity.* www.worldhistory.org/Silver/.

[14] Reuters Staff. *Brief History of Silver.* www.reuters.com/article/us-silver-history-idUSTRE73O13O20110425.

Rulers later practiced debasement—mixing precious metals with cheaper metals, like copper or zinc. For some, it was a way to create more coins, increasing the number in circulation. For others, it was greed. Why use all that gold when they could save it for themselves while still producing a viable currency? The problem with debasement is that it led to inflation. Although the face value remained unchanged, the intrinsic value was lowered, resulting in the need to pay out more coins for goods and services.[15]

Paper Becomes King

The first paper money came from China in AD 800 during the Tang dynasty (AD 600–918),[16] which reduced the need to transport coins over long distances. When redeemed, the holder received an equivalent sum in hard currency. Because the certificates were transferrable, merchants found it easier to swap the notes with others rather than to redeem them.[17] During the Song dynasty (AD 960–1279), wealthy merchants and financiers from Szechuan introduced paper money featuring pictures of people, trees, and homes. It was later modified over time with other distinctive markings.[18] This use of paper (made from the bark of Mulberry trees) was chronicled by Venetian merchant and explorer Marco Polo in the latter half of the 13th century.[19] Yet, paper currency wouldn't make its European debut until 1661.

As a result of its financial success abroad, England found itself awash in gold in the second half of the 17th century,[20] about the time paper money was making its way into Europe. As gold piled up, the question became where to store it all. Goldsmiths answered the call, agreeing to

[15] Halton. *Debasement.* www.investopedia.com/terms/d/debasement.asp.

[16] Silkroad.com. *Chinese Paper Money.* www.silk-road.com/artl/papermoney.shtml.

[17] Ibid.

[18] Ibid.

[19] Harford. *Chinese Money and Mulberry Bark.* www.bbc.com/news/business-40879028.

[20] NatWest Group History 100. *Goldsmith's Ledger 1671–72.* www.natwest-group.com/heritage/history-100/objects-by-theme/turning-points/goldsmiths-ledger-1671-72.html.

put the gold and other valuables in their vaults for safekeeping. Eventually they agreed to make payments on behalf of their clients based on the value of what had been stored. These practices were the precursors to today's banks.[21]

The value of gold has been perpetuated by societies that agreed it was valuable then and always would be. As time progressed, the perception of scarcity and the difficulty in mining gold added to its value.[22]

By the 18th century, gold in Europe was rivaled by paper money. This led to the adoption of the gold standard, pegging the value of paper currency to the gold it held. The formation of the gold standard got its start between 1696 and 1812.[23] The gold standard was formally adopted in England in 1821, followed by the adoption of the International Gold Standard in 1871.[24] A strong silver lobby kept the United States from being the sole precious metal standard through the 19th century.[25]

The newly minted government of the United States, which adopted its Constitution in 1789, was awash in foreign currencies up to the early 1800s when it was finally able to rid itself of foreign money. The new country used gold, silver, and paper money issued by private banks as its currency.[26] The government did not back the money, so the value of the paper could easily slip, resulting in inflation. That changed in the early 1860s when the U.S. Congress adopted the U.S. Note as a legal tender to pay for the Civil War (1861–1865). It was nicknamed the *greenback* because it was printed on green paper.[27]

---

[21] Ibid.

[22] Tardi. *Value of Gold.* www.investopedia.com/articles/investing/071114/why-gold-has-always-had-value.asp#:~:text=Gold's%20value%20is%20ultimately%20a,gold%20as%20a%20valuable%20commodity.

[23] Lioudis. *What Is the Gold Standard.* www.investopedia.com/ask/answers/09/gold-standard.asp.

[24] Ibid.

[25] Ibid.

[26] Chen. *Greenback.* www.investopedia.com/terms/g/greenback.asp#:~:text=A%20greenback%20is%20a%20slang,help%20finance%20the%20civil%20war.

[27] Wikipedia. *Greenback.* https://en.wikipedia.org/wiki/Greenback_(1860s_money).

Before the notes were created, the government issued U.S.$50 million in the form of a bond called *Demand Notes*, which paid no interest but could be redeemed before March 1862.[28] These notes, used by the government to pay salaries and cover expenses,[29] became untenable, draining the U.S. Treasury of funds. As a result, they were replaced with paper notes under the Legal Tender Act of 1862.[30] Still, the move was controversial and met with stiff opposition from bankers who argued that if the North lost the war, it could result in financial disaster.[31] To curb paper money, which saw its value rise and fall over short periods, Congress voted to pass *The Redemption Act*, a law in 1875 that limited the number of notes in circulation to U.S.$382 million. The law included a provision to buy back greenbacks for gold beginning January 1, 1879. The move prompted strong opposition from those who favored the greenback. The 45th Congress (1877–1879) amended the law, allowing more paper money to be placed into circulation and a limited number of silver coins to be minted for use.

The gold standard reached its zenith between 1871 and 1914.[32] What started as sensible economics quickly soured, however. Vibrant economies found themselves hamstrung by gold reserves that lagged behind the amount of paper needed to be printed to expand their heated economies. The situation darkened when many of those same governments had to fund the First World War (July 28, 1914–November 11, 1918). Consequently, the West abandoned the gold standard in the early and latter 20th century. Britain ended it in 1931, followed by the United States in 1933, with the last vestiges of the practice ending during the Nixon administration (January 20, 1969–August 8, 1974) in 1973. The gold standard was replaced by *fiat* money—government-issued currency backed by the government, rather than physical commodities like precious metals.[33]

---

[28] Ibid.

[29] Chen. *Greenback*. www.investopedia.com/terms/g/greenback.asp#:~:text=A%20 greenback%20is%20a%20slang,help%20finance%20the%20civil%20war.

[30] Ibid.

[31] Ibid.

[32] Ibid.

[33] Chen. *Fiat Money*. www.investopedia.com/terms/f/fiatmoney.asp.

Today, governments control the printing presses, allowing them to churn out as much cash as they deem necessary to keep their economies humming while simultaneously adhering to sound monetary policies to avoid rampant inflation. It's a balancing act that only gets noticed when food, gasoline, and energy prices rise. Barring financial crises like the Great Depression (1929–1939) and Great Recession (December 2007–June 2009), the machinations surrounding monetary policy are of little interest to consumers who don't think twice about the availability of cash. They know the paper, readily available at any ATM, will be accepted wherever they spend it.

Money in the Modern Era

How the check, another form of a promissory note, came about is unknown but credited to ancient Rome.[34] Checks were recorded in Holland in the 16th century, while the first printed check was recorded in England in 1762.[35]

While still widespread in the United States, today's use of checks worldwide is declining.[36] Although widely used in the United States, German banks, for example, don't offer them to their customers. Instead, residents either pay online or use terminals at bank branches to make electronic payments.

The early and mid-20th century brought about revolutionary changes that made financial transactions more convenient and hassle-free, beginning with the creation of *plastic*—credit cards that offered extended credit to credit-worthy consumers. A precursor to credit cards was called *metal money*, created by Western Union in 1914. This card allowed customers to pay auto loans, mortgages, and other bills.[37]

---

[34] Infoplease Staff. *Brief History of Checking.* www.infoplease.com/business/consumer-resources/brief-history-checking.

[35] Ibid.

[36] Bedell. *Checks.* www.gfmag.com/global-data/economic-data/hquidd-payment-instruments-checks.

[37] Hendrix. *Western Union History.* www.westernunion.com/blog/en/6-fascinating-things-about-western-unions-history/.

The forerunner of the credit card was created in 1946 by American banker John Biggens while working at Flatbush National Bank in Brooklyn, N.Y.,[38] and made available for local merchants.[39]

The Diners Club card was the first to offer a multipurpose card in 1950, American Express in 1958, followed by Visa and MasterCard.

The debit card, a plastic check that allows consumers to dip into their checking account in lieu of cash or check, was first issued in 1978 by The First National Bank of Seattle.[40]

Western Union pioneered wire transfers in 1872 on its telegraph system.[41] The growing power of the Internet gave rise to PayPal. Founded in 1998, PayPal, an online payment system that supports money transfers, began to see worldwide growth after eBay acquired it in 2002.[42]

The introduction of the iPhone in 2007 would later offer consumers greater ease in using cash, with the company introduction of Apple Pay in 2014, followed by Android Pay and Google Pay in 2015.[43]

Although bitcoin and other forms of cryptocurrency are proving wildly popular today, especially among the young, the idea of electronic money has been around for 30 years.

David Chaum, a computer scientist behind several ideas involving encryption, wrote a paper in 1982 entitled *Blind Signatures for Untraceable Paper*.[44] In 1990, he launched DigiCash, a digital currency *designed exclusively for electronic use*.[45]

---

[38] Wikipedia. *John C. Biggens*. https://en.wikipedia.org/wiki/John_C._Biggins.

[39] Steele. *History of Credit Cards*. www.creditcards.com/statistics/history-of-credit-cards/.

[40] Moorwand Team. *History of Debit Card*. www.moorwand.com/a-history-of-payments-the-growth-of-the-debit-card/.

[41] Wikipedia. *Wire Transfers*. https://en.wikipedia.org/wiki/Wire_transfer#:~:text=The%20first%20widely%20used%20service,on%20its%20existing%20telegraph%20network.&text=Because%20the%20earliest%20wire%20transfers,still%20used%20in%20some%20countries.

[42] Global Data. *PayPal History*. www.electronicpaymentsinternational.com/news/paypal-history-milestones/.

[43] Steele. *History of Credit Cards*. www.creditcards.com/statistics/history-of-credit-cards/.

[44] Smith. *DigiCash*. https://shortformernie.medium.com/before-there-was-bitcoin-there-was-digicash-fc2668c1d457.

[45] Ibid.

Chaum's invention, *Blind Signature*, technology based on cryptography, provided its users with improved security while making untraceable payments.[46]

The company only lasted 10 years, however. The reasons for its demise are debatable. Some attribute it to Chaum's management style. Another possible reason was a lack of capital. And yet another suggestion was that he was ahead of his time. Whatever the reason, Chaum's invention can also be linked to cryptocurrency.[47]

Coming Full Circle

The means of swapping goods and services has undergone a massive transformation since the days of bartering for food. What began as a P2P transaction quickly grew to state-organized trading, creating powerful centralized business empires with equally dominant centralized banking systems.

The means of transmitting cash may have undergone a revolution, but control levers remain the same. To access your money, you must go through centralized corporations and institutions, providing them with personal data before you can be taken on as a customer. And there are fees related to processing that transaction. Banks, which loan out your money for a hefty profit, charge you, their depositor, for the privilege. Wire and electronic transfers can also demand high fees. If you need to move your money quickly, that costs extra. Otherwise, you could find that your transaction—sending or receiving cash, could take several days.

Taking on centralized systems regarding disputed charges is also a source of consternation, even in today's online world. Remember the last time you had a dispute with your bank or a merchant regarding a questionable charge? Rectifying that grievance probably proved exhausting. You had to comb through mounds of paper and hopefully locate just the right piece of paper you needed to prove your case. Then there were all the letters and now e-mails that seemed to take forever to be answered. It most likely felt like an uphill battle to rectify their mistake.

---

[46] Frankenfield. *DigiCash*. www.investopedia.com/terms/d/digicash.asp.
[47] Ibid.

What if that could be changed? What if we could go back to a P2P payment method that guaranteed transparency and proof of purchase while assuring anonymity? What if it was possible to reduce third-party control and put that power back into the hands of the consumer? Cryptocurrency offers just that—two chickens and a cow at a time.

The Age of Cryptocurrency

It's graduation time, and you want to send that special person—a grand-child, niece, nephew, a little something to let them know you are thinking about them. So, you send them a graduation card with a check. You fill out the check, write a special message on the card, then enclose it in the envelope. Your address goes in the upper left-hand corner, the recipient's name in the center, and a stamp in the upper right-hand corner that allowed the envelope to be transmitted through the U.S. Postal Service.

Sender → Trusted Source → Receiver

The idea behind Satoshi's notion is just as simple, but with his method, there is no trusted third-party service. The currency arrives in short order, albeit without a card.

A Little More About Satoshi's White Paper

In his 2008 whitepaper, *Bitcoin: A Peer-to-Peer Electronic Cash System*, Satoshi outlined a means of sending cash through the Internet and deliv-ered to the recipient without complication. Wait, you say. That's being done now. What's the difference between traditional methods of sending electronic cash and Satoshi's method?

It's about trusting a trustless system rather than an established one.

The Merriam-Webster dictionary defines *trust* as the "belief that someone or something is reliable, good, honest, effective, etc." That definition didn't fit traditional centralized institutions as far as Satoshi was concerned. Well, maybe some, but certainly not all, especially regarding Internet sales, which was a primary focus in his white paper. He supported the idea of relying on a trustless system. In this case, it means the user doesn't need to have trust in a third party. Transactions are verified through consensus.

Specifically, Satoshi believed that the merchant, not the customer, held all the power.

Doing business online can be difficult, especially if you are seeking a resolution to a problem.

Remember, while it seems we've had the Internet forever, it really wasn't so long ago. The first sale over the Internet was recorded on August 11, 1994,[1] when Dan Kohn sold a CD of Sting's *Ten Summoner's Tales* to a friend in Philadelphia through his website NetMarket. The buyer used encrypted software to send his credit card number to pay for it.[2]

In July 1995, Jeff Bezos launched Amazon from his garage, selling books online.[3] By 2007, a year before Satoshi published his whitepaper, e-commerce sales reached U.S.$175 billion, with U.S.$204 billion expected the following year.[4] That's a lot of services and merchandise with, to be sure, a healthy amount of consumer complaints.

Recognizing the growing reliance on trusted financial institutions for online sales "as a trusted third party to process electronic payments,"[5] he determined inherent weaknesses in this model, including the difficulty of mediation on behalf of consumers who make small purchases. Resolving a dispute, he wrote, increased the *transaction costs*[6] associated with buying or selling goods or services.[7] Basically, the dispute costs more than the item itself. Satoshi surmised that the broader issue was "the loss of the ability to make non-reversible payments for non-reversible services."[8] Irreversible payments ensure merchants are paid because customers cannot cancel their payments. He wrote that services that can be reversed

[1] Fessenden. *First Thing Sold on the Internet.* www.smithsonianmag.com/smart-news/what-was-first-thing-sold-internet-180957414/.
[2] Ibid.
[3] Wikipedia. *History of Amazon.* https://en.wikipedia.org/wiki/History_of_Amazon.
[4] Briggs. 2007. *Online Retail Sales.* www.digitalcommerce360.com/2008/01/28/2007-online-retail-sales-hit-175-billion-forrester-research-sa/.
[5] Satoshi. *White Paper.* https://nakamotoinstitute.org/bitcoin/.
[6] Ibid.
[7] Downey. *Transaction Costs.* www.investopedia.com/terms/t/transactioncosts.asp.
[8] Satoshi. *White Paper.* https://nakamotoinstitute.org/bitcoin/.

require *wary* merchants to *harass* their customers for more information than necessary.[9]

The answer, Satoshi concluded, was the use of encrypted virtual currency he called bitcoin, which could be transferred electronically from one person to another without involving a bank. But even this solution had a weakness. He referred to that shortcoming as *double spending*, defined as spending or attempting to use the same digital coin twice. This was the problem Szabo recognized when he proposed bit gold. Think of it as another form of counterfeiting. Someone copies the digital information of a piece of legitimate electronic currency, makes a copy, and then attempts to spend it.

To solve this problem, Satoshi proposed that all transactions would be distributed on an open ledger called a *blockchain* to be verified by a decentralized network of computers, called nodes, that receive, analyze, and verify bitcoin transactions. Verification could be strengthened by using a timestamp, a process developed in 1991 to timestamp digital documents. A timestamp would show when the coin was first spent, so it could not be used again. Neither the time nor the date can be altered, which would give the blockchain even more security.

To keep the system honest, the process would require no less than six confirmations, each resulting in a new block forming the blockchain, allowing the transaction to be completed.

Let's talk about the currency.

What Exactly Is a Bitcoin?

The pictures of the big shiny coin associated with bitcoin look inviting, but the image merely represents the idea of a virtual currency. It's not physical money you can hold, fold, and drop into your pocket. You can't go to the bank or ATM and withdraw these particular *coins* to jingle in your pocket or purse. Cryptocurrency represents virtual money built with code on the blockchain.

Bitcoin, like a number of other cryptocurrencies, is a virtual currency created using a computer program by mining. The creators, called miners, don't dig the coins out of the ground. They create the coins by solving a

---

[9] Ibid.

mathematical algorithm that produces the right amount of zeros at the beginning of the solution.

The program used to create bitcoins and prove each transaction is the cryptographic program SHA-256, which was discussed in a previous chapter. Each bit represents a 0 or a 1. Computers calculating the predetermined answer compete with one another to find the predetermined answer. SHA-256 creates a 2^{256} or 32-byte signature.[10] Once information is converted, no matter the length, 256 characters are created.

Satoshi knew that finding the right combination of zeros and ones in 10 minutes would require much computer power and be expensive. But he reasoned this method was the most egalitarian method of distributing wealth. Miners, he believed, would pay high costs to earn even more money.[11] The first miner to get the correct answer earns bitcoins. When proving individual blocks of transactions, they earn bitcoin and the transaction fees associated with processing bitcoin transactions. What he didn't foresee was that his program would result in the demand for greater energy sources and be blamed for contributing to global warming.

So, what gives bitcoins and other cryptocurrencies value? Why are people clamoring to spend hard-earned money for pieces of code?

As mentioned earlier, speculation is one key factor adding to bitcoin's value. Only 21 million bitcoins were to be created, with no more to follow. Human nature being what it is, people want to own something that's a limited edition. But if there are only 21 million coins and more than eight billion people on the planet, won't those coins quickly disappear? As the price for coins goes up, the system allowed bitcoins to be broken down into smaller units, much like dollars can be broken down into change. Unlike dollars, which can only break down into 100 cents, a single bitcoin "is divisible by eight decimal places, or one-hundredth millionth of a Bitcoin" called Satoshis.[12] When one does the math, there are 100 million Satoshis in one bitcoin. Multiply that by 21 million bitcoins, and you come up with 2.1×10^{15}, or 2.1e+15 Satoshis.

---

[10] Wagner. *What Is SHA-256.* https://blog.boot.dev/cryptography/how-sha-2-works-step-by-step-sha-256/.

[11] Hamacher. *Bitcoin Energy Consumption.* https://decrypt.co/62338/satoshi-nakamotos-view-on-bitcoins-energy-consumption-resurfaces.

[12] Luno. *Bitcoin Divided.* https://discover.luno.com/how-many-satoshis-make-a-bitcoin/.

To get the ball rolling, those decentralized computers with powerful central processing units (CPUs) first downloaded a copy of SHA-256, the open code software necessary to solve the algorithm essential to create bitcoins. The first to get the correct algorithm is awarded bitcoins putting more into circulation.

Finding the correct algorithm, which becomes more complex as more and more bitcoins are produced, requires a lot of computer power and energy, something Satoshi predicted. In 2010, miners turned to more powerful processors—graphic processing units (GPUs) to improve computing power.[13] A year later, miners began mining with field-programmable gate array (FGPA), which was programmable and used less energy. However, it required users to have a deeper understanding of programming and wasn't available everywhere.[14] In 2011, miners turned to application-specific integrated circuits (ASICs) to create the correct algorithm necessary to make the coin. One ASIC processor today can cost between U.S.$500 to just over U.S.$1,000 retail in the United States but is much more expensive, sometimes twice the U.S. retail cost, in other countries.[15] Cryptocurrency farms use hundreds, if not thousands, of ASIC processing units on one site.

Following the release of Satoshi's white paper, the first of those 21 million bitcoins were mined in January of 2009 to a waiting community eager to embrace a new form of commerce, one that could lead to the end of financial domination of banking institutions and Wall Street; returning real purchasing power back to Main Street.[16] For bitcoin supporters, the high production costs are worth it if the result is creating a new financial system government cannot interfere with.[17]

As the value of bitcoin has risen, followed by other cryptocurrencies like Ethereum, speculators who only follow trends found an investment

---

[13] Coin Gossip. *Bitcoin Mining Hardware.* https://ccoingossip.com/history-of-bitcoin-mining-hardware/.

[14] Ibid.

[15] Cryptopedia Staff. *Retail Vs Industrial Mining.* www.gemini.com/cryptopedia/crypto-mining-operation-crypto-mining-rig-asic-miner.

[16] Lewis. *Bitcoin Is the Great Definancialization.* nakamotoinstitute.org/mempool/bitcoin-is-the-great-definancialization/.

[17] Rooks. *Bitcoin Mining Power.* www.dw.com/en/why-does-bitcoin-need-more-energy-than-whole-countries/a-56573390.

opportunity. They began moving their capital into this mysterious market, hoping to catch the next big wave to ease them into early retirement. To put it another way, some see utility, while others see profitability.

Once a lucrative venture for a handful of speculators, individual miners now find themselves up against powerful *mining farms* that can outman and outspend them, buying more powerful computers with more than enough to pay the high energy costs associated with mining. As more and more coins are created, the reward for their creation declines by design. As of November 2023, 19.545 million bitcoins had been created.

Altcoins

The success of bitcoin ushered in a wave of competitors eager to seize on the idea of creating a currency to compete with fiat money. These alternative currencies, referred to as altcoins (alternative cryptocurrencies), have the same properties and function as Bitcoin.

As of Novmber 2023, there were 10,748 cryptocurrencies, of which 8,848 were considered active or valuable.[18] The number of active cryptocurrency users worldwide numbered around 420 million with 18,000 businesses accepting cryptocurrency for payment. The market cap (total value) for all cryptocurrency at U.S.$1.32 trillion. Bitcoin led with a market cap of around U.S.$650 billion.[19] Some cryptocurrencies, like Ethereum, were created through premining. That is, the developer mined them to reward investors, programmers, and developers before they were released to the public.[20] Ethereum, the second leading crypto coin producer behind bitcoin, issued premined coins to great effect.

Some argue that because these coins were not independently created but rather offered through a *centralized* port, the company could

---

[18] Howarth. *Cryptocurrencies in 2024.* https://explodingtopics.com/blog/number-of-cryptocurrencies.

[19] Ibid.

[20] Bitpanda. *Pre-Mined Coins.* www.bitpanda.com/academy/en/lessons/what-does-pre-mined-mean/.

be *pumping and dumping* their currency—offering it for a low price and *artificially inflated* to sell it for a higher price.[21]

Then there is a form of cryptocurrency, called tokens, that are not mined but can only be bought. They have value like coins but are designed to be used within the developer's platform.[22]

Stablecoins

The cryptocurrency market can be wildly unpredictable. Between 2019 and early 2022, bitcoin soared from a low of just over U.S.$3,000 in January 2019 to a high of U.S.$65,000 in February, April, and November of 2021, followed by a steep dive and prices leveled to almost U.S.$19,000 as of November 8, 2022.[23]

Some cryptocurrencies have chosen to peg their value to fiat money (such as U.S. dollars) or commodities like gold and silver to avoid that rollercoaster ride. These forms of cryptocurrencies are referred to as stablecoins. Exchanges offering stablecoins must keep reserves of those physical assets as collateral.[24]

These reserves are held by third-party custodians that are regularly audited.[25]

Coins Versus Tokens

Coins and tokens are the same, in that they can be used to make payments. They can also be swapped. However, there are clear differences. One key difference is that coins were created to replace fiat currency, while tokens represent physical objects like property or art.[26]

---

[21] Ibid.

[22] Bonpay. *Difference Between Coins and Tokens.* https://medium.com/@bonpay/what-is-the-difference-between-coins-and-tokens-6cedff311c31.

[23] de Best. *Bitcoin Price April 2013—December 2022.* www.statista.com/statistics/326707/bitcoin-price-index/.

[24] Hayes. Stablecoins. www.investopedia.com/terms/s/stablecoin.asp#:~:text=Stablecoins%20are%20cryptocurrencies%20that%20attempt,a%20commodity%20such%20as%20gold.

[25] Ibid.

[26] Liquid. *Crypto Coins Vs Tokens.* https://blog.liquid.com/coin-vs-token.

Coins offer universal crossover.[27] While tokens are readily bought and sold on exchanges, they don't have the same universal appeal as coins. To sell your tokens, you need to find an exchange that trades them. Unlike coins, not all tokens are available from all exchanges.

Tokens offer more versatility. For example, they can also represent services like a rewards program where holders can use their tokens to stream music or videos.[28]

Online gamers, for example, use tokens. Players who need tools, weapons, or other game pieces, use tokens to buy them.

We take a closer look at tokens in the next chapter.

[27] Bonpay. *Difference Between Coins and Tokens.* https://medium.com/@bonpay/what-is-the-difference-between-coins-and-tokens-6cedff311c31.

[28] Frankenfield. *What Are Crypto Tokens.* www.investopedia.com/terms/c/crypto-token.asp#:~:text=Tokens%20are%20created%20through%20an,company%20can%20purchase%20these%20tokens.

A Token Economy

Almost everyone is familiar with tokens. There was a time when tokens—small metal disks the size of an American quarter or a euro coin, were issued for admittance to theaters. Pay your money, get a token, and drop it in the turnstile allowing the theater to keep count of attendees. For fans of video arcades, visitors bought tokens used to play games. Winners were issued a slew of tickets, which could then be redeemed for a prize. To get through a subway, you needed a token.

Grocery carts in Germany require a fiat coin or a token to release the buggy from its chain lock as a means of keeping up with the carts. When the customer is done and replaces the chain lock, they get their coin or token back.

These tokens have no value outside the establishments where they are issued. Once you bought your movie ticket, you walked through the turnstile, guaranteed a seat in the theater. Nothing more.

Subway tokens issued by a municipality could be used at any station there or traded or sold in the city that recognized them.[1]

In many cases, metal tokens have been replaced by paper or plastic tickets, but the purpose is the same.

Casino chips are another type of token that represents cash. Rather than putting money on a table or in a machine, visitors buy chips representing the value of the game they are playing.[2]

We think of tokens as these plastic or metal coins in this way, which has a rich history dating back to ancient days.

However, the first tokens were created for a different purpose. They were created for use as accounting tools in the ancient agricultural region of the Near East. They were used to measure quantities of farm products such as cereal, cattle, and oil. Unlike today's tokens, these tokens, made of clay, had different shapes and sizes. Some were circular, like small

---

[1] Coates. *Token History.* https://medium.com/@fooyay/a-history-of-tokens-a064b28d5af2.

[2] Ibid.

balls. Others were cone-shaped and triangular, not the flat, circular coin we know today. Some tokens were more defined.[3] Use the QR code to find images.

Ancient tokens

The first clay tokens dating back to between 9000 and 8700 BC were discovered in ancient Syria in an agricultural region known for growing cereal.[4] Newer, intricately designed tokens dating between 3500 and 3100 BC were discovered alongside the plain tokens on archeological sites between Syria to Persia and from Palestine to Anatolia.[5] The more intricate tokens were associated with more sophisticated goods, such as textiles, made in urban workshops.[6]

Different shaped tokens representing different quantities of grain were impressed onto tablets representing quantity. Over time, finding tokens difficult to store and keep up with, merchants pressed the tokens onto clay tablets creating impressions that provided an easier method for keeping up with transactions, a precursor to today's accounting ledger.

The use of tokens led to the advancement of counting, which evolved into accounting and data processing methods that, by the fourth century, led to writing while forever changing urban centers into centers of commerce and trade.[7]

---

[3] Schmandt-Besserat. *Invention of Tokens.* https://sites.utexas.edu/dsb/tokens/the-invention-of-tokens/.

[4] Ibid.

[5] Schmandt-Besserat. *Significance of Tokens, Counting and Writing.* https://sites.utexas.edu/dsb/tokens/tokens/.

[6] Ibid.

[7] Ibid.

The use of coin-shaped tokens as we know them reaches back to the days of the Roman Empire when tokens were issued to provide services that were forbidden to be paid with using Roman coins.[8]

Coins were expensive to mint, so tokens were also used in exchange for small purchases and services.[9] The use of copper tokens came into use following the English Civil War in the mid-17th century. Following the beheading of Charles I in 1649, Cromwell was named *Lord Protector* of the Commonwealth. Now then, a king held the sole right to issue coins. Anyone attempting to mint coins faced the death penalty.[10] Since Cromwell was not a king, there were no death sentences, allowing the use of copper tokens to explode.[11]

Cryptocurrency tokens are simply a modern-day extension of an old idea traced to 9000 BC. As in ancient times, they represent physical assets and services. These digital assets are stored on a blockchain rather than a clay tablet.

Types of Cryptocurrency Tokens

Tokens fall into four categories:

- Utility tokens: Used to raise capital for projects that can later be redeemed for goods or services offered on the developer's platform.[12]
- Security/equity tokens: Used like stock or shares to generate capital.[13]
- Asset-backed tokens: Tokens backed by tangible assets such as gold, real estate, or bonds.[14]
- Reward tokens: Used to redeem goods and services.[15]

---

[8] Feetham. *Brief History of Tokens*. www.lexology.com/library/detail.aspx?g=57e3ba14-ae4b-45a5-95cb-e14d0eb92caf.
[9] Ibid.
[10] InCoins. *Early Token History*. www.jncoins.co.uk/Shop/content/26-early-token-history.
[11] Ibid.
[12] Medipedia. *Types of Crypto Tokens*. https://medium.com/@medipedia/the-various-types-of-crypto-tokens-26bab8f6622c.
[13] Ibid.
[14] Ibid.
[15] BBC News. *Rewards Tokens*. www.bsc.news/post/rewards-token-living-up-to-their-name.

Utility Tokens

These tokens are issued as an ICO by a company looking for money to finance a project. In exchange, the tokens can be redeemed for goods or services offered by the company.[16] The investor can also elect to hold onto them. If the project is successful and demand for those tokens increases, so does the token's value. On the other hand, if the project fails, the investor is left with worthless tokens.[17]

Examples of utility tokens include the BAT, discussed in the previous section. Another utility token type is the Golem (GNT), which allows users to pay or be paid for agreeing to share spare computer processing power.[18]

Security/Equity Tokens

Like stock shares, equity tokens represent an equity stake in the issuing company. The token may receive dividends, have voting rights, or both.[19]

Security tokens include a wide array of financial products to fit most investors' portfolios.[20] To find a *complete* list of global security token exchanges, go to stomarket.com.

Asset-Backed Tokens

Asset-backed tokens represent physical assets such as precious metals, crude oil, real estate, equity, or anything with a value that can be tokenized. The value of the token is directly related to the asset's value.[21]

---

[16] Bit2Me Academy. *What Are Utility Tokens.* https://academy.bit2me.com/en/ what-is-utility-token/ https://academy.bit2me.com/en/what-is-utility-token/.

[17] Ibid.

[18] Kraken. *What Is Golem.* www.kraken.com/learn/what-is-golem-gnt golem/#:~: text=Golem%20is%20a%20blockchain%2Dbased,that%20demand%20great %20computing%20power.

[19] Moneyland.ch. *Equity Token.* https://blog.stomarket.com/quick-guide-to-buying-security-tokens-8bea7f6fbed7 www.moneyland.ch/en/equity-token-definition.

[20] Pittman. *Best Place to Buy Security Tokens.* https://blog.stomarket.com/quick-guide-to-buying-security-tokens-8bea7f6fbed7.

[21] Schweifer. *Asset-Backed Tokens and Business and Wealth Creation.* www.linkedin .com/pulse/what-asset-backed-tokens-mean-business-wealth-johannes-schweifer/.

These tokens represent an investment opportunity, particularly for small-time investors who can own a portion of a real-world asset at minimum cost.[22] The seller gets the liquidity they need while the buyer obtains a portion of that asset. For example, they could be used to raise capital for a commercial building with the owner(s) selling square feet/ meters to buyers looking for an opportunity to have a stake in commercial real estate.

Reward Tokens

Rewards tokens are linked to payback/ loyalty cards, which reward users with purchase points that can be redeemed later.

It seems like rewards programs for loyal customers keep growing. Go shopping, and when you are in the checkout line, don't forget your payback card. Use your bank card and earn points. Are you flying somewhere? Don't forget your frequent flyer card, and earn those extra points.

Payback points reached close to U.S.$5.2 billion in the United States in 2022, while in Germany, for example, between March 2000 and January 2021, customers collected points worth five billion euros.[23] A study conducted in the UK found that customers with higher income levels (£75,000 and up) were far more likely to swipe their payback cards than those with lower incomes. The lower their income, the less likely they will use these cards.[24]

Businesses win, too, as loyal customers represent 40 percent of their revenue.[25] On the other hand, points represent an asset that must be stored and paid out later. On the ledger sheet, they fall in the minus

[22] Shareworks. *Asset Tokenization.* https://discover.shareworks.com/ipo-and-liquidity-events/asset-tokenization.

[23] Research and Markets. *Germany Loyalty Programs 2022.* www.globenewswire.com/en/news-release/2022/05/17/2444806/28124/en/Germany-Loyalty-Programs-Market-Report-2022-Retailers-are-Building-Partnerships-with-Multi-Brand-Loyalty-Program-Providers-as-a-Business-Differentiator.html.

[24] D. Tighe. *Loyalty Card Usage.* www.statista.com/statistics/1125748/loyalty-card-usage-rate-for-top-up-shopping-in-the-uk-by-income/.

[25] Fowler. *Loyalty Cards Next Level.* www.forbes.com/sites/forbesbusinessdevelopmentcouncil/2021/08/02/building-the-next-level-of-customer-loyalty-through-tokenization/?sh=4f77daa5132b.

column as a liability. To counter this, some companies put an expiration date on them, wiping them from books if the points are not used.

On average, 60 percent of customers redeem their points[26] which shows that a lot of cash value is left unused. Other surveys put that redemption average closer to 50 percent.

There is also the issue of payback card fatigue. One survey of loyalty card membership in the United States between 2015 and 2022 found that the average consumer belonged to 16.6 loyalty programs in 2022 but used less than half.[27]

Still, another issue is privacy. The information retrieved from customers using cards is valuable to businesses and the loyalty they inspire. Each swipe provides companies with valuable purchasing information they can use to bolster their offerings. An online Harris Poll conducted in 2019 found that 71 percent of respondents said they were less likely to join a loyalty rewards program that required personal information.[28] The poll also found that 76 percent said they were more likely to join such a program if they only had to provide their name and phone number.[29]

One popular way to encourage card usage has been for businesses to come together and offer a card that can be used with multiple vendors. It is convenient for customers who don't have to carry a wallet full of cards or hunt for the correct app on their smartphone.

Customers may love it, but a multivendor payback card presents challenges. For one, participating vendors have to share, collate, and audit usage from each customer while guarding against fraud.[30]

---

[26] Spendgo. *Understanding Loyalty Programs*. https://resources.spendgo.com/blog/understanding-average-loyalty-program-redemption-rate-tips-for-improving-yours.

[27] A. Guttmann. *U.S. Loyalty Programs 2015—2022*. www.statista.com/statistics/618744/average-number-of-loyalty-programs-us-consumers-belong-to/.

[28] Press Release PR Newswire. *U.S. Loyalty Program Usage Survey*. https://markets.businessinsider.com/news/stocks/most-americans-less-likely-to-join-customer-loyalty-program-that-collects-personal-information-71-or-requires-an-app-58-according-to-survey-on-behalf-of-wilbur-1028114529.

[29] Ibid.

[30] Tokened. *Tokenization Solution for Loyalty*. https://tokend.io/loyalty/.

Blockchain could solve several of these problems by providing tokens that can easily be exchanged between providers and won't lose value or expire while protecting customer privacy.[31]

NFTs

NFTs are digitized tokens representing one-of-a-kind items one can purchase online, storing them on a blockchain. These items include art, collectible digital cards and figures, music, online game pieces, and property.

We'll take a more in-depth look at NFTs in the next section.

Summing Up

Tokens are wide and varied as the platforms that produce them. As blockchains grow and develop, tokens will play an integral part in fueling their development and have a significant role in economic development.

Getting Started

Although several prominent players have been working hard to create some semblance of order, it's still the *Wild West* in crypto land. At this writing, there's no such thing as *one-stop shopping* where novices can go to have all questions answered on one platform. There is so much credible information online in articles, videos, and podcasts. There is a lot of hype, too. Be discerning when doing research.

Several exchanges offer free courses, including some that allow you to earn a little cryptocurrency as you learn, so consider taking one. Even though they represent a private exchange, their courses offer a plethora of information to prepare one for this market. Signing up in no way obligates one to do business with them. If the idea of learning through private exchanges troubles you, the Massachusetts Institute of Technology has several cryptocurrency courses posted on YouTube.

---

[31] Fowler. *Loyalty Cards Next Level.* www.forbes.com/sites/forbesbusinessdevelopmentcouncil/2021/08/02/building-the-next-level-of-customer-loyalty-through-tokenization/?sh=4f77daa5132b.

Be aware that, for the most part, no U.S. government regulators oversee the cryptocurrency market other than taxing authorities like the Internal Revenue Service (IRS). The IRS regards cryptocurrency as an investment to be taxed. That said, the U.S. Securities and Exchange Commission is calling for regulatory oversight.[32]

As with any investment, you need to be aware of risks. Don't get into a hurry. Do your homework. Never spend money you are not prepared to lose.

Once again, be reminded that this book is solely intended to serve as information based on research and personal experience. It in no way endorses cryptocurrency investment.

Finding a Currency That's Right for You

The first step you need to take is to decide which cryptocurrency you want to own. There's no shortage of advice from so-called experts online ready to shower you with their prognostications. So, beware. Don't rely on just one or even two sources. Find as many as you can to validate the initial predictions. Use the footnotes found in this book. Work your information the way bitcoin miners work to validate transactions.

Verify! Verify! Verify!

If you are interested in cryptocurrency, you can start by looking at Coin-MarketCap.com, which lists all available cryptocurrencies (coins and tokens) in ranking order, like a stock exchange. Here you will get a good idea of what's out there. The site is comprehensive, offering a trading history and valuable information about each currency listed. When looking at the prices, know they reflect one coin. Several crypto coins, like bitcoin and Ethereum, can be purchased in smaller units offering ownership at affordable prices. So don't pass up something you are interested in just because the price for one coin appears out of reach.

---

[32] Barton, Mcnamara, and Ward. *Are Cryptocurrencies Securities.* www.reuters .com/legal/transactional/are-cryptocurrencies-securities-sec-is-answering-question-2022-03-21/.

Like stocks, cryptocurrencies are subject to market volatility resulting in short- or long-term losses. To help ease some of that volatility, some cryptocurrencies, called *stablecoins*, are pegged to fiat currencies such as the U.S. dollar or other stable assets like gold and other precious metals. They can also be tied to other cryptocurrencies and other financial instruments like commercial paper.[33]

One potential drawback to stablecoins could be the entity holding the coin doesn't have enough reserves to back each unit of currency it issues, potentially shaking confidence in those coins that lack adequate reserves.[34]

In April 2023, the European Parliament passed rules governing cryptocurrency. The rules, set to go into effect sometime in 2024, require said entities issuing stablecoins to maintain enough reserves to cover major withdrawals.[35] As of this writing, 23 firms that issued stablecoins since 2021 have collapsed, resulting in the loss of billions of dollars.[36]

Finding the Right Exchange

Once you have decided on a cryptocurrency you want, the next step is to sign up with a cryptocurrency exchange where you buy and sell cryptocurrency and crypto assets like NFTs. Again, you'll have to do some research. Start online and look for recommendations. Some exchanges have strict residency requirements or are closed to nonresidents looking for exchanges outside their borders. You may find even fewer options if you are a citizen of one country living as a legal resident in another. Also, it can be even more restrictive if you hold tokens that limit your choices

---

[33] Hertig. *What Is a Stablecoin.* www.coindesk.com/learn/what-is-a-stablecoin/.
[34] Ibid.
[35] Browne. *EU Parliament Passes Comprehensive Crypto Asset Regulations.* www.cnbc .com/2023/04/20/eu-lawmakers-approve-worlds-first-comprehensive-crypto-regulation.html#:~:text=the%20cryptocurrency%20industry.-,In%20a%20 vote%20Thursday%2C%20the%20EU%20Parliament%20voted%20517%20 in,lose%20investors'%20crypto-assets.
[36] ChainSec. *Comprehensive List of Failed Stablecoins (2021–22).* https://chainsec .io/failed-stablecoins/.

more because the exchange you are interested in may not trade those particular tokens.

If you are only interested in NFTs, these sites most likely offer their own token, so all you need is a wallet, which can be downloaded for free.

Fees are another issue to consider. Exchanges charge fees for transactions, with some charging more than others. So, check around and compare.

There are three types of cryptocurrency exchanges: centralized, decentralized, and hybrid.

Centralized exchanges (CEX) act as intermediaries between buyers and sellers for which they earn a commission.[37] They buy and sell cryptocurrency based on the market price at the time of the transaction. This is the best place to start if you are new to cryptocurrency. CEX include Crypto.com, Coinbase, Gemini, and Kraken.

Decentralized exchanges (DEX) offer P2P transactions without the middleman.[38] Transactions include using a smart contract, a self-executing program that approves a transaction if all conditions are met or deny it otherwise.[39]

In this system, when cryptocurrency owners want to swap their cryptocurrency for another, they choose a selling price, the number of coins or tokens they want to sell, and set a time limit. Those looking to buy this currency make bids the seller can accept or reject.[40]

DEX include PanCake Swap, Curve, Airswap, Bancor, and dydX.

A hybrid exchange is a mix of CEX and DEX, pulling the best elements of the two into one. Members do not rely on custodians. Rather, they have full control over their assets. One can trade digital assets directly from their wallet while contributing tokens to a smart contract.[41]

Hybrid exchanges include Legolas Hybrid Exchange, Eidoo Hybrid Exchange, and Qurrex Hybrid Exchange.[42]

---

[37] CFI Team. *Cryptocurrency Exchanges.* https://corporatefinanceinstitute.com/resources/knowledge/other/cryptocurrency-exchanges/.

[38] Ibid.

[39] Ibid.

[40] ZenLedger. *Decentralized Vs Centralized Exchange.* www.zenledger.io/blog/decentralized-exchange-vs-centralized-exchange.

[41] Innocent. *Hybrid Cryptocurrency Exchanges.* https://medium.com/xord/hybrid-cryptocurrency-exchanges-what-are-they-8c9849f50b9f.

[42] Ibid.

There are pros and cons to CEX and DEX.

CEX are more user-friendly, offers greater layers of security, is faster, and is trustworthy.[43] On the other hand, they can be targets of hackers, charge service fees, and, like any business, can go out of business.[44] The exchange holds your currency, not you.

DEX are private with no intermediary, with fees distributed to liquidity providers, those who stake their cryptocurrency for transaction fees.[45] DEX don't accept fiat currency.[46] Due to its complexity, experts suggest beginners start with a centralized exchange.[47]

Signing up for a CEX account requires patience. You must fill out what is referred to as a *know your customer* (KYC) form. The purpose is to prevent illegal funding of activities such as money laundering, funding terrorism, or tax evasion.[48] You must prove residency, so make sure to have personal documents, like a valid driver's license, residency card, or passport, on hand to upload. You will be instructed to upload a photo of yourself using the video camera on your computer or smartphone camera. A copy of these documents must then be uploaded to their platform as part of your application. A few might even ask to include additional documents like a utility bill to further prove your residency.

Bank information is also required, so have your account information handy.

Decentralized authorities do not require a KYC.[49]

Once you've submitted your application, you wait. Your application could be approved within an hour or a day. In other cases, it can take 7 to 10 business days. The reality is some exchanges could take weeks, if not longer, depending on where you live, your nationality, or the quality of the documents you submit.

Once approved, you will need to finish setting up your account, including the method of payment for your currency, which could be your

---

[43] Ibid.

[44] Ibid.

[45] Abrol. *Liquidity Provider Guide.* www.blockchain-council.org/defi/liquidity-provider-tokens/.

[46] Ibid.

[47] Ibid.

[48] Veriff. *What Is KYC.* www.veriff.com/blog/what-is-kyc-in-crypto.

[49] Ibid.

credit card or bank account. You have to make a minimum purchase of cryptocurrency to activate the account

Ask Questions

Like any enterprise, exchanges are out to make money. And like any consumer, you need to be aware of the difference between hype and fact. So, do your due diligence and research the products and services you are considering.

When examining an exchange, see how they are rated. Check multiple sources, not just one. Compare their prices for conducting transactions, referred to by the industry as *gas* prices. Check to see how they protect your assets and whether they offer insurance. Find out if they are insured for losses. Finally, ensure they are available to answer your questions in real time. Nothing is more frustrating than starting something new and having no one to answer specific questions.

Fast Cash

For some, cryptocurrency is seen as an investment. For others, it's an alternative means to get the cash you need to buy the things you want without going through a bank.

Accessing cash is simple: selling some cryptocurrency and then transferring it to your bank account, which could take as little as half a day.

Several exchanges offer debit cards, providing security as well as convenience. Instead of accessing your wallet on an unsecured network, you conduct your transaction with their debit card.

Debit cards from these exchanges operate just like your bank debit card. You pay for your purchase by entering your PIN or using it at an ATM to withdraw cash. Crypto is moved from your wallet, sold, and converted into currency. Some debit cards take the money directly from your wallet, while others must be loaded with cash before being used.[50]

---

[50] Crypto.com. *Best Crypto Debit Cards*. www.benzinga.com/money/best-crypto-debit-cards.

In addition to storing money, some cards offer cashback rewards on purchases, no fees or low fees for transactions, *hassle-free sharing*, which allows you to send cash to others from your card, and worldwide acceptance. One card provider includes an app enabling you to create virtual cards for online shopping.

When shopping around for exchanges, you might consider one that offers flexibility. Be aware that small merchants may not have the means to accept your crypto debit card. Help on this front comes from Visa and MasterCard, both of which support crypto debit cards, making transactions easier as they are taken wherever Visa and MasterCard are accepted.

Taxes

No matter where you live in the world, your cryptocurrency is considered income and subject to taxation. However, not all taxation is equal. Some countries are more lenient, while others are far less forgiving.

A 2022 study conducted by Coincub[51] ranked countries in terms of taxation. Ranked from one to five are Germany, Italy, Switzerland, Singapore, and Slovenia as the most crypto-friendly countries. Germany earned top honors because it doesn't charge a capital gains tax if the cryptocurrency is held for at least one year.

The bottom five, levying the heaviest taxes on cryptocurrency profits, are, in order, Japan, The Philippines, Israel, Iceland, and Belgium. Belgium, ranked the worst for cryptocurrency traders, charges a capital gains tax of 33 percent. Cryptocurrency gains that fall under *professional income* can be charged up to 50 percent under the country's progressive tax rate system.[52]

In this survey, the United States was among six countries with high taxes on cryptocurrency gains. Depending on their tax bracket, those selling crypto within a year are taxed between 10 and 33 percent. If held for

---

[51] Lea. *Crypto Tax Ranking 2022*. https://coincub.com/ranking/coincub-annual-crypto-tax-ranking-2022/.

[52] Ibid.

more than a year, the maximum tax burden is 20 percent, depending on their tax bracket.[53]

If you live in the United States, the IRS treats cryptocurrency like property and therefore taxed like property.[54] You must report the profit if you sell your cryptocurrency and make a profit. If you lose money, the loss is also reported.[55]

In 2022, one had to pay a short-term capital gains tax if they held cryptocurrency for less than a year and a long-term capital gains tax if it held after one year.[56] Check with the IRS for 2023 and beyond.

The Coincub survey also ranked the top six tax havens for crypto. They are, in order, The Bahamas, Bermuda, Belarus, UAE, the Cordillera Administrative Region (CAR) of the Philippines, and Lichtenstein.[57]

The Bahamas earned the top spot because it does not tax its citizens or alien residents for personal income or capital gains.[58]

Check with your tax advisor or tax office for more information if you want to hold cryptocurrency in one of these countries.

Conclusion

The virtual currency revolution is still a work in progress. While it offers anonymity and ensures fairness, holders must still provide personal information regarding identity and finance to exchanges that are not household names.

Like stocks, some currencies are subject to market volatility, gaining and losing value based on investors' feelings, and are taxable income.

---

[53] Ibid.

[54] Daly. *How Is Cryptocurrency Taxed.* www.fool.com/investing/stock-market/market-sectors/financials/cryptocurrency-stocks/crypto-taxes/.

[55] Ibid.

[56] Ibid.

[57] Lea. *Crypto Tax Ranking 2022.* https://coincub.com/ranking/coincub-annual-crypto-tax-ranking-2022/.

[58] Ibid.

Remember, as of November 2023, there were 10,748 cryptocurrencies, of which only 8,848 were considered active or valuable.[59] Some do very well, while others go bust. So, before you invest, do your homework. Track the coins or tokens you want to trade like you would track a stock or mutual fund. Like a stock prospectus, read the company's white paper (a sign that the developers are serious) and track currencies on CoinMarketCap.com. Know what you are getting into before you buy.

Regarding taxes, if cryptocurrency is to become a viable alternative currency, there needs to be a fixed amount not subject to taxation.

---

[59] Howarth. *Cryptocurrency Numbers in 2024.* https://explodingtopics.com/blog/number-of-cryptocurrencies.

Tools for Trading

Think back to your first hobby. Maybe it was photography. Perhaps it was woodworking. Maybe it was cooking. It could have been camping, hunting, or fishing. Whatever it was, when you hit the shops, there wasn't anything on their store shelves you didn't *need* to get yourself started.

No doubt your credit or debit card got a real workout by the time you got home with all those shiny sealed boxes of *essentials* you just had to make this new journey into personal growth work for you.

It's easy to get caught up by all the extra stuff they say you need or what you think you will need. What gets forgotten is that all you wanted was to learn something or experience something new and not the stuff that goes with it.

Now you find yourself wanting to be part of the world of cryptocurrency. Of course, many electronic peripherals, software, and apps promise to make this experience much more accessible for a price. But relax, the primary tools you will need, including virtual wallets, are free.

Sure, good tools are great to have if you know how to use them. Just like having the most expensive camera won't make you a great photographer, having all the bells and whistles attached to crypto trading won't ensure a smooth ride.

Start with what you need.

Wallets

You will need a virtual wallet if you conduct any business on the blockchain. As mentioned in earlier chapters, you must have a crypto wallet to store your coins and/or tokens, including NFTs. Remember, these assets aren't pieces of paper or metal you fold up and tuck away or drop into a glass jar when your pockets get too full. They are pieces of digital code that are stored in your wallet until you use them.

There's a plethora of advice on what type of wallet to get and why a particular wallet is right for you. First and foremost, it's all about security.

The idea behind blockchain technology is privacy and security. Rather than a centralized institution that keeps up with your money, the onus is on you to keep up with your account.

Cryptocurrency wallets come in the form of either sophisticated software downloaded into your computer or smart device to serve as virtual wallets, or hardware—USB storage devices set up to store your tokens. These devices can be ordered online.

Custodial or Noncustodial Wallet, That Is the Question

When looking for a cryptocurrency wallet, one of the first questions you need to answer is this: Do you want to be personally responsible for your cryptocurrency and assorted tokens, or are you willing to let others care for them?

If you are not good about keeping up with things, maybe a custodial wallet is your best bet to get started. Most cryptocurrency exchanges will store your currency on their site for you. In other words, they are the custodians of your money, much like a bank keeps custody of your funds.[1] In this case, the exchange *owns* the currency you buy until you decide to transfer amounts to your wallet.[2]

Cryptocurrency is kept in a virtual wallet with only one key holder. If you choose a custodial wallet, you relinquish control of your funds and the private key in exchange for the exchange's security measures that keep your account safe. In other words, you are trusting a third party to take care of your assets, which is the very concern Satoshi raised.

The upside of this control is that the custodian of your wallet has made it easier for you to access your account. If, say, you lose your password, you can reset it.[3] When you set up your account, ensure you

---

[1] Cryptopedia Staff. *Custodial Vs Non-Custodial Wallets.* www.gemini.com/cryptopedia/crypto-wallets-custodial-vs-noncustodial.

[2] Locke. *Hackers Threaten Crypto Wallets.* www.cnbc.com/2021/06/11/tips-to-help-keep-your-crypto-wallet-secure.html.

[3] Cryptopedia Staff. *Custodial Vs Non-Custodial Wallets.* www.gemini.com/cryptopedia/crypto-wallets-custodial-vs-noncustodial#section-custodial-crypto-wallets-pro-and-cons.

understand how to recover it should you lose or forget your access code. You will be sent an e-mail with those instructions after you sign up, so make sure to file it away. You will need it, especially if you routinely clean your cookies.

If you choose to use a custodial wallet, some recommend using one with *cold storage*. That means the bulk of your holdings is kept on the service's storage devices that are not connected to the Internet, making them more secure.[4]

When setting up your passcode, experts recommend using a two-factor identification method, which offers the best security. Your identity is verified by a password and a code generated on an authenticator app on your smart device. This two-factor password could also be a numerical code sent to your smartphone to be re-entered on their site. As with any password, keeping your data private and safe is crucial, especially when it involves your assets.

Holders of custodial wallets should be aware the exchanges they do business with are targets for hackers. As the value of cryptocurrency rises, so does the temptation to steal it.[5] Although easier prey in the early days, hacks are up, although the amount stolen is down due to increased security measures exchanges have put into place. Since 2012, 47 CEX have been hacked, with thieves making off with U.S.$2.72 billion.[6] Changes in storage security measures saw decreases in hacking attempts in 2021.[7]

It's a constant race between hackers exploiting weaknesses to gain access to exchanges and the exchanges themselves working to find ways to close those breaches ahead of time.[8]

Even with improved security, cryptocurrency holders need to safeguard their passcodes. Always be skeptical of any message purported to be from your exchange asking sensitive questions about your account.

---

[4] Ibid.

[5] Cryptopedia Staff. *Learning From Crypto Hacks*. www.gemini.com/cryptopedia/mt-gox-bitcoin-exchange-hacked.

[6] Groves. *Cryptocurrency Exchange Hacks 2022*. www.hedgewithcrypto.com/cryptocurrency-exchange-hacks/.

[7] Ibid.

[8] Cryptopedia Staff. *Learning From Crypto Hacks*. www.gemini.com/cryptopedia/mt-gox-bitcoin-exchange-hacked.

In those cases, leave the message and log into the exchange homepage to check for messages.

If you choose a noncustodial wallet, you retain control of your private key. When activating your digital wallet, prepare to spend time getting it set up. Once you create a username and password, you will get an e-mail with your recovery key. After you are set up, if you find yourself logged out, you will need to go back to that e-mail and follow the link to access your account, as there is no traditional login. File that e-mail where you can find it.

However, if you lose that e-mail, you can recover your account if you took care and wrote down that security phrase the platform generated for you after you signed up. That security phrase, a list of 12 to 24 words such as *ball, fence, feed, cliff, vanish*, and so on, will get you back into your account. Make sure they are copied down in the correct word order. If you were to need to use your security phrase and, using the above words, type in *ball, feed, fence, cliff, vanish*, you would be denied access because you did not follow the correct word order. So, don't get in a hurry. Make sure you copy your phrase in the correct order.

After copying down your security phrase, put it somewhere safe and secure. Don't leave it lying around where it might accidentally get thrown out. Better yet, make several copies and put them in different locations, with one possibly going into your safety deposit box. Yes, it's that big of a deal.

If you lose your private key and security phrase, you lose access to your assets. Customer service can't help you as they don't have a copy of your private key or security phrase. No key. No security phrase. No access. No assets.

Noncustodial wallets can be *hot* or *cold*. If your wallet is *hot*, that means your wallet is connected to the Internet. Conversely, a cold storage wallet is not.

You can download a wallet to your personal computer or laptop or as an app on your mobile devices. Remember, when you are connected to the Internet, you are vulnerable to hackers.

Cold wallet or cold storage refers to a USB storage device programmed to store cryptocurrency and attached by a USB cable. Just like hot wallets, these devices need to be set up. You'll need to create your password and then copy down the security phrase generated by the device. Unlike hot wallets, your key is stored inside these devices. Again, don't get in a hurry. Check and double-check your codes. Once you've copied the information, it might be a good idea to copy it a second time before tucking them away in a secure location. Some cold wallets now include a Bluetooth function. When your device is not in use, it is highly recommended to disconnect it from your computer and keep it turned off when not in use. Also, because it looks like other USB sticks, keep it separated in a secure location.

If the device is lost, stolen, or damaged, you can recover your assets using your security phrase and importing that phrase into your new device.

The following anecdote is a cautionary tale of what can go wrong if one is careless. It's probably the most quoted story of all crypto horror stories. It's a tale about James Howells, a then thirtysomething information technology engineer from Newport, Wales, who had stored 7,500 bitcoins (worth U.S.$354 million in December 2021) he had mined on his laptop hard drive, but in 2013, mistakenly discarded it as rubbish.

Howells told *CNBC* that he had two identical laptop hard drives, but only one had his key. He discarded what he thought was the damaged hard drive, only to discover too late it was the one that contained his private key.[9] Howells petitioned local authorities in January 2021 to excavate the landfill. He sweetened the deal by offering the town 25 percent of the proceeds (worth U.S.$70 million at that time) from selling those bitcoins to fund a COVID-19 relief effort. However, his offer was rejected. They told him it would be too difficult to dig up the landfill due to environmental concerns.[10]

Of course, there are other stories, but this one stands out due to the size of the loss. So, be careful if you store your assets on your hard drive or a cold wallet. Keep your password and security phrases safe and secure.

---

[9] Poonia. *Discarded Hard Drive Held Crypto*. www.deseret.com/2021/12/10/22827963/james-howells-threw-away-hard-drives-with-bitcoin-password.

[10] Murray. *Reward Offered to Find Hard Drive*. www.businessinsider.com/man-offers-council-70-million-dig-up-bitcoin-hard-drive-2021-1.

Even though experts say cold storage wallets are more secure, both hot and cold storage wallets are prone to hacks during cryptocurrency transfers.[11]

Because cryptocurrency is not recognized as a legal tender issued by the government, it is not insured. There are only a handful of insurers offering cryptocurrency insurance at this writing. Many insurers are wary as the entire structure is based on a decentralized system. This leaves the door open for large crypto exchanges to create their own.[12]

Other Wallet Considerations

When considering a wallet, make sure it is compatible with the cryptocurrency or the NFTs you want to hold. Some wallets offer compatibility with multiple coins and tokens. So, check to ensure the wallet you want supports your currency, while others may only support specified coins and tokens.

You may want more than one wallet, one dedicated to cryptocurrency and one to NFTs for such things as game pieces or Graphics Interchange Format (GIFs).

Third-Party Offerings

Research tools are available for serious investors.

Once you are comfortable with trading and want to broaden your portfolio, trading tools are available. These add-ons may serve you or be a confusing hindrance while you start. You'll have to determine that for yourself. Again, do your research. Ask questions. Know your objectives. Stay focused. Save your money to buy cryptocurrency, not promises.

---

[11] CoinBeam. *Cold Vs Hot Wallets.* www.coinbeam.com/cold_wallets_vs_hot_wallets/#:~:text=Hot%20wallets%20are%20also%20more,have%20easier%20access%20to%20them.&text=A%20hot%20wallet%20is%20a,easily%20access%20your%20crypto%20holdings.

[12] O'Connell. *Cryptocurrency Insurance Guide.* www.insurancethoughtleadership.com/emerging-technologies/guide-insurance-cryptocurrency.

Summing Up

Whether you are looking for an exchange, a wallet, or additional services to trade your cryptocurrency, do your homework first. Yes, it might take extra time, but don't let crypto fever get the best of you. It will still be available when you are ready. As anxious as you are, so are the hucksters who are more than willing to take advantage of you.

We'll dive deeper into regulatory issues and taxes in the next chapter.

Risk and Regulation

The depiction most associated with the cryptocurrency market is that of the *wild west*, a description of a chaotic market still trying to find its footing following bitcoin's successful introduction to the world stage in 2009, followed by its tumultuous market gyrations that followed.

While your teenager or twentysomething may be hip to crypto, passing tokens around the way you traded collectible cards, the truth is that crypto is a relatively new, evolving frontier. It is a largely unregulated ecosystem marked by colossal profitability and massive losses that can occur within the same week, if not on the same day. Watching the market can feel like riding a rollercoaster until you get used to the constant gyrations it produces.

Even insiders will admit it's a mess in need of reform. Despite what the crypto market sites promise, navigating this landscape that lacks an agreed-upon roadmap can be daunting. Still, it's a challenge many see as worth taking.

The Need for Regulation

The crypto market has been around for over a decade, while uniform regulations governing cryptocurrency are only now trying to catch up.

As the market has soared to record highs and lows, regulators are still trying to figure out what cryptocurrency is all about and what rules need to be implemented to ensure consumer protection.

Experienced regulators view the cryptocurrency market skeptically, citing the lack of controls necessary to prevent fraud and criminality. On the other hand, even with their decades of experience, these same regulators are, like you, finding themselves having to learn something new. It certainly wasn't something they learned about during their days in business school. Their judgments are based on what they know of a system they grew up with and how it is supposed to work. The worldview proposed by Satoshi in October 2008 just doesn't comport with their understanding of what is.

Aside from deciding that cryptocurrency is property and, therefore, subject to capital gains taxation, the U.S. Congress is struggling to understand the market.[1] Remember, these lawmakers still don't understand the Internet well enough to reign it in. Now, they are trying to wrap their heads around the idea of equating pieces of virtual data with cash.

Unlike centralized institutional financial markets, the cryptocurrency model is based on decentralization operated by an independent network of nodes. Working independently, they make a portion of their living by proving that blockchain transactions are valid. Their reward comes from the cryptocurrency they receive for giving their stamp of approval to each transaction they process.

Unlike traditional jobs, they cannot get away with cheating. If they attempt to alter or change a transaction displayed for all to see on an open distributed ledger, their work can readily be discredited by their peers. It takes a 51 percent majority to reach a consensus, which Satoshi assumed would be ample. He wrote that altering blocks would be difficult given the computer power necessary to validate a transaction and the sheer number of miners committed to upholding the process.

Compare this system to traditional banks—centralized systems that can track any transaction through a paper trail; a system Satoshi suggested favored the merchant rather than the consumer.[2] Yet, the guardrails surrounding the traditional banking system don't currently exist in the crypto world. Because the value of the cryptocurrency has no institutional backing, good fortune can turn to dust in short order leaving the investor with nothing but their dreams of what could have been or should have been.[3]

---

[1] UKTN. *Bitcoin Challenges and Regulations.* www.uktech.news/bitcoin-and-the-challenges-for-financial-regulation.

[2] N. Satoshi. *White Paper.* https://nakamotoinstitute.org/bitcoin/.

[3] Reiff. *Cryptocurrency Legal Risks.* www.investopedia.com/tech/what-are-legal-risks-cryptocurrency-investors/.

Cryptocurrency Exchange Collapses

Some catastrophic collapses that grab the headlines boil down to irre-sponsible management, fraud, successful hacks, or they simply disappear. In 2020, 75 cryptocurrency exchanges fell into one of these categories.[4]

The most recent and notorious case is FTX, one of the largest crypto-currency exchanges.

In November 2022, FTX, a Bahamian-based cryptocurrency exchange worth U.S.$32 billion that year, went bankrupt following questions about its bookkeeping.[5] The company was created and led by Sam Bankman-Fried, a young MIT graduate hailed as the next J.P. Morgan. Bankman-Fried also owned Almeda, a separate business described as a quantitative cryptocurrency firm.

A review of Almeda's balance sheet by *CoinDesk* showed that a large por-tion of its equity was based on a large amount of FTX's tokens. The tokens, FTTs, were issued to traders to reduce trading costs.[6] FTX declared bank-ruptcy shortly thereafter. Bankman-Fried was arrested after being placed under criminal investigation by Bahamian officials for criminal misconduct.[7] He was indicted, charged with multiple charges filed by the U.S. Department of Justice, and extradited to the United States in December 2022 for trial. His trial began on October 4, 2023, on November 2, after 15 days of testimony, Bankman-Fried was found guilty on all seven federal charges of fraud, con-spiracy, and money laundering, each count carrying a maximum sentence of 20 years in prison. Sentencing was scheduled for March 28, 2024.

Cryptocurrency Failures

In some cases, cryptocurrencies just fail. The reasons for their failure can be that they have a weak base that is not committed to the goals of the

---

[4] Young. *Crypto Exchanges Closures 2020*. cointelegraph.com/news/75-crypto-exchanges-have-closed-down-so-far-in-2020.

[5] Tidy. *Fall of FTX*. www.bbc.com/news/technology-63612489.

[6] Allison. *Divisions in FTX*. www.coindesk.com/business/2022/11/02/divisions-in-sam-bankman-frieds-crypto-empire-blur-on-his-trading-titan-alamedas-balance-sheet/.

[7] Egan. *FTX Under Criminal Investigation*. https://edition.cnn.com/2022/11/13/business/ftx-bahamas-criminal-investigation/index.html.

company creating the coin or token. It could be that the founder abandons the projects or use their platform to scam investors and make off with the cash. It could also be due to a successful hack that drains the exchange of significant amounts of currency.[8]

Fraud and Money Laundering

Let's be clear. The cryptocurrency market is not snow-white. But what market is? There have been, and continue to be, unscrupulous actors looking to take advantage of wide-eyed speculators and novices looking to enter the market. Money is to hucksters as blood is to sharks. They smell it and go wild, unapologetically gorging themselves on their unsuspecting prey.

According to reports from the Federal Trade Commission, one of the most brazen online scams involved Elon Musk impersonators who duped investors out of U.S.$2 million in cryptocurrency over six months.[9] Musk is a proponent of cryptocurrency, and a Twitter fan (a platform he purchased in late October 2022), which gave credibility to the deception. These investors were drawn in by the promise of *multiplying* the amount of crypto they held in exchange for sending in what they had.[10]

In a report issued in May 2021, the FTC reported that between October 2020 and March 2021, consumers lost more than U.S.$80 million to cryptocurrency investment scams.[11] As egregious as this is, according to the Consumer Financial Protection Bureau, cryptocurrency cons don't make the top ten fraud list. This federal agency, created under the Obama administration (January 20, 2009–January 20, 2017), listed identity theft as number one.[12] Other forms of theft among the top 10 include credit and debit card fraud, fake charities, prize and lottery fraud, and debt collection.[13] Identity fraud alone cost American consum-

---

[8] Boluwatife. *Cryptos That Failed.* https://sortter.com/blog/article/failed-cryptocurrencies/.

[9] Iacurci. *$2 Million Stolen in Crypto Scams.* www.cnbc.com/2021/05/17/elon-musk-impersonators-stole-more-than-2-million-in-crypto-scams-.html.

[10] Ibid.

[11] Kolhatkar. *Challenges of Regulating Cryptocurrency.* www.newyorker.com/business/currency/the-challenges-of-regulating-cryptocurrency.

[12] Fontinelle. *Common Types of Consumer Fraud.* www.investopedia.com/financial-edge/0512/the-most-common-types-of-consumer-fraud.aspx.

[13] Ibid.

ers U.S.$56 billion in 2020, according to the *2021 Identity Fraud Study* by Javelin Strategy & Research.[14]

Critics of cryptocurrency, who have long warned of abuses, saw those concerns realized two-fold when on November 21, 2023, Binance, the world's largest cryptocurrency exchange, agreed to pay around U.S.$4 billion to settle U.S. federal charges of money laundering. In addition, founder and CEO Changpeng Zhao pleaded guilty to one count of "failing to prevent money laundering" on the platform. As part of the deal, Zhao had to step down as CEO. Binance was charged with processing transactions from drug traffickers, members of terrorist organizations, and those contributing to child sexual abuse, U.S. Treasury Secretary Janet Yellen said in a statement.[15]

Government Regulation

Following the Wall Street Crash of 1929, the federal government stepped in to regulate Wall Street and the banking system. This was accomplished with the passage of the Glass-Steagall Act in 1933, separating banks from brokerage houses.[16] However, it was essentially repealed in 1999 in the waning years of the Clinton administration (January 20, 1993–January 20, 2001). The repeal removed protections that kept the country from financial calamity at the hands of financial institutions.

The Savings and Loan collapse in 1989 cost U.S.$160 billion, of which taxpayers footed U.S.$132 billion. It was considered the greatest financial failure since the 1929 crash.[17]

With no meaningful laws protecting consumers, financial institutions converged during the George W. Bush administration (January 20, 2001–January 20, 2009) to offer risky housing loans in the form of

---

[14] Leonhardt. *$56 Billion Lost to Identity Theft.* www.cnbc.com/2021/03/23/consumers-lost-56-billion-dollars-to-identity-fraud-last-year.html.

[15] Tucker, Whitehurst, Johnson, and Hussein. *Cryptocurrency Exchanged Fined U.S.$4 Billion for Money Laundering.* https://apnews.com/article/cryptocurrency-exchange-binance-justice-department-settlement-sec-8314e9697b98cfe3a9827c78e5720914.

[16] Wikipedia. *Wall Street Reform.* https://en.wikipedia.org/wiki/Wall_Street_reform.

[17] Amadeo. *Savings and Loan Crisis.* www.thebalance.com/savings-and-loans-crisis-causes-cost-3306035.

mortgage-backed securities and "sophisticated derivative products"[18] to people with poor or no credit. The housing market collapsed in 2007, leading to the Great Recession (December 2007–June 2009), when those mortgage-backed securities and derivatives plummeted in value.[19]

In the end, a few of the nation's leading investment firms went bankrupt. Banks got bailed out to the tune of U.S.$498 billion[20] again, leaving taxpayers holding the bag. More than six million people lost their homes,[21] while millions more watched the value of their retirement plans evaporate when the stock market tanked. Despite the calamity, no financial institutions were held liable. No one was held accountable, except for an executive at Credit Suisse who admitted to concealing millions in bank losses in its mortgage-backed securities portfolio and was sent to jail.[22]

Congress responded to the financial crisis with U.S.$787 billion to fund the American Recovery and Reinvestment Act of 2009 to stimulate the stalled economy.[23]

In 2010, Congress passed the Dodd-Frank Wall Street Reform and Consumer Protection Act to reform financial institutions that brought about the economic collapse two years earlier. The reform package included the creation of the Consumer Financial Protection Bureau. The bureau provides educational material and accepts consumer complaints.[24]

---

[18] The Investopedia Team. *2008 Recession*. www.investopedia.com/terms/g/great-recession.asp.

[19] Ibid.

[20] Harbert. *Cost of 2008 Bailouts*. https://mitsloan.mit.edu/ideas-made-to-matter/heres-how-much-2008-bailouts-really-cost.

[21] Ohlrogge. *Home Foreclosures in Great Recession*. www.law.nyu.edu/news/ideas/michael-ohlrogge-great-recession-foreclosures.

[22] Eisinger. *Banker Convicted in Financial Crisis*. www.nytimes.com/2014/05/04/magazine/only-one-top-banker-jail-financial-crisis.html.

[23] Wikipedia. *2009 American Recovery and Reinvestment Act*. https://en.wikipedia.org/wiki/American_Recovery_and_Reinvestment_Act_of_2009#:~:text=The%20approximate%20cost%20of%20the,billion%20between%202009%20and%202019.https://en.wikipedia.org/wiki/American_Recovery_and_Reinvestment_Act_of_2009%23:~:text=The approximate cost of the,billion between 2009 and 2019.

[24] USA.gov. *Consumer Financial Protection Bureau*. www.usa.gov/federal-agencies/consumer-financial-protection-bureau.

Then in 2018, Congress rolled back much of the act, freeing up thousands of small- and medium-sized banks from strict oversight rules.[25]

Now, these same lawmakers are weighing in on cryptocurrency, citing reports that investors have been victims of fraud and further galvanized by the collapse of FTX. Other complaints focus on concerns that cryptocurrency is being used to evade taxes, launder money, and fund other nefarious purposes.

In September 2022, the Biden-Harris administration (January 20, 2021–Present) released its first-ever framework to find ways to regulate cryptocurrency. While looking to curb fraud, the administration's efforts are also looking for ways to make digital transactions easier.[26] Targets include completing assessments of financial risk relating to DeFI by the end of February 2023 and looking at NFTs by the end of July 2023.[27] As of this writing, no new information was available.

While the U.S. government struggles with legislation, state legislatures are taking matters into their own hands. In 2021, 17 states were found to have adopted regulations, while the other 33 and Puerto Rico introduced legislation to regulate the currency.[28]

The United States is not alone in grappling with this emerging market. Governments worldwide, such as the UK, are looking for ways to reign in a market that is gaining maturity.

While some look to reform the system, others are banning it outright.

To reign in financial crime, the European Commission has introduced a series of proposals requiring exchanges to collect identifying information about their traders.[29] The law would establish oversight by creating an EU-wide anti-money laundering authority (AMLA).[30]

---

[25] Rappeport and Flitter. *Dodd-Frank Rollback.* www.nytimes.com/2018/05/22/business/congress-passes-dodd-frank-rollback-for-smaller-banks.html.

[26] Sigalos. *Biden White House to Regulate Crypto.* www.cnbc.com/2022/09/16/heres-whats-in-biden-framework-to-regulate-crypto.html.

[27] Ibid.

[28] Morton. *Cryptocurrency 2021 Legislation.* www.ncsl.org/research/financial-services-and-commerce/cryptocurrency-2021-legislation.aspx.

[29] Bateman and Reuters. *EU Bitcoin Regulations.* www.euronews.com/next/2021/07/21/eu-will-make-bitcoin-traceable-and-ban-anonymous-crypto-wallets-in-anti-money-laundering-d.

[30] Ibid.

The European Parliament took its first steps to regulate cryptocurrency assets in March 2022, approving a provision requiring traceable crypto transfers. The new regulations are part of its proposed Transfer of Funds regulations. The proposals outlaw noncustodial wallets whose owners cannot be confirmed, like custodial wallets held by exchanges that identify customers through the KYC review.[31] The move was made to combat money laundering and using crypto to fund terrorism.

Remember, a noncustodial wallet (also referred to as an unhosted wallet) is a digital wallet solely managed by the owner who holds the keys to the wallet.

Critics countered that the regulations require crypto asset service providers (exchanges) to verify information about the wallet holders, and to ensure that the transaction is legitimate.[32] The proposal requires that crypto transactions over 1,000 euros from a noncustodial wallet be reported to the appropriate AMLAs.[33]

Exchanges, as you recall, require verifiable personal information from official government sources before an account can be opened. Critics argue that keeping up with every transaction could produce undue burdens on those exchanges.[34]

This provision was so alarming 40 crypto companies sent an open letter to the European Parliament, the European Commission, and other EU principals urging commonsense legislation. The group is particularly concerned about the threat to privacy if noncustodial wallets are outlawed.[35]

In April 2023, the EU Parliament, following up on that provisional agreement made in 2022, overwhelmingly approved comprehensive legislation to regulate cryptocurrency assets, which include measures to

---

[31] Dinsmore. *EU Votes to Regulate Crypto Wallets.* www.dinsmore.com/publications/eu-lawmakers-vote-to-regulate-digital-wallets/.

[32] Attlee. *EU Parliament to Regulate Crypto Wallets.* https://cointelegraph.com/news/eu-parliament-can-outlaw-transacting-with-unhosted-wallets-crypto-advocate-warns.

[33] Ibid.

[34] Attlee. *Unhosted Crypto Wallets Unwelcome in EU.* https://cointelegraph.com/news/unhosted-is-unwelcome-eu-s-attack-on-noncustodial-wallets-is-part-of-a-larger-trend.

[35] Attlee. *Web3 in Europe.* https://cointelegraph.com/news/let-s-build-a-europe-where-web3-can-flourish-crypto-companies-sign-an-open-letter-to-eu-regulators.

provide transparency, protect customers, and prevent fraud and money laundering.[36] The rules, known as the Markets in Crypto Act (MiCA), include requiring cryptocurrency exchanges to be licensed in each of those European countries where they do business. These exchanges will, for example, be required to inform customers of the potential risks associated with cryptocurrency.[37] The European Securities and Markets Authority (ESMA) will oversee exchanges to ensure they protect both investors and the industry.[38]

Suspicious transfers will be subject to trace and can be blocked. Transactions of more than 1,000 euros between the holders of noncustodial wallets and crypto exchanges (referred to by the EU as crypto-assets service providers) must be reported.[39] On the other hand, the rule does not apply to *person-to-person* transfers that do not require a *provider* or *providers acting on their own behalf.*[40]

The comprehensive package, which goes into effect sometime in 2024, also requires that firms provide information about energy consumption.[41]

For now, NFTs, which represent tangible assets, are exempted from these rules but are expected to be addressed later.

Countries in Southeast Asia are also moving to control this market. In Singapore, for example, a license will be required to process any transaction, storage, or exchange.[42] In Malaysia, cryptocurrency trades must comply with Security Commission Malaysia.[43]

---

[36] Browne. *European Parliament Passes Comprehensive Cryptocurrency Regulation.* www.cnbc.com/2023/04/20/eu-lawmakers-approve-worlds-first-comprehensive-crypto-regulation.html#:~:text=the%20cryptocurrency%20industry.-,In%20 a%20vote%20Thursday%2C%20the%20EU%20Parliament%20voted%20 517%20in,lose%20investors'%20crypto-assets.

[37] Ibid.

[38] Ibid.

[39] EU Parliament. *Crypto Asset Regulations Approved.* www.europarl.europa.eu/ news/en/press-room/20230414IPR80133/crypto-assets-green-light-to-new-rules-for-tracing-transfers-in-the-eu.

[40] Ibid.

[41] Ibid.

[42] The Crystal Marketing Team. *2021 Crypto Regulations in SE Asia.* https:// crystalblockchain.com/articles/2021-crypto-regulations-in-south-east-asia/.

[43] Ibid.

China banned crypto mining and trading in September 2021, joining eight other countries and making cryptocurrency illegal, while another 42 countries have implicit bans. That is, it is understood that this activity is prohibited.[44] Another 103 countries are moving toward regulation.[45]

Aside from the revelations regarding Binance, fears that bad actors are overrunning the crypto market are not rooted in fact. Figures collected in the Chainalysis' 2021 report painted a far different picture. The report found that in 2019, criminal transactions totaling U.S.$21.4 billion accounted for only 2.1 percent of all cryptocurrency transactions.[46] That number fell significantly in 2020 when illegal transactions accounted for only 0.34 percent, or U.S.$10 billion, of total crypto transactions.[47]

Cash and the use of established financial institutions remain the primary go-to choice for those looking to launder money. Capital One, for example, was charged with a U.S.$390 million Enforcement Action "for engaging in both willful and negligent violations of the Bank Secrecy Act (BSA)." They *willingly* failed "to implement and maintain an effective Anti-Money Laundering (AML) program to guard against money laundering."[48] The financial giant was also cited for other related activities.[49]

While governments grapple with what to do, crypto watchers understand that the cryptocurrency market must be regulated to attain the legitimacy it needs to survive.[50]

---

[44] Bajpai. *Countries Where Bitcoin Is Legal and Illegal.* www.investopedia.com/articles/forex/041515/countries-where-bitcoin-legal-illegal.asp.

[45] Ibid.

[46] Lennon. *Bitcoin's Bad Rap.* www.forbes.com/sites/haileylennon/2021/01/19/the-false-narrative-of-bitcoins-role-in-illicit-activity/?sh=649487c33432.

[47] Ibid.

[48] Lennon. *The False Narrative of Bitcoin's Role in Illicit Activity.* www.forbes.com/sites/haileylennon/2021/01/19/the-false-narrative-of-bitcoins-role-in-illicit-activity/?sh=649487c33432.

[49] Ibid.

[50] Gebbing and Nöffke. *Regulating Crypto Essential for Legitimacy.* https://techcrunch.com/2021/08/16/regulating-crypto-is-essential-to-ensuring-its-global-legitimacy/.

Do I Need This?

The answer depends on your goals and your sense of the future, as cryptocurrency and NFTs challenge our historical understanding of traditional forms of assets. But as history shows, the representation of money, considered a general purpose technology (one that can affect an entire economy), has, like other technologies, changed radically over the centuries. Civilization has moved from bartering and trading to using precious metals, paper money and checks, credit and debit cards, electronic money, and now cryptocurrency.

Even with the criticism and fear surrounding the cryptocurrency market, an equally obstinate group of supporters and backers are determined to make it work.

Since the first bitcoin was mined in January 2009, the value of bitcoin and other altcoins (alternative coins launched after the success of bitcoin) has created millionaires overnight. At the same time, others lured by the prospect of overnight riches have lost big betting on one of the thousands of cryptocurrencies that failed to live up to investor expectations. That was true in the California Gold Rush in the mid-19th century and the booms and busts of the emerging oil markets in the late 19th and early 20th centuries.

It was reported that in the first five months of 2022 alone, 2,421 cryptocurrencies failed.[1] The number is higher than most years, which typically report a thousand or more cryptocurrencies fail only to be replaced by others. These failed coins and tokens are referred to as *dead coins* and can be tracked on coinopsy.com.

Other problems include that wallets can be lost, damaged, or corrupted, as in the case of cold storage wallets. Without a private key and recovery phase generated when one sets up their noncustodial wallet, they won't be able to recover their currency. Cryptocurrency can be lost without a recovery tool in a custodial wallet or hard drive.

---

[1] Wanguba. *Cryptocurrencies Failures 2022.* https://e-cryptonews.com/how-many-cryptocurrencies-have-failed/#:~:text=Mostly%2C%20they%20come%20in%20the,Coinopsy%20which%20tracks%20such%20failures.

Because transactions are irreversible, if you make a mistake and list an incorrect or invalid address for the receiver, there is no way to recover your currency, which is ironic given that the blockchain is an open ledger and can be tracked from sender to receiver.

On the plus side, cryptocurrency offers the hope of financial safety. Unlike traditional financial institutions, which have brought the world economy to its knees more than once, including during the Great Recession of 2008, cryptocurrency holders oversee their money.[2]

Other advantages are the fact that transactions are secure and irreversible. A transaction can be made anonymously, and transaction fees are low.[3]

One of the biggest draws to the decentralization thesis is that personal information remains with individuals.[4] While that remains true in transactions, there's a good deal one must disclose when signing up with an exchange. This is done, in part, to ensure that transactions are not used to perpetrate nefarious activities.

Although the use of cryptocurrency outside the crypto world is limited, it is gaining appeal in the mainstream markets, with some businesses now offering to exchange services for cryptocurrency. For example, one can use cryptocurrency to buy a Netflix gift card. Some exchanges offer Visa and MasterCard debit and credit cards. NFTs, which offer many opportunities, require cryptocurrency. More about NFTs in the next section.

Suppose you decide to go forward, whether as a currency trader or if you plan to use cryptocurrency to make purchases, or take part in the NFT market, do your homework. Take a free crypto course offered by several exchanges or other reputable learning platforms like MIT. Read articles from trusted news and financial sites, including the extensive bibliography at the end of this book. Read the white papers from developers offering cryptocurrency. Check with those you know who trade crypto. Join crypto communities and ask questions.

---

[2] Reiff. *Paying With Cryptocurrency.* www.investopedia.com/ask/answers/100314/what-are-advantages-paying-bitcoin.asp.

[3] Ibid.

[4] The European Press Review. *Pros and Cons of Cryptocurrency 2021.* www.europeanbusinessreview.com/major-pros-and-cons-of-cryptocurrency-in-2021/.

NFTs

What Are NFTs?

Nonfungible tokens, or NFTs, represent unique digital or physical assets. They can represent a piece of art, a dinner for two, or even a house. As digital assets, they are easier to trade on the Internet.

To better understand nonfungibles, let's first look at their opposite—fungibles.

A fungible is something interchangeable like dollar bills, shares of common stock, or commodities like corn and oats. For example, you go to a vending machine to buy a soda, put in a dollar bill, press the button, and get your drink. Depending on the price, you get change back. Put in another dollar bill, press the button, and you get another soda and change.[1] The dollar bills are fungibles, in that they are interchangeable and represent equal value. The value of that can of soda is also fungible as cans of the same beverage are of equal value.

Nonfungibles, on the other hand, cannot be exchanged equally.[2] Take works of art, for example. Vincent van Gogh's *The Starry Night* is unique and cannot be swapped for, say, *La Danse* by Henri Matisse, which is unique in and of itself and carries a unique specified monetary value.

Other examples of nonfungibles include such things as land and diamonds.[3] Land is land, but the value of the land depends on use, location, and condition. Diamonds may look alike, but factors such as cut, color, and carat weight separate them in quality, value, and price.

Like nonfungible physical items, NFTs represent one-of-a-kind objects digitized and placed on tokens and stored on the blockchain—the unalterable open ledger where information is recorded and stored.

The first NFT was a piece of generative art entitled *Quantum* by digital artists Kevin and Jennifer McCoy. Kevin minted it as an NFT in 2014.[4]

---

[1] Kenton. *What Are Fungible Goods*. www.investopedia.com/terms/f/fungibles.asp.

[2] Ibid.

[3] Ibid.

[4] Exmundo. *The Story of Quantum, the First NFT*. https://nftnow.com/art/quantum-the-first-piece-of-nft-art-ever-created/#:~:text=So%20what%20was%20the%20first,NFT%20by%20Kevin%20in%202014.

As mentioned in the previous sections, digital assets—coins and tokens, were initially created to represent fiat money (currency backed by governments). Developers like Ethereum quickly realized that tokens could be made for other things, spawning a new industry for artists, musicians, and entrepreneurs looking for new avenues to share their work. Consumers looking for collectibles or investment opportunities obliged.

The Ethereum blockchain took nonfungibles to a new level inviting artists of all stripes to share their creations as NFTs on its blockchain. NFTs, as mentioned earlier, are unique, noninterchangeable data made in the form of digitized assets. They include paintings, drawings, generative art, music, photographs, audio snipes, video game collectibles, and GIFs[5] created on a PC or with a device app. Once created, they are stored on a decentralized ledger, where ownership and authenticity cannot be disputed. On the other hand, when one buys an NFT, they own it but do not have a say as to who can see or share it.[6] As these ledgers are public, they can be shared and viewed by anyone on the blockchain.

If you are thinking there's no way this could translate into a business opportunity, you couldn't be more mistaken. Believe it or not, NFTs sales reached U.S.$25 billion in 2021 compared to just U.S.$95 million in 2020. No, that's not a typo. NFT sales went from U.S.$95 million to U.S.$25 billion in just one year.[7]

The rise and fall of values are based on the fact that, for the most part, NFTs are purchased with cryptocurrency, which has enjoyed both meteoric rises and catastrophic crashes. Despite the setbacks, the work of NFT artists continues, gaining more and more popularity among those who believe in the work.

In this section, we will look at how NFTs are being used and how they are changing the marketplace.

---

[5] TRG Datacenters. *Popular NFTs of 2021*. www.trgdatacenters.com/the-most-popular-nfts-of-2021/.

[6] N26. *What Is an NFT*. https://n26.com/en-eu/blog/what-is-an-nft.

[7] Fatemi. *NFTs and Music*. www.forbes.com/sites/falonfatemi/2022/01/24/nfts-and-the-future-of-music/?sh=1436c3af5677.

NFTs

Art, Music, and Those Adorable Collectibles

While crypto art has been around for a decade, it has only been in the last year or two that the market has reached a fever pitch. NFT art sales brought in U.S.$2.57 billion in 2021 compared to U.S.$20 million in 2020.[1]

In March 2021, an NFT entitled *Everydays: The First 5,000 Days*, a collage created by the digital artist Mike Winkelmann, a.k.a. Beeple, was sold at Christie's for a record U.S.$69 million.[2]

A few months prior, Beeple sold a series in December 2020 for U.S.$3.5 million.[3]

You can find images of the collage using your search engine or by scanning this QR code.

Everydays: The First 5,000 Days—Beeple

The rush to NFT art is yet another avenue for investors looking for new investment opportunities.[4]

---

[1] Statista Research Department. *NFT Sales 2019–2021.* www.statista.com/statistics/1299636/sales-value-art-and-collectibles-nfts-worldwide/ www.google.com/search?q=NFT+ART+SALES+IN+DOLLARS&oq=NFT+ART+SALES+IN+DOLLARS&aqs=chrome..69i57.6988j0j15&sourceid=chrome&ie=UTF-8.
[2] Kastrenakes. *Beeple NFT Sells for $69 Million.* www.theverge.com/2021/3/11/22325054/beeple-christies-nft-sale-cost-everydays-69-million.
[3] Ibid.
[4] Kay. *Why People Spend Millions on NFT Art.* www.businessinsider.com/why-are-people-buying-nfts-investing-in-nft-crypto-art-2021-3.

Perspective

Who hasn't been taken aback by the works of David, whose mammoth paintings blanket the walls of the Louvre in Paris, or struck by Pablo Picasso's mural *Guernica* at the Museo Reina Sofía in Madrid?

It's one thing to thumb through a coffee table catalog and enjoy glossy reproductions but quite another to stand before those works boldly displayed as the artist intended. Stand in front of a work, and you have one perspective. Move to the side and get another. Change the lighting, and the conveyance of the work could completely change your perspective.

That perspective has changed over the past few years with the advent of digital art—unique works of pixel art placed on tokens wrapped up in blocks and sold, with the owner having the distinction of being the holder of a unique piece of art shrouded in computer coding. You'll need a good monitor with an electric socket nearby if you want to display it.

Some see NFTs as another avenue to convey an artistic vision. Others see it as a traditional means of investment. And others see it as a passing fad.

However you may view it, NFTs are capturing the imagination of a range of artists eager to share their work on a platform that stretches the globe. Several platforms have subsequently sprung up to provide those artists with a venue from which to share their work.

For example, music legend Bob Dylan, his son Jesse Dylan, and two others have created a platform where leading artists, publishers, and brands can convert their work into NFTS. The platform is called *Snowcrash*, a Web3 studio[5] dedicated to what is referred to as the metaverse or digital space.[6]

The term *metaverse* comes from the 1992 science fiction novel *Snow Crash* by Neal Stephenson.[7] *Snowcrash* features several NFT illustrations that can be purchased with SOL tokens.

---

[5] Snowcrash. *Snowcrash.* https://snowcrash.com/.

[6] Kahn. *Bob Dylan Creates NFT Project.* https://faroutmagazine.co.uk/bob-dylan-revealed-as-founder-of-new-nft-project/.

[7] Wiseman. *NFTs for Writers.* www.novlr.org/the-reading-room/nfts-for-writers-new-ways-to-publish-in-a-digital-world.

The success of NFT art has caught the eye of a real estate developer planning to add it as an amenity. In 2022, Lofty Brickell Residences, a 44-story luxury condominium in Miami, FL, where condominiums price between U.S.$500,000 and U.S.$1.7 million, announced it had commissioned NFT works of art which it plans to transfer to buyers, which they can display and share within the building.[8]

What Is Art? An Aesthetic Point of View

The purpose of art is to inspire. The question is whether or not that inspiration can be fully appreciated on a monitor limited by the number of pixels a graphics card can generate.

Is this format something a collector should consider? Does it move the senses? Can it be appreciated like the works of Matisse that lifts the spirit or the works of Picasso that stirs unsettled passions? Or is it just about value? These are questions aestheticians are asking. Those images, their form, color, and perspective cast into pixels are, in the strict sense, considered art. But there is more to art than the image. There's the marriage with the experience to feel, said Dr. Michael Mitias, Emeritus Professor of Philosophy at Millsaps College, Jackson, MS, in an e-mail exchange. Mitias spent his career as a professor and scholar delving into the humanities, which included the study of aesthetics (the philosophical study of beauty and taste). His long list of book titles includes *Aesthetic Quality and Aesthetic Experience (Elementa 42)* and *Possibility of the Aesthetic Experience.*

While *aesthetically beautiful* and *valuable* to the admirer, the fact is that NFTs are *restrictive*, in that the image is confined to a fixed space—a computer screen that is contrary to how art should be experienced, he wrote.

"Again, although the computer is a viable means of artistic expression, as in architectural design, having an aesthetic experience at the computer is limited to the language of the computer, which is not

---

[8] Reynolds. *Miami Condo Offers NFT Art.* www.forbes.com/sites/emmareynolds/2022/04/05/this-luxury-miami-condo-building-is-launching-an-nft-art-collection-for-its-owners/?sh=4636d7a235c9.

as abundant or versatile as the plastic or temporal media are," Mitias wrote.

Let's compare. Enter an art gallery, and one is met with works teeming with vibrant energy, enhanced by nuanced lighting and spacing, finetuning its essence in ways that can leave one breathless. Then there is the computer screen and its limited pixels. How can this medium offer the same experience? Mitias asked. "The meaning it (art) communicates is, after all, a human meaning. Even the literary work of art, which is read in the privacy of one's soul, is essentially communal because the book is a public object," he said. "Some critics would argue that digital art fosters the value of selfish orientation and pleasure in life because it detracts rather than promotes the human bond in a particular society or in human society at large."

In the end, it comes down to the question we first asked. What is art, and how will this new medium reflect it? "Whether the possibilities of the formal organization of the digits can compete with the capacity of the human voice, human motion, colors, and lines, marble, wood, or bronze, or space is an open question," Mitias wrote.

NFTs and Music

The global music industry is a multibillion-dollar business bolstered by streaming services, raking in between 50 and 70 percent profits. In 2021, the industry earned U.S.$25.9 billion in 2021, up 18.5 percent in 2020, where earnings reached U.S.$21.9 billion.[9] The figures represented the seventh consecutive year of growth for the industry.

Artists earn a fraction of that amount. As noted, streaming has been a significant factor in lifting profits. Published reports say Spotify, for example, paid 90 percent of its royalties to 0.8 percent of the artists it carries.[10]

---

[9] Richter. *Global Streaming Resurgence.* www.statista.com/chart/4713/global-recorded-music-industry-revenues/.
[10] Willings. *Spotify's Top Earners.* https://musictech.com/news/most-of-spotifys-top-0-8-of-artists-earn-less-than-50k-in-streaming-revenue/.

Of the 23,900 artists making up this group, 13,400 earned more than U.S.$50,000 that year, while 7,800 earned more than U.S.$100,000. Moving up, 1,870 earned more than U.S.$500,000, while 870 earned more than U.S.$1 million.[11]

To gain oversight over their music, several artists are turning to NFTs where they can control their work and earn more. Offering their music as NFTs combined with converting artwork for that album into one-of-a-kind JPGs or GIFs could give them more control and more money.[12] Kings of Leon, in 2021, became the first group to launch an album as an NFT. It's not just for millennials. Snoop Dogg plans to convert his newly acquired record label, *Death Row Records*, into an NFT recording label.[13] Also, country music legend Dolly Parton came together with FOX Entertainment's Blockchain Creative Labs to produce Dollyverse, a collection of certified Dolly NFT collectibles, which includes limited-edition work from her album *Run Rose Run* and artwork.[14]

NFTs: Books and Literature

NFTs could open the world of publishing for independent writers and poets who can use this medium to sell their work directly to the public, bypassing traditional publishing methods.[15]

---

[11] Ibid.

[12] Wolfson. *NFTs Hot 2022 Grammy Topic*. https://cointelegraph.com/news/grammys-2022-nfts-hot-topic-of-discussion-amongst-musicians-and-industry-experts.

[13] Campbell. *Snoop Dogg's NFT Release*. www.nme.com/news/music/new-death-row-records-owner-snoop-dogg-teases-labels-first-nft-release-3196189#:~:text=New%20Death%20Row%20Records%20owner%20Snoop%20Dogg%20teases%20label's%20first%20NFT%20release&text=Snoop%20Dogg%20has%20shared%20plans,Snoop%2C%20and%20peaked%20at%20No.

[14] Needham. *Dolly Parton's Dollyverse*. www.musicbusinessworldwide.com/dolly-parton-to-launch-the-dollyverse-a-web3-experience-offering-limited-edition-nfts1/#:~:text=Parton%20has%20partnered%20with%20FOX,and%20certified%20Dolly%20NFT%20collectibles%E2%80%9D.

[15] Wiseman. *NFTs for Writers*. www.novlr.org/the-reading-room/nfts-for-writers-new-ways-to-publish-in-a-digital-world.

NFTs allow the author the opportunity to deviate from traditional works a publisher may reject due to marketing data. The digital world offers them different options and different formats than traditional publishers. Writers, for example, can use flickering to produce flashing pages with content suddenly appearing on the pages, replacing what was there before. Once ready for sale, the writer can control how many copies they release, numbering each like a lithograph for collectors. In February 2021, Blake Butler released his novel, *DECADE*, as a GIF, then digitized the work, creating an NFT, which he quickly sold to a willing buyer for five ERC-20 (Ethereum tokens) then valued at U.S.$7,560.50. The work featured flashing pages and included a PDF version of the book.[16] Butler originally completed the novel in 2008, but publishers found the language too dense and the structure too complicated, so they rejected the book. The rise of NFTs allowed Butler to put it on the market.[17]

While NFTs and e-books are delivered similarly, NFTs are like physical books. Once you buy them, they are yours forever. You can give them away, share them or sell them. When you buy an e-book, you are simply purchasing the license to the book. Should you break the terms and conditions of the seller, or if the seller ever goes out of business, you lose those e-books. Your Kindle e-books, for example, cannot be resold, transferred, or donated.[18]

Another cited benefit for NFT books is the use of smart contracts created to share profits. When you buy a book, a percentage goes to the publisher, who intermittently sends a percentage to the authors and others involved. With a smart contract, payments are made immediately. What's more, contingencies can be built into the program to make changes in payments over time, if necessary.[19]

---

[16] Caplan. *Rise of the Crypto Writer*. https://lithub.com/the-rise-of-the-crypto-writer-on-what-literary-nfts-might-mean-for-the-book-world/.

[17] Ibid.

[18] Jarrard. *Where e-Books Go When You Do*. www.nytimes.com/2012/05/11/opinion/where-do-e-books-go-when-you-do.html#:~:text=Here's%20what%20I%20got%20back,be%20accessed%20by%20that%20person.

[19] Wenstrom. *NFTs for Books*. https://bookriot.com/nfts-for-books/.

The possibilities for writers may be growing, but will readers follow? One question that begs for an answer is cost. Obviously, the average reader cannot afford to spend U.S.$7,560.50 for a book, nor would they buy one unless they are serious collectors. This is where economic terms like *economies of scale* come into play. Like widgets produced in a factory, the more books produced, the lower the cost of the goods produced. The average book publication time ranges between nine months and two years, with self-publishing siding on a quicker release date.[20]

That's a lot of time and energy by a cadre of people, with most of the work done by the writer who wants to earn money from their endeavor. Take the book example *DECADE* from above. Obviously, this was not a book generated in a few months. Let's say it took a year—365 days. Divide 365 into U.S.$7,560.50, and you see the author earned a whopping U.S.$20.71 per day writing.

The good news is that not all original NFT books cost U.S.$7,000. Creatokia, a digital website based in Frankfurt, Germany, offers NFT books, audiobooks, works of art, and other literary items at hardcover book prices. The platform takes tokens or credit cards. The site also accepts dollars and euros. The books are downloaded to one's crypto wallet, the same wallet necessary to store crypto.

Creatokia is supported by Bookwire GmbH, Frankfurt, Germany. Founded in 2009 and now international, the company converts print to e-books, audiobooks, and print-on-demand for publishers. Creatokia is one of the first platforms to offer NFT books.[21] So, yes, while NFTs offer greater control and creativity, in the end, it's still about making money. The goal is to exceed the breakeven point. Anything less is a loss. Even new technology can't change the rules of business fundamentals.

---

[20] Writer's Digest. *Getting Published.* www.writersdigest.com/getting-published/ how-long-does-it-take-to-get-a-book-published#:~:text=With%20our%20 rules%20established%20above,they%20plan%20their%20production%20 schedule.

[21] The Creative Penn. *Creatokia and NFT Originals.* www.thecreativepenn.com/ 2021/11/05/creatokia-digital-originals-nfts/.

NFTs and Poetry

Poetry is the perfection of storytelling, blending emotions with beautifully scripted words and cadence. Passed through the ages, it heralds the triumphs and tragedies of King Odysseus of Ithaca on his journey home after the Trojan War in Homer's *The Odyssey*. It rebukes intractable thinking that led to calamity in the Anglo-Boer War, as told in Rudyard Kipling's *The Old Men*. It acknowledges the reckoning a man has with his fate, underscored in Robert Penn Warren's *Audubon*. It looks deep into the soul of a young man whose actions bring him closer to his love in Pablo Neruda's *If You Forget Me*. And it offers hope for a young girl who seized on the beauty of words to overcome the harsh realities faced in life in Maya Angelou's *I Know Why the Caged Bird Sings*. The list is endless.

So, it's no wonder today's poets are gravitating to blockchain technology, where they can convey their timeless messages of love, hope, pain, longing, and suffering, married to a technology that is believed to be timeless.

One of the leading sites created to share this timeless art form is *theVERSEverse*, created by two poets and an artist whose purpose, according to their website mission statement, is to equate poetry with works of art. It's a haven where "we celebrate the rise of crypto-native poetry" while building on the movement to "build the future of literature on the blockchain."[22]

The founders are Ana Maria Caballero, an internationally recognized poet who has received several international awards for her work; Kalen Iwamoto, a crypto writer and artist; and Sasha Stiles, a poet, artist, and AI researcher.[23]

The NFT Poet's Society provides poets and writers a platform to exhibit their work on the metaverse.

For those looking to gift written forms of art, NFT poetry offers one-of-a-kind original works to one-of-a-kind people.

---

[22] TheVERSEverse. *Website.* https://theverseverse.com/mission/.
[23] Ibid.

NFT Images and GIFs

Stickers, animated video clips, and images produced by artists worldwide have become another money-making opportunity. Anyone with a computer and a software program or app can create NFTs held in wallets or transferred and displayed on T-shirts. There's even a line of NFTs called *wearables*, which are fashion lines of clothing and accessories created for avatars.

Costs for these lines of NFTs can run from a few dollars up to hundreds of thousands of dollars. The most famous piece of pop art, *Nyan Cat*, sold for 300 Ethereum coins, then valued at U.S.$560,000.[24] Others put the amount at U.S.$600,000. You can find the video on YouTube or follow the QR code.

Nyan Cat video—Chris Torres

Other NFT Collectables

Collectibles, like beauty, are in the eye of the beholder. The rise of NFTs suggests that just about anything written, photographed, drawn, or recorded can become an NFT. Twitter cofounder Jack Dorsey's first tweet fetched an unprecedented U.S.$2.9 million when he put it on the market as an NFT in March 2021. The tweet, created in 2006, was auctioned for charity.[25]

Time, which has grown increasingly interested in the NFT movement, issued its first interactive NFT magazine on March 23, 2022,

[24] Kinsella. *Nyam Cat GIF Sold for U.S.$560,000.* https://news.artnet.com/market/nyan-cat-nft-sells-for-560000-1945679.

[25] Harper. *First Tweet Sells for U.S.$2.9m.* www.bbc.com/news/business-56492358.

with a cover story featuring Ethereum cofounder Vitalik Buterin.[26] The move came seven months after it launched *TIMEPieces* NFT collection, which opened with 4,676 pieces of NFT art derived from the works of 40 influential artists.[27]

While *Time* is the largest media company to focus on Web3, the third generation of the World Wide Web, it's not the first magazine to enter the NFT domain. The first was traced to Sam J., who launched *ISSUE 1* in October 2020.[28]

There's even the first-ever NFT for dogs. It features a stick between the front paws of Remy, a dog owned by a married couple who created the image.[29]

Love has also found its way to the blockchain. Some unique traditional methods couples have used to signify their eternal love and devotion have included clicking a lock on a bridge and throwing the key into the water below. The tradition, believed to have begun in Hungary, soon spread to other parts of the world.[30] No bridge is more famous than the Pont des Arts, or *lock bridge* in Paris, one of many that cross the River Seine, where couples long flocked to click their lock and toss the key below. The weight of the locks, which grew to 45 tons, caused part of the railing to collapse in 2014. The following year, the city began replacing the bridge with graffiti depicting messages of love and hope. Locks are forbidden.[31]

---

[26] Time PR. Time NFT Edition. https://time.com/6158525/time-releases-first-ever-nft-magazine-issue/#:~:text=Founder%20Vitalik%20Buterin-,TIME%20Releases%20First%2DEver%20Full%20Magazine%20Issue%20as%20an%20NFT,Ethereum%20Co%2DFounder%20Vitalik%20Buterin&text=On%20Wednesday%2C%20March%202023,an%20NFT%20on%20the%20blockchain.

[27] Thomas. *TIMEPieces NFT Collection*. https://nftnow.com/news/time-magazine-timepieces-nft-collection/.

[28] Ibid.

[29] Ibid.

[30] City Wonders Team. *Paris Love Lock Bridge*. https://citywonders.com/blog/France/Paris/paris-love-lock-bridge-story#:~:text=The%20'lock%20bridge'%20is%20a,ritual%20symbolizes%20love%20locked%20forever.

[31] Desbiens. *Love Lock's Prohibited on Pont Des Arts*. www.thetravel.com/pont-des-arts-can-you-still-do-love-locks-in-paris/.

Symbols of love may be too weighty in the physical world but are weightless measurements in the virtual world. When *Coinbase* employees Rebecca Rose and Peter Kacherginsky got married, they added an engaging trapping that could find a foothold in future wedding ceremonies. Their traditional Jewish wedding included the exchange of not-so-traditional virtual rings. The two pulled out their smartphones and sent virtual wedding rings to each other's digital wallets, which will forever be stored on a blockchain.[32]

The VCR Group, a mix of entrepreneurs and restauranteurs, may be paving the wave of the future. The group has created the world's first NFT members-only restaurant, the Flyfish Club, which opened in 2023. Those buying in are treated to private dining and succulent sushi and sashimi dishes.[33]

NFTs are also being used for branding opportunities and memorabilia.

As you see, NFTs offer a wide range of utilities. If you can imagine it, then an NFT is possible.

Where to Buy NFTs

There are dozens of platforms where one can buy or sell NFTs. Here are a handful representing a wide array of interests. Again, this is just a sampling. An online search will bring up several lists of prospective buyers from which to choose.

Unlike fiat money, not all sites accept the same cryptocurrency, so be prepared to swap yours out at your exchange, if you don't have the right coins or tokens.

One of the most popular platforms is OpenSea, an open marketplace that offers virtual land, digital pets, trading cards, games, and photographs, to name a few categories. The site also offers artists the opportunity to create NFTs on their site.

---

[32] Clark. *NFT Wedding Rings Exchanged.* www.theverge.com/tldr/2021/4/2/22364647/coinbase-employees-nft-wedding-exchange-romance.

[33] Sutton. *First NFT Restaurant Planned.* www.theartnewspaper.com/2022/01/14/nft-restaurant-new-york-city-flyfish-club.

The site reported monthly sales of U.S.$5 billion in February 2022, up from U.S.$3.4 billion in August 2021.[34] The platform earns most of its revenue from a 2.5 percent service fee charged when NFTs are sold.[35]

Mintable is another popular marketplace where NFTs can be bought, sold, and created. This platform is comparable in content, but OpenSea charges less commission, while Mintable charges range from 2.5 percent to 10 percent. On the other hand, artists displaying on Mintable can earn higher royalties.[36] Mintable also offers online courses.[37]

Crypto.com, a cryptocurrency exchange, also includes a marketplace where users can buy and sell collectibles. Like cryptocurrency purchases, buyers can also use credit or debit cards to buy NFTs.[38]

For those interested in digital art, there's SuperRare, a site that specializes in selling single-edition digital artwork.[39] The platform is very selective about whom it represents, putting artists through a screening process and choosing a minimum number to provide works on the site.[40] For sports fans, there's NBA Top Shot for basketball fans,[41] Fan Zone Sports Club for football (soccer) enthusiasts, Ferrari and Velas for Formula One fans, and Battle Infinity for the hockey crowd, to name a few.[42]

If you are interested in collectibles, chances are you can find an NFT site that meets your needs. But before you buy, do your research. Treat these purchases the way you would treat any other online purchase. Be skeptical.

---

[34] Hyperbeast. *OpenSea U.S.$5 Billion in Monthly NFT Sales.* https://hypebeast.com/2022/2/opensea-new-record-nft-sales-january-2022.

[35] Cuofano. *How OpenSea Market Make Money.* https://fourweekmba.com/how-does-opensea-make-money-opensea-business-model/.

[36] Houston. *OpenSea Vs Mintable.* www.businessinsider.com/personal-finance/opensea-vs-mintable.

[37] Ibid.

[38] Brooke. *Crypto.com NFT Marketplace.* www.business2community.com/nft/cryptocom-nft-marketplace.

[39] Newbery. *SuperRare NFT Marketplace Review.* www.fool.com/the-ascent/cryptocurrency/nfts/superrare-review/.

[40] Ibid.

[41] Lehman. *Where to Buy NFTs.* https://seekingalpha.com/article/4482960-where-to-buy-nfts.

[42] Jennings. *Best Sport NFT Collectibles 2022.* www.business2community.com/nft/sport-nft-drops.

Use a well-known platform, which is an indication it is trusted. While browsing the platform, check to see that the sellers have been verified.[43] As noted earlier, platforms like OpenSea and Mintable charge commission fees. Be aware of how much you are asked to pay.

Are NFTs a Fad?

Answers for the surge in interest in NFTs can be traced to the impact of the COVID-19 pandemic that began in early 2020, the rising value of bitcoin, and mistrust of the U.S. dollar.[44] Like other economies around the world, the U.S. dollar took a beating due to pandemic-related inflation.

So, should you buy an NFT? Rest assured, if you are a collector, you won't have to pay millions if you extend your collection to include elements from the digital world. But whatever it is that drives our desires to corner the market on knick-knacks is undoubtedly rooted in psychology.[45] Do you remember the Beanie Babies craze between 1995 and 1999? People flocked to stores to hunt for these tiny plush animals that sold for U.S.$5 apiece as an investment after prices rose on the suggestion that they were valuable collectibles. That notion was fueled after some of the toys were *retired* and no longer made available for sale. A handful of Beanie Babies alone reached values of between U.S.$9,500 and U.S.$40,000 following their planned discontinuation. That bubble burst in 1999 when values plummeted, and sales declined by more than 90 percent. Values tumbled even further to 1 percent of their value in the early 2000s.[46]

So, here we are again with an eager public willing to embrace what some see as a novelty with their cash. Once an NFT is created, it is placed on the blockchain that cannot be altered or destroyed. This permanence verifies ownership. But, you say, what's the difference between these

---

[43] Rees. *Check Before Buying NFTS.* www.makeuseof.com/things-check-before-buying-nft/.

[44] Ibid.

[45] Stern. *Beanie Baby Fad.* https://slate.com/technology/2015/02/beanie-babies-bubble-economics-and-psychology-of-a-plush-toy-investment-craze.html.

[46] Crockett. *Beanie Baby Bubble of '99.* https://thehustle.co/the-great-beanie-baby-bubble-of-99/.

originals and copies? Let's go back to our Van Gogh example. Sure, we've all seen copies of *The Starry Night* in the form of prints and posters. They all look the same though some have better quality than others. Yet, they are just that. They are copies. There's only one original that's recognized around the world. That is the same for the works prepared for the blockchain. There's only one.

Still, you note, yes, there's only one *The Starry Night*, but that's real art! Now you are treading in that gray area of what people find valuable. Remember our Beanie Babies example. Like Beanie Babies, only time will tell whether the money was well spent or just another plush toy left to gather dust in a virtual dustbin.

NFTs and Gaming

There's this scene toward the end of the iconic 1988 smash hit movie *Big* where Josh (Tom Hanks) and Susan (Elizabeth Perkins) are toy executives pitching the concept of a new electronic game to other company members. The concept was a simple comic book adventure game where, in the end, players could move on to other adventures by plucking down U.S.$18.95 for a new disk to resume the game with a new adventure. Josh's rival, Paul (John Heard), anxious over the meteoric rise of Josh at the company after only a few weeks, smugly chimed in, "I don't get it."

The unit would be expensive, and what kid could afford to buy game disks? (Never mind that the film's opening scene show Josh at his true age of 12 playing a video game.)

Electronic gaming has come a long way since *Big* was released. With the advent of the Internet and the explosion of Web 2.0, online gaming is now a multibillion dollar industry, generating U.S.$160 billion alone in 2021.[1] Instead of relying on retail outlets to get the latest games, eager customers can download those games on demand, or join online platforms. Moreover, gamers no longer have to share the controls or buy additional controllers. Today they meet and play online.

Technology has evolved, but the basics remain the same. For the hero to defeat the enemy or overcome the obstacle, they need tools to succeed and get to the next level. Maybe they can earn game pieces by meeting a challenge, or they are offered the opportunity to buy the pieces they need. Ultimately, they are customers who have no real control over their accounts. This is how blockchain gaming is becoming a real (no pun intended) game changer. Creating games for blockchain allows players to have a stake in the platforms. They have a say in the storyline, and they have a say in the rules. Moreover, the NFT pieces they buy or earn are theirs to keep or resell.

---

[1] Kothari. *Gaming in Web3 Economy.* https://yourstory.com/the-decrypting-story/gaming-ecosystem-evolve-web3-economy/amp.

NFT games can be free to download, but the pieces cost extra and must be purchased with cryptocurrency. What's different from traditional online games is that the players own the pieces they collect, so they can resell them. As one moves up levels, the reward may include bits of cryptocurrency the player can use to buy more game pieces or cash out.[2]

Some games are referred to as play-2-earn (P2E) games or *crypto games*, where they can acquire weapons, tools, magical potions and rings, powers, avatars, and so forth just by playing the game.

Some of you may be thinking, "I don't get it." Ok, look at it like this. Imagine you are a gamer who spends hours, days, or weeks playing one of these seemingly never-ending online games. When you finally reach the end, you have nothing tangible to show for your effort. On the other hand, if you play games on the blockchain, those unique one-of-a-kind game pieces you collected have a monetary value that could provide a healthy payout.[3]

The rise of NFT online gaming, like the interest in NFT collectibles, is attributed to the COVID-19 pandemic. People who could not go to work or wander about due to mandatory closures and lockdowns went online to find something to ease their boredom at home. Many found relief in a game called *Axle Infinity*. Like *Pokémon*, players "collect, breed, raise, battle, and trade digital creatures."[4] Players reportedly spent an average of U.S.$400 per month on game pieces to stay in the game.[5]

The company reported that the game's popularity as of August 2021 had attracted 1.8 million people daily.[6]

Other popular NFTs are card-based trading card games (TCGs), including *Exploding Kittens* (which was originally released as a board game in 2015), *Splinterlands*, *Dr. Who – Worlds Apart*, *Gods Unchained*, *Crypto Strikers* (*Wrapped Strikers*) featuring football (soccer) players, and Major League Baseball's *Candy Digital*.

---

[2] Morales. *NFTs and Gaming*. www.makeuseof.com/nfts-gaming-revolution/.

[3] Sensorium. *Top Blockchain Games*. https://sensoriumxr.com/articles/best-blockchain-games.

[4] Morales. *NFTs and Gaming*. www.makeuseof.com/nfts-gaming-revolution/.

[5] Ibid.

[6] D'Anastasio. *Making Money With NFT Games*. www.wired.co.uk/article/escapist-fantasy-of-nft-games-is-capitalism.

Many of these games are free to play, and players are rewarded with cards they can keep. Some platforms require a minimum investment of U.S.$5 or so for starter card packs. Like any physical collectible trading card, some cards can increase in value, which can be sold and traded.

As with collectibles, there are a number of NFT sites devoted to gaming, too many to list in their entirety. A few of the favorites in 2022 include the aforementioned *Axie Infinity* (which allows players to earn AXS tokens), *Alien Worlds*, another play-to-earn game, and *The Walking Dead Empires*, based on the popular AMC TV series.[7]

With millions of dollars on the table, corporate toy makers have decided to get in on the action, like Hasbro, whose CEO Brian Goldner informed his board in April 2021 that the company was *actively developing* plans to utilize NFT technology.[8]

Virtual Worlds

For those interested in spending time in Xanadu, many startup companies have created virtual worlds where investors can purchase virtual property and build virtual residences. Some top virtual real estate platforms include Fantasy Islands, The Sandbox, Decentraland, Cryptovoxels, Fraction, and Somnium Space.[9] Getting started can be expensive. Someone paid U.S.$450,000 on The Sandbox platform to have a virtual property next to Snoop Dog.[10]

One note of caution. Under the terms and conditions for use, The Sandbox reserves the right to suspend or terminate a member if it believes that member is causing harm. It can then delete a banned user's property.[11]

Republic Realm, a major investor in the virtual real estate ecosystem with some 3,000 NFTs on 24 virtual platforms, found that the

[7] Geyser. *Top 11 NFT Games 2022*. https://influencermarketinghub.com/nft-games/.

[8] Carter. *NFT Magic*. www.dicebreaker.com/companies/hasbro/news/magic-the-gathering-nft-earnings-call.

[9] Mileva. *Top NFT Real Estate Companies to Follow*. https://influencermarketinghub.com/nft-real-estate-companies/.

[10] Williamson. *NFT Real Estate in the Metaverse*. www.financemagnates.com/cryptocurrency/nfts-markets-in-2022-from-trading-volumes-to-real-estate/.

[11] Brassell. *Legal Worries in the Metaverse*. www.beyondgames.biz/22138/legal-worries-in-the-metaverse-as-nfts-and-blockchains-dont-protect-virtual-property/.

average price for a parcel of virtual land from one of the leading plat-forms can run around U.S.$12,684.[12] Overall, virtual property sales in the Metaverse reached U.S.$500 million, a figure that was projected to double by the end of 2022.[13]

Taking it one step further, ONE Sotheby's International Realty, an international company with 1,000 offices in 40 countries,[14] teamed up with Voxel Architects of Coral Gables, FL, and Metaverse artist developer Gabe Sierra of Meta Residence, to offer the first luxury mansion that is both a real-world property (offered by ONE Sotheby's International Realty) and an identical virtual mansion, created by Voxel and Meta Residence, to be located on The Sandbox. The 11,000-square-foot man-sion, located in Miami, FL, was expected to be completed by the end of 2022.[15] Because it has an NFT component, the mansion, based on the virtual design, could be bought with cryptocurrency.[16]

India Sotheby's International Realty, which caters to the wealthy, is following suit, working with Delhi-based architect Arjun Sodhi who will design virtual properties for the metaverse.[17]

While the world of NFT collectibles is booming, those looking to invest in this virtual world should take care. Like any virtual collectible, the value can plummet should interest in them diminish. And like any item of value, this domain has its share of cyber criminals and scammers eager to pass off fakes or copies to the unsuspecting.

Like any investment, weigh the risks and don't spend what you cannot afford to lose.

---

[12] Williamson. *NFT Real Estate in the Metaverse.* www.financemagnates.com/cryptocurrency/nfts-markets-in-2022-from-trading-volumes-to-real-estate/.

[13] Frank. *Metaverse Real Estate Sales Top $500 Million.* www.cnbc.com/2022/02/01/metaverse-real-estate-sales-top-500-million-metametric-solutions-says.html.

[14] DEEDS.com. *Sotheby's International and the Metaverse.* www.deeds.com/articles/sothebys-international-realty-gives-its-blessing-to-the-metaverse/.

[15] Niland. *ONE Sotheby's NFT Home Project.* https://archinect.com/news/article/150293580/one-sotheby-s-unveils-new-digital-twin-nft-home-project.

[16] Ibid.

[17] Haidar. *India Sotheby's to Enter Metaverse.* https://economictimes.indiatimes.com/industry/services/property-/-cstruction/india-sothebys-international-realty-to-enter-metaverse-with-virtual-design-and-nft-real-estate/articleshow/92315573.cms?from=mdr.

NFTs as Real Estate

As you have been reading, NFTs are digital assets that represent physical objects like art, music, literature, and other collectibles that are traded, bought, and sold in the digital world.

The story of blockchain trades began with the creation of bitcoin, which was created to replace fiat currency. So, it was no wonder that the next step forward was to create digital representations of other physical objects.

Then, of course, the next big idea was, why not physical real estate? This concept, discussed in the section on blockchain, launched a number of startups—some unique, while others are partnerships between traditional realtors and blockchain platforms.

As discussed, NFTs are being used to sell property, fractional shares of properties, and provide mortgages.[1] In this chapter, we will continue our discussion and look at three uses.

Because it's on the blockchain, buyers can rest assured the asset is legitimate and the seller is the true owner.[2]

Using NFTs also cuts down on paperwork. NFTs allow one to buy a property in minutes instead of days or weeks. If you are a buyer, you can borrow against the value of the NFT or finance your purchase through traditional lending institutions.[3]

NFTs offer real estate buyers and sellers the option to deal with one another directly without the need for a middleman. The transaction is created in a smart contract. The information is placed on a transparent, open ledger where every action taken can be seen by participants.

[1] Joshi. *NFT Real Estate Applications.* www.bbntimes.com/financial/3-applications-of-nfts-in-real-estate.

[2] Waterworth. *Investing in NFT Real Estate.* www.fool.com/investing/stock-market/market-sectors/financials/non-fungible-tokens/nft-real-estate/#:~:text=NFTs%20in%20the%20real%20estate,in%20fact%2C%20own%20a%20thing.

[3] Sonenreich. *NFTs and Commercial Real Estate.* www.forbes.com/sites/forbesbusinesscouncil/2022/02/16/nfts-and-the-future-of-commercial-real-estate/?sh=739dd3d89bac.

It is then verified by nodes, those network stakeholders who use their computers to verify the authenticity of those transactions for a cryptocurrency fee.

The smart contract includes a digital copy of all the property details and the sale, including location, construction plans, price and payment schedule, ownership, and owner's rights.[4] If all the conditions outlined in the contract are met, then funds are released, and property ownership is legally transferred to the buyer.

If you are an investor looking for a way to raise capital for commercial building and traditional methods are failing you, then NFTs might be the way to go. Entering the market is much easier and faster and can save you money as it cuts out the intermediary, their fees, and commissions.

Real Estate

Are you looking for a new house? There are traditional methods. You can scour the classifieds or go through a realtor who can show you around.

Perhaps you have a new job in another city, and your circumstances require you to find a home as quickly as possible.

Some realtors are turning to blockchain to help would-be buyers streamline the process and achieve home ownership quickly, recognizing that NFTs can expedite sales.

To sell a property on the blockchain, one must create the NFT—a digital representation of that property and a smart contract.

Propy, Palo Alto, CA, mentioned previously, sold its first home in the United States, a five-bedroom, three-and-a-half bath, 2,165-square-foot (201.04 square meters) property in Gulfport, FL, as an NFT. The house was sold for cryptocurrency totaling 210 ETH, valued at U.S.$654,309.60. The sale was made on February 8, 2022, and was one of two properties Propy auctioned.[5]

---

[4] Kunzi. *NFT in Real Estate Industry*. www.forbes.com/sites/forbesbizcouncil/2021/10/25/nft-in-the-real-estate-industry-short-term-trend-or-an-investment-in-the-future/?sh=14e46c478d28.

[5] Palasciano. *Florida Home Sold as NFT*. https://thesmartwallet.com/how-a-florida-house-became-the-first-ever-sold-as-an-nft/?articleid=82292#:~:text=Now%2C%20for%20the%20first%20time,associated%20with%20digital%20assets!).

The title and transaction for the home in Gulfport were recorded on a blockchain and with the county administrator. The title document includes a QR code with the address of the blockchain record, said Propy Chief Operating Officer Kelly Dolyniuk in a message exchange.

Propy's second NFT auction, a condominium in Tampa, FL, worth between U.S.$200,000 and U.S.$300,000, had yet to be finalized at the time of this writing.[6]

Auction participants had to complete a KYC form, which assures the seller of the buyers' identity while helping deter financial crime such as money laundering.

While this sale was Propy's first in the United States, it made its first-ever NFT real estate sale in May 2021. They sold a one-bedroom, one-bathroom, 505.9-square-foot (48 square meters) studio apartment owned by TechCrunch Founder Michael Arrington in Kyiv, Ukraine.[7] The flat, which included an NFT art piece on the wall and a licensed cyberpunk picture, sold for 36 ETH or U.S.$93,429.72.[8]

The growing interest in blockchain real estate transactions has also attracted the attention of traditional real estate companies like RE/MAX, which incorporates NFTs as part of its sales strategy.

In May 2021, OMNI Estate Group, Spain, launched Europe's first real estate token, the OMNI Real Estate Token ($ORT). The tokens, created to allow real estate investors to expedite investment in the market, sold out within five minutes after the announcement of the sale.[9]

Fractional Shares

These days, people are looking for passive income. It may or may not make them rich, but it could provide added income that helps pay bills or provide extras.

---

[6] Tan. *NFT-Linked House Sells for $650K.* www.coindesk.com/business/2022/02/11/nft-linked-house-sells-for-650k-in-propys-first-us-sale/.

[7] Arrington. *First Real Estate NFT.* https://seen.haus/drops/first-real-estate-nft.

[8] Ibid.

[9] Passive Income. *OMNI Tokenized Real Estate Offers Passive Income.* www.globe-newswire.com/en/news-release/2021/05/28/2238333/0/en/ORT-Launching-Europe-s-First-Tokenized-Real-Estate-Assets-by-OMNI-Estate-Group-Passive-Income.html.

Some investors are turning to NFT fractional shares. What are these? Simply put, an NFT is broken down into a fixed number of tokens, or shares, with each share representing a percentage of the value of the sold object. Investors can rest assured that the number of tokens is fixed because the information is held in the smart contract, which keeps up with the token transactions.

Let's say you are interested in commercial real estate but don't have the money to buy a building. You could partner with others, but it would still require a lot of capital. Or, say you think about buying or partnering to buy an existing building. Again, making that happen will require a lot of upfront money. Buying in with fractionalized NFTs means you can buy shares of that building on a Tuesday and, if necessary, theoretically be able to turn around and sell your token on a Friday. No papers to sign. No banks to serve as middlemen. Just like other digitized assets, you buy and trade with others directly.[10]

Ekta Real Estate, Bali, which began in 2021, bridges the real and digital divide with a platform that allows investors to invest in real-world properties that fit their budgets. The assets they represent are tokenized and placed on their blockchain allowing investors to purchase real estate on their NFT marketplace. The company, which has its own blockchain, allows investors to buy and sell long-term leases.[11]

Mortgages

The mortgage business is a multitrillion-dollar business that generates huge profits for mortgage lenders. In 2020, independent mortgage banks earned more than U.S.$4,200 per loan.[12]

NFT-created mortgages offer borrowers an alternative for securing the money they need to buy residential property at lower rates, cutting out

---

[10] CNBCTV18.com. *Fractional NFT Real Estate.* www.cnbctv18.com/crypto-currency/how-ekta-blockchains-fractional-real-estate-nft-aims-to-tokenise-real-world-properties-12738702.htm.

[11] Ibid.

[12] Rubinstein. *Mortgage Lenders Timed Market Perfectly.* www.bloomberg.com/opinion/articles/2022-06-21/mortgage-lenders-timed-the-market-perfectly.

the middleman while offering investors a way to grow their portfolios.[13] LoanSnap, a decentralized mortgage lending platform in the United States, offered the first NFT mortgages through its platform, Bacon Protocol.[14] The platform provides pooled funds from investors to creditworthy borrowers who meet Fannie Mae (Federal National Mortgage Association) and Freddie Mac (Federal Home Loan Mortgage Association) guidelines.[15]

The platform uses its own cryptocurrency, bHome, a stablecoin. Stablecoins are those pegged to reserve assets like money or other commodities, rising and falling on the value of those assets the stablecoins are tied to and, therefore, less likely to experience wild fluctuations in price.

Borrowers also benefit by paying slightly lower interest rates while cutting fees that would go to centralized lending institutions handling the deal. Borrowers approved by Bacon Protocol mine their mortgage, which the lender whimsically refers to as *Eggs*, holding to the traditional American breakfast motif. This mining process (the proof of verification) requires the borrower to verify they are the actual owner, the home value, and they must sign a deed of trust. Then, the borrower must record that lien in the county where the home is located.[16]

In 2022, Miami, FL-based Milo announced a 30-year crypto mortgage that allows cryptocurrency holders to invest in real estate in the United States.[17] Open to foreign investors, as well, the plan offers investors the opportunity to leverage their cryptocurrency rather than having to sell it to make a purchase.[18]

---

[13] Bourgi. *Bacon Protocol NFT Mortgages*. https://cointelegraph.com/news/bacon-protocol-offers-industry-first-nft-mortgages.

[14] Cooling. *Loansnap Offers Smart Mortgages*. https://finance.yahoo.com/news/loansnap-launch-bacon-protocol-smart-073013376.html.

[15] White-Gomez. *Bacon Protocol Explained*. www.one37pm.com/nft/what-is-the-bacon-protocol.

[16] Ibid.

[17] Wojno. *Milo Secures $17M Financing for Mortgages*. www.zdnet.com/finance/blockchain/crypto-mortgage-lender-milo-secures-17m-financing-to-expand-operations-enabling-crypto-holders-to-buy-real-estate/.

[18] Wright. *Milo Offering 30-year Crypto Mortgages*. https://cointelegraph.com/news/fintech-startup-milo-is-offering-30-year-crypto-mortgages.

As of this writing, Milo only accepted bitcoin, Ethereum, and the USD Coin.[19]

As interest grows, so will mortgage platforms, catering to a new generation of borrowers and investors who have planted their flag in the blockchain ecosystem.

Last Thoughts

NFT mortgages are a paradigm shifter. This relatively new instrument allows borrowers and investors alike to enter the real estate market faster, easier, and cheaper without all the mounds of paperwork or cadre of mediators to complete the sale. Buyers can be assured that the information they receive is accurate and up to date as the information is on the blockchain and available for all participating parties to see. Also attractive is that these digital assets can be sold faster than traditional methods.

But, of course, buyers and investors should always do their due diligence before parting with their money. Research the company you want to do business with the same way you would seek information if seeking a traditional mortgage.

If you are selling and want to use blockchain and sell it yourself, you should consider getting help if the asset represents a significant value. You can easily find an online program to create the transaction and tokenize your property. Still, you should consider legal advice from a real estate attorney who understands blockchain and can help you with your smart contract. At this time, finding that expert in your hometown may be difficult as this marketplace is still in its infancy. The laws of your state may not be up to date, so check.

This is a new market, so, of course, there will be growing pains. Like any new technology, there will be successes and failures. For would-be homeowners denied credit by traditional lenders, NFT mortgages offer another avenue. Investors don't need a reason. They look for opportunity, and if the yields are what companies say they are, this group will gladly open their wallets.

---

[19] Conroy. *Milo Reaches $10M Crypto-Mortgage Milestone.* www.housingwire .com/articles/milo-reaches-10m-crypto-mortgage-milestone/#:~:text=Milo's%20 crypto%2Dloan%20program%2C%20however,price%20appreciation%20 in%20both%20assets.

NFT Pros and Cons

NFTs are a young market, far from maturity. What NFTs lack in identity, they make up for in sales. Billions of dollars are being spent on everything from NFT artworks, stickers, and video loops to physical property.

Let's take a moment to recap the benefits and concerns related to NFTs.

On the plus side, NFTs are digital assets representing physical objects that can be quickly and securely sold and traded to anyone worldwide without an intermediary. NFTs are transportable. Turning physical assets into digital assets improves market efficiency by opening doors between buyers and sellers while eliminating the middleman and doing so through enhanced security.[1]

These improvements allow developers and entrepreneurs a relatively easy platform to access a worldwide audience regardless of their stature. Their work feeds new platforms that offer more opportunities for those who might otherwise be ignored.

Improved security is a crucial benefit of blockchain technology. NFTs are placed onto a blockchain—a transparent ledger open to the parties involved. They are immutable and are, therefore, secure. The block is overseen by a network of operators (nodes) who verify transactions. Remember, the only way to alter the transaction is to lead an attack requiring 51 percent of nodes' support. An attack of that magnitude, especially on large blockchains, would be highly costly.

NFTs offer investors a wide range of opportunities. Options include art, books, music, collectibles, virtual real estate, gaming, fractional ownership in just about any NFT, and physical property without needing physical inspection or paperwork. Costs are reduced as approval is shifted from third parties to smart contracts. If the conditions for the sale are met, then the transaction is approved. Otherwise, the sale is declined.

---

[1] Brock. *8 Pros and Cons of NFTs*. www.annuity.org/2022/01/14/from-the-experts-8-pros-and-cons-of-nfts/.

The downside to NFTs is, understandably, their volatility. Like any collector, one needs to appreciate the asset they purchase regardless of market forces.

Yes, NFTs are liquid because they are digital assets that represent physical ones. They are one-of-a-kind objects bought for investment that can easily be bought and sold, but they are not particularly liquid in the traditional sense.[2] Suppose someone pays several thousand in currency for a digital painting. In that case, they are most likely art collectors who see both aesthetic value and investment potential in holding on to that painting. The same can be said for collectors of trading cards. Over time, some emerge as being extremely valuable.

As you know, liquidity is quickly converting a physical asset into cash. Here, the rules of supply and demand take front and center. If you need money fast, you can always place a classified ad, put the item online, or take it to a pawn shop. Of the three scenarios, you are more likely to succeed at a pawn shop that can tell you immediately what they will give you for your item. None of the three scenarios will likely meet your asking price. You will most likely recoup a fraction of the amount you paid for it. That's how the market works.

If your physical asset is a property, you could wait for months, even years, before you get an offer, even with the help of St. Joseph. Again, it all depends on the market, not to mention location, location, location. The benefit of owning an asset tokenized as an NFT is that you can move it without delay once you identify your buyer.

The NFT collectible market is smaller than its physical counterpart. Sellers must rely on the buyers in the virtual world, earning U.S.$15.7 billion in 2021.[3] Real-world collectibles, by contract, accounted for U.S.$412 billion that same year, representing 5 to 10 percent of an

---

[2] Dev. *Understanding NFT Liquidity.* https://medium.com/metapherse/how-to-understand-liquidity-when-it-comes-to-nfts-4f605098de8f.

[3] SkyQuest Technology Consulting Pvt. Ltd. *Global NFT Market to Reach $122.43 Billion by 2028.* www.globenewswire.com/en/news-release/2022/05/26/2451426/0/en/The-Global-Non-Fungible-Tokens-NFTs-Market-is-expected-to-reach-a-value-of-USD-122-43-Billion-by-2028-at-a-CAGR-of-34-10-over-the-forecast-period-2022-2028-SkyQuest-Technology.html.

investor's income.[4] Because the virtual buyer's market is much smaller, you may have to hold on to your asset for a while before finding a buyer.

If you want to buy NFT art, you need to know that while you are buying the image, the rights to that image remain with the artist who created it.[5] Like physical pieces of art, for example, owners don't have the right to display the purchased works in public without permission. Nor can they claim copyright infringement if the NFT is copied. In 2021, Kevin McCoy put his NFT, *Quantum* (mentioned earlier) on auction at Sotheby's for $1.47 million. But there was a challenge regarding ownership. After creating the NFT, McCoy stored it on the blockchain, Namecoin, which required McCoy to periodically renew his ownership rights. He failed to do so in 2015, whereby Free Holdings, a Canadian concern, claimed the rights. So, in 2022, they sued McCoy and Sotheby's. On March 17, 2023, a U.S. District Court judge in the Southern District of New York, dismissed the case, ruling the company "failed to establish ownership, malice, or damages."[6] So, know your rights ahead of time. If you want the copyright, you have to ask the owner and get it in writing, including the artist's signature.[7]

NFTs: Death and Taxes

For buyers and sellers of NFTs, one will need to check how the government sees their purchase. Is it a capital gain or a one-off purchase requiring one to pay sales tax?[8] It's not a simple question to gloss over. Like stocks or other financial instruments cashed in that bring a profit,

---

[4] Market Decipher. *Collectibles Market and NFT Size and Growth Trends*. www.marketdecipher.com/report/collectibles-market.

[5] The Conversation. *NFT Owner's Rights*. https://theconversation.com/when-you-buy-an-nft-you-dont-completely-own-it-heres-why-166445.

[6] Escalante-De Mattei. *Lawsuit Challenging Ownership of First NFT Dismissed*. www.artnews.com/art-news/news/kevin-mccoy-quantum-case-dismissed-free-holdings-sothebys-1234662076/.

[7] The Conversation. *NFT Owner's Rights*. https://theconversation.com/when-you-buy-an-nft-you-dont-completely-own-it-heres-why-166445.

[8] Stelzner. *What Web3 Projects Need to Consider*. www.socialmediaexaminer.com/web3-legal-what-projects-need-to-consider/.

the sellers are subject to capital gains taxes.[9] Or, if the token loses value, they can claim a loss.

Virtual assets are like physical assets and can be passed on in the event of the owner's death as long as the owner leaves instructions on what to do with those virtual assets. This includes access to keys and passwords to their digital wallet. If family members or others don't know the assets exist or lack a key or password, then they can remain lost on a blockchain for eternity. One can be named as a beneficiary to a digital asset, but without the key, the gift is worthless.[10]

[9] Chandrasekera. *Taxing NFTs*. https://news.bloombergtax.com/daily-tax-report/how-are-non-fungible-tokens-nfts-taxed.

[10] Bury. *NFTs After Death*. https://techcrunch.com/2021/04/05/what-happens-to-your-nfts-and-crypto-assets-after-you-die/.

Web 3.0 The Next Generation

Web 3.0 The Next Generation

Web 3.0, or as some refer to it—the Semantic Web, represents the third generation of the World Wide Web built on blockchain technology—that decentralized system of public blockchains where information is stored on an immutable public ledger. There are no barriers and no centralized third parties deciding who gets access to platforms. Rather, websites will be *permissionless*. They will be controlled from the bottom up instead of the top down. Community users will set the rules, not CEOs and boards of directors.

Social platform members won't have their posts removed due to some broad arbitrary policy or an algorithm, much less be locked out of that account due to that post. These platforms will no longer be able to block or censor thought.

Decentralized search engines will play an important role in Web3. Browsers today operate on centralized systems, the most dominant being Google, which controls 80 percent of the market.[1] While Google uses algorithms, critics note that the global search engine collects data about users, which affects search results. Two people can search for the same information but be presented with different search results.[2]

Decentralized search engines don't have access to a user's search history and, therefore, cannot track them. Instead, the information is stored on a blockchain where the user has complete control.[3] Web 3.0 will offer

---

[1] Bitcoinist. *Cyber: Web3 Search Engine for Web 3*. https://bitcoinist.com/cyber-a-search-engine-for-web-3/?utm_source=rss&utm_medium=rss&utm_campaign=cyber-a-search-engine-for-web-3.
[2] Ibid.
[3] World Crypto Index. *Decentralized Search Engines*. www.worldcryptoindex.com/decentralized-search-engines/#:~:text=With%20a%20decentralized%20search%20engine,it%20with%20a%20private%20key.

equality to all by incorporating all the elements discussed so far—blockchain technology, cryptocurrency, NFTs, AI, and machine learning.

Some might see it as a natural, technological evolution that comports with a growing list of wireless devices. Others may see it as a rebellion by a younger generation longing to reclaim their privacy. However viewed, this move promises to disrupt the status quo, forcing today's major players to adapt or disappear.

The financial stakes are high. The Web3 market, which is still emerging, was valued at U.S.$2.9 billion in 2021 and is expected to jump to U.S.$23.3 billion by 2028.[4] By the same token, companies built on today's Web 2.0 technology have an estimated worth of U.S.$14.8 trillion, a value some argue they could lose if they hold on too tightly to the past.[5]

The goal for Web3 is lofty but poses several questions and concerns. If transactions are carried out without third parties, what's to prevent them from being used to carry out unlawful acts?

If speech is unregulated, does that mean there are no boundaries for willful misinformation and hate speech? Here, Web 3.0 presents a paradox that must be addressed through honest and open discussions.

The concept of Web 3.0, for which there is no definitive description, is also a work in progress. What is gospel today could well be a footnote in tech history tomorrow.

The best way to go forward is to look back. So, in this chapter, we'll take a brief look at the history of the Web and how we got here.

The Worldwide Web

The World Wide Web (www), or the Web, is the information system we use to share documents and information, videos, conduct business, and

---

[4] Wolfson. *Decentralized Storage Providers.* https://cointelegraph.com/news/decentralized-storage-providers-power-the-web3-economy-but-adoption-still-underway.

[5] Sephton. *Metaverse Value.* https://coinmarketcap.com/alexandria/article/revealed-how-much-metaverse-industry-could-be-worth.

make use of online resources. One opens, clicks on a URL link, or clicks on an app that takes them to the needed information.

The Internet, or *net* for short, represents the network of computers used to connect with other computers to collect information from websites.

Internet Speed

It seems obvious, but it bears mentioning that this movement would not be possible without high-speed Internet. Anyone who has sat in front of a screen trying to download files using a dial-up modem will tell you that. What takes seconds or, worse, minutes used to take hours. Tech users today take for granted that a text message is delivered instantaneously, or that a video can be viewed effortlessly. Those conveniences result from hundreds of thousands of hours of work and research and millions, if not billions, of dollars in research and development. Like any enduring technology, Internet speed has evolved.

First introduced in 1997, wireless Internet is now entering its fifth generation (5G), significantly increasing data transfer speeds. As technology improves, the speed and the specificity of where that data are sent, will allow more smart devices in one's home to be operated by a virtual assistant, such as Amazon's Alexa or Apple's Siri. Just give the command and any smart device—be it an oven, television, thermostat, refrigerator, oven, or coffee maker, can also be activated or deactivated.[6] The evolution of smart devices will be a boon to manufacturing as consumers race to embrace the new technology.

Beyond the home, 5G makes driverless cars plausible. The constant data flow will allow vehicles to receive a constant barrage of information regarding the location of the vehicle as well as the road conditions—weather, congestion, construction, and then make adjustments to those

---

[6] Fabricating Metalworking. 2022. *5G Smart Home Appliances.* www.fabricatingandmetalworking.com/2018/04/theres-no-place-like-home-5g-heralds-the-rise-of-smart-home-appliances/#:~:text=We're%20entering%20a%20brave,or%20by%20using%20a%20mobile (accessed August 8, 2022).

conditions.[7] Deutsche Telekom (Germany) reports it plans to connect the 5G network to all main roads, highways, and rail tracks by 2025.[8]

This connectivity is called the *Internet of things* or IoT.

Now then, with progress comes issues. In the case of 5G, some serious security issues must be addressed. With more data flowing, there is more opportunity for thieves and hackers to steal data and cause mischief. Malware could be transmitted faster, resulting in crippling shutdowns of vital infrastructure.[9] Enhancing security is, for now, simply a matter of extending existing security policies that take the upgrade into account.[10]

On the other hand, Web 3.0 and its components offer safety and security to protect consumers from malicious actors.

The Vision

Web development is more methodical and requires discussion and direction than the latest software updates or upgrades for computers, smartphones, and tablets. This third wave of the Internet represents that direction. It's as much evolution as it is revolution.

Let's look at a work from Hollywood to get a glimpse of what could be.

Set in the not-too-distant future, the 2013 futuristic movie, *Her* tells the story of Theodore (Joaquin Phoenix), a lonely man going through a divorce who buys a new operating system that promises to be the first artificially intelligent program. The system's voice, he named Samantha (voiced by Scarlett Johansson), begins by organizing his e-mails and then comments on his writings. The program not only served as a virtual assistant but also as a confidant. The story's theme was loneliness, set against the backdrop of advanced technology. That was then. Looking at the film today, one can see it also touches on the vision of Web3 and beyond. Sir Tim Berners-Lee, credited with coining the term

---

[7] Deutsche Telekom. *5G and Autonomous Driving.* www.telekom.com/en/company/details/5g-network-as-foundation-for-autonomous-driving-561986/.
[8] Ibid.
[9] Gupta. *Security Challenges in the 5G World.* www.forbes.com/sites/forbestechcouncil/2021/07/05/security-challenges-in-the-5g-world-and-how-to-overcome-them/?sh=58a68185ee9c.
[10] Ibid.

Web 3.0 in 1999, envisioned an Internet that could actively respond to user requests in a human-like fashion through skills made possible by machine learning.[11]

Too unbelievable? Remember Dick Tracy's two-way wristwatch radio?

It took some time, but today, we have watches that go far beyond Dick Tracy's wildest dreams.

Let's look back.

---

[11] Aurora. *Web 3.0.* www.ongraph.com/what-is-web-3-how-it-is-going-to-change-the-future-of-the-internet/.

A Brief History of the
World Wide Web

Like computers and microwave ovens, it seems like we've always had Internet access. We take it for granted that our computers and smart devices can easily access platforms connecting us to our family and friends. The truth is, Internet access, as we know it today, has only been around for just a generation.

Before we move forward, let's take a moment to look back at the evolution of the Web and where we are today.

Web 1.0 (1989–2005)

Web 1.0, or in those days, simply the Web or World Wide Web, created by Sir Tim Berners Lee in 1989, consisted of a hodgepodge of decentralized read-only websites, which, beginning in August 1991, could be joined together with hyperlinks.[1] There were no centralized corporate servers as we know them today. Instead, the content was "hosted on web servers run by an Internet service provider (ISP) on free web hosting devices."[2] It lacked the interactivity users enjoy today, but it was a start.

The push toward commercial connectivity began in the mid-to-late 1980s when programmers began putting up their own web pages. Consumers with little or no technical experience could finally be a part of that experience in 1988 when Prodigy Communications[3] introduced an online service that allowed computer users with modems to connect to their platform. The service, which grew, by one account, to one million subscribers before it was shut down in 1999, took users to their platform

---

[1] Abbany. *Web Creation*. www.dw.com/en/hyperlink-when-tim-berners-lee-invented-the-world-wide-web-not-the-internet/a-19448729.

[2] Technopedia. *Web 1.0*. www.techopedia.com/definition/27960/web-10.

[3] Edwards. *Online Services No More*. www.theatlantic.com/technology/archive/2014/07/where-online-services-go-when-they-die/374099/.

where they could access news, weather, business, games, bulletin boards, and shopping, among others.[4]

All users needed was a desktop computer, a modem, a communications disk, and a telephone line to connect to a telephone jack. Connecting was part of the experience. The cacophony of sounds of the modem, its cadence replete with beeps, pings, whirs, gargling tones, the honking sound of a fire truck, and finally, a flat tone indicating you were *in*. Otherwise, you would get an error message and have to start the process over. If someone in the house picked up an extension while you were online, they were greeted by the sound of static.

It couldn't take you to other sites, nor was it interactive. But it was exciting as it opened the door to what was possible. The home page was basically an electronic bulletin board that gave you access to basic information.

Prodigy was the second-largest online provider in 1993, with 465,000 subscribers, trailing CompuServe, an online service that provided access to its database of information, which claimed 600,000 subscribers. As part of its business model, CompuServe charged 13 cents per minute during the day and 10 cents per minute at night.[5]

While the numbers don't sound that impressive today, in 1993, only 22.9 percent of American households owned home computers, up from 15 percent in 1989.[6]

Both would be eclipsed by America Online (AOL). The online service started in 1985 and grew to around three million users by 1995, offering such things as instant messaging. In 1993, AOL was the first to offer access to the Web through a system called Usenet, a worldwide distributed discussion network.[7] AOL then created its own browser, which it released in 2005.[8]

---

[4] Wikipedia. *Prodigy*. https://en-academic.com/dic.nsf/enwiki/200655.

[5] Paleotronic. *CompuServe's Business Model*. https://paleotronic.com/2019/09/24/pay-by-the-minute-the-compuserve-era/.

[6] Statista Research Department. *Home Computer Owners 1984–2010*. www.statista.com/statistics/184685/percentage-of-households-with-computer-in-the-united-states-since-1984/.

[7] Wikipedia. *AOL*. https://en.wikipedia.org/wiki/AOL#:~:text=AOL%20was%20one%20of%20the,1993%20began%20adding%20internet%20access.

[8] Wikipedia. *AOL Explorer*. https://en.wikipedia.org/wiki/AOL_Explorer#:~:text=AOL%20Explorer%2C%20previously%20known%20as,Microsoft's%20Trident%20browser%20engine.

In 1996, Americans were introduced to WebTV, an online service for those without computers who wanted to be part of the online experience.[9] The system included a standalone device connected to one's television, a telephone cable, a remote control, and an optional wireless keyboard, which made typing easier.

Sitting on one's couch, one could search for information by typing keywords into the search bar. In addition to print content from contributing publishers, subscribers could access video clips related to various topics.[10] They could also set up an e-mail account.

By the mid-to-late 1990s, increased modem speeds made it easier for households to surf the Web. Consider this. In 1995, only 0.04 percent of the world's population had Internet access, with more than half of the users living in the United States. By 2014, that figure had risen to 41 percent worldwide.[11]

Online access reached a fever pitch between 1998 and 1999, with venture capitalists throwing no less than U.S.$1 trillion[12] into online startups in what was referred to as the *dot.com* era. Between 1996 at the start of this new revolution, and 2000, when the bubble burst, 2,288 companies in the United States had gone public. Venture capital for Internet companies accounted for a whopping 39 percent of investment.[13] It was raining money, and no one wanted to get in out of the coming storm.

There were no bad ideas as venture capitalists who pumped trillions of dollars into this new market, eager to create new IPOs for that opening payday. Never mind that most of these companies lacked a solid business plan. They were out to change the future and do so in a big way. The fundamentals would take care of themselves, or so they thought. By the

---

[9] Smith. *WebTV.* www.vice.com/en/article/4xaqe9/why-webtvs-remote-controlled-internet-failed-to-take-off.

[10] (^W^)/, Getting started with WebTV 1998. www.youtube.com/watch?v=MhzojvS4B5I&t=100s.

[11] Wikipedia. *Internet Access.* https://en.wikipedia.org/wiki/Internet_access.

[12] McCullough. *The Dot-Com Bubble.* https://ideas.ted.com/an-eye-opening-look-at-the-dot-com-bubble-of-2000-and-how-it-shapes-our-lives-today/.

[13] International Banker. 2000. *Dotcom Bubble Burst.* https://internationalbanker.com/history-of-financial-crises/the-dotcom-bubble-burst-2000/#:~:text=And%20it%20was%20this%20overvaluation,1999%20and%20380%20in%202000.

time the dust settled, trillions of dollars had disappeared, with average investors left to pick up the tab.[14]

A number of memorable companies caught the public's attention, including Pets.com, which started operations in 1998, selling pet food and supplies online. The company raised U.S.$82.5 million in a February 2000 IPO only to go out of business that November.[15]

The crash created an economic tsunami that would take more than a decade for markets, hit again by the Great Recession, to recover.[16]

While most companies went by the wayside, many survived, including Amazon and eBay. The boon may have sucked trillions out of the market and put some 200,000 techs in Silicon Valley out of work, but, ironically, it set the stage heralding the second generation of the Web, known as Web 2.0.

How? Through overcapacity. During this same period, several global telecom companies, such as WorldCom and Global Crossing, both of which would later go out of business due to fraud, but not before installing some 80.2 million miles of fiber optic cable across the United States.[17] There was more infrastructure than needed, resulting in lower prices for access while allowing a new wave of companies to stake their claim.[18]

Web 2.0 (2004–Present)

This next generation of the Internet, known as Web 2.0, a term coined by author and Web designer Darcy DeNucci in 1999 and popularized by book publisher Tim O'Reilly in 2004,[19] is marked by the introduction of broadband.

---

[14] McCullough. *The Dot-Com Bubble.* https://ideas.ted.com/an-eye-opening-look-at-the-dot-com-bubble-of-2000-and-how-it-shapes-our-lives-today/.

[15] Beattie. *Pets.com Crash.* www.investopedia.com/ask/answers/08/dotcom-pets-dot-com.asp#:~:text=The%20company%20raised%20%2482.5%20million, such%20as%20dog%20food%20bags.

[16] McCullough. *The Dot-Com Bubble.* https://ideas.ted.com/an-eye-opening-look-at-the-dot-com-bubble-of-2000-and-how-it-shapes-our-lives-today/.

[17] Ibid.

[18] Ibid.

[19] Wikipedia. *Web 2.0.* https://en.wikipedia.org/wiki/Web_2.0.

No longer would one have to choose the telephone over the Internet. The signal was split, allowing consumers to use both simultaneously.[20] This speed galvanized static websites into lively, interactive sites, allowing users to engage with platforms directly. This opened the door for creating wireless devices that could log in and share home networks.

Consumers were not only able to quickly download music, texts, and videos at greater speed, but they were also able to participate actively and enjoy a wide range of streaming services like YouTube which went online February 14, 2005.

Social media platforms, which got started in 1997, began to blossom under the awnings of free services, including Facebook (2004), MySpace (2003), LinkedIn (2003), Google+ (2011),[21] Twitter (now called X) (2006),[22] and WhatsApp in 2009. Others included Flickr (2004), a site for amateur photographers and professionals, Instagram (2010), and Roblox (2006). Snapchat went online in 2011, and TikTok in 2016. All of these popular sites, among others, allowed users to interact with others on those sites.

Static decentralized platforms were replaced by large, centralized platforms where companies like Facebook, Twitter, Amazon, and Google (1998), the largest search engine, control 88 percent of the market share.[23] One of the largest social media platforms is owned by Facebook founder Mark Zuckerberg who bought Instagram in 2012 and WhatsApp in 2014 and placed them all under the umbrella company he created in 2021 named Meta. Meta is a Greek word that means *after* or *beyond*. It is a prefix for *more comprehensive* or *transcending*.[24] Therein lies the rub for consumers. While it's free to search, join, and post, somebody has to pay the bills. And those somebodies are the users who agree to give up their personal information to participate. That personal information is sold to commerce, which tracks users to sell their products.

---

[20] Beckett. *History of the Internet.* www.uswitch.com/broadband/guides/broadband-history/.

[21] Ngak. *A History of Social Networking.* www.cbsnews.com/pictures/then-and-now-a-history-of-social-networking-sites/.

[22] Pennington Creative. *The Origins of Twitter.* https://penningtoncreative.com/the-origins-of-twitter/.

[23] Davies. *Popular Search Engines.* www.searchenginejournal.com/seo-guide/meet-search-engines/#:~:text=1.,any%20list%20of%20search%20engines.

[24] Wikipedia. *Meta.* https://en.wikipedia.org/wiki/Meta.

Social media platforms have also been used to manipulate public opinion, sowing further social divisions. Couple this with these platforms acting as *walled gardens*, controlling content and delivery on their platforms.

Centralized systems also control user behavior. Make a snarky comment that violates the terms and conditions of use, and the user could find themselves booted out of the platform for a determined period of time, if not permanently. Such actions have raised the ire of free speech advocates who call these acts of censorship.[25]

Conversely, users could be trolled and bullied by an invisible mob protected by their online anonymity. Young people are particularly vulnerable to online bullying, resulting in disasterous consequences.

The information posted, photographs, in particular, are the site's property once uploaded. Content stored on sites by users also faces the potential for deletion. Flickr, for example, was struggling financially, so Yahoo sold it to SmugMug in 2018. Under the new terms, terabyte storage was discontinued. Accounts were restricted to 1,000 photos, with the excess deleted.[26]

In short, the platforms we use today are on the one had quite sophisticated, allowing users immediate access to content and communities. On the other side is that these platforms control the information users provide about their personal lives and the additional information they provide along the way. What's more, content can be deleted.

Web 3.0 (Present)

The goal of Web 3.0, also referred to as the Semantic Web, is to return control to the users and give them a greater voice in how information is controlled. Machines will not only be able to accept instructions, but they will be able to analyze that data and understand it, allowing for

---

[25] Bailey. *Web3 Vs Web2.* https://supplain.io/news/web3-solve-web2-problems.
[26] Tiffany. *Flickr.* www.vox.com/the-goods/2019/2/6/18214046/flickr-free-storage-ends-digital-photo-archive-history.

the creation of open, intelligent websites that will enhance the users' experience.[27]

Semantic Web

Today, computers *know* what you want by the words you type into your address or search bar, although they don't understand what you are typing.

Computer programs can read the syntax, those words or phrases arranged to create sentences but don't understand its semantics or meaning. For example, "It is a beautiful day!" In this example of syntax, you have a subject, linking verb, indefinite article, adjective, and object rounded off with an exclamation mark to amplify the statement.

A conversation involves syntax and semantics, or understanding, which can form or break bonds depending on the semantics. Simply put, this is communication.

When computers communicate with each other, they process what we want without understanding what it means. When we type in the address of one of our favorite websites into the address bar, the computer recognizes the address and then sends a request to that website. The site replies with the information we want, written in HTML, a computer language (syntax) the computer can read, and one that allows our computer to display that information. The computer doesn't understand what the information means. It simply responds and retrieves what we want.[28]

If our computers could understand what we are looking for—people, places,[29] and things, they could actively assist our search rather than passively retrieving information. The computer can't pause and suggest something else.

[27] Howell. *Internet of Things and Web 3.0.* https://101blockchains.com/internet-of-things-and-web-3-0/.

[28] Sporny. *Intro to the Semantic Web.* www.youtube.com/watch?v=OGg8A2zfWKg&ab_channel=ManuSporny.

[29] Ibid.

The goal of Web3 is to make it possible for online data to do just that and be *machine-readable*.[30]

Although a dream, several semantic technologies are currently used in companies representing different industries worldwide representing supply chain management, media management, and data distribution.[31]

[30] Ozarde. *Tim Berners-Lee, Semantic Web 3.0.* www.linkedin.com/pulse/tim-berners-lee-semantic-web-30-sandeep-ozarde/?trk=public_post.

[31] Cambridge Semantics. *Semantic Technologies Applied.* https://cambridgesemantics.com/blog/semantic-university/semantic-technologies-applied/example-semantic-web-applications/.

Web 3.0

Under the Hood

What makes Web 3.0 tick? It combines all the technologies discussed: blockchain, decentralization, cryptocurrency, NFTs, AI, machine learning, and the Internet of things (IoT). Information is collected and shared between machines, which can sort, collate, and process that information to provide an answer and make improvements without being programmed to do so.[1]

This chapter looks at these elements and their role in the next generation of the worldwide web. Much of the material will be review.

Blockchain

Web 3.0 is about privacy serving as a conduit for one's ability to conduct a P2P transaction without needing a third party to oversee that transaction. The blockchain serves as the backbone that makes this possible.[2]

Blockchain, as you recall, is a transparent ledger containing immutable transactions stored on a decentralized network of computers, referred to as nodes. The computer operators on whose computers the information is stored verify the transaction's validity by solving an algorithm, referred to as PoW, or validating the transaction by putting up a large share of cryptocurrency for the chance to verify the transaction, referred to as PoS. PoA is a third consensus method, using an algorithm that provides an efficient solution for blockchains. Nodes using proof of authority must undergo a vigorous vetting process before verifying transactions.

---

[1] Howell. *Internet of Things and Web 3.0.* https://101blockchains.com/internet-of-things-and-web-3-0/.
[2] Blockchain Hub Berlin. *Tokenized Networks and Web 3.0.* https://blockchain-hub.net/web3-decentralized-web/.

Transactions are between two parties (P2P) without needing confirmation from a third party, such as a bank. Agreements are set out in smart contracts, which automatically activate if the conditions are met. Using blockchain technology, one can trade cryptocurrency for investment purposes or use it to buy goods and services. NFTs are tokenized assets stored on the blockchain.

Recognizing the digital asset market explosion, the United Arab Emirates (UAE), in March 2022, passed its first law related to Web3, cryptocurrency and NFTs to advance itself as a significant player in this new digital world. The country established the Virtual Assets Regulatory Authority (VARA) to regulate, supervise, and oversee digital services in Dubai. The law, designed to balance the growth and development of this new frontier along with regulation, applies to all free zones, except for the Dubai International Financial Center.[3]

Free zones are geographical areas within the UAE that permit 100 percent foreign ownership. Usually, these zones are dedicated to a specific business or industry.[4]

With this new law, the UAE is looking to attract Web3 entrepreneurs from around the world.[5]

Decentralized Networks

Under the current system, centralized platforms make the rules. They set the terms of the agreement by which the user can participate. If the user decides to leave the platform or is ousted due to a breach of those terms and conditions, all of their assets—their photos, passwords,

---

[3] Rowaad. *Virtual Assets Law in UAE*. www.legal500.com/developments/thought-leadership/what-you-need-to-know-about-virtual-assets-law-in-the-uae/#:~:text=Dubai%20Virtual%20Assets%20Law%20has,virtual%20asset%20services%20in%20Dubai.

[4] Hammad and Al-Mehdar Law Firm. *Legal Impact of Web3*. www.lexology.com/library/detail.aspx?g=bf5a9c9c-dee6-40e1-be70-dd81d688dfa0.

[5] Ocorian. *10 Benefits of UAE Free Zones*. www.ocorian.com/article/explained-uae-free-zones#:~:text=What%20is%20a%20free%20zone,dedicated%20to%20a%20specific%20industry.

contact lists, game pieces, whatever, are lost. In other words, those assets don't belong to the owner. Yes, it's their information, but they are housing it on a platform that can lock them out at any hint of impropriety and keep them out.

This new generation of the Web acknowledges the rights of ownership. Personal data are protected and free from centralized control.[6]

Decision making is put into the hands of platform members, not the creators of these decentralized platforms. They refer to this as a decentralized autonomous organization (DAO); as an inverted power pyramid.

Decentralized Autonomous Organizations (DAOs)

DAOs are Internet groups and organizations governed by their members. There is no central authority to oversee that organization. Instead, decisions are made from the bottom up.[7] In other words, DAOs are members who don't know one another, with no leader but are committed to the DAO and how it operates. They create and legislate using smart contracts encoded with policies that require action. The weight of one's vote is based on the amount of native DAO tokens they have.[8] All decisions are recorded on the blockchain.

DAOs are viewed by many in this new digital world as a replacement for traditional corporate governing bodies providing more transparency and efficiency to the governing process. There are eight major types of DAOs, each representing a need such as social, financial, political, and philanthropic. For this book, that's a discussion for another day. Follow

---

[6] Ferraro. *Ownership in Web3.* www.figment.io/resources/what-does-ownership-mean-in-web3.

[7] CoinTelegraph. *Decentralized Autonomous Organizations.* https://cointelegraph.com/daos-for-beginners/what-is-a-dao#:~:text=A%20decentralized%20autonomous%20organization%20(DAO,and%20managed%20by%20their%20members.

[8] Reiff. *Decentralized Autonomous Organizations.* www.investopedia.com/tech/what-dao/.

this footnote if you find DAOs interesting and want to know more about them.[9]

With responsibility comes liability. DAOs do more than vote on rules and governing procedures. They also raise capital, which can run in the millions. Unlike corporations whose governance is built on four centuries of law,[10] DAOs are seen by some as lacking the same *legal personality* (legal rights and responsibilities granted to individuals and organizations). Instead, they are seen by some as an entity living on a blockchain. This perception could make it difficult to carry out daily functions.[11] These functions include contracting with entities outside the DAO, filing or paying taxes, holding assets off the blockchain, and protecting intellectual property.[12] How they operate or are perceived as operating is a legal issue that needs to be addressed, allowing the DAO to do business and protect its members.[13]

Recognizing that current legal structures don't fit DAOs, a few U.S. states—Vermont (July 2018), Wyoming (July 2021), and Tennessee (April 2022)—passed legislation to create new legal entities to govern DAOs.[14] While recognized as a good start, some experts believe the laws are flawed because they do not believe lawmakers fully understand blockchain technology or its workings.[15] That's understandable, given that most lawmakers do not know how today's Web works.

Like the United States, governments worldwide are taking up legislation to regulate DAOs.

---

[9] Hennekes. *The 8 Important Types of DAOs.* www.alchemy.com/blog/types-of-daos#:~:text=There%20are%20eight%20main%20types,Protocol%20DAOs.

[10] Singer. *Are DAOs the New Corporate Paradigm.* https://cointelegraph.com/magazine/dao-challenge-business-model-become-new-corporate-paradigm/.

[11] Ellis. *What Is a Legal Personality.* www.mylawquestions.com/what-is-a-legal-personality.htm.

[12] O'Melveny. *What Is the DAO.* www.omm.com/resources/alerts-and-publications/alerts/what-the-dao-why-everyone-is-talking-about-decentralized-autonomous-organizations/.

[13] Ibid.

[14] Teague. *DAO Legislation in USA.* https://thedefiant.io/starting-a-dao-in-the-usa-steer-clear-of-dao-legislation.

[15] Ibid.

Switzerland offers four different operating structures for DAOs: The Swiss Foundation, the Swiss Association, the Decentralized Autonomous Association, and the Private International Act, each designed to fit the needs of the DAO.[16]

When it comes to blockchain, Switzerland is a major player. By the close of 2021, Zug, Switzerland, referred to as *Crypto Valley*, had attracted around 1,000 blockchain companies valued at U.S.$254.9 billion. Switzerland is a favorite crypto world due to its favorable tax and regulatory structures.[17]

The Cayman Islands, which has a long history of offshore banking, now offers a haven for DAOs. In 2017, the government passed the Cayman Islands Foundation Companies Law, which allows foundation companies to be structured without shareholders, just like DAOs.[18] Anyone interested in setting up a DAO in the Cayman Islands should consult a tax attorney for help.

AI

The great British mathematician Alan Turing posed a test that ignited a movement. It was called the Turing test. Simply stated, it is a test to determine if machines can demonstrate intelligence. The machine has to be able to speak like a human and fool human beings into believing the machine is human.[19] The test itself requires the computer to be convincing by more than 33 percent of the time during a series of five-minute keyboard conversations. A computer program named Eugene Goodman met that test on June 7, 2014, by convincing 33 percent of the Royal Society in London it was a 13-year-old Ukrainian boy.[20]

---

[16] Rau. *Legal Frameworks for DAOs Worldwide.* https://mirror.xyz/0x43d06b9e BFB0c76A448fBd5B6faa2cfba81901d6/CYm-hNaniW0C1Mn9KR677jn4o9ok GugkKC3C8iD9k28.

[17] Ibid.

[18] Ibid.

[19] Frankenfield. *The Turing Test.* www.investopedia.com/terms/t/turing-test.asp.

[20] Veselov. *Computer AI Passes Turing Test.* www.bbc.com/news/technology-27762088.

The results drew criticism from experts. They disputed the results, suggesting that the answers were weighted to favor the program.[21] The larger question remains whether machines can mimic human thought. In that respect, AI is moving in that direction, playing a vital role in today's Web experience, making it easy to connect to friends, products, and services offered on the Web.

AI, based on algorithms, which are unstructured (information generated by a variety of sources such as social media sites or those creating records) instructions able to "cope with unforeseen circumstances,"[22] that allows a search engine to direct one to the topic of their choice. It could be someone searching for their perfect match or like-minded friends. Algorithms can direct them to find unknown addresses, suggest online games or music based on their current choices, or offer products they may be interested in purchasing.[23] The latest breakthrough arrived in November 2022 with ChatGPT from OpenAI. Using their language models, the program allows users to do such things as get answers to questions, create programs, correspond, create papers, art, and videos by simply typing in the instructions. The program then scours the internet and immediately delivers results. The list goes on and on. However, there are concerns that users are directed to sites that may be controlled by bad actors who want to cause them harm.[24] On the other hand, AI made it possible to produce the last single song by The Beatles. "Now and Then," was released November 2, 2023, more than 50 years after the infamous break up of the Fab Four. AI was used to isolate the vocals of the late John Lennon from an old demo track, making it possible to complete the song.

Now then, when that algorithmic-based machine can opine on that input and make changes to offer its own choices, that's true AI.[25]

[21] Ibid.

[22] Quinyx. *Differences Between AI, ML and Algorithms*. www.quinyx.com/blog/difference-between-ai-ml-algorithms#:~:text=To%20summarize%3A%20algorithms%20are%20automated,receive%20is%20structured%20or%20unstructured.

[23] Scott. *Difference Between Algorithm and Artificial Intelligence*. www.datasciencecentral.com/difference-between-algorithm-and-artificial-intelligence/.

[24] Rainie and Anderson. *Pros and Cons of the Algorithm Age*. www.pewresearch.org/internet/2017/02/08/code-dependent-pros-and-cons-of-the-algorithm-age.

[25] Ibid.

Another issue with algorithms is that they steer people with similar values and interests together. That might seem appealing if one is interested in a particular sport, hobby, or something similar. However, it has further divided societies politically and socially, insulating people from any facts with which they do not agree.[26]

Cognizant of privacy and security, Web3 will build on AI, combining it with machine learning to create what developers believe will be a more intuitive Internet.[27]

Machine Learning

Machine learning, which is a part of AI but differs from AI,[28] is also algorithms that can take structured data (fixed data organized to follow fixed instructions) and build on that information and make improvements without requiring additional instructions to be added by a programmer.[29] Today, it is used in search engines to separate spam from necessary e-mails, make recommendations, and be on guard for suspicious activity that could harm the user.[30]

Machine learning will also be used for privacy protection when using online applications referred to as dApps, or decentralized applications. When you download an app today, you do so through your provider's app store, such as Apple, Google, Microsoft, Firefox, Chrome, and so forth. When you download that app, you typically must give permission.[31]

---

[26] ReverseAds. *Algorithms Pros and Cons*. https://reverseads.com/blog/algorithms-the-good-the-bad-the-ugly/.

[27] Fauna. *What Is Web3 and Why It's Important*. https://fauna.com/blog/what-is-web3-and-why-is-it-important.

[28] Quyni. *Differences Between AI, ML and Algorithms*. www.quinyx.com/blog/difference-between-ai-ml-algorithms#:~:text=To%20summarize%3A%20algorithms%20are%20automated,receive%20is%20structured%20or%20unstructured.

[29] Selig. *What Is Machine Learning*. www.expert.ai/blog/machine-learning-definition/.

[30] The Royal Society. *What Is Machine Learning*. https://royalsociety.org/topics-policy/projects/machine-learning/videos-and-background-information/.

[31] Federal Trade Commission Consumer Advice. *How to Protect Your Privacy on Apps*. https://consumer.ftc.gov/articles/how-protect-your-privacy-apps.

You get access to the game or the restaurant location, but unless checked, the app gathers information about you, whether it's related to the app's purpose or not. That developer can then take that information and share or sell it to other third parties without you being the wiser.[32] While you have a certain amount of control, let's be honest, you probably don't care if the app knows where you are or who you associate with, so you click *okay* when prompted without realizing you are providing a backdoor to your personal information.

Decentralized apps, on the other hand, operate on the blockchain which protects your privacy. Machine learning, used today by the likes of IBM, Google, and Microsoft, could help improve that privacy wall allowing you to enjoy the tips and recommendations an app might provide while keeping your personal information under your control.[33]

Machine learning could identify malicious activity that could harm the user.[34] It could also be used to develop other apps.[35]

The goal is for machines to take all that data generated and shared on the Web and act on that information without human oversight. Today, you can type a query into the search bar and choose the appropriate link based on the information you have read. Perhaps you are looking to book a trip. The algorithms take you to travel sites where you read the information and choose. The next step is for you to enter your travel information (arrival, length of stay, room size, and so forth) before finally entering your payment information.

Imagine a machine interpreting the questions and filling in all the blanks without needing a human pair of eyes to respond. No *reading* is required. The machine, loaded with information from all quarters, could share that data instantaneously with other machines. With a vocabulary aid, futurists say computers could take all that information and develop an appropriate result.[36]

---

[32] Gutermuth. *Information Mobile Apps Collect.* https://slate.com/technology/2017/02/how-to-understand-what-info-mobile-apps-collect-about-you.html.

[33] Tilbe. *Machine Learning, Web3 and AI.* https://medium.com/illumination/web3-and-ai-top-3-most-important-machine-learning-methods-d1cf4374a965.

[34] Ibid.

[35] Ibid.

[36] Tehcnopedia. *Semantic Web.* www.techopedia.com/definition/27961/semantic-web.

The IoT

The IoT is a term used to describe the connectivity of one or more devices to others and sending that information through the Internet without human input.[37]

These devices contain sensors, processors, software, or other programs that interact with other devices.[38] It can be as simple as today's sensor measuring the efficiency of a motor in a machine or keeping tabs on light and energy usage in a home or factory. IoT includes sensors installed by farmers to measure soil moisture. It's the sensor in smoke alarms. It's a chip in a pet's ear to store identification and medical information. Implants can be used in humans to monitor health. There are built-in sensors in today's automobiles that alert drivers they are too close to another object or that something or that the vehicle needs attention.[39]

Web 3.0 will be able to take all the information provided by the machines, analyze that data, and make the necessary adjustments to improve the efficiency of a particular device, all without the need for human intervention.

The marriage of IoT and Web3 is designed to increase productivity, leaving more and more responsibilities to machines to analyze data instead of people.[40] The technology will serve as that critical personal assistant corporate executives clamor for, only to discover they need more to get their jobs done.

Homelife will also be enhanced.

The connectivity of a smart home already allows devices to be connected to appliances such as lights, thermostats, home entertainment systems, and kitchen appliances. Amazon's Alexa, Apple's Siri, Microsoft's

---

[37] Gillis. *What Is the Internet of Things*. www.techtarget.com/iotagenda/definition/ Internet-of-Things-IoT.

[38] Wikipedia. *Internet of Things*. https://en.wikipedia.org/wiki/Internet_of_things.

[39] Gillis. *What Is the Internet of Things*. www.techtarget.com/iotagenda/definition/ Internet-of-Things-IoT.

[40] IMS Technology Services. *Internet of Things, Web 3.0 and Meetings*. https:// imsts.com/internet-of-things-and-web-3-0-how-they-will-affect-your-meeting.

Cortana, or Google Assistant can respond to voice commands.[41] And yes, the IoT makes driverless cars possible.

Household appliances are being developed to incorporate machine learning to help improve efficiency with voice connectivity, incorporating Amazon's Alexa and Google Assistant.[42] Imagine coming home, uncertain of what to eat, so you ask Siri to offer suggestions based on past meals and what's available in your refrigerator. Google Assistant summarizes the day's events while your smart kitchen prepares dinner. After dinner, you relax in front of the television, watching programs Alexa has already chosen for you based on your interests. Or perhaps Siri plays your favorite music without your need to choose.

Imagine you need to go to the grocery store but are unsure what to buy. Your smart refrigerator, which keeps up with what it has stored, provides a list to your smart device. Today's smart refrigerators now include an app that allows you to monitor and change its temperature, get recipes based on available ingredients, and even alert you when the door is open.[43]

With Web3, no third party—no food producers or entertainment executives will see that data representing a gold mine of information. What you eat, drink, and watch are kept private. You are nobody's product.

The Metaverse

You've probably heard a lot about the metaverse. For this conversation, it is only mentioned.

In short, the metaverse is a 3D virtual world created through augmented reality (AR), virtual reality (VR), and extended reality (XR) where people can meet, learn, work, and play together in a virtual landscape.

---

[41] De Marco. *Voice Control in IoT.* www.techtarget.com/iotagenda/blog/IoT-Agenda/The-rise-of-voice-control-in-the-internet-of-things#:~:text=The%20 current%20players%20in%20the,controlled%20applications%20within%20 the%20iPhone.

[42] Thomas. *IoT Examples.* https://builtin.com/internet-things/iot-examples.

[43] Rabbitte. *Smart Refrigerators.* https://150sec.com/smart-fridges-set-to-get-smarter-with-iot-ai-functionalities/13576/.

The metaverse incorporates blockchain technology overseen by DAOs to set policies and manage disputes.[44]

While some argue Web3 and the metaverse are the same, or one dominates the other, other experts see differences in these two worlds, although both include the same elements. Web3 is about conducting one's affairs in privacy, while the metaverse is about bringing people together in a virtual space.[45]

[44] XR Today Team. *Seven Layers of the Metaverse*. www.xrtoday.com/virtual-reality/what-are-the-seven-layers-of-the-metaverse/.
[45] Patrizio. *Differences Between Web3 and Metaverse*. www.techtarget.com/whatis/feature/Web3-vs-metaverse-Whats-the-difference#:~:text=Web3%20is%20about%20decentralized%20ownership,t%20care%20who%20owns%20it.

Web 3.0 Today

As you have been reading, to a limited degree, Web3 is already here. Many startups offer various services promoting their sites that use Web3 technology. There are sites for banking, monitoring supply chains, and insurance providers. There are platforms for trading, social media, messaging, cloud storage, and even provide a virtual private network (VPN), to name a few. In addition, some sites offer opportunities for web designers and coders to ply their trade in this emerging ecosystem.

While some sites are online and available today, others host websites on centralized platforms while incorporating Web3 elements.

As time goes on, more and more companies will follow, creating that *hard fork* that will take our virtual experience to a new level and leave the old version of the Web behind.

The examples listed are examples of what is available and in no way an endorsement of those sites. Similar platforms are also available. If you are interested, look using your search engine.

Search Engines

One essential element needed for Web3 is decentralized browsers. Several are under development, such as Cyber and Neeva.xyz. Neeva, founded by two former Google executives, currently operates an ad-free search engine that is private and can be customized. They offer both free access and monthly subscriptions that provide extra benefits. The company is working on neeva.xyz, a browser that conforms to Web3. Information will be stored on a blockchain instead of centralized computers. Their continued goal is to provide service to users, not advertisers.[1]

---

[1] The Neeva Team. *Neeva.xzy Web3 Search Engine.* https://neeva.com/blog/neeva-xyz-the-web3-search-engine.

Social Media

Several decentralized social media sites allow users to share posts and content without fear of censorship.

Minds, which has been referred to as the *anti-Facebook*, is a blockchain open-source, decentralized social media site where members earn tokens for their contributions. Tokens are earned by contributing content to others or paying others to share one's content.[2] However, users cannot target specific members. Instead, one's posts are sent out randomly to 1,000 people for each token spent. Minds does not censor content or promote groups.[3] The site offers paid subscriptions.

Discord offers channels, subchannels, unlimited file storage, and a verification process that has made it a favorite among crypto developers, although the site is open to everyone.[4] Community administrators must approve access to outsiders looking to connect to specific communities.

Videos

PeerTube is a video-sharing program that offers access to some 600,000 videos over a decentralized P2P network.[5] Viewers can participate, offering comments through the P2P network. Viewers are not tracked. Although unnecessary, signing up for an account is free. Simply choose the categories you are interested in watching. Video offerings are referred to as *instances* so follow the arrows. Otherwise, look for *see instances list* box, which will take you to several platforms.

If you are interested in showing videos, sign up on their homepage and choose the platform or *instances* that fit your offerings.

---

[2] Matsakis. *Minds, the Anti-Facebook*. www.wired.com/story/minds-anti-facebook/#:~:text=Minds%20doesn't%20let%20you,for%20each%20token%20you%20spend.

[3] Ibid.

[4] Ebiekutan. *Best Social Media Platforms for Web3 Communities*. www.signvm.io/post/the-best-social-media-platforms-for-web3-communities.

[5] Chocobozzz. *PeerTube Concerns*. https://medium.com/@chocobozzz/why-should-you-feel-concerned-about-peertube-bb4a55cd8c7c.

Odysee allows content creators to upload videos without fear of that content being removed. The platform operates on the LBRY blockchain, so the content cannot be altered or removed.[6]

Content providers, who in 2021 numbered around 300,000, can earn anywhere from U.S.$100 to U.S.$5,000 per month. Uploading videos requires contributors to deposit a minimum of 0.01 LBRY Credits (LBC), ensuring they are registered and their content discoverable.[7] In November 2022, they were valued at around U.S.$0.02 per credit.

Content providers can set an LBC price for viewing their videos, which requires users to have a wallet to buy LBC.[8]

Blogs

Fair Data Society has a self-hosted blog hosted by Swarm (a decentralized data storage and distribution technology), which is *permission-less*. The content creator not only produce their content, but they control it and are responsible for it.[9] The site includes decentralized storage, allowing content providers control over who has access to it.[10]

Messaging

Matrix is a decentralized, encrypted messaging service built on an open-source platform. Users connect to a server that includes chat rooms. The server is linked to other servers so that they can share messages. Users are also invited to create servers, giving them more control over their data.[11]

Secretum is a decentralized, encrypted messaging service that uses blockchain technology for messaging and over-the-counter (OTC)

---

[6] Brown. *Blockchain-Based Odysee*. www.zdnet.com/finance/blockchain/block chain-based-odysee-keeps-your-social-media-content-online/.

[7] Ibid.

[8] Status. *Frequently Asked Questions*. https://status.im/docs/FAQs.html#:~:text= Status%20currently%20uses%20Whisper%2C%20the,network%20for%20 a%20set%20time.

[9] Žavcer. *Cancel Culture and Censorship*. www.datacenterdynamics.com/en/ opinions/cancel-culture-and-censorship-freeing-the-content-through-web3/.

[10] Ibid.

[11] Matrix.org. *What Is Matrix*. https://matrix.org/docs/guides/introduction.

trading. The system combines the functionality of several popular centralized messaging services, combined with features to make cryptocurrency and NFT trades.[12]

Status is a P2P messaging service that operates on Ethereum. Like others, messages are encrypted. For added safeguards, an encryption key is sent with each message, so if someone intercepts and decrypts a message, they only have access to that message. Unlike other instant messaging services that store messages on their servers, no messages are stored on the Ethereum blockchain. Messages are stored on a mail server for two weeks and on the users' phones.[13]

Compared to other messaging apps, setting up Status requires time and patience. For instance, users must create a three-word identity. If the user wants a recognizable identity, they can use an Ethereum Name Service (ENS) address, which requires them to purchase one with ETH.[14] Otherwise, the app is free. Users can earn SNT tokens for use on the network.[15]

Web3 Browsers

Centralized web browsers can threaten your privacy, tracking every site you visit and every click you make. That information is held by these providers and sold to advertisers. Yes, you can take steps to reduce this oversight, but that requires constant diligence on your part. Decentralized browsers release you of that need. You decide what to share and what to keep private.

---

[12] BeinCrypto Team. *Secretum Web3 Messaging App.* https://beincrypto.com/secretum-the-messaging-app-of-the-web-3-0-era/.

[13] ProPrivacy. *Status.im Review.* https://proprivacy.com/privacy-service/review/statusim.

[14] Graves. *Status Want Private Messaging App.* https://decrypt.co/25629/status-wants-to-be-the-worlds-most-private-instant-messaging-app.

[15] ProPrivacy. *Status.im Review.* https://proprivacy.com/privacy-service/review/statusim.

Web3 browsers allow users to access decentralized platforms and use dApps that run on the blockchain.[16]

There are a growing number of Web3 browsers out today. Following are two of many that enjoy popularity.

Brave, considered one of the leading Web3 browsers, strips away ads with ad-blocking software and replaces them with optional private ads.[17] If a user chooses to participate in the program, they earn Brave Rewards in the form of BATs, which can be used to purchase gift cards or sent as tips to content creators. The browser easily integrates information from one's existing browser, simplifying use. The home page is a news feed that follows one's interests. Brave was discussed at length in the blockchain section.

The browser also includes Brave Talk, a video chat line that lets users hold video chats with up to four people for free. Users who need more lines can purchase a U.S.$7 monthly subscription.

Opera, one of the first browsers to include an ad blocker and built-in VPN, now offers two other browsers—Opera GX for gamers and Opera Crypto for those who trade cryptocurrency and NFTs.[18] Opera Crypto includes links to DAOs. It also includes an optional wallet for cryptocurrency and NFTs, relieving users of the need to attach a wallet app to trade directly from the site.

Other features include the Crypto Corner, which keeps up with crypto news, and an education page. The homepage contains buttons for popular messaging sites with the option to add additional websites.

Cloud Storage

Today's cloud storage services hold our information on servers connected to networks owned by the providers. There are several different types of

---

[16] CyberScrilla. *What Is a Web3 Browser*. https://cyberscrilla.com/what-is-a-web3-wallet-and-why-is-it-important/#:~:text=What%20is%20the%20difference%20between,the%20internet%20and%20multiple%20servers.

[17] Jain. *7 Best Web 3.0 Browsers 2022*. https://browsertouse.com/blog/5098/best-web-3-0-browsers/.

[18] Batt. *Opera's New Web3 Crypto Browser*. https://blogs.opera.com/crypto/2022/01/opera-crypto-browser-project-web3/.

architecture for cloud servers that can be an exciting topic for some. Our focus is on personal storage—that far-away place you send your photos, videos, music, and papers, so they don't get lost. Like centralized services, decentralized services offer free storage space but charge for excessive amounts.

Web3.storage is a decentralized cloud service that offers 5 GB of free storage at no cost.[19] Files are uploaded on their website with a password.[20]

Summing Up

If and when you have the chance, visit these sites or conduct a search and look for Web3 services that interest you. Download them and play around with them. Get your feet wet. There's nothing to buy, no commitments. You are simply looking for the Web3 experience. Yes, some of the sites are a bit more labor-intensive than you might be accustomed to and, for sure, could use some refinement. But remember, this is the dawn of Web3. As time goes on, improvements and ease of use will follow.

---

[19] Preface. *How Web Companies Used Web 3.0.* www.preface.ai/blog/trend/web3-examples/.
[20] Ibid.

Web3

The Battle for Control

Free speech, a central tenant to Web3, is a seemingly simple idea but is fraught with complexity, especially regarding the Internet.

Is government control over the Internet really necessary to regulate questionable speech? It's an easy answer if the question includes authoritarian nations like China, Iran, and Russia, which so fear their people that they monitor every aspect of their lives, including what they see, read, and say online. If someone enjoys democratic liberties, then, of course, they find the actions of these governments are reprehensible. Who can be against free speech? This is where things get complicated.

Those in power, regardless of ideology, want to keep power. To do so, they need to control the narrative and remove any message of dissent. Methods, also used in democracies, include ridding schools and libraries of books contrary to the authorities' personal beliefs. It includes editing or removing films, videos, television, or radio programs deemed contrary to the establishment view. It includes removing works of art from museums that provoke controversy.

Efforts to police the Internet are no different. For some, it's about halting the spread of disinformation that can cause irreparable harm if followed, curbing the dissemination of hate speech, or protecting children from predators and bullies. For others, it's about calling out expressed thoughts they find objectionable, which usually forces the *offender* to cry *uncle* and apologize. If their actions are seen as going too far, these *offenders* are *canceled*. They are banished from the tribe, shunned, and forced to wear a scarlet letter tattooed to their forehead for the rest of their days.

If it's not complicated enough, let's not forget the posted writings of those whose self-absorbed treatises filled with hate and misinformation are followed by bloody violence.

The common strain in this mix is the originators of these works begin with thoughts that emerge as ideas. Just like other communication conduits, the Internet has become an equal opportunity disseminator that those in places of authority would like to see regulated, much like the established media platforms that are held responsible for their content.

Those committed to Web3 take issue with the idea that any idea should be censored. They have criticized social media sites like Facebook and the platform formerly known as Twitter, that, for better or worse, removed content, suspended members, or kicked them off their sites for the content they decided was unacceptable.

To be fair, these platforms reluctantly implemented those actions following public pressure to do something to control content deemed harmful and false. After buying Twitter, Musk, who changed Twitter's name to X in 2023, reversed course, reinstating the accounts of those who had been removed.

For Web3 proponents, contrasting ideas should be open for debate.[1] Still, some recognize a moderation system is necessary. If hate speech and bullying go unchecked, it quells other voices. On the other hand, driving out controversial figures limits the conversation.[2] Where to draw the line?

There are proponents of Web3 who support using decentralized platforms governed by its members as a DAO. Members use tokens to determine voting rights. Those who *behave* and show respect are rewarded with tokens.[3] Web3 also offers *interoperability*. Ifs someone chooses to leave a platform because they disagree with the rules, they are still free to be part of other platforms without fear of rejection. Compare that to centralized entities that own more than one platform so could ban offending members from all platforms they control.[4]

Interoperability, in this case, is the idea of allowing communications across blockchain platforms.[5]

While not available in the past, centralized social media platforms are now offering connectivity between different platforms.

---

[1] Cudos. *Moderating Free Speech in Web3.* www.cudos.org/blog/censorship-moderation-and-free-speech-in-web3/.

[2] Ibid.

[3] Polkastarter. *Web3, Cancel Culture and Censorship.* https://blog.polkastarter.com/how-can-web3-help-with-cancel-culture-and-content-censorship/.

[4] Ibid.

[5] Ibid.

Net Neutrality

Another issue that has dogged the Internet since the 1990s is the idea of network (net) neutrality, which guarantees equal access to all Internet providers regardless of the device or platform used, and the content consumed. In other words, a community website is treated no differently than a corporate movie site. Broadband providers cannot block lesser-known sites or charge them more for better service. It's a level playing field where anyone can share their platform content without fear of being blocked because it might compete with a major platform. What's more, the Internet speed must be shared equally. Broadband providers cannot reduce the speed for smaller, unfamiliar platforms and shift it to more prominent platforms that require faster downloads.[6]

There are no tiers of access. No platform gets preferential treatment.

Web neutrality is an egalitarian principle embodied in one of the last available territories. Broadband providers have balked at sharing the digital highway with smaller upstarts that want to keep Internet access free and open to all, which led to contentious senate hearings in the United States, pitting David against Goliath for control of the Internet.

For the most part, net neutrality has been respected for the past two decades in many countries.[7] Well, almost. After a contentious debate, the Federal Communications Commission, under the Trump administration, voted 3-2 on December 14, 2017, to end net neutrality. The rule went into effect on June 11, 2018.[8]

Despite predictions to the contrary, Internet access in the United States has not dramatically changed. However, some argue minor changes have been made to benefit providers, including a study that found telecom companies slowed down Internet traffic from apps such as Netflix and YouTube while charging more for higher speeds.[9]

---

[6] Awati and Gerwig. *Net Neutrality*. www.techtarget.com/searchnetworking/definition/Net-neutrality#:~:text=Net%20neutrality%20is%20the%20concept,internet%20data%20and%20users%20equally.

[7] Wikipedia. *Net Neutrality by Country*. https://en.wikipedia.org/wiki/Net_neutrality_by_country#Summary.

[8] Collins. *Repeal of Net Neutrality*. www.nytimes.com/2018/06/11/technology/net-neutrality-repeal.html.

[9] Stern. *Broadband Providers Taking Advantage of Net Neutrality Repeal*. https://publicknowledge.org/broadband-providers-are-quietly-taking-advantage-of-an-internet-without-net-neutrality-protections/.

Web3 could also be affected, providing special services to large, well-capitalized platforms, while smaller sites with fewer means could be charged for access.

Cryptocurrency exchanges operating in areas without net neutrality could find the need to charge more for transactions or slow down the speed at which those transactions are made.[10]

FCC Chair Jessica Rosenworcel, who serves in the Biden-Harris administration, announced on September 26, 2023, the FCC would introduce a proposal to reverse the 2017 decision and re-establish rules restoring net neutrality.[11]

But It's Not What You Promised!

Although aspects of Web3 are being utilized today, the promise of Web3 as this decentralized egalitarian system has yet to materialize. Sure, some sites, like the ones listed earlier, operate on a decentralized system, while others still rely on centralized computers to run their business. Some are already dismissing Web3 and looking to Web5 as fulfilling the promise.

Like Web3, Web5 is committed to personal privacy and giving individuals control over their private information. Unlike Web3, the vision of Web5 is where decentralized web applications (DWAs), built on blockchain, interact with what is referred to as decentralized web nodes (DWNs) that create a P2P connection independent of public blockchains.[12] Users run DWNs on their devices, which makes it possible to share information with others.[13]

The advent of Web3 has not stopped critics from complaining that it isn't living up to its promise before it began.

Web3 is an emerging technology. Nothing more. Nothing less. It's the technology we supposedly use to make lives easier. Like any technology, it's subject to abuse. Anyone believing otherwise is fooling themselves. The idea is to keep trying, keep building, and keep moving forward.

---

[10] Newsbtc. *How Net Neutrality Could Affect Cryptocurrency.* www.newsbtc.com/opinion/end-net-neutrality-mean-cryptocurrency/.

[11] Stella. *Rules to reinstate net neutrality to be reintroduced.* https://publicknowledge.org/fcc-chairwoman-rosenworcel-announces-plan-to-reinstate-title-ii-broadband-authority-net-neutrality-rules/.

[12] Adede. *Web5 Explained.* https://beincrypto.com/learn/web5-explained/.

[13] Ibid.

Resources

A curated directory of the best cryptocurrency resources. *Crypto Minded.* https://cryptominded.com/.

A guide to the best crypto resources on the internet. *Brex.* www.brex.com/journal/crypto-reading-list.

Beginner's Guide to NFTs: What Are Non-Fungible Tokens? *Decrypt.* https://about.fb.com/news/2022/06/what-are-nfts-beginners-guide-by-meta/#:~:text=NFT%20stands%20for%20non%2Dfungible,trading%20cards%20and%20even%20memes.

CoinDesk. *Online News and Information About Cryptocurrency, Digital Assets, and the Future of Money.* www.coindesk.com/.

CoinTelegraph. *Online Magazine Covering Blockchain, Cryptocurrency and Related Topics.* https://cointelegraph.com/.

Cryptocurrency Online Short Course. *MIT Media Lab.* https://mit-online.getsmarter.com/presentations/lp/mit-cryptocurrency-online-short-course/?ef_id=c:518876724464_d:c_n:g_ti:kwd-1894291486731_p:_k:mit%20media%20lab%20crypto_m:e_a:125007125447&gclid=CjwKCAiAzKqdBhAnEiwAePEjkkW2WCjDFUmG1qV8pVByriSNDkTuT395KOLOMrg1eufcRHE9sQUulxoCgfMQAvD_BwE&gclsrc=aw.ds.

Cryptocurrency Resources: Glossary. Texas State Securities Board.

Investopedia.com. *Web Source for Financial Content.* www.investopedia.com/.

Simply Explained. *YouTube Tutorial Series That Takes Complicated Topics and Breaks Them Down Into Simple Language.* www.youtube.com/@simplyexplained.

Virtual currency tax guidance and resources. *AICPA.* www.aicpa.org/resources/article/virtual-currency-tax-guidance-and-resources.

Bibliography

(^W^)/. January 31, 2019. "Getting Started With WebTV [1998]." *YouTube* video, 12:28. www.youtube.com/watch?v=MhzojvS4B5I&t=100s.

99Bitcoins. August 4, 2015. "What Are Digital Bitcoin Signatures." *Youtube video*, 1:11. www.youtube.com/watch?v=hv-nz8jJlTA&ab_channel=99Bitcoins.

Abazorius, A. February 13, 2020. "MIT Researchers Identify Security Vulnerabilities in Voting App." *MIT News.* https://news.mit.edu/2020/voting-voatz-app-hack-issues-0213.

Abbany, Z. August 4, 2016. "Worldwide Dispute: When Tim Invented the Web." *DW.* www.dw.com/en/hyperlink-when-tim-berners-lee-invented-the-world-wide-web-not-the-internet/a-19448729.

ABC Legal Services. October 5, 2020. "Legal Tech: How Blockchain Can Easily Transform the Legal Profession." *ABC Legal.* www.abclegal.com/blog/legal-tech-blockchain.

Abrol, A. April 13, 2022. "A Complete Guide of Liquidity Provider (LP) Tokens." *Blockchain Council.* www.blockchain-council.org/defi/liquidity-provider-tokens/.

Academic Dictionaries and Encyclopedias. 2022. "Prodigy (Online Service)." *Academic Dictionaries and Encyclopedias.* https://en-academic.com/dic.nsf/enwiki/200655 (accessed August 10, 2022).

Accenture Technology. April 15, 2020. "WEF: Known Traveller Digital Identity." *YouTube* video, 3:46. www.youtube.com/watch?v=cnUAQKKnEAU&ab_channel=AccentureTechnology.

Adede, C. November 17, 2022. "Web5 Explained: What It Is and How It Is Different From Web3." *BeinCrypto.* https://beincrypto.com/learn/web5-explained/.

Ahmed, E and M. Shabani. November 5, 2019. "DNA Marketplace: An Analysis of the Ethical Concerns Regarding the Participation of the Individuals." *Frontiers in Genetics.* www.frontiersin.org/articles/10.3389/fgene.2019.01107/full#B3.

Allison, I. November 9, 2022. "Divisions in Sam Bankman-Fried's Crypto Empire Blur on His Trading Titan Alameda's Balance Sheet." *CoinDesk.* www.coindesk.com/business/2022/11/02/divisions-in-sam-bankman-frieds-crypto-empire-blur-on-his-trading-titan-alamedas-balance-sheet/.

Alsup, D., S. Almasy, and G. Sands. August 17, 2019. "US Customs Computers Coming Back Online After Outage Leads to Long Lines." *CNN.* https://edition.cnn.com/2019/08/16/politics/us-customs-computers/index.html.

Altaweel, M., C. Sandvick, and E. Lambrecht. 2022. "How Did Gold Become Desired by Ancient Civilizations." *DailyHistory.org*. https://dailyhistory .org/How_Did_Gold_Become_Desired_by_Ancient_Civilizations (accessed November 8, 2022).

Amadeo, K. February 27, 2021. "Savings and Loan Crisis Explained." *The Balance*. www.thebalance.com/savings-and-loans-crisis-causes-cost-3306035.

Andrews, E.L. October 24, 2019. "Cryptocurrencies Could Eliminate Banking's Easiest Moneymaker." *Graduate School of Stanford Business*. www.gsb.stanford .edu/insights/cryptocurrencies-could-eliminate-bankings-easiest-moneymaker.

Antolin, M. June 2, 2022. "What Is Proof-of-Authority?" *CoinDesk*. www .coindesk.com/learn/what-is-proof-of-authority/.

Anwar, H. February 8, 2021. "Blockchain Consortium: Top 20 Consortia You Should Check Out." *101 Blockchains*. https://101blockchains.com/ blockchain-consortium/.

Anzalone, R. September 30, 2020. "Blockchain Voting Can Work, Both Republican and Democrats Use Voatz." *Forbes*. www.forbes.com/sites/ robertanzalone/2020/09/30/blockchain-voting-can-work-both-republican-and-democrats-use-voatz/?sh=2b8a4964ee9e.

Apla Blockchain Platform Guide. 2022. "Proof-of-Authority Consensus." *Apla Blockchain Platform Guide*. https://apla.readthedocs.io/en/latest/concepts/ consensus.html (accessed October 28, 2022).

Ariella, S. November 13, 2022. "25 Incredible Nonprofit Statistics [2022]: How Many Nonprofits Are in the US?." *Zippia*. www.zippia.com/advice/nonprofit-statistics/#:~:text=There%20are%20over%201.5%20million,around%20 10%20million%20nonprofits%20worldwide.

Arijit, S. October 29, 2022. "The Merge Brings Down Ethereum's Network Power Consumption by Over 99.9%." *Cointelegraph*. https://cointelegraph.com/ news/the-merge-brings-down-ethereum-s-network-power-consumption-by-over-99-9.

Armstrong, E. January 31, 2022. "Hashing Vs Encryption: What's the Difference?." *NordLocker* (blog). https://nordlocker.com/blog/hashing-vs-encryption/#:~:text=Hashing%20is%20not%20a%20type,the%20case%20 with%20encrypted%20messages.

Arrington, M. 2022. "First Real Estate NFT." *Seen.Haus*. https://seen.haus/ drops/first-real-estate-nft (accessed July 11, 2022).

Arthur, R. May 10, 2017. "From Farmed to Finished Garment: Blockchain Is Aiding This Fashion Collection With Transparency." *Forbes*. www .forbes.com/sites/rachelarthur/2017/05/10/garment-blockchain-fashion-transparency/?sh=3fee631974f3.

Artificial Lawyer. November 25, 2021. "UK Law Commission Gives Smart Contracts the Green Light." *Artificial Lawyer*. www.artificiallawyer.com/ 2021/11/25/uk-law-commission-gives-smart-contracts-the-green-light/.

Artificial Lawyer. October 16, 2018. "Integra Ledgers Launches Tools to Add Blockchain Tech to All Legal Software." *Artificial Lawyer*. www.artificiallawyer .com/2018/10/16/integra-ledger-launches-tools-to-add-blockchain-tech-to-all-legal-software/.

Arvelaiz, J. April 2022. "Why Top International Banks Partnered to Use Ripple Network." *Bitcoinist*. https://bitcoinist.com/why-top-international-banks-partnered-to-use-ripple/.

Attlee, D. April 20, 2022. "'Let's Build a Europe Where Web3 Can Flourish:' Crypto Companies Sign an Open Letter to EU Regulators." *Cointelegraph*. https://cointelegraph.com/news/let-s-build-a-europe-where-web3-can-flourish-crypto-companies-sign-an-open-letter-to-eu-regulators.

Attlee, D. March 28, 2022. "EU Parliament Can Outlaw Transacting With 'Unhosted' Wallets, Crypto Advocate Warns." *Cointelegraph*. https:// cointelegraph.com/news/eu-parliament-can-outlaw-transacting-with-unhosted-wallets-crypto-advocate-warns.

Attlee, D. April 6,2022. "Unhosted Is Unwelcome: EU's Attack on Noncustodial Wallets Is Part of a Larger Trend." *Cointelegraph*. https://cointelegraph.com/ news/unhosted-is-unwelcome-eu-s-attack-on-noncustodial-wallets-is-part-of-a-larger-trend.

Aufrichtig, A. October 25, 2021. "The Blockchain Easement: Benefits and Drawbacks of Blockchain Technology in Real Estate." *CARDOZOAELJ Arts & Entertainment Law Journal* (blog). https://cardozoaelj.com/2021/10/25/the-blockchain-easement-benefits-and-drawbacks-of-blockchain-technology-in-real-estate/.

Aurora, V. January 4, 2022. "What Is Web 3.0 and How It Is Going to Change the Future of the Internet." *OnGraph Technologies*. www.ongraph.com/what-is-web-3-how-it-is-going-to-change-the-future-of-the-internet/.

Auxier, B., L. Rainie, M. Anderson, A. Perrin, M. Kumar, and E. Turner. November 15, 2019. "Americans and Privacy: Concerned, Confused and Feeling Lack of Control Over Their Personal Information." *Pew Research Center*. www.pewresearch.org/internet/2019/11/15/americans-and-privacy-concerned-confused-and-feeling-lack-of-control-over-their-personal-information/.

Avidor, J. July 2012, 2018. "Is Blockchain HIPPA Compliant?" *MGA* (blog). https://masur.com/lawtalk/is-blockchain-hipaa-compliant/.

Awati, R. and K. Gerwig. 2022. "Net Neutrality." *TechTarget*. www.techtarget.com/ searchnetworking/definition/Net-neutrality#:~:text=Net%20neutrality%20 is%20the%20concept,internet%20data%20and%20users%20equally (accessed September 7, 2022).

Ayers, J. August 8, 2022. "Do Closing Costs Include Realtor Fees?" *Clever Real Estate* (blog). https://listwithclever.com/real-estate-blog/do-closing-costs-include-realtor-fees/.

Back, A. August 1, 2002. "A Denial of Service Counter-Measure." *Satoshi Nakamoto Institute*. https://nakamotoinstitute.org/static/docs/hashcash.pdf

Bailey, D. May 22, 2022. "Can Web 3.0 Solve the Problems of Web 2.0?" *Supplain*. https://supplain.io/news/web3-solve-web2-problems.

Bajpai, P. December 14, 2021. "Countries Where Bitcoin Is Legal and Illegal." *Investopedia*. www.investopedia.com/articles/forex/041515/countries-where-bitcoin-legal-illegal.asp.

Barth, S. and M.D.T. de Jong. November 2017. "The Privacy Paradox— Investigating Discrepancies Between Expressed Privacy Concerns and Actual Online Behavior—A Systematic Literature Review." *Telematics and Informatics* 34, no. 7, pp. 1038–1058. www.sciencedirect.com/science/article/pii/S0736585317302022.

Barton, R.E., C.J. Mcnamara, and M.C. Ward. March 21, 2022. "Are Cryptocurrencies Securities? The SEC Is Answering the Question." *Reuters*. www.reuters.com/legal/transactional/are-cryptocurrencies-securities-sec-is-answering-question-2022-03-21/.

Bateman, T. and Reuters. August 26, 2021. "EU Will Make Bitcoin Traceable and Ban Anonymous Crypto Wallets in Anti-Money Laundering Drive." *Euronews.Next*. www.euronews.com/next/2021/07/21/eu-will-make-bitcoin-traceable-and-ban-anonymous-crypto-wallets-in-anti-money-laundering-d.

Batista, M. August 14, 2018. "Healthcare Blockchain Startup Coral Health Announces Healthcare App and Upcoming Token Sale (Interview)." *Medgadget*. www.medgadget.com/2018/08/healthcare-blockchain-startup-coral-health-announces-health-records-app-and-upcoming-token-sale-interview.html#:~:text=Categories-,Healthcare%20Blockchain%20Startup%20Coral%20Health%20Announces%20Health,and%20Upcoming%20Token%20Sale%20(Interview)&text=Once%20using%20the%20app%2C%20patients,%2C%20healthcare%20organizations%2C%20and%20researchers.

Batt, S. January 9, 2022. "Introducing Opera's New Web3 Initiative: Crypto Browser Project Now Available in Public Beta for Windows, Mac and Android." *Opera Blogs*. https://blogs.opera.com/crypto/2022/01/opera-crypto-browser-project-web3/.

BBC News. July 30, 2021. "Rewards Token—Living UP to Their Name." *BBC News*. www.bsc.news/post/rewards-token-living-up-to-their-name.

Beattie, A. October 31, 2021. "Why Did Pets.com Crash so Drastically?" *Investopedia*. www.investopedia.com/ask/answers/08/dotcom-pets-dot-com.asp#:~:text=The%20company%20raised%20%2482.5%20million,such%20as%20dog%20food%20bags.

Becher, B. September 29, 2022. "What Are Blockchain Nodes and How Do They Work?" *Built In*. https://builtin.com/blockchain/blockchain-node.

Beckett, M. May 19, 2022. "History of the Internet: A Timeline Throughout the Years." *U switch*. www.uswitch.com/broadband/guides/broadband-history/.

Beckles, C.A. 2022. "From Ancient to Modern: The Changing Face of Personal Data." *Iapp*. https://iapp.org/news/a/from-ancient-to-modern-the-changing-face-of-personal-data/ (accessed January 18, 2022).

Bedell, D. June 14, 2013. "Payment Instruments: Checks." *Global Finance*. www.gfmag.com/global-data/economic-data/hquidd-payment-instruments-checks.

Beedham, M. March 21, 2019. "Here's the Difference Between ICOs and IEOs." *Hard Fork*. https://thenextweb.com/news/initial-exchange-offering-ieo-ico.

BeinCrypto Team. April 4, 2022. "Secretum: The Messaging App of Web 3.0 Era." *BeinCrypto*. https://beincrypto.com/secretum-the-messaging-app-of-the-web-3-0-era/.

Berkley Law. 2022. "The Common Law and Civil Law Traditions." *Berkeley Law*. www.law.berkeley.edu/wp-content/uploads/2017/11/CommonLaw CivilLawTraditions.pdf (accessed March 16, 2022).

Berman, A. September 3, 2018. "Japanese City Tsukuba Trials Blockchain-Based Voting System." *Cointelegraph*. https://cointelegraph.com/news/japanese-city-tsukuba-trials-blockchain-based-voting-system.

Bhattacharya, A. July 17, 2018. "Blockchain Is Helping Build a New Indian City, But It's No Cure for Corruption." *Quartz India*. https://qz.com/india/1325423/indias-andhra-state-is-using-blockchain-to-build-capital-amaravati.

Bit2Me Academy. 2021. "What Is a Utility Token?" *Bit2Me Academy*. https://academy.bit2me.com/en/what-is-utility-token/ (accessed December 1, 2021).

Bitcoin Magazine. July 4, 2022. "What Is the Bitcoin Blocksize Limit?" *Bitcoin Magazine*. https://bitcoinmagazine.com/guides/what-is-the-bitcoin-block-size-limit.

Bitcoinist. November 2021. "Cyber: A Search Engine for Web 3." *Bitcoinist*. https://bitcoinist.com/cyber-a-search-engine-for-web-3/?utm_source=rss&utm_medium=rss&utm_campaign=cyber-a-search-engine-for-web-3.

Bitpanda. 2021. "What Does Pre-Mined Mean?" *Bitpanda*. www.bitpanda.com/academy/en/lessons/what-does-pre-mined-mean/ (accessed November 23, 2021).

Biz Vlogs. September 17, 2017. "HashCash: The Original Bitcoin (Live)." *Youtube video*, 7:21. www.youtube.com/watch?v=YUTwqG6e8LY&ab_channel=BizVlogs.

Blockchain Hub Berlin. 2022. "Tokenized Networks, Web3, the Stateful Web." *Blockchain Hub*. https://blockchainhub.net/web3-decentralized-web/ (accessed August 19, 2022).

Blockchain Support Center. 2022. "How Can I Look Up a Transaction on the Blockchain?" *Blockchain.com*. https://support.blockchain.com/hc/en-us/signin?return_to=https%3A%2F%2Fsupport.blockchain.com%2Fhc%2Fen-us%2Farticles%2F211160663-How-can-I-look-up-a-transaction-on-the-blockchain-#:~:text=To%20look%20up%20a%20bitcoin,your%20search%20query%20will%20display (accessed February 3, 2022).

Blockchain.com. 2022. "Average Transactions Per Block." *Blockchain.com.* www .blockchain.com/charts/n-transactions-per-block (accessed October 11, 2022).

Blocknative. January 14, 2020. "What Is the Mempool?—Your Intro to In-Flight Transactions." *Blocknative.* www.blocknative.com/blog/mempool-intro.

Blocknative. October 27, 2020. "Liquidty 2020: Manpool 101 With Matt Cutler, CEO of Blocknative." *YouTube* video, 30:30. www.youtube.com/ watch?v=aZPx7K8XI68&t=932s&ab_channel=Blocknative.

BlockstreetHQ Team. September 6, 2018. "Before Blockchain, There Was Distributed Ledger Technology." *Blockstreet HQ.* https://medium.com/ blockstreethq/before-blockchain-there-was-distributed-ledger-technology-319d0295f011#:~:text=But%20the%20concept%20was%20not,which%20 has%20a%20rich%20past.

Bloomberg Law. Updated September 7, 2023. "Which States Have Consumer Data Privacy Laws? *Bloomberg Law.* https://pro.bloomberglaw.com/brief/ state-privacy-legislation-tracker/#:~:text=Browse%20all%20privacy%20 articles&text=Currently%2C%20there%20are%2011%20states,data%20 privacy%20laws%20in%20place.

Волков, Николай. May 27, 2017. "Patientory—Making Healthcare Personal." *Medium.com.* https://medium.com/@BtcetHmaker/patientory-how-it-work-f3e22fad50f0.

Bolt, W. and M.R.C. van Oordt. April 21, 2019. "On the Value of Virtual Currencies." *Journal of Money, Credit and Banking.* https://onlinelibrary .wiley.com/doi/full/10.1111/jmcb.12619.

Boluwatife, F. May 24, 2022. "Top 10 Biggest Cryptos That Failed." *Sortter* (blog). https://sortter.com/blog/article/failed-cryptocurrencies/.

Bonpay. March 13, 2018. "What Is the Difference Between Coins and Tokens?" *Bonpay.* https://medium.com/@bonpay/what-is-the-difference-between-coins-and-tokens-6cedff311c31.

Bond, C. Updated August 11, 2023. "Good News: The Average Savings Account Interest Rate Is Still on the Rise." *Fortune.* https://fortune.com/recommends/ banking/average-savings-account-interest/.

Bourgi, S. November 17, 2021. "Bacon Protocol Offers Industry-First 'NFT Mortgages'." *Cointelegraph.* https://cointelegraph.com/news/bacon-protocol-offers-industry-first-nft-mortgages.

Bowles, C. May 8, 2020. "Smart Contracts—Legally Enforceable?" *EM Law* (blog). https://emlaw.co.uk/smart-contracts-legally-enforceable/.

Brassell, J. May 4, 2022. "Legal Worries in the Metaverse as NFTs and Blockchains Don't Protect Virtual Property." *BeyondGames.biz.* www.beyondgames.biz/ 22138/legal-worries-in-the-metaverse-as-nfts-and-blockchains-dont-protect-virtual-property/.

Brave Software. February 10, 2021. "Basic Attention Token (BAT) Blockchain Based Digital Advertising." *Basicattentiontoken.org*. https://basicattentiontoken.org/static-assets/documents/BasicAttentionTokenWhitePaper-4.pdf.

Brett, C. May 8, 2018. "MediLedger, Chronicled, and blockchain." *Enterprise Times*. www.enterprisetimes.co.uk/2018/05/08/mediledger-chronicled-and-blockchain/.

Briggs, B. January 28, 2008. "2007 Online Retail Sales Hit $175 Billion, Forrester Research Says." *Digital Commerce 360*. www.digitalcommerce360.com/2008/01/28/2007-online-retail-sales-hit-175-billion-forrester-research-sa/.

Brock, T.J. January 14, 2022. "From the Experts: 8 Pros and Cons of Non-Fungible Tokens and How They Compare to Traditional Investments." *Annunity.org*. www.annuity.org/2022/01/14/from-the-experts-8-pros-and-cons-of-nfts/.

Brooke, C. September 8, 2022. "Crypto.com NFT Marketplace—How to Buy NFTs on Crypto.com App." *Business 2 Community*. www.business2community.com/nft/cryptocom-nft-marketplace.

Brown, E. April 8, 2021. "Blockchain-Based Odysee Keeps Your Social Media Content Online." *ZDNet*. www.zdnet.com/finance/blockchain/blockchain-based-odysee-keeps-your-social-media-content-online/.

Browne, R. April 20, 2023. "EU Lawmakers Approve World's First Comprehensive Framework for Crypto Regulation." *CNBC*. www.cnbc.com/2023/04/20/eu-lawmakers-approve-worlds-first-comprehensive-crypto-regulation.html#:~:text=the%20cryptocurrency%20industry.-,In%20a%20vote%20Thursday%2C%20the%20EU%20Parliament%20voted%20517%20in,lose%20investors'%20crypto-assets.

Built In. 2022. "Hi, We're Blockpharma." *Built In*. https://builtin.com/company/blockpharma (accessed February 23, 2022).

Bury, E. April 5, 2021. "What Happens to Your NFTs and Crypto Assets After You Die?" *TechCrunch*. https://techcrunch.com/2021/04/05/what-happens-to-your-nfts-and-crypto-assets-after-you-die/.

Buy Bitcoin Worldwide. 2022. "How Many Bitcoin Miners Are There?" *buybitcoinworldwide.com*. https://buybitcoinworldwide.com/how-many-bitcoins-are-there/#:~:text=How%20Many%20Bitcoin%20Miners%20Are,1%2C000%2C000%20unique%20individuals%20mining%20bitcoins (accessed October 28, 2022).

Buylaert, F. and J. Haemers. November 11, 2016. "Record-Keeping and Status Performance in the Early Modern Low Countries." *Oxford Academic* 230, no.11, pp. 131–150. https://academic.oup.com/past/article/230/suppl_11/131/2884255.

Cambridge Semantics. 2022. "Semantic Technologies Applied." *Cambridge Semantics*. https://cambridgesemantics.com/blog/semantic-university/semantic-technologies-applied/example-semantic-web-applications/ (accessed November 10, 2022).

Campbell, E. April 1, 2022. "New Death Row Records Owner Snoop Dogg Teases Label's First NFT Release." *NME*. www.nme.com/news/music/new-death-row-records-owner-snoop-dogg-teases-labels-first-nft-release-3196189#:~:text=New%20Death%20Row%20Records%20owner%20Snoop%20Dogg%20teases%20label's%20first%20NFT%20release&text=Snoop%20Dogg%20has%20shared%20plans,Snoop%2C%20and%20peaked%20at%20No.

Campbell, R. August 21, 2019. "Blockchain Voting Platform Horizon State Shuts Down After Lawsuit." *Yahoo! Finance*. https://finance.yahoo.com/news/blockchain-voting-platform-horizon-state-140552054.html?guccounter=1.

Cant, J. October 18, 2019. "Two More US Jurisdictions Launch Blockchain-Based Mobile Voting." *Cointelegraph*. https://cointelegraph.com/news/two-more-us-jurisdictions-launch-blockchain-based-mobile-voting.

Caplan, W. June 25, 2021. "The Rise of the Crypto Writer? On What Literary NFTs Might Mean for the Book World." *Literary Hub*. https://lithub.com/the-rise-of-the-crypto-writer-on-what-literary-nfts-might-mean-for-the-book-world/.

Carter, C. April 29, 2021. "The NFT Scourge Could One Day Hit Magic: The Gathering." *Dicebreaker*. www.dicebreaker.com/companies/hasbro/news/magic-the-gathering-nft-earnings-call.

Cartwright, M. September 19, 2017. "Silver in Antiquity." *World History Encyclopedia*. www.worldhistory.org/Silver/.

Cassell, A. March 25, 2022. "3 Blockchain Startups to Watch in the Travel Industry as Vacations Make a Comeback." *InvestorPlace*. https://investorplace.com/newdigitalworld/2022/03/3-blockchain-startups-to-watch-in-the-travel-industry-as-vacations-make-a-comeback/.

Cassiopeia Services. May 9, 2022. "Web3 Banking Has Arrived—Meet Fiat24." *Cassiopeia Services*. https://cassiopeiaservicesltd.medium.com/web3-banking-has-arrived-meet-fiat24-3ff07592036e.

CB Insights Research Briefs. February 11, 2021. "How Blockchain Could Disrupt Banking." *CB Insights*. www.cbinsights.com/research/blockchain-disrupting-banking/.

CB Insights Research Briefs. March 9, 2022. "Banking Is Only the Beginning: 65 Big Industries Blockchain Could Transform." *CB Insights*. www.cbinsights.com/research/industries-disrupted-blockchain/.

CBS LA Staff. May 21, 2021. "Massive Computer Outage Causes Frustrating Delays at Airport Nationwide, Including LAX." *CBS Los Angeles*. www

.cbsnews.com/losangeles/news/massive-computer-outage-causes-frustrating-delays-at-airport-nationwide-including-lax/.

CFI Team. October 9, 2022. "Hard Forks." *CFI*. https://corporatefinanceinstitute.com/resources/cryptocurrency/hard-fork/.

CFI Team. November 28, 2022. "Cryptocurrency Exchanges." *CFI*. https://corporatefinanceinstitute.com/resources/knowledge/other/cryptocurrency-exchanges/.

ChainSec. 2023. "Comprehensive List of Failed Stablecoins (2021–2022)." *ChanSec*. https://chainsec.io/failed-stablecoins/ (accessed May 29, 2023).

Chan, K. May 22, 2023. "Meta Fined Record $1.3 Billion and Ordered to Stop Sending European User to US." *The Associated Press*. https://apnews.com/article/meta-facebook-data-privacy-fine-europe-9aa912200226c3d53aa293dca8968f84?user_email=f5ff8be8d0fa22bbafcffab811c1fcbb897c1533ead9d835682c1e6db1fbf7a7&utm_medium=Morning_Wire&utm_source=Sailthru&utm_campaign=MorningWire_May22_2023&utm_term=Morning%20Wire%20Subscribers.

Chandler, S. February 8, 2019. "Smart Contracts Are No Problem for the World's Legal Systems, So Long as They Behave Like Legal Contracts." *Cointelegraph*. https://cointelegraph.com/news/smart-contracts-are-no-problem-for-the-worlds-legal-systems-so-long-as-they-behave-like-legal-contracts.

Chandran, R. July 29, 2020. "Deadly Land Conflicts Seen Rising as Threat From Industry Grows." *Reuters*. www.reuters.com/article/us-global-landrights-violence-idUSKCN24U005.

Chandrasekera, S. May 26, 2021. "How Are Non-Fungible Tokens (NFTs) Taxed?" *Bloomberg Tax*. https://news.bloombergtax.com/daily-tax-report/how-are-non-fungible-tokens-nfts-taxed.

Charles, X. November 15, 2021. "Upgrading Real Estate Tokenization to the Next Level." *Finextra* (blog). www.finextra.com/blogposting/21252/upgrading-real-estate-tokenization-to-the-next-level#:~:text=The%20process%20of%20real%20estate,raise%20capital%20for%20investment%20development.

Chauhan, S. Dr., S. Malhotra, S. Chandak, and students of the International Institute of health Management Research. March 18, 2021. "What Is Estonia Doing With Block Chain in Providing Healthcare to Its Citizens?" *InnoHEALTH magazine*. https://innohealthmagazine.com/2021/in-focus/what-is-estonia-doing-with-block-chain-in-providing-healthcare-to-its-citizens/.

Chavez-Dreyfuss, G. November 22, 2017. "Air New Zealand, Swiss Travel Platform Winding Tree in blockchain Tie-Up." *Reuters*. www.reuters.com/article/us-blockchain-travel-airnewzealand-idUSKBN1DM2KQ.

Chen, J. April 19, 2022. "Fiat Money: What It Is, How It Works, Example, Pros & Cons." *Investopedia*. www.investopedia.com/terms/f/fiatmoney.asp.

Chen, J. June 19, 2022. "Greenback: Definition, Origin, and History." *Investopedia*. www.investopedia.com/terms/g/greenback.asp#:~:text=A%20 greenback%20is%20a%20slang,help%20finance%20the%20civil%20war.

Chocobozzz. June 20, 2018. "Why Should You Feel Concerned About PeerTube?" *Medium*. https://medium.com/@chocobozzz/why-should-you-feel-concerned-about-peertube-bb4a55cd8c7c.

Cision. September 21, 2017. "Chronicled and the LinkLab Announce the MediLedger Project, a Revolutionary Blockchain-backed System to Safeguard the Pharmaceutical Industry." *Chronicled*. www.prnewswire.com/ news-releases/chronicled-and-the-linklab-announce-the-mediledger-project-a-revolutionary-blockchain-backed-system-to-safeguard-the-pharmaceutical-industry-300522426.html.

City Wonders Team. March 9, 2015. "The True Story of the Paris Love Lock Bridge." *City Wonders, CW on the Go* (blog). https://citywonders.com/ blog/France/Paris/paris-love-lock-bridge-story#:~:text=The%20'lock%20 bridge'%20is%20a,ritual%20symbolizes%20love%20locked%20forever.

Clark, M. April 2, 2021. "Two Coinbase Employees Exchange NFT Rings With Their Wedding Vows." *The Verge*. www.theverge.com/tldr/2021/4/2/22364647/ coinbase-employees-nft-wedding-exchange-romance.

Clifford, R. August 13, 2020. "Competitors for Airbnb: Who's Stealing Market Share From the Industry Giant?" *Hospitable*. https://hospitable .com/competitors-for-airbnb/#:~:text=Airbnb%20market%20 share&text=Statistics%20from%202019%20estimate%20that,the%20 realms%20of%20%2420Billion.

CNBCTV18.com. March 7, 2022. "How Ekta blockchain's Fractional Real Estate NFT Aims to Tokenize Real World Properties." *CNBCTV18.com*. www.cnbctv18.com/cryptocurrency/how-ekta-blockchains-fractional-real-estate-nft-aims-to-tokenise-real-world-properties-12738702.htm.

Coates, S. August 15, 2018. "A History of Tokens." *Medium.com*. https:// medium.com/@fooyay/a-history-of-tokens-a064b28d5af2.

COE-EDP. April 30, 2021. "Blockchain in Healthcare: Opportunities and Challenges." *Devdiscourse*. www.devdiscourse.com/article/technology/1553504-blockchain-in-healthcare-opportunities-and-challenges.

Coin Gossip. May 10, 2020. "History of Bitcoin Mining Hardware." *Coingossip .com* (blog). https://ccoingossip.com/history-of-bitcoin-mining-hardware/.

Coinbase. January 26, 2022. "Why Digital Signatures Are Essential for Blockchains." *Coinbase*. www.coinbase.com/de/cloud/discover/dev-foundations/ digital-signatures#:~:text=Digital%20signatures%20are%20a%20 fundamental,other%20users%20from%20spending%20them.

CoinBeam. August 23, 2022. " Cold Wallets Vs. Hot Wallets." *CoinBeam*. www.coinbeam.com/cold_wallets_vs_hot_wallets/#:~:text=Hot%20

wallets%20are%20also%20more,have%20easier%20access%20to%20
them.&text=A%20hot%20wallet%20is%20a,easily%20access%20
your%20crypto%20holdings.

CoinTelegraph. 2022. "What Is a Bitcoin Node? A beginner's Guide on Blockchain Nodes." *CoinTelegraph*. https://cointelegraph.com/bitcoin-for-beginners/what-is-a-bitcoin-node-a-beginners-guide-on-blockchain-nodes (accessed October 28, 2022).

CoinTelegraph. 2022. "What Is a Decentralized Autonomous Organization, and How Does a DAO Work?" *CointTelegraph*. https://cointelegraph .com/daos-for-beginners/what-is-a-dao#:~:text=A%20decentralized%20 autonomous%20organization%20(DAO,and%20managed%20by%20 their%20members (accessed September 14, 2022).

Collins, K. June 11, 2018. "Net Neutrality Has Officially Been Repealed. Here's How That Could Affect You." *The New York Times*. www.nytimes .com/2018/06/11/technology/net-neutrality-repeal.html.

Conaghan, J. May 17, 2017. "Young, Old, and In-Between: Newspaper Platform Readers Ages Are Well-Distributed." *News Media Alliance*. www .newsmediaalliance.org/age-newspaper-readers-platforms/.

ConcenSys Media. July 25, 2017. "Introducing OpenLaw." *ConcenSys Media*. https://media.consensys.net/introducing-openlaw-7a2ea410138b.

ConcenSys. April 17, 2019. "Forbes Releases Top 50-Billion-Dollar Companies Exploring Blockchain." *ConcenSys* (blog). https://consensys.net/blog/ enterprise-blockchain/forbes-releases-top-50-billion-dollar-companies-exploring-blockchain-over-half-are-working-with-ethereum/2021.

Congi. 2022. "Congi: Your Money. Your Lifestyle. One App." *Congi*. https:// getcogni.com/ (accessed August 30, 2022).

Conroy B. July 19, 2022. "Milo Reaches $10M Crypto-Mortgage Milestone." *HW*. www.housingwire.com/articles/milo-reaches-10m-crypto-mortgage-milestone/#:~:text=Milo's%20crypto%2Dloan%20program%2C%20 however,price%20appreciation%20in%20both%20assets.

Consensys. 2022. "Blockchain for Global Trade and Commerce." *Consensys*. https://consensys.net/blockchain-use-cases/global-trade-and-commerce/ (accessed February 22, 2022).

Consensys. 2022. "Blockchain in Digital Identity." *Consensys*. https://consensys .net/blockchain-use-cases/digital-identity/ (accessed March 1, 2022).

Consensys. 2022. "Blockchain in the Legal Industry." *Consensys*. https:// consensys.net/blockchain-use-cases/law/ (accessed March 16, 2022).

Conway, L. October 4, 2022. "What Is Bitcoin Halving? Definition, How It Works, Why It Matters." *Investopedia*. www.investopedia.com/bitcoin-halving-4843769#:~:text=Bitcoin%20last%20halved%20on%20 May,maximum%20supply%20of%2021%20million.

Cooling, S. September 30, 2021. "Loansnap Launch Bacon Protocol Smart Mortgages and First Stable+ Coin." *Yahoo! Finance.* https://finance.yahoo .com/news/loansnap-launch-bacon-protocol-smart-073013376.html.

Cooper, C. August 16, 2010. "For 20 Million Americans, One Social Security Number's Not Enough." *CBS News.* www.cbsnews.com/news/for-20-million-americans-one-social-security-numbers-not-enough/.

Cooper, D., M. Mkhize, S.J. Choi, and S. Naidoo. December 9, 2021. "Tech Regulation in Africa: Recently Enacted Data Protection Laws." *Inside Privacy.* www.insideprivacy.com/data-privacy/tech-regulation-in-africa-recently-enacted-data-protection-laws/.

CoreLedger. January 22, 2020. "Land Registry on Blockchain." *Coreledger.* https:// medium.com/coreledger/land-registry-on-blockchain-a0da4dd25ea6.

Corrigan, J. November 6, 2018. "CDC Is Testing Blockchain to Monitor the Country's Health in Real Time." *Nextgov.* www.nextgov.com/emerging-tech/ 2018/11/cdc-testing-blockchain-monitor-countrys-health-real-time/152622/.

Cowley, S. November 7, 2023. "Cyberattack Disrupts Mortgage Payments for Millions of Mr. Cooper Customers." *The New York Times.* www.nytimes.com/ 2023/11/07/business/cyberattack-mr-cooper-mortgages.html#:~:text=7%2C %202023-,Mr.,31.

Credentialing Provider Management. November 18, 2021. "What Is Physician Credentialing?" *Verisys* (blog). https://verisys.com/what-is-physician-credentialing/#:~:text=In%20healthcare%2C%20physician%20 credentialing%20is,%2C%20work%20history%2C%20and%20more.

Crockett, Z. May 19, 2018. "The Beanie Baby Bubble of '99." *The Hustle.* https:// thehustle.co/the-great-beanie-baby-bubble-of-99/.

Crypto.com. 2021. "Best Crypto Debit Cards." *Benzinga.* www.benzinga.com/ money/best-crypto-debit-cards (accessed December 5, 2021).

Cryptonews.com. 2022. "Travala.com." *Cryptonews.com.* https://cryptonews .com/coins/travala/#:~:text=Travala%20promises%20to%20combat%20 high,as%20Expedia%20or%20Booking.com (accessed April 4, 2022).

Cryptopedia Staff. May 6, 2021. "Custodial Vs. Non-Custodial Wallets." *Cryptopedia.* www.gemini.com/cryptopedia/crypto-wallets-custodial-vs-noncustodial.

Cryptopedia Staff. August 15, 2021. "Crypto Hacks and What We Can Learn From Them." *Cryptopedia.* www.gemini.com/cryptopedia/mt-gox-bitcoin-exchange-hacked.

Cryptopedia Staff. November 30, 2021. "Retail Vs. Industrial-Scale Crypto Mining." *Cryptopedia.* www.gemini.com/cryptopedia/crypto-mining-operation-crypto-mining-rig-asic-miner.

Cryptopedia Staff. June 28, 2022. "What Are Public and Private Keys?" *Cryptopedia.* www.gemini.com/cryptopedia/public-private-keys-cryptography.

Cryptoslate. 2022. "Proof of Work (PoW) Cryptocurrencies." *Cryptoslate*. https://
cryptoslate.com/cryptos/proof-of-work/ (accessed November 25, 2022).

Cudos. 2022. "Censorship, Moderation and Free Speech In Web3." *Cudos* (blog).
www.cudos.org/blog/censorship-moderation-and-free-speech-in-web3/
(accessed September 7, 2022).

Cuofano, G. October 9, 2022. "How Does OpenSea Market Make Money? The
OpenSea Business Model in a Nutshell." *FourWeekMBA*. https://fourweekmba
.com/how-does-opensea-make-money-opensea-business-model/.

Custom Market Insights. August 25, 2022. "Global Blockchain Technology
Market Size Worth $69 Billion by 2030 at a 68% CAGR Check Blockchain
Industry Share, Growth, Trends, Value & Analysis: Custom Market Insights."
Custom Market Insights. www.globenewswire.com/en/news-release/2022/08/25/
2504745/0/en/Global-Blockchain-Technology-Market-Size-Worth-69-Billion-
by-2030-at-a-68-CAGR-Check-Blockchain-Industry-Share-Growth-Trends-
Value-Analysis-Custom-Market-Insights.html#:~:text=The%20blockchain%20
technology%20market%20size,a%20number%20of%20driving%20factors.

Cuthbertson, A. December 11, 2017. "Bitcoin Mining on Track to Consume
All of the World's Energy By 2020." *Newsweek*. www.newsweek.com/bitcoin-
mining-track-consume-worlds-energy-2020-744036.

CyberScrilla. 2022. "What Is a Web3 Browser? A Complete Beginner's Guide."
CyberScrilla. https://cyberscrilla.com/what-is-a-web3-wallet-and-why-is-it-
important/#:~:text=What%20is%20the%20difference%20between,the%20
internet%20and%20multiple%20servers (accessed September 6, 2022).

D'Anastasio, C. November 30, 2021. "The Escapist Fantasy of NFT Games Is
Capitalism." *Wired UK*. www.wired.co.uk/article/escapist-fantasy-of-nft-games-
is-capitalism.

Daley, S. September 19, 2022. "8 Crypto Loan Companies Using Blockchain
for Lending." *Built In*, Updated by Jessica Powers. https://builtin.com/
blockchain/lending-loans-borrowing-mortgages.

Daly, L. June 28, 2022. "What Is Proof of Stake (PoS) in Crypto?" *The
Motley Fool*. www.fool.com/investing/stock-market/market-sectors/financials/
cryptocurrency-stocks/proof-of-stake/.

Daly, L. November 4, 2022. "How Is Cryptocurrency Taxed? 2022 and 2023
IRS Rules." *The Motley Fool*. www.fool.com/investing/stock-market/market-
sectors/financials/cryptocurrency-stocks/crypto-taxes/.

Daniel, D. and C.I. Speranza. May 12, 2020. "The Role of Blockchain in Documenting Land Users' Rights: The Canonical Case of Farmers in the Vernacular Land
Market." *Frontiers in Blockchain*. www.frontiersin.org/articles/10.3389/fbloc
.2020.00019/full#:~:text=Land%20Administration%20Context-,Blockchain
%20technology%20is%20a%20peer%2Dto%2Dpeer%20protocol%20that
%20can,the%20management%20of%20land%20rights.

Darby, N. July 27, 2021. "The Nuisance of Eavesdroppers. Dr. Neil Darby Criminal Historian." *Dr. Neil Darby Criminal Historian* (blog). www .criminalhistorian.com/the-nuisance-of-eavesdroppers/.

Davies, D. March 3, 2021. "Meet the 7 Most Popular Search Engines in the World." *Search Engine Journal.* www.searchenginejournal.com/seo-guide/ meet-search-engines/#:~:text=1.,any%20list%20of%20search%20engines.

de Best, R. July 27, 2022. "Size of the Bitcoin Blockchain From January 2009 to July 11, 2022." *Statista.* www.statista.com/statistics/647523/worldwide-bitcoin-blockchain-size/.

de Best, R. December 2, 2022. "Bitcoin (BTC) Price Per Day From April 2013 to December 1, 2022." *Statista.* www.statista.com/statistics/326707/bitcoin-price-index/.

De Groot, J. August 22, 2022. "The History of Data Breeches." *Digital Guardian.* https://digitalguardian.com/blog/history-data-breaches.

De Marco, N. September 27, 2018. "The Rise of Voice Control in the Internet of Things." *TechTarget.* www.techtarget.com/iotagenda/blog/IoT-Agenda/The-rise-of-voice-control-in-the-internet-of-things#:~:text=The%20current%20players %20in%20the,controlled%20applications%20within%20the%20iPhone.

Dean, B. March 8, 2021. "Google Chrome Statistics for 2022." *Backlink.* https:// backlinko.com/chrome-users.

Dean, B. March 9, 2021. "Ad Blocker Usage and Demographic Statistics in 2022." *Backlink.* https://backlinko.com/ad-blockers-users.

DeCambre, M. May 22, 2021. "Bitcoin Pizza Day? Laszlo Hanyecz Spent $3.8 Billion on Pizzas in the Summer of 2010 Using the Novel Crypto." *MarketWatch.* www.marketwatch.com/story/bitcoin-pizza-day-laszlo-hanyecz-spent-3-8-billion-on-pizzas-in-the-summer-of-2010-using-the-novel-crypto-11621714395.

DEEDS.com. February 3, 2022. "Sotheby's International Realty Gives Its Blessing to the Metaverse." *DEEDS.com.* www.deeds.com/articles/sothebys-international-realty-gives-its-blessing-to-the-metaverse/.

Deign, J. October 29, 2018. "WePower Is the First Blockchain Firm to Tokenize an Entire Grid." *Blockchain.* www.greentechmedia.com/articles/read/wepower-is-the-first-blockchain-firm-to-tokenize-an-entire-grid.

Deloitte. 2022. "Using blockchain to Drive Supply Chain Transparency." *Deloitte.* www2.deloitte.com/us/en/pages/operations/articles/blockchain-supply-chain-innovation.html (accessed February 19, 2022).

Dentons. April 26, 2023. "Worldwide Wednesdays: Dentons Tech Talks|Global Cryptocurrency Laws: Mica Regulation in the EU." *Dentons.* www .dentons.com/en/insights/articles/2023/april/26/worldwide-wednesdays-dentons-tech-talks-global-cryptocurrency-laws-mica-regulation-in-the-eu#:~:text=EU%20legislators%20aim%20to%20restore,to%201-8-month%20transition%20period.

Desbiens, V. March 16, 2022. "You Can't Put a Love Lock on Pont Des Arts, and Here's What Else to Plan for Before Visiting." *The Travel*. www.thetravel.com/pont-des-arts-can-you-still-do-love-locks-in-paris/.

Deutsche Telekom. n.d. "5G Network as Foundation for Autonomous Driving." *Deutsche Telekom* (blog). www.telekom.com/en/company/details/5g-network-as-foundation-for-autonomous-driving-561986/.

Dev. November 8, 2021. "How to Understand Liquidity When It Comes to NFTs." *Metapherse*. https://medium.com/metapherse/how-to-understand-liquidity-when-it-comes-to-nfts-4f605098de8f (accessed July 26, 2022).

Di Gregorio, M. February 3, 2022. "Blockchain: A New Tool to Cut Costs." *PWC*. www.pwc.com/m1/en/media-centre/articles/blockchain-new-tool-to-cut-costs.html.

Dinsmore. April 5, 2022. "EU Lawmakers Vote to Regulate Digital Wallets." *Dinsmore*. www.dinsmore.com/publications/eu-lawmakers-vote-to-regulate-digital-wallets/.

Doc.ai: a Sharecare company. January 6, 2018. "Doc.ai for Patients and Consumers to Initiate Data Trials." *YouTube video*, 2:16. www.youtube.com/watch?v=nWMfRnqr_cA&ab_channel=doc.ai%3AaSharecarecompany.

Downey, L. April 30, 2021. "What Are Transaction Costs? Definition, How They Work and Example." *Investopedia*. www.investopedia.com/terms/t/transactioncosts.asp.

Dquindia Online. September 17, 2021. "Top 5 Uses of Blockchain in Banking." *Dataquest*. www.dqindia.com/top-5-uses-blockchain-banking/.

Dragonchain. August 27, 2019. "Self Sovereign Identity and Decentralized Identity—Control Your Data." *Dragonchain*. https://dragonchain.com/blog/decentralized-identity-self-sovereign-identity-explained.

EAS Intelligence. November 14, 2019. "Blockchain Likely to Make a Safe Landing in Aviation Sector." *EAS Intelligence*. www.eos-intelligence.com/perspectives/transportation/blockchain-likely-to-make-a-safe-landing-in-aviation-sector/.

Ebiekutan, M. August 5, 2022. "The Best Social Media Platforms for Web3 Communities—4 Social Media to Launch Your Community." *SignVM*. www.signvm.io/post/the-best-social-media-platforms-for-web3-communities.

Edwards, B. July 12, 2014. "Where Online Services Go When They Die." *The Atlantic*. www.theatlantic.com/technology/archive/2014/07/where-online-services-go-when-they-die/374099/.

Edwards, J. July 2, 2022. "Bitcoin's Price History." *Investopedia*. www.investopedia.com/articles/forex/121815/bitcoins-price-history.asp.

Egan, M. November 14, 2022. "Bankrupt Crypto Exchange FTX Is Under Criminal Investigation in the Bahamas." *CNN Business*. https://edition.cnn.com/2022/11/13/business/ftx-bahamas-criminal-investigation/index.html.

Eisinger, J. April 30, 2014. "Why Only One Top Banker Went to Jail for the Financial Crisis." *The New York Times Magazine*. www.nytimes .com/2014/05/04/magazine/only-one-top-banker-jail-financial-crisis.html.

Ellis, J. November 2, 2022. "What Is a Legal Personality?" *MyLawQuestions.com*. www.mylawquestions.com/what-is-a-legal-personality.htm.

Ellsmoor, J. April 27, 2019. "Meet 5 Companies Spearheading Blockchain for Renewable Energy." *Forbes*. www.forbes.com/sites/jamesellsmoor/2019/ 04/27/meet-5-companies-spearheading-blockchain-for-renewable-energy/? sh=5c5f37d9f2ae.

Emergen Research. April 7, 2022. "Top 7 Leading Companies in the Blockchain Supply Chain Industry." *Emergen Research*. www.emergenresearch .com/blog/top-7-leading-companies-in-the-blockchain-supply-chain-industry.

Enerdata. 2022. "Norway Energy Information." *Enerdata*. www.enerdata.net/ estore/energy-market/norway/ (accessed October 26, 2022).

Escalante-De Mattei, S. March 23, 2023. "Code Is Not Law: Case on Who Owns the First NFT Dismissed by Judge." *ARTnews*. www.artnews.com/art-news/news/kevin-mccoy-quantum-case-dismissed-free-holdings-sothebys-1234662076/.

Euromoney Learning. 2022. "The Rise of Private Blockchains." *Euromoney Learning*. www.euromoney.com/learning/blockchain-explained/the-rise-of-private-blockchains (accessed February 5, 2022).

European Parliament News. April 20, 2023. "Crypto-Assets: Green Light to New Rules for Tracing Transfers In the EU." *European Parliament News*. www .europarl.europa.eu/news/en/press-room/20230414IPR80133/crypto-assets-green-light-to-new-rules-for-tracing-transfers-in-the-eu.

Everledger. 2022. "How Fashion Brands Are Taking Advantage of Blockchain Apparel." *Everledger*. https://everledger.io/how-fashion-brands-are-taking-advantage-of-blockchain-apparel/ (accessed February 22, 2022).

Exmundo, J. March 21, 2023. "Quantum: The Story Behind the World's First NFT." *NFT Now*. https://nftnow.com/art/quantum-the-first-piece-of-nft-art-ever-created/#:~:text=So%20what%20was%20the%20first,NFT%20by%20 Kevin%20in%202014.

Fabricating Metalworking. April 27, 2018. "There's No Place Like Home: 5G Heralds the Rise of Smart Home Appliances." *Fabricating Metalworking*. www.fabricatingandmetalworking.com/2018/04/theres-no-place-like-home-5g-heralds-the-rise-of-smart-home-appliances/#:~:text=We're%20 entering%20a%20brave,or%20by%20using%20a%20mobile.

Fatemi, F. January 24, 2022. "Here's How NFTs Could Define the Future of Music." *Forbes*. www.forbes.com/sites/falonfatemi/2022/01/24/nfts-and-the-future-of-music/?sh=1436c3af5677.

Fauna. October 31, 2021. "What Is Web3 and Why Is It important?" *Fauna*. https://fauna.com/blog/what-is-web3-and-why-is-it-important.

Federal Bureau of Investigation. 2022. *Skimming*. Federal Bureau of Investigation. www.fbi.gov/how-we-can-help-you/safety-resources/scams-and-safety/common-scams-and-crimes/skimming#:~:text=Criminals%20use%20the%20data%20 to,than%20%241%20billion%20each%20year (accessed October 7, 2022).

Federal Trade Commission Consumer Advice. 2022. "How to Protect Your Privacy on Apps." *Federal Trade Commission Consumer Advice*. https://consumer.ftc .gov/articles/how-protect-your-privacy-apps (accessed August 24, 2022).

Feetham, N. February 2, 2022. "A Brief History of Tokens and How They Converge With Modern Crypto." *Lexology*. www.lexology.com/library/detail .aspx?g=57e3ba14-ae4b-45a5-95cb-e14d0eb92caf.

Ferenstein, G. November 25, 2015. "The Birth and Death of Privacy: 3,000 Years of History Told Through 46 Images." *The Ferestein Wire*. https://medium .com/the-ferenstein-wire/the-birth-and-death-of-privacy-3-000-years-of-history-in-50-images-614c26059e.

Ferraro, E. May 28, 2022. "What Does Ownership Mean in Web3?" *Figment* (Blog). www.figment.io/resources/what-does-ownership-mean-in-web3.

Ferreira, A. June 19, 2021. "Smart Contracts and the Law: Tech Developments Challenge Legal Community." *Cointelegraph*. https://cointelegraph.com/news/ smart-contracts-and-the-law-tech-developments-challenge-legal-community.

Fessenden, M. November 30, 2015. "What Was the First Thing Sold on the Internet?" *Smart News*. www.smithsonianmag.com/smart-news/what-was-first-thing-sold-internet-180957414/.

Fontinelle, A. June 9, 2022. "The Most Common Types of Consumer Fraud." *Investopedia*. www.investopedia.com/financial-edge/0512/the-most-common-types-of-consumer-fraud.aspx.

Forbes. May 31, 1999. "Dig More Coal—The PCs Are Coming." *Forbes*. www .forbes.com/forbes/1999/0531/6311070a.html?sh=697e414a2580.

Forman-Katz, N., E. Shearer, and K.E. Masta. April 29, 2022. "Nonprofit News Outlets Are Playing a Growing Role in Statehouse Coverage." *Pew Research Center*. www.pewresearch.org/fact-tank/2022/04/29/nonprofit-news-outlets-are-playing-a-growing-role-in-statehouse-coverage/#:~:text=Pew%20 Research%20Center's%20accounting%20of,outlets%20that%20cover%20 U.S.%20statehouses.

Fowler, G. August 2, 2021. "Building the Next Level of Customer Loyalty Through Tokenization." *Forbes*. www.forbes.com/sites/forbesbusiness developmentcouncil/2021/08/02/building-the-next-level-of-customer-loyalty-through-tokenization/?sh=4f77daa5132b.

Fractal. April 27, 2022. "Decentralized Identity Challenges and How to Tackle Them." *Fractal*. https://medium.com/frctls/decentralized-identity-challenges-how-to-tackle-them-7bf1f36e5f2c.

Frank, R. February 1, 2022. "Metaverse Real Estate Sales Top $500 Million, and Are Projected to Double This Year." *CNBC*. www.cnbc.com/2022/02/01/ metaverse-real-estate-sales-top-500-million-metametric-solutions-says.html.

Frankenfield, J. July 20, 2021. "DigiCash." *Investopedia*. www.investopedia.com/terms/d/digicash.asp.

Frankenfield, J. August 24, 2021. "What Is a Merkel Root (Cryptocurrency)? How It Works in Blockchain." *Investopedia*. www.investopedia.com/terms/m/merkle-root-cryptocurrency.asp.

Frankenfield, J. November 3, 2021. "Ripple." *Investopeida*. www.investopedia.com/terms/r/ripple-cryptocurrency.asp#:~:text=Ripple%20is%20a%20blockchain%2Dbased,owned%20servers%2C%20to%20confirm%20transactions.

Frankenfield, J. November 12, 2021. "What Is Sharding? Purpose, How It Works, Security, and Benefits." *Investopedia*. www.investopedia.com/terms/s/sharding.asp.

Frankenfield, J. January 3, 2022. "Initial Coin Offering (ICO): Coin Lunch Defined, With Examples." *Investopedia*. www.investopedia.com/terms/i/initial-coin-offering-ico.asp#:~:text=Initial%20coin%20offerings%20(ICOs)%20are,have%20yielded%20returns%20for%20investors.

Frankenfield, J. March 24, 2022. "Virtual Currency: Definition, Types, Advantages and Disadvantages." *Investopedia*. www.investopedia.com/terms/v/virtual-currency.asp#:~:text=Virtual%20currencies%20are%20a%20form,physical%20incarnation%20like%20paper%20money.

Frankenfield, J. March 24, 2022. "What Are Smart Contracts on the Blockchain and How They Work." *Investopedia*. www.investopedia.com/terms/s/smart-contracts.asp.

Frankenfield, J. May 20, 2022. "What Are Crypto Tokens, and How Do They Work?" *Investopedia*. www.investopedia.com/terms/c/crypto-token.asp#:~:text=Tokens%20are%20created%20through%20an,company%20can%20purchase%20these%20tokens.

Frankenfield, J. August 13, 2022. "The Turing Test: What Is It, What Can Pass It, and Limitations." *Investopedia*. www.investopedia.com/terms/t/turing-test.asp.

Frankenfield, J. September 27, 2022. "What Does Proof-of-Stake (PoS) Mean in Crypto?" *Investopedia*. www.investopedia.com/terms/p/proof-stake-pos.asp.

FreshByte Software. November 4, 2021. "Food Fraud Costs Billions Each Year." *FreshByte Software*. www.freshbyte.com/blog/food-fraud-costs-billions-each-year.

Froehlich, A. 2022. "Walled Garden." *TechTarget*. www.techtarget.com/searchsecurity/definition/walled-garden#:~:text=On%20the%20internet%2C%20a%20walled,prevent%20access%20to%20other%20material (accessed November 6, 2022).

Fuentes, R. September 6, 2022. "What Is Sharding and How Is It Helping Blockchain Protocols?" *Rootstrap*. www.rootstrap.com/blog/what-is-sharding-and-how-is-it-helping-blockchain-protocols/#:~:text=The%20most%20important%20advantage%20of,significantly%20slowing%20down%20transaction%20times.

Gaur, V. and A. Gaiha. May–June 2020 "Building a Transparent Supply Chain." *Harvard Business Review.* https://hbr.org/2020/05/building-a-transparent-supply-chain.

GDPR.EU. 2022. "What Is GDPR, the EU's New Data Protection Law?" *GDPR. EU.* https://gdpr.eu/what-is-gdpr/ - :~:text=The%20General%20Data %20Protection%20Regulation,to%20people%20in%20the%20EU (accessed January 18, 2022).

Gebbing, H. and W. Nöffke. August 16, 2021. "Regulating Crypto Is Essential to Ensuring Its Global Legitimacy." *TechCrunch.com.* https://techcrunch .com/2021/08/16/regulating-crypto-is-essential-to-ensuring-its-global-legitimacy/.

Geeks for Geeks. June 1, 2022. "Blockchain Protocols and Their Working." *GeeksforGeeks.org.* www.geeksforgeeks.org/blockchain-protocols-and-their-working/.

Geroni, D. January 28, 2021. "Hybrid Blockchain: The Best of Both Worlds." *101 Blockchains.* https://101blockchains.com/hybrid-blockchain/.

Geroni, D. April 5, 2021. "Blockchain Nodes: An In-Depth Guide." *101 Blockchains.* https://101blockchains.com/blockchain-nodes/.

Geroni, D. August 16, 2021. "Everything You Need to Know About Tokenization." *101 Blockchains.* https://101blockchains.com/tokenization-blockchain/.

Geyser, W. May 16, 2022. "The Top 11 NFT Games You Should Check Out in 2022." *Influencer Marketing Hub.* https://influencermarketinghub.com/nft-games/.

Gillis, A.S. 2022. "Biometrics." *TechTarget.* www.techtarget.com/searchsecurity/definition/biometrics (accessed October 7, 2022).

Gillis, A.S. 2022. "What Is the Internet of Things (IoT)?" *TechTarget.* www .techtarget.com/iotagenda/definition/Internet-of-Things-IoT (accessed August 25, 2022).

Global Data. April 18, 2022. "PayPal History: Looking Back at the Milestones." *Electronic Payments International.* www.electronicpaymentsinternational .com/news/paypal-history-milestones/.

GoCardless. September 2021. "How to Validate Bitcoin Transactions." *GoCardless.* https://gocardless.com/en-us/guides/posts/bitcoin-transaction-verification/#:~:text=Some%20exchanges%20will%20process%20 a,confirmed%20at%20least%20three%20times.

Google Cloud. 2022. "doc.ai: A Mobile AI App Blazes Trails in Medical Research." *Google Cloud.* https://cloud.google.com/customers/doc-ai (accessed February 22, 2022).

GovChain. 2022. "Ghana." *GovChain.* https://govchain.world/ghana/ (accessed March 4, 2022).

Grauer, Y. July 11, 2019. "What Really Happened With West Virginia's Blockchain Voting Experiment?" *Slate.* https://slate.com/technology/2019/07/west-virginia-blockchain-voting-voatz.html.

Graves, S. April 16, 2020. "Status Want to Be the World's Most Private Instant Messaging App." *Decrypt.* https://decrypt.co/25629/status-wants-to-be-the-worlds-most-private-instant-messaging-app.

Greenwood, M. June 21, 2021. "One-Third of Americans Believe Biden Won Because of Voter Fraud: Poll." *The Hill.* https://thehill.com/homenews/campaign/559402-one-third-of-americans-believe-biden-won-because-of-voter-fraud-poll/.

Groves, K. November 23, 2022. "Cryptocurrency Exchange Hacks (Updated 2022 List)." *HedgewithCrypto.* www.hedgewithcrypto.com/cryptocurrency-exchange-hacks/.

Grundy, A. June 7, 2022. "Service Annual Survey Shows Continuing Decline in Print Publishing Revenue." *United States Census Bureau.* www.census.gov/library/stories/2022/06/internet-crushes-traditional-media.html.

Gupta, P. July 5, 2021. "Security Challenges in the 5G World and How to Overcome Them." *Forbes.* www.forbes.com/sites/forbestechcouncil/2021/07/05/security-challenges-in-the-5g-world-and-how-to-overcome-them/?sh=58a68185ee9c.

Gutermuth, L. February 24, 2017. 2 "How to Understand What Info Mobile Apps Are Collecting About You." *Slate.* https://slate.com/technology/2017/02/how-to-understand-what-info-mobile-apps-collect-about-you.html.

Guttmann, A. November 11, 2022. "Average Loyalty Program Membership in the United States From 2015 To 2022." *Statista.* www.statista.com/statistics/618744/average-number-of-loyalty-programs-us-consumers-belong-to/.

Haidar, F. June 19, 2022. "India Sotheby's International Realty to Enter Metaverse With Virtual Design and NFT Real Estate." *The Economic Times.* https://economictimes.indiatimes.com/industry/services/property-/-cstruction/india-sothebys-international-realty-to-enter-metaverse-with-virtual-design-and-nft-real-estate/articleshow/92315573.cms?from=mdr.

Halton, C. August 27, 2021. "Debasement." *Investopedia.* www.investopedia.com/terms/d/debasement.asp.

Hamacher, A. March 22, 2021. "Satoshi Nakamoto's View on Bitcoin's Energy Consumption Resurfaces." *Decrypt.* https://decrypt.co/62338/satoshi-nakamotos-view-on-bitcoins-energy-consumption-resurfaces.

Hamilton, L. July 1, 2022. "Privacy Laws in Southeast Asia." *TermsFeed.* www.termsfeed.com/blog/privacy-laws-southeast-asia/.

Hammad & Al-Mehdar Law Firm. May 29, 2022. "What Is the Legal Impact of Web 3?" *Lexology.* www.lexology.com/library/detail.aspx?g=bf5a9c9c-dee6-40e1-be70-dd81d688dfa0.

Hanson, J. April 9, 2021. "The Keys to Decentralized Identity." *YouTube video,* 32:46. www.youtube.com/watch?v=gWfAIYXcyH4&t=1369s&ab_channel=Okta.

Harbert, T. February 21, 2019. "Here's How Much the 2008 Bailouts Really Cost." *MIT Sloan School of Management.* https://mitsloan.mit.edu/ideas-made-to-matter/heres-how-much-2008-bailouts-really-cost.

Harford, T. September 11, 2017. "How Chinese Mulberry Bark Paved the Way for Paper Money." *BBC News.* www.bbc.com/news/business-40879028.

Harper, J. March 23, 2021. "Jack Dorsey's First Ever Tweet Sells for $2.9M." *BBC News.* www.bbc.com/news/business-56492358.

Hayes, A. February 13, 2022. "What Is a Basic Attention Token (BAT)? How It Tracks Consumers." *Investopedia.* www.investopedia.com/terms/b/basic-attention-token.asp.

Hayes, A. October 4, 2022. "Stablecoins: Definition, How They Work, and Types." *Investopedia.* www.investopedia.com/terms/s/stablecoin.asp#:~:text=Stablecoins%20are%20cryptocurrencies%20that%20attempt,a%20commodity%20such%20as%20gold.

Heasman, W. April 23, 2020. "Power Leger Rolls Out Blockchain-Based Microgrid in Australia." *Decrypt.* https://decrypt.co/26478/power-ledger-rolls-out-blockchain-based-microgrid-in-australia.

Helen You, G. December 7, 2021. "Why Congress Should Regulate Cryptocurrency Now." *Foreign Policy.* https://foreignpolicy.com/2021/12/07/cryptocurrency-regulation-congress-hearing-stablecoin-digital-currency/.

Henderson, J. May 17, 2020. "De Beers Tracks 100 Diamonds Through Supply Chain Using Blockchain." *Supply Chain.* https://supplychaindigital.com/technology/de-beers-tracks-100-diamonds-through-supply-chain-using-blockchain.

Hendrix, C. October 8, 2019. "6 Fascinating Things About Western Union's History." *Western Union.* www.westernunion.com/blog/en/6-fascinating-things-about-western-unions-history/.

Hennekes, B. April 6, 2022. "The 8 Most Important Types of DAOs You Need to Know." *Alchemy* (Blog). www.alchemy.com/blog/types-of-daos#:~:text=There%20are%20eight%20main%20types,Protocol%20DAOs.

Hereward, J. and C. Curtis. February 1, 2018. "Your DNA Could Become the Next Cryptocurrency." *World Economic Forum.* www.weforum.org/agenda/2018/02/new-cryptocurrencies-could-let-you-control-and-sell-access-to-your-dna-data.

Hertig, A. September 16, 2022. "What Is a Stablecoin?" *CoinDesk.* www.coindesk.com/learn/what-is-a-stablecoin/.

Home Loan Experts. 2022. "Blockchain Mortgage." *Home Loan Experts.* www.homeloanexperts.com.au/home-loan-articles/blockchain-mortgage/ (accessed February 9, 2022).

Hooper, A. November 2, 2020. "Transaction Fees, Explained." *Cointelegraph.* https://cointelegraph.com/explained/transaction-fees-explained.

Hosoi, J. February 10, 2017. "What Is Timestamping?" *GlobalSign.* www .globalsign.com/en/blog/what-is-timestamping-how-does-it-work.

Houston, R. March 25, 2022. "OpenSea Vs. Mintable: How the NFT Marketplaces Compare." *Insider.* www.businessinsider.com/personal-finance/ opensea-vs-mintable.

Howarth, J. November 3, 2023. "How Many Cryptocurrencies Are There in 2024?" (Blog). *Exploding Topics.* https://explodingtopics.com/blog/number-of-cryptocurrencies.

Howell, J. February 25, 2022. "Internet of Things and Web 3.0." *101 Blockchains.* https://101blockchains.com/internet-of-things-and-web-3-0/.

Howell, J. June 23, 2022. "Blockchain Sharding a Comprehensive Guide." *101 Blockchains.* https://101blockchains.com/what-is-blockchain-sharding/#:~: text=In%20the%20case%20of%20sharding,latency%20and%20 prevent%20data%20overload.

Huang, J., C. O'Neill, and H. Tabuchi. September 3, 2021. "Bitcoin Uses More Electricity Than Many Countries. How Is That Possible?" *The New York Times.* www.nytimes.com/interactive/2021/09/03/climate/bitcoin-carbon-footprint-electricity.html.

Hyperbeast. February 2, 2022. "OpenSea Sets New Record With $5 Billion in Monthly NFT Sales." *Hyperbeast.* https://hypebeast.com/2022/2/opensea-new-record-nft-sales-january-2022.

Iacurci, G. May 17, 2021. "Elon Musk Impersonators Stole More Than $2 Million in Crypto Scams, Regulator Says." *CNBC.* www.cnbc.com/2021/05/17/elon-musk-impersonators-stole-more-than-2-million-in-crypto-scams-.html.

Ian Porter Museum of Art. 2022. "'Easedropping': A Collaboration Between Liquid Architecture and Melbourne Law School." *Digicult.* https://digicult.it/ articles/sound/eavesdropping-a-collaboration-between-liquid-architecture-and-melbourne-law-school/ (accessed January 18, 2022).

Ibrisevic, I. July 29, 2022. "Nonprofit Journalism: Funding, Surviving, and Thriving." *Donorbox* (Blog). https://donorbox.org/nonprofit-blog/nonprofit-journalism-funding#:~:text=Nonprofit%20news%20organizations%20 focus%20on,media%20organizations%20are%20decades%2Dold.

IDC. April 19, 2021. "Global Spending on Blockchain Solutions Forecast to Be Narly $19 Billion in 2024, According to New IDC Spending Guide." *International Data Corporation.* www.businesswire.com/news/ home/20210419005059/en/Global-Spending-on-Blockchain-Solutions-Forecast-to-be-Nearly-19-Billion-in-2024-According-to-New-IDC-Spending-Guide.

IDnow. 2022. "EU Extends TFR to Crypto, Requiring KYC for All Crypto Transactions." *IDnow.* www.idnow.io/blog/transfer-of-funds-crypto/#:~:text=

Updates%20to%20the%20TFR%20regulation,European%20licensing%20
scheme%20for%20CASPs (accessed December 27, 2022).

IMS Technology Services. 2022. "Internet of Things and Web 3.0: How They
Will Affect Your Meeting." *IMS Technology Services.* https://imsts.com/
internet-of-things-and-web-3-0-how-they-will-affect-your-meeting (accessed
August 25, 2022).

InCoins. 2022. "Early Token History." *InCoins.* www.jncoins.co.uk/Shop/
content/26-early-token-history (accessed October 24, 2022).

Index Mundi. April 2, 2022. "International Expenditures, Tourism (Current
US$)—Country Ranking." *Index Mundi.* www.indexmundi.com/facts/
indicators/ST.INT.XPND.CD/rankings.

Infoplease Staff. February 11, 2017. "A Brief History of Checking."
Infoplease. www.infoplease.com/business/consumer-resources/brief-history-
checking.

Information Governance. April 16, 2019. "Yes, Blockchain Can Be Hacked:
3 Ways It Can Be Done." *Epiq Global* (Blog). www.epiqglobal.com/en-us/
resource-center/articles/blockchain-can-be-hacked.

International Banker. September 29, 2021. "The Dotcom Bubble Burst (2000)."
International Banker. https://internationalbanker.com/history-of-financial-
crises/the-dotcom-bubble-burst-2000/#:~:text=And%20it%20was%20
this%20overvaluation,1999%20and%20380%20in%202000.

Iredale, G. January 10, 2021. "Public Vs Private Blockchain: How Do They
Differ?" *101 Blockchains.* https://101blockchains.com/public-vs-private-
blockchain/.

Iryo. December 18, 2017. "Iryo Is Bringing Medical Records in the Hands of
the Patients."*Youtube video.* www.youtube.com/watch?v=6irGhqNZj68&ab_
channel=Iryo.

Iryo. March 9, 2018. "Healthcare Blockchain Startup Iryo Aims to Disrupt
Medical Data Ownership by Giving Full Control to the Patient." *Iryo.*
www.prnewswire.com/in/news-releases/healthcare-blockchain-startup-iryo-
aims-to-disrupt-medical-data-ownership-by-giving-full-control-to-the-
patient-676361703.html.

Ivy, K. March 18, 2022. "What Is Compound Finance?" *The Defiant.* https://
thedefiant.io/what-is-compound-crypto.

Jain, A. November 9, 2022. "List of 7 Best Web 3.0 Browsers (2022)." *browsertouse.
com* (Blog). https://browsertouse.com/blog/5098/best-web-3-0-browsers/.

Jarrard, K. May 10, 2012. "Where Do E-Books Go When You Do?" *The New
York Times.* www.nytimes.com/2012/05/11/opinion/where-do-e-books-go-
when-you-do.html#:~:text=Here's%20what%20I%20got%20back,be%20
accessed%20by%20that%20person. July 4, 2022.

Jatain, V. August 12, 2020. "Countering the Revenue Loss Caused by Ad Blockers." *Digital Content Next.* https://digitalcontentnext.org/blog/2020/08/12/countering-the-revenue-loss-caused-by-ad-blockers/.

Jennings, P. October 24, 2022. "Best Sport NFT Drops and Collectibles in 2022." *Business 2 Community.* www.business2community.com/nft/sport-nft-drops.

Jiang, S., Y. Li, Q. Lu, Y. Hong, D. Guan, Y. Xiong, and S. Wang. April 6, 2021. "Policy Assessments for the Carbon Emission Flows and Sustainability of Bitcoin Blockchain Operation in China." *Nature Communications.* www.nature.com/articles/s41467-021-22256-3.

Joshi, N. June 6, 2022. "3 Applications of NFTs in Real Estate." *BBN Times.* www.bbntimes.com/financial/3-applications-of-nfts-in-real-estate.

Balakumar, K. May 26, 2021. "Google Chrome Browser Now Has More Than 3 Billion Users." *Techradar.* www.techradar.com/news/google-chrome-browser-now-has-more-than-3-billion-users.

Kahn, J. March 2, 2022. "Bob Dylan Revealed as Founder of New NFT Project." *Far Out.* https://faroutmagazine.co.uk/bob-dylan-revealed-as-founder-of-new-nft-project/.

Kamiya, G. July 5, 2019. "Bitcoin Energy Use—Mined the Gap." *International Energy Association.* www.iea.org/commentaries/bitcoin-energy-use-mined-the-gap.

Kasireddy, P. February 19, 2018. "What Do Me Mean by "Blockchains Are Trustless"?" *Preethi Kasireddy* (Blog). www.preethikasireddy.com/post/what-do-we-mean-by-blockchains-are-trustless.

Kastrenakes, J. March 11, 2021. "Beeple Sold an NFT for $69 Million." *The Verge.* www.theverge.com/2021/3/11/22325054/beeple-christies-nft-sale-cost-everydays-69-million.

Kay, G. March 20, 2021. "We Talked to Crypto-Art Investors to Figure Out What's Driving People to Spend Millions on NFTs, Despite No Guarantee Their Value Will Increase." *Insider.* www.businessinsider.com/why-are-people-buying-nfts-investing-in-nft-crypto-art-2021-3.

Keiser, G. April 8, 2021. "The Brave Browser Basics: What It Does, How It Differs From Rivals." *Computerworld.* www.computerworld.com/article/3292619/the-brave-browser-basics-what-it-does-how-it-differs-from-rivals.html#:~:text=The%20web%20browser%20from%20Brave,money%20to%20sites%20they%20like.&text=Boutique%20browsers%20try%20to%20scratch,underserved%20by%20the%20usual%20suspects.

Keller, L. October 19, 2022. "EU Targets Bitcoin With Energy Efficiency Labeling for Crypto." *Forkast.* https://forkast.news/eu-bitcoin-energy-efficiency-labelling-crypto/.

Kenney, A. March 8, 2019. "Denver Offers Blockchain Voting to Military, Overseas Voters." *Government Technology.* www.govtech.com/dc/denver-offers-blockchain-voting-to-military-overseas-voters.html.

Kenny. January 30, 2019. "The Blockchain Scalability Problem and the Race for Visa-Like Transaction Speed." *Towards Data Science*. https:// towardsdatascience.com/the-blockchain-scalability-problem-the-race-for-visa-like-transaction-speed-5cce48f9d44.

Kenton, W. April 18, 2022. "What Are Fungible Goods? Meaning, Examples and How to Trade." *Investopedia*. www.investopedia.com/terms/f/fungibles.asp.

Khodaei, A. September 2, 2021. *Utilities Assess Benefits and Challenges of Decentralizing the Power Grid Through Blockchain Technology*. Utility Analytics Institute. https://utilityanalytics.com/2021/09/utilities-assess-benefits-and-challenges-of-decentralizing-the-power-grid-through-blockchain-technology/.

Kim, C. September 13, 2021. "Sweden's Land Registry Demos Live Transactions on a Blockchain." *CoinDesk*. www.coindesk.com/markets/2018/06/15/swedens-land-registry-demos-live-transaction-on-a-blockchain/.

Kinsella, E. February 22, 2021. "Is This the Next Art Market Bubble? A Unique NFT for the Popular 'Nyam Cat' GIF Just Sold for a Whopping $560,000." *Artnet news*. https://news.artnet.com/market/nyan-cat-nft-sells-for-560000-1945679.

Klosowski, T. September 6, 2021. "The State of Consumer Data Privacy Laws in the US (and Why It Matters)." *The New York Times Wirecutter* (Blog). www.nytimes.com/wirecutter/blog/state-of-privacy-laws-in-us/.

Knapp, A. April 16, 2019. "This Bud's for Blockchain: AB InBev Is Banking on African Farmers." *Forbes*. www.forbes.com/sites/alexknapp/2019/04/16/this-buds-for-blockchain/?sh=62d944845966.

Kolhatkar, S. October 6, 2021. "The Challenges of Regulating Cryptocurrency." *The New Yorker*. www.newyorker.com/business/currency/the-challenges-of-regulating-cryptocurrency.

Kothar, L. January 28, 2022. "How the Gaming Ecosystem Will Evolve in the Web 3.0 Economy." *The Decrypting Story*. https://yourstory.com/the-decrypting-story/gaming-ecosystem-evolve-web3-economy/amp.

Kraken. 2021. "What Is Golem? (GNT) The Beginner's Guide." *Kraken*. www.kraken.com/learn/what-is-golem-gnt golem/#:~:text=Golem%20is%20a%20blockchain%2Dbased,that%20demand%20great%20computing%20power (accessed December 1, 2021).

Kukkuru, M.G. 2022. *Smart Contracts: A Transparent Way to Do Business*. Infosys. www.infosys.com/insights/digital-future/smart-contracts.html (accessed September 27, 2022).

Kunz, D. April 3, 2019. "Why Identity Is a Human Right." *TED Conference Video*, 16:55. www.ted.com/talks/dominique_kunz_why_identity_is_a_human_right.

Kunzi. October 25, 2021. "NFT in the Real Estate Industry: Short-Term Trend or an Investment in the Future?" *Forbes*. www.forbes.com/sites/forbesbizcouncil/2021/10/25/nft-in-the-real-estate-industry-short-term-trend-or-an-investment-in-the-future/?sh=14e46c478d28.

Kyle. June 7, 2018. "Blockchain Issues|#2 Human Error Breeds Catastrophe." *Medium.com* (Blog). https://medium.com/@Kyle.May/blockchain-issues-2-human-error-breeds-catastrophe-679948072da4.

Lea, J. September 2022. "Coincub Annual Crypto Tax Ranking 2022." *Coincub.* https://coincub.com/ranking/coincub-annual-crypto-tax-ranking-2022/.

Leary, K. September 28, 2017. "Illinois Is Experimenting With Blockchains to Replace Physical Birth Certificates." *Futurism.* https://futurism.com/illinois-is-experimenting-with-blockchains-to-replace-physical-birth-certificates.

Ledger Insights. December 10, 2018. "Abu Dhabi Oil Reveals IBM Blockchain Supply Chain Pilot." *Ledger Insights.* www.ledgerinsights.com/abu-dhabi-oil-ibm-blockchain/.

Ledger Insights. January 14, 2019. "Spain's Iberdrola Adopts Blockchain to Prove Energy Is Renewable." *Ledger Insights.* www.ledgerinsights.com/iberdrola-blockchain-renewable-energy-proof/.

Ledger Insights. June 10, 2021. "Leading Healthcare Firms Launch Blockchain Utility Avaneer Health." *Ledger Insights.* www.ledgerinsights.com/leading-healthcare-firms-launch-blockchain-utility-avaneer-health/.

Lehman, R. June 21, 2022. "Where to Buy NFTs: Top 10 Marketplaces." *Seeking Alpha.* https://seekingalpha.com/article/4482960-where-to-buy-nfts.

Lei, N., E. Masanet, and J. Koomey. September 2021. "Best Practices for Analyzing the Direct Energy Use of Blockchain Technology Systems: Review and Policy Recommendations." *Elsevier Energy Policy* 156. www.sciencedirect.com/science/article/pii/S0301421521002925.

Leimer, B. June 2015, 2022. "Web3, DeFI, and the Atonement of Purpose: Is Banking Ready to Answer Tomorrow's Questions?" *International Banker.* https://internationalbanker.com/banking/web3-defi-and-the-atonement-of-purpose-is-banking-ready-to-answer-tomorrows-questions/.

Lennon, H. January 19, 2021. "The False Narrative of Bitcoin's Role in Illicit Activity." *Forbes.* www.forbes.com/sites/haileylennon/2021/01/19/the-false-narrative-of-bitcoins-role-in-illicit-activity/?sh=649487c33432.

Leonhardt, M. March 23, 2021. "Consumers Lost $56 Billion to Identity Fraud Last Year—Here's What to Look Out for." *CNBC Make It.* www.cnbc.com/2021/03/23/consumers-lost-56-billion-dollars-to-identity-fraud-last-year.html.

Lewis, P. December 19, 2020. *Bitcoin Is the Great Definancialization.* Satoshi Nakamoto Institute. https://nakamotoinstitute.org/mempool/bitcoin-is-the-great-definancialization/.

Liebkind, J. March 22, 2020. "How Blockchain Technology Is Changing Real Estate." *Investopedia.* www.investopedia.com/news/how-blockchain-technology-changing-real-estate/.

Liebkind, J. September 22, 2021. "5 Companies Using Blockchain to Change Travel." *Investopedia.* www.investopedia.com/news/6-companies-using-blockchain-change-travel-0/.

Lioudis, N. March 4, 2022. "What Is the Gold Standard? Advantages, Alternatives, and History." *Investopedia.* www.investopedia.com/ask/answers/09/gold-standard.asp.

Liquid. 2022. "Crypto Coin Vs. Token: Understanding the Difference." *Liquid.* https://blog.liquid.com/coin-vs-token (accessed October 11, 2022).

Locke, T. June 11, 2021. "You Could Be Leaving Your Crypto Wallet Open to Hackers—Here's How to Protect It." *CNBC Make It.* www.cnbc.com/2021/06/11/tips-to-help-keep-your-crypto-wallet-secure.html.

Yaqub, M. August 8, 2022. "13 Eye-Opening Average Vacations Cost and Spending Statistics in 2021." *Smart Insights.* www.renolon.com/average-vacations-cost-and-spending-statistics/.

Mafi, N. June 9, 2021. "This Miami Beach Home Is the Most Expensive Ever to Be Bought With Cryptocurrency." *Architectural Digest.* www.architecturaldigest.com/story/miami-beach-home-most-expensive-bought-cryptocurrency.

Magyar, V. September 27, 2020. "Blockchain, Cryptocurrencies, and Vacation Rentals: The Path to Decentralisation." *Rentals United* (Blog). https://rentalsunited.com/blog/blockchain-vacation-rentals/.

Market Decipher. 2022. "Collectibles Market and NFT Market Size, Statistics, Growth Trend Analysis and Forecast Report, 2022—2032." *Market Decipher.* www.marketdecipher.com/report/collectibles-market (accessed July 25, 2022).

Matrix.org. 2022. "Introduction: What Is Matrix?" *Matrix.org.* https://matrix.org/docs/guides/introduction (accessed September 6, 2022).

Matsakis, L. April 19, 2018. "Minds Is the Anti-Facebook That Pays You for Your Time." *Wired.* www.wired.com/story/minds-anti-facebook/#:~:text=Minds%20doesn't%20let%20you,for%20each%20token%20you%20spend.

Matthews, K. July 10, 2018. "How Blockchain Technology Could Help Prevent Medical Fraud." *Health IT.* https://hitconsultant.net/2018/07/10/blockchain-technology-medical-fraud/.

Mavadiya, M. October 13, 2017. "Blockchain Ballot Boxes and Democratizing Distributed Ledger Technology." *Forbes.* www.forbes.com/sites/madhvimavadiya/2017/10/13/blockchain-ballot-boxes/?sh=48aa64e9140d.

McCormick, M. August 30, 2019. "Finally, One Blockchain Solution That Deserves the Buzz." *Forbes.* www.forbes.com/sites/meghanmccormick/2019/08/30/finally-one-blockchain-solution-that-deserves-the-buzz/?sh=496bf5684f9b.

McCullough, B. December 4, 2018. "A Revealing Look at the Dot-com Bubble of 2000—and How It Shapes Our Lives Today." *Ideas. TED.com*. https:// ideas.ted.com/an-eye-opening-look-at-the-dot-com-bubble-of-2000-and-how-it-shapes-our-lives-today/.

McGovern, T. June 1, 2023. "How Many Blockchains Are There in 2023?" *Earthweb*. https://earthweb.com/how-many-blockchains-are-there/.

Medichain. January 19, 2018. "Medichain Showcase Video." *YouTube video*, 2:01. www.youtube.com/watch?v=cO-prfZBmyw&ab_channel=Medicalchain.

Medichain. 2022. "Own Your Health." *Medichain*. https://medicalchain.com/en/ (accessed February 27, 2022).

Medipedia. August 8, 2018. "The Various Types of Crypto Tokens." *Medipedia*. https://medium.com/@medipedia/the-various-types-of-crypto-tokens-26bab8f6622c.

Mehra, A. and J.G. Dale. May 20, 2020. "How Humanitarian Blockchain Can Deliver Fair Labor to Global Supply Chains." *Reliefweb.intl OSHA Services*. https://reliefweb.int/report/world/how-humanitarian-blockchain-can-deliver-fair-labor-global-supply-chains.

Metadium. July 4, 2019. "Decentralized Identifiers: The Easy Guide." *Metadium*. https://medium.com/metadium/decentralized-identifiers-the-easy-guide-fb96429e8b24.

MetaJure Team. January 28, 2016. "Lawyers Waste as Much as Six Hours a Week on Document Management Issues." *Metajure*. https://metajure.com/lawyers-waste-six-hours-a-week-on-document-management-issues-2/.

Micky News. November 6, 2018. "Blockchain Voting to Be Used in New Zealand Politics." *Micky News*. https://micky.com.au/blockchain-voting-to-be-used-in-new-zealand-politics/.

Mikulic, M. December 10, 2020. "Estimated U.S. Economic Loss Due to Counterfeit Drugs as of 2020, By Scenario*." *Statista*. www.statista.com/statistics/1181283/us-cost-due-to-counterfeit-drugs-by-scenario/#:~:text=Based%20on%20estimates%20saying%20the,revenues%20in%20the%20United%20States.

Mileva, G. July 13, 2022. "Top 12 NFT Real Estate Companies to Follow." *Influencer Market Hub*. https://influencermarketinghub.com/nft-real-estate-companies/.

Miller, B. August 7, 2022. "Here's What a Blockchain Property Deed Looks Like." *Government Technology*. www.govtech.com/biz/heres-what-a-blockchain-property-deed-looks-like.html.

Millward, S. May 1, 2018. "Alibaba Rolls Out Blockchain Pilot to Tackle Fake Food Products." *Tech in Asia*. www.techinasia.com/alibaba-fake-food-blockchain-pilot.

Mintlife. March 31, 2021. "Guide to the Barter Economy & the Barter System History." *Intuit MintLife.* https://mint.intuit.com/blog/personal-finance/guide-to-the-barter-economy-the-barter-system-history/.

Moneyland.ch. 2021. "Equity Token." *Moneyland.ch.* www.moneyland.ch/en/equity-token-definition (accessed December 2, 2021).

Moorwand Team. 2021. "A History of Payments: The Growth of the Debit Card." *Moorwand.* www.moorwand.com/a-history-of-payments-the-growth-of-the-debit-card/ (accessed November 12, 2021).

Mora, C., R.L. Rollins, K. Taladay, M.B. Kantar, M. Chock, M. Shamada, and E.C. Franklin. October 2018. "Bitcoin Emissions Alone Could Push Global Warming Above 2°C." *ResearchGate.* www.researchgate.net/publication/328581842_Bitcoin_emissions_alone_could_push_global_warming_above_2C.

Morales, J. October 15, 2021. "NFTs and Gaming: Is Ready Player One Coming True in Our Lifetime?" *MUO.* www.makeuseof.com/nfts-gaming-revolution/.

Moreland, K. September 11, 2020. "How to Read a Blockchain Transaction History." *Ledger Academy.* www.ledger.com/academy/how-to-read-a-blockchains-transaction-history.

Morpheus Labs. December 23, 2020. "Bridging Supply Chain and Its Future With Blockchain." *Morpheus Labs.* www.morpheuslabs.io/bridging-supply-chain-and-its-future-with-blockchain/.

Morrison, S. June 8, 2021. "How a Major Pipeline Got Held for Ransom." *Vox.* www.vox.com/recode/22428774/ransomeware-pipeline-colonial-darkside-gas-prices.

Morton, H. December 16, 2021. "Cryptocurrency 2021 Legislation." *National Conference of State Legislatures.* www.ncsl.org/research/financial-services-and-commerce/cryptocurrency-2021-legislation.aspx.

Moskvitch, K. October 25, 2018. "Estonia May Actually Have a Use for the Blockchain: Green Energy." *Wired UK.* www.wired.co.uk/article/blockchain-energy-renewables-estonia-tokenisation.

Munro, A. August 20, 2019. "Australian Cryptocurrency Horizon State Collapses Under Lawsuit From Founder Oren Alazraki." *Finder.* www.finder.com.au/australian-cryptocurrency-horizon-state-collapses-under-lawsuit-from-founder-oren-alazraki.

Murray, T. January 16, 2021. "A Man Who Says He Threw Away a Hard Drive Loaded With 7,500 Bitcoins in 2013 Is Offering His City $70 Million to Dig It Up From the Dump." *Insider.* www.businessinsider.com/man-offers-council-70-million-dig-up-bitcoin-hard-drive-2021-1.

N26. November 15, 2021. "What Is an NFT, and Should You Invest in Them?" *N26.* https://n26.com/en-eu/blog/what-is-an-nft.

Napoletano, E. and B. Curry. April 8, 2022. "Proof of Stake Explained." *Forbes Advisor.* www.forbes.com/advisor/investing/cryptocurrency/proof-of-stake/.

NatWest Group History 100. 2021. "Goldsmith's Ledger 1671-72." *NatWest Group Heritage Hub.* www.natwestgroup.com/heritage/history-100/ objects-by-theme/turning-points/goldsmiths-ledger-1671-72.html (accessed November 12, 2021).

NCSL. December 2017. "Combatting Health Care Fraud, WASTE and Abuse—Health Cost Containment." *National Conference of State Legislatures.* www.ncsl.org/research/health/combating-health-care-fraud-and-abuse.aspx#:~:text=%22%20Health%20Care%20Fraud%20Is%20 Costly,harming%20both%20patients%20and%20taxpayers.

Needham, J. March 3, 2022. "Dolly Parton to Launch the 'Dollyverse', A Web3 Experience Offering 'Limited-Edition NFTS'." *Music Business Worldwide.* www.musicbusinessworldwide.com/dolly-parton-to-launch-the-dollyverse-a-web3-experience-offering-limited-edition-nfts1/#:~:text=Parton%20has%20 partnered%20with%20FOX,and%20certified%20Dolly%20NFT%20 collectibles%E2%80%9D.

New America. December 15, 2020. "Restoring Trust in Public Land Registries." *New America* (Blog). www.newamerica.org/digital-impact-governance-initiative/digital-impact-and-governance-initiative/digi-blogs/project-capsule-georgia-land-titling-system/.

Newbery, E. July 22, 2022. "SuperRare NFT Marketplace Review: A Serious Art-Focused Platform." *The Ascent.* www.fool.com/the-ascent/cryptocurrency/ nfts/superrare-review/.

Newsbtc. 2017. "ATLANT Is Using Blockchain to Disrupt the Real Estate Ecosystem." *Newsbtc.* www.newsbtc.com/news/atlant-blockchain-real-estate-ecosystem/#:~:text=ATLANT's%20blockchain%20platform%20is%20 designed,property%20on%20a%20distributed%20ledger.

Newsbtc. 2022. "What Does the End of Net Neutrality Mean for Cryptocurrency." *Newsbtc.* www.newsbtc.com/opinion/end-net-neutrality-mean-cryptocurrency/ (accessed September 7, 2022).

Ngak, C. July 6, 2011. "Then and Now: A History of Social Networking Sites." *CBS News.* www.cbsnews.com/pictures/then-and-now-a-history-of-social-networking-sites/.

Niland, J. January 7, 2022. "ONE Sotheby's Unveils New Digital Twin NFT Home Project." *Archinect News.* https://archinect.com/news/article/150293580/ one-sotheby-s-unveils-new-digital-twin-nft-home-project.

O'Brien, K. 2018. "Japanese City Introduces Blockchain-Based Voting System." *Bitcoinist.* https://bitcoinist.com/japanese-city-introduces-blockchain-based-voting-system/.

O'Connell, B. March 3, 2021. "Guide to Insurance on Cryptocurrency." *Insurance Thought Leadership.com.* www.insurancethoughtleadership.com/emerging-technologies/guide-insurance-cryptocurrency.

O'Melveny. April 11, 2022. "What the DAO? Why Everyone Is Talking About Decentralized Autonomous Organizations." *O'Melveny.* www.omm.com/resources/alerts-and-publications/alerts/what-the-dao-why-everyone-is-talking-about-decentralized-autonomous-organizations/.

Ocorian. October 30, 2018. "10 Benefits of UAE Free Zones." *Ocorian.* www.ocorian.com/article/explained-uae-free-zones#:~:text=What%20is%20a%20free%20zone,dedicated%20to%20a%20specific%20industry.

Office of the Privacy Commissioner of Canada. May 2019. *PIPEDA in Brief.* Office of the Privacy Commissioner of Canada. www.priv.gc.ca/en/privacy-topics/privacy-laws-in-canada/the-personal-information-protection-and-electronic-documents-act-pipeda/pipeda_brief/.

Office of Vermont Secretary of State. January 15, 2019. *Blockchains for Public Recordkeeping and for Recording Land Records.* Vermont Secretary of State. https://sos.vermont.gov/media/r3jh24ig/vsara_blockchains_for_public_recordkeeping_white_paper_v1.pdf .

Ohlrogge, M. 2021. "Starting Over: Michael Ohlrogge Tracks Post-Foreclosure Outcomes During the Great Recession." *NYU|Law.* www.law.nyu.edu/news/ideas/michael-ohlrogge-great-recession-foreclosures (accessed December 14, 2021).

Okereke Innocent. January 12, 2021. "Hybrid Cryptocurrency Exchanges: What Are They?" *Medium.com.* https://medium.com/xord/hybrid-cryptocurrency-exchanges-what-are-they-8c9849f50b9f.

Okta. 2022. "Practical Thoughts on Blockchain and Identity." *Okta.* www.okta.com/resources/whitepaper/practical-thoughts-on-blockchain-and-identity/ (accessed March 2, 2022).

Orcutt, M. February 19, 2019. "Once Hailed as Unhackable, Blockchains Are Now Getting Hacked." *MIT Technology Review.* www.technologyreview.com/2019/02/19/239592/once-hailed-as-unhackable-blockchains-are-now-getting-hacked/.

Ozarde, S. May 8, 2022. "Tim Berners-Lee, Semantic Web 3.0." *LinkedIn Warp Drive blog.* www.linkedin.com/pulse/tim-berners-lee-semantic-web-30-sandeep-ozarde/?trk=public_post.

Pahulje, M. May 11, 2021. "Achieving Supply Chain Transparency Through Blockchain." *Flexis.* https://blog.flexis.com/achieving-supply-chain-transparency-through-blockchain.

Palasciano, A. August 18, 2022. "How a Florida House Became the First Ever Sold as an NFT." *The Smart Wallet.* https://thesmartwallet.com/how-a-florida-house-became-the-first-ever-sold-as-an-nft/?articleid=82292#:~:text=Now%2C%20for%20the%20first%20time,associated%20with%20digital%20assets!).

Paleotronic. September 24, 2019. "Pay by the Minute: The CompuServe Era." *Paleotronic.* https://paleotronic.com/2019/09/24/pay-by-the-minute-the-compuserve-era/.

Passive Income. May 28, 2021. "$ORT—Launching Europe's First Tokenized Real Estate Assets By OMNI Estate Group & Passive Income." *Global Newswire.* www.globenewswire.com/en/news-release/2021/05/28/2238333/0/en/ORT-Launching-Europe-s-First-Tokenized-Real-Estate-Assets-by-OMNI-Estate-Group-Passive-Income.html.

Patientory Inc. June 11, 2018. "Patientory Introduction Video." *YouTube video*, 4:43. www.youtube.com/watch?v=a464XQSGmDQ&ab_channel=PatientoryInc.

Patrizio, A. November 18, 2022. "Web3 Vs. Metaverse: What's the Difference?" *TechTarget.* www.techtarget.com/whatis/feature/Web3-vs-metaverse-Whats-the-difference#:~:text=Web3%20is%20about%20decentralized%20ownership,t%20care%20who%20owns%20it.

Pattnaik, B. December 5, 2021. "Hackers Steal $200M Worth of Shiba Inu, Saitama, and Other Tokens From Bitmart Exchange." *Benzinga.* www.benzinga.com/markets/cryptocurrency/21/12/24449490/hackers-steal-200m-worth-of-shiba-inu-saitama-and-other-tokens-from-bitmart-exchange.

Pauw, C. February 21, 2019. "What Is an STO, Explained." *Cointelegraph.* https://cointelegraph.com/explained/what-is-an-sto-explained.

Pennington Creative. 2022. "The Origins of Twitter." *Pennington Creative.* https://penningtoncreative.com/the-origins-of-twitter/ (accessed August 15, 2022).

Petersson, D. October 24, 2018. "How Smart Contracts Started and Where They Are Heading." *Forbes.* www.forbes.com/sites/davidpetersson/2018/10/24/how-smart-contracts-started-and-where-they-are-heading/?sh=4fb0539537b6.

Pew Research Center. September 14, 2020. "Americans' Views of Government: Low Trust, But Some Positive Performance Ratings." *Pew Research Center.* www.pewresearch.org/politics/2020/09/14/americans-views-of-government-low-trust-but-some-positive-performance-ratings/.

Pew Research Center. February 20, 2020. "The U.S. Census and Privacy Concerns." *Pew Research Center.* www.pewresearch.org/social-trends/2020/02/20/the-u-s-census-and-privacy-concerns/.

Pisani, B. July 21, 2017. "Bank Fees Have Been Growing Like Crazy." *CNBC.* www.cnbc.com/2017/07/21/the-crazy-growth-of-bank-fees.html.

Pitchforth, J. May 1, 2017. "5 Ways Theme Parks Could Embrace Blockchain (and Why They Should)." *CoinDesk.* www.coindesk.com/tech/2017/05/16/5-ways-theme-parks-could-embrace-blockchain-and-why-they-should/.

Pittman, J. September 16, 2021. "The Best Place to Buy Security Tokens." *Security Token Market* (Blog). https://blog.stomarket.com/quick-guide-to-buying-security-tokens-8bea7f6fbed7.

Polkastarter. August 16, 2022. "Web3 Interoperability: The Truth, the Promise & the Importance." *Polkastarter.* https://blog.polkastarter.com/web3-interoperability-the-truth-the-promise-the-importance/.

Polkastarter. October 14, 2022. "How Can Web3 Help With Cancel Culture and Content Censorship?" *Polkastarter.* https://blog.polkastarter.com/how-can-web3-help-with-cancel-culture-and-content-censorship/.

Poonia, G. December 10, 2021. "The Reason Not to Throw Away Old Hard Drives Might Be Surprising—There Could Be Bitcoin on There." *Deseret News.* www.deseret.com/2021/12/10/22827963/james-howells-threw-away-hard-drives-with-bitcoin-password.

Power Technology. September 28, 2018. "Acciona Uses Blockchain Technology at Two Storage Facilities in Spain." *Power Technology.* www.power-technology.com/news/acciona-uses-blockchain-technology-two-storage-facilities-spain/.

Practice Panther in Security. 2022. "How Blockchain Technology Will Drive Clients to Your Law Firm." *Practice Panther.* www.practicepanther.com/blog/how-blockchain-technology-will-drive-clients-to-your-law-firm/ (accessed March 19, 2022).

Preface. 2022. "How Do Web Companies Used Web 3.0? Uses Cases and Examples." *Preface.* www.preface.ai/blog/trend/web3-examples/ (accessed September 5, 2022).

Press Release PR Newswire. April 16, 2019. "Most Americans Less Likely to Join Customer Loyalty Program That Connects Information (71%) or Requires an APP (58%), According to Survey on Behalf of Wilbur." *Insider.* https://markets.businessinsider.com/news/stocks/most-americans-less-likely-to-join-customer-loyalty-program-that-collects-personal-information-71-or-requires-an-app-58-according-to-survey-on-behalf-of-wilbur-1028114529.

Pressgrove, J. October 20, 2020. "Utah County Makes History With Presidential Blockchain Vote." *Government Technology.* www.govtech.com/products/utah-county-makes-history-with-presidential-blockchain-vote.html.

Preveil. January 12, 2021. "Public—Private Key Pairs & How They Work." *Preveil* (Blog). www.preveil.com/blog/public-and-private-key/.

Price, S. 2022. "Average Cost of a Vacation." *Value Penguin.* www.valuepenguin.com/average-cost-vacation (accessed April 3, 2022).

ProPrivacy. January 28, 2021. "Status.im Review." *ProPrivacy.* https://proprivacy.com/privacy-service/review/statusim.

Providentmetals.com. January 9, 2018. "How Precious Metals Were Used in Ancient Egypt." *Provident Metals*. https://blog.providentmetals.com/how-precious-metals-were-used-in-ancient-egypt.htm#.Y2-sTXaZND9.

Puckett, C. 2009. "The Story of the Social Security Number." *Social Security Bulletin* 69, no. 2. www.ssa.gov/policy/docs/ssb/v69n2/v69n2p55.html#:~:text=The%20Social%20Security%20number%20(%20SSN%20)%20was%20created%20in%201936%20for,the%20SSN%20has%20expanded%20substantially.

PVS Admin. October 22, 2019. "Important Economic Factors Affecting Housing Market." *PVS Builders & Developers* (Blog). https://pvsbuilders.com/economic-factors-affecting-housing-market/.

Qi-Long, C., Y. Rong-Hua, and L. Fei-Long. 2019. "A Blockchain-Based Housing Rental System." *Scitepress Papers*. www.scitepress.org/Papers/2019/80972/80972.pdf.

Quinyx. 2023. "What's the Difference Between AI, ML, and Algorithms?" *Quinyx*. www.quinyx.com/blog/difference-between-ai-ml-algorithms#:~:text=To%20summarize%3A%20algorithms%20are%20automated,receive%20is%20structured%20or%20unstructured (accessed September 23, 2023).

Rabbitte, P. January 27, 2020. "Smart Fridges Set to Get Smarter With IoT & AI functionalities." *150 SEC*. https://150sec.com/smart-fridges-set-to-get-smarter-with-iot-ai-functionalities/13576/.

Rainie, L. and J. Anderson. February 8, 2017. "Code-Dependent: Pros and Cons of the Algorithm Age." *Pew Research Center*. www.pewresearch.org/internet/2017/02/08/code-dependent-pros-and-cons-of-the-algorithm-age.

Rappeport, A. and E. Flitter. May 22, 2018. "Congress Approves First Big Dodd-Frank Rollback." *The New York Times*. www.nytimes.com/2018/05/22/business/congress-passes-dodd-frank-rollback-for-smaller-banks.html.

Kaur, R. November 15, 2021. "Blockchain in Real Estate: How This Disrupts the Market?" *DataDrivenInvestor*. https://medium.datadriveninvestor.com/blockchain-in-real-estate-how-this-disrupts-the-market-394ea2a230ac.

Rau, A. November 22, 2021. "The Best Legal Frameworks for DAOs From Around the World." *Mirror.xyz*. https://mirror.xyz/0x43d06b9eBFB0c76A448fBd5B6faa2cfba81901d6/CYm-hNaniW0C1Mn9KR677jn4o9okGugkKC3C8iD9k28.

Redfin. 2022. "How Real Estate Commission Works." *Redfin*. www.redfin.com/guides/how-much-is-real-estate-agent-commission-buyer-seller (accessed April 6, 2022).

Redolfi, A. October 7, 2021. "The Future of Real Estate Transactions on the Blockchain." *Forbes*. www.forbes.com/sites/forbesbizcouncil/2021/10/27/the-future-of-real-estate-transactions-on-the-blockchain/?sh=362a55b49387.

Rees, K. June 20, 2022. "The Top 6 Things to Check Before Buying an NFT." *MUO*. www.makeuseof.com/things-check-before-buying-nft/.

Reiff, N. January 28, 2022. "What Are the Legal Risks to Cryptocurrency Investors?" *Investopedia.* www.investopedia.com/tech/what-are-legal-risks-cryptocurrency-investors/.

Reiff, N. September 23, 2022. "Decentralized Autonomous Organization (DAO): Definition, Purpose, and Example." *Investopedia.* www.investopedia .com/tech/what-dao/.

Reiff, N. September 6, 2022. "How to Pay With Cryptocurrency." *Investopedia.* www.investopedia.com/ask/answers/100314/what-are-advantages-paying-bitcoin.asp.

Research and Markets. May 17, 2022. "Germany Loyalty Programs Market Report 2022: Retailers Are Building Partnerships With Multi-Brand Loyalty Program Providers as a Business Differentiator." *Global Newswire.* www.globenewswire .com/en/news-release/2022/05/17/2444806/28124/en/Germany-Loyalty-Programs-Market-Report-2022-Retailers-are-Building-Partnerships-with-Multi-Brand-Loyalty-Program-Providers-as-a-Business-Differentiator.html.

Reuters Staff. April 25, 2011. "Timeline: A Brief History of Silver." *Reuters.* www .reuters.com/article/us-silver-history-idUSTRE73O13O20110425.

ReverseAds. May 19, 2021. "Algorithms…The Good, the Bad & the Ugly." *ReverseAds* (Blog). https://reverseads.com/blog/algorithms-the-good-the-bad-the-ugly/.

Reynolds, E. April 5, 2022. "This Luxury Miami Condo Building Is Launching an NFT Art Collection for Its Owners." *Forbes.* www.forbes.com/sites/ emmareynolds/2022/04/05/this-luxury-miami-condo-building-is-launching-an-nft-art-collection-for-its-owners/?sh=4636d7a235c9.

Richter, F. April 8, 2022. "Streaming Drives Global Music Industry Resurgence." *Statista.* www.statista.com/chart/4713/global-recorded-music-industry-revenues/.

Roberts, J.J. October 31, 2018. "Is There Any Doubt This Man Created Bitcoin?" *Fortune.* https://fortune.com/2018/10/31/satoshi-identity/.

Robeznieks, A. August 26, 2019. "Insurers Want Patients to Use Wearables. That could Be a Problem." *American Medical Association.* www.ama-assn.org/practice-management/digital/insurers-want-patients-use-wearables-could-be-problem.

Robyn. May 22, 2018. "Who Needs Your Social Security Number? (and When to Refuse to Give It Out)." *Money Care, LLC.* https://moneycarevt.com/ who-needs-your-social-security-number-and-when-to-refuse-to-give-it-out/#:~:text=You%20do%20need%20to%20give,Security%20number%20 (SSN)%20to%3A&text=The%20three%20main%20credit%20 reporting,Medicaid%2C%20and%20other%20aid%20programs%60.

Rodriguez, K. and V. Alimonti. September 21, 2020. *A Look-Back and Ahead on Data Protection in Latin America and Spain.* Electronic Frontier Foundation. www.eff.org/deeplinks/2020/09/look-back-and-ahead-data-protection-latin-america-and-spain.

Rooks, T. February 16, 2021. "The Power Needed to Run Bitcoin." *DW*. www.dw.com/en/why-does-bitcoin-need-more-energy-than-whole-countries/a-56573390.

Room, J. October 29, 2018. "Experts Debunk 'Dangerous and Misleading' Study Hyping Bitcoin Energy Use." *Think Progress*. https://thinkprogress.org/experts-debunk-dangerous-and-misleading-study-hyping-bitcoin-energy-use-8f8744672611/.

Rousey, M. September 1, 2019. "A Complete Guide to the Proof of Authority (PoA) Algorithm." *Changelly* (Blog). https://changelly.com/blog/what-is-proof-of-authority-poa/.

Rowaad, A. August 15, 2022. "What You Need to Know About the Virtual Assets Law in the UAE?" *The Legal 500*. www.legal500.com/developments/thought-leadership/what-you-need-to-know-about-virtual-assets-law-in-the-uae/#:~:text=Dubai%20Virtual%20Assets%20Law%20has,virtual%20asset%20services%20in%20Dubai.

Rubinstein, M. June 21, 2022. "Mortgage Lenders Timed the Market Perfectly." *Bloomberg*. www.bloomberg.com/opinion/articles/2022-06-21/mortgage-lenders-timed-the-market-perfectly.

Satariano, A. April 22, 2022. "E.U. Takes Aim at Social Media's Harms With Landmark New Law." *The New York Times*. www.nytimes.com/2022/04/22/technology/european-union-social-media-law.html.

Satoshi, N. October 31, 2008. *Bitcoin: A Peer-To-Peer Electronic Cash System*. Satoshi Nakamoto Institute. https://nakamotoinstitute.org/bitcoin/.

SC& SCAND. February 15, 2022. "The Future of Real Estate Transactions on the Blockchain Technology." SC& *SCAND* (Blog). https://scand.com/company/blog/the-future-of-real-estate-transactions-on-the-blockchain/#:~:text=But%20why%20do%20more%20and,property%20history%20and%20its%20status.

Schatsky, D., A. Arora, and A. Dongre. September 28, 2018. "Blockchain and the Five Vectors of Progress." *Deloitte*. www2.deloitte.com/us/en/insights/focus/signals-for-strategists/value-of-blockchain-applications-interoperability.html.

Schmandt-Besserat, D. 2019. "The Invention of Tokens." *Royal Numismatic Society*, no 51. https://sites.utexas.edu/dsb/tokens/the-invention-of-tokens/.

Schmandt-Besserat, D. 2019. "Tokens: Their Significance for the Origin of Counting and Writing." *Royal Numismatic Society*, no. 51. https://sites.utexas.edu/dsb/tokens/tokens/

Schmidt, J. May 18, 2022. "Why Does Bitcoin Use so Much Energy?" *Forbes Advisor*. www.forbes.com/advisor/investing/cryptocurrency/bitcoins-energy-usage-explained/#:~:text=It's%20estimated%20that%20Bitcoin%20consumes,annual%20electricity%20consumption%20of%20Norway.

Schweifer, J. January 21, 2021. *What Asset-Backed Tokens Mean for Business & Wealth Creation*. LinkedIn. www.linkedin.com/pulse/what-asset-backed-tokens-mean-business-wealth-johannes-schweifer/.

Scott, A. July 7, 2021. "Difference Between Algorithm and Artificial Intelligence." *Data Science Central*. www.datasciencecentral.com/difference-between-algorithm-and-artificial-intelligence/.

Sedlmeir, J., H.U. Buhl, G. Fridgen, and R. Keller. June 19, 2020. "The Energy Consumption of Blockchain Technology: Beyond Myth." *Springer Link*. https://link.springer.com/article/10.1007/s12599-020-00656-x#Sec9.

Selig, J. March 14, 2022. "What Is Machine Learning? A Definition." *expert.ai*. www.expert.ai/blog/machine-learning-definition/.

Sensorium. March 1, 2022. "Top Blockchain Games." *Sensorium* (Blog). https://sensoriumxr.com/articles/best-blockchain-games.

Senti, F. August 1, 2019. *The Denver Mobile Voting Pilot: A Report*. The National Cybersecurity Center. https://cyber-center.org/wp-content/uploads/2019/08/Mobile-Voting-Audit-Report-on-the-Denver-County-Pilots-FINAL.pdf.

Sephton, C. November 23, 2021. "Revealed: How Much Metaverse Industry Could Be Worth." *Alexandria*. https://coinmarketcap.com/alexandria/article/revealed-how-much-metaverse-industry-could-be-worth.

Setupad. December 2, 2021. "Ad Blocker Trends for 2022 | Statistics and Most Useful Tips." *Setupad* (Blog). https://setupad.com/blog/ad-blockers-trends-tips/.

Shahbandeh, M. February 17, 2022. "Worldwide Sales of Organic Foods 1999-2020." *Statistica*. www.statista.com/statistics/273090/worldwide-sales-of-organic-foods-since-1999/.

Shang, Q. and A. Price. January 1, 2019. "A Blockchain-Based Land Titling Project in the Republic of Georgia: Rebuilding Public Trust and Lessons for Future Pilot Projects." *Massachusetts Institute of Technology Press Journals* 12, no. 3–4. https://direct.mit.edu/itgg/article/12/3-4/72/9852/A-Blockchain-Based-Land-Titling-Project-in-the.

Share&Charge Foundation. November 14, 2018. "Share&Charge—EV Charging Via the Blockchain." *YouTube* video, 3:48. www.youtube.com/watch?v=7TBR1nq83tE&ab_channel=Share%26ChargeFoundation.

Shareworks. 2021. "Asset Tokenization: A Short Overview." *Morgan Stanley at Work Shareworks*. https://discover.shareworks.com/ipo-and-liquidity-events/asset-tokenization (accessed December 2, 2021).

Sharma, R. August 15, 2021. "Running a Full Bitcoin Node for Investors." *Investopedia*. www.investopedia.com/news/running-full-bitcoin-node-investors/#:~:text=While%20there%20are%20no%20monetary,bitcoin%20transactions%20in%20a%20day.

Sharma, T.K. December 30, 2019. "Blockchain Land Registries Across the Globe." *Blockchain Council.* www.blockchain-council.org/blockchain/ blockchain-land-registeries-across-the-globe/.

Shen, T. May 18, 2022. "China Banned Bitcoin Mining and Became the World's No.2 Bitcoin Miner." *Forkast.* https://forkast.news/china-banned-bitcoin-mining-became-no-2-bitcoin-miner/.

Sherbina, M. March 20, 2020. "Opportunities and Risks of Using Blockchain Technology." *Blaize* (Blog). https://blaize.tech/article-type/blockchain-in-healthcare-opportunities-and-risks-of-using-blockchain-technology/.

Short Term Rentalz. August 4, 2022. "Dtravel Processes First Travel Booking on the Blockchain." *Short Term Rentalz.* https://shorttermrentalz.com/news/ dtravel-first-travel-booking-blockchain/.

Shou, D. December 10, 2021. "How Decentralized Identity Is Reshaping Privacy for Digital Identities." *Forbes.* www.forbes.com/sites/ forbestechcouncil/2021/12/10/how-decentralized-identity-is-reshaping-privacy-for-digital-identities/?sh=3819ba0e3226.

Sigalos, M. September 16, 2022. "Biden White House Just Put Out a Framework on Regulating Crypto—Here's What's in It." *CNBC.* www.cnbc .com/2022/09/16/heres-whats-in-biden-framework-to-regulate-crypto.html.

Silkroad.com. 2021. "Chinese Paper Money." *Silkroad.com.* www.silk-road.com/ artl/papermoney.shtml (accessed November 12, 2021).

Simplilearn. August 19, 2022. "Merkle Tree in Blockchain: What Is It, How Does It Work and Benefits." *Simplilearn.* www.simplilearn.com/tutorials/blockchain-tutorial/merkle-tree-in-blockchain#:~:text=It's%20a%20mathematical%20 data%20structure,and%20content%20of%20the%20data.

Simply Explained. November 13, 2017. "How Does a Blockchain Work." *YouTube video*, 5:59. www.youtube.com/watch?v=SSo_EIwHSd4&t=4s&ab_ channel=SimplyExplained.

Sinclair, S. March 2, 2020. "West Virginia Ditches Blockchain Voting App Provider Voatz." *CoinDesk.* www.coindesk.com/policy/2020/03/02/west-virginia-ditches-blockchain-voting-app-provider-voatz/.

Singer, A. February 22, 2022. "Year 1602 Revisited: Are DAOs the New Corporate Paradigm?" *CoinTelegraph.* https://cointelegraph.com/magazine/ dao-challenge-business-model-become-new-corporate-paradigm/.

Singh, P. 2020. *Role of Blockchain Technology in Digitalization of Land Records in Indian Scenario.* IOP Publishing Ltd. https://iopscience.iop.org/ article/10.1088/1755-1315/614/1/012055/pdf#:~:text=Blockchain%20in%20 the%20land%20registry,buyer%20through%20an%20application%20form.

Singh, O. March 26, 2022. "What Is Front-Running in Crypto and NFT trading?" *Cointelegraph.* https://cointelegraph.com/explained/what-is-front-running-in-crypto-and-nft-trading.

Siriwardena, P. October 15, 2017. "The Mystery Behind Block Time." *Medium* (Blog). https://medium.facilelogin.com/the-mystery-behind-block-time-63351e35603a.

SkyQuest Technology Consulting Pvt. Ltd. May 26, 2022. "The Global Non-Fungible Tokens (NFTs) Market Is Expected to Reach a Value of USD 122.43 Billion by 2028, at a CAGR of 34.10% Over the Forecast Period (2022–2028)—SkyQuest Technology." *Global Newswire.* www .globenewswire.com/en/news-release/2022/05/26/2451426/0/en/The-Global-Non-Fungible-Tokens-NFTs-Market-is-expected-to-reach-a-value-of-USD-122-43-Billion-by-2028-at-a-CAGR-of-34-10-over-the-forecast-period-2022-2028-SkyQuest-Technology.html.

Smith, E. December 5, 2017. *Before There Was Bitcoin, There Was DigiCash.* https://shortformernie.medium.com/before-there-was-bitcoin-there-was-digicash-fc2668c1d457.

Smith, E. September 16, 2016. "The Story of WebTV, the Smart TV of the 90s." *Vice.* www.vice.com/en/article/4xaqe9/why-webtvs-remote-controlled-internet-failed-to-take-off.

Snowcrash. 2022. *Snowcrash.* https://snowcrash.com/ (accessed June 28, 2022).

Software Testing Help. October 25, 2022. "Blockchain Explorer Tutorial—What Is a Blockchain Explorer." *Software Testing Help.* www.softwaretestinghelp .com/blockchain-explorer-tutorial/#:~:text=A%20blockchain%20explorer%20is%20a,user%20in%20a%20searchable%20format.

Sonenreich, A. February 16, 2022. "NFTs and the Future of Commercial Real Estate." *Forbes.* www.forbes.com/sites/forbesbusinesscouncil/2022/02/16/nfts-and-the-future-of-commercial-real-estate/?sh=739dd3d89bac.

Spanu, A. July 19, 2018. "Embleema Propels Healthcare Into the Future: New Platform Empowers Patients to Own & Share Their Medical Data." *Healthcare Weekly.* https://healthcareweekly.com/embleema-blockchain-healthcare/.

Spendgo. March 13, 2020. "Understanding Average Loyalty Program Redemption Rate & Tips for Improving Yours." *Spendgo.* https://resources.spendgo.com/blog/understanding-average-loyalty-program-redemption-rate-tips-for-improving-yours.

Sporny, M. December 25, 2007. "Intro to the Semantic Web." *Youtube video*, 6:06. www.youtube.com/watch?v=OGg8A2zfWKg&ab_channel=ManuSporny.

Sristy, A. 2022. "Blockchain in the Food Supply Chain—What Does the Future Look Like?" *Walmart.com* (Blog). https://one.walmart.com/content/globaltechindia/en_in/Tech-insights/blog/Blockchain-in-the-food-supply-chain.html (accessed February 19, 2022).

Statista Research Department. n.d. "Leisure Tourism Spending Worldwide From 2019 to 2021." *Statista.* www.statista.com/statistics/1093335/leisure-travel-spending-worldwide/.

Statista Research Department. February 1, 2010. "Percentage of Households With a Computer at Home in the United States From 1984 to 2010." *Statista.* www.statista.com/statistics/184685/percentage-of-households-with-computer-in-the-united-states-since-1984/.

Statista Research Department. February 17, 2022. "Average Sales Price of New Homes Sold in the United States From 1965 to 2021." *Statista.* www.statista.com/statistics/240991/average-sales-prices-of-new-homes-sold-in-the-us/.

Statista Research Department. June 27, 2022. "Number of Existing Homes Sold in the United States From 2005 to 2023." *Statista.* www.statista.com/statistics/226144/us-existing-home-sales/.

Statista Research Department. May 12, 2022. "Total Sales Value of Art and Collectibles Non-Fungible Tokens (NFTs) Worldwide From 2019 to 2021." *Statista.* www.statista.com/statistics/1299636/sales-value-art-and-collectibles-nfts-worldwide/. www.google.com/search?q=NFT+ART+SALES+IN+DOLLARS&oq=NFT+ART+SALES+IN+DOLLARS&aqs=chrome..69i57.6988j0j15&sourceid=chrome&ie=UTF-8.

Status. 2022. "Frequently Asked Questions." *Status.* https://status.im/docs/FAQs.html#:~:text=Status%20currently%20uses%20Whisper%2C%20the,network%20for%20a%20set%20time (accessed November 6, 2022).

Steele, J. July 11, 2022. "The History of Credit Cards." *Creditcards.com.* www.creditcards.com/statistics/history-of-credit-cards/.

Stella, S. September 26, 2023. "FCC Chairwoman Rosenworcel Announces Plan To Reinstate Title II Broadband Authority, Net Neutrality Rules." *Public Knowledge.* https://publicknowledge.org/fcc-chairwoman-rosenworcel-announces-plan-to-reinstate-title-ii-broadband-authority-net-neutrality-rules/.

Stelzner, M. July 22, 2022. "Web3 Legal: What Projects Need to Consider." *Social Media Examiner.* www.socialmediaexaminer.com/web3-legal-what-projects-need-to-consider/.

Stern, L. January 29, 2019. "Broadband Providers Are Quietly Taking Advantage of an Internet Without Net Neutrality Protections." *Public Knowledge.* https://publicknowledge.org/broadband-providers-are-quietly-taking-advantage-of-an-internet-without-net-neutrality-protections/.

Stern, M.J. February 3, 2015. "Plush Life Why Did People Lose Their Minds Over Beanie Babies?" *Slate.* https://slate.com/technology/2015/02/beanie-babies-bubble-economics-and-psychology-of-a-plush-toy-investment-craze.html.

Stewart, E. December 10, 2019. "Why Every Website Wants You to Accept Its Cookies." *Vox.* www.vox.com/recode/2019/12/10/18656519/what-are-cookies-website-tracking-gdpr-privacy.

Stoll, C., L. Klaaßen, and U. Gallersdörfer. June 12, 2019. "The Carbon Footprint of Bitcoin." *Joule* 3, no.17, pp.1647–1661. www.cell.com/joule/fulltext/

S2542-4351(19)30255-7?_returnURL=https%3A%2F%2Flinkinghub.elsevier
.com%2Fretrieve%2Fpii%2FS2542435119302557%3Fshowall%3Dtrue.

Strack, B. August 24, 2022. "New Web3 Head at Digital Bank Congi Braces for More Regulation." *Blockworks*. https://blockworks.co/new-web3-head-at-digital-bank-cogni-braces-for-more-regulation/.

Sullivan, D. March 9, 2012. "Pew Survey: 68% View Targeted Ads Negatively; 59% Have Noticed Targeting." *Martech*. https://martech.org/pew-survey-targeted-ads-negatively/?utm_campaign=tweet&utm_source=socialflow&utm_medium=twitter.

Sundaramoorthy, T. July 4, 2017. "Hashing and Public Key Cryptography for Beginners." *Medium.com*. https://medium.com/@thyagsundaramoorthy/hashing-and-public-key-cryptography-for-beginners-292aaf14efae.

Sutton, B. January 14, 2022. "Caviar With Your Crypto? Word's 'First NFT Restaurant' Planned in New York." *The Art Newspaper*. www.theartnewspaper.com/2022/01/14/nft-restaurant-new-york-city-flyfish-club.

Swiss Federal Office of Energy. September 27, 2021. "Blockchain Energy Consumption an exploratory study." *Swiss Federal Office of Energy*. www.vs.inf.ethz.ch/publ/papers/Coroama2021_BlockchainEnergy.pdf.

Swissinfo.ch. July 2, 2018. "Switzerland's First Municipal Blockchain Vote Hailed a Success." *Swissinfo.ch*. www.swissinfo.ch/eng/business/crypto-valley-_-switzerland-s-first-municipal-blockchain-vote-hailed-a-success/44230928.

Szabo, N. December 29, 2005. *Bit Gold*. Satoshi Nakamoto Institute. https://nakamotoinstitute.org/bit-gold/.

Tabora, V. November 21, 2019. "A Decomposition of the Bitcoin Block Header." *Data Driven Investor*. www.datadriveninvestor.com/2019/11/21/a-decomposition-of-the-bitcoin-block-header/#.

Tan, E. February 11, 2022. "NFT-Linked House Sells for $650K in Propy's First US Sale." *CoinDesk*. www.coindesk.com/business/2022/02/11/nft-linked-house-sells-for-650k-in-propys-first-us-sale/.

Tapscott, A. and D. Tappscott. March 1, 2017. "How Blockchain Is Changing Finance." *Harvard Business Review*. https://hbr.org/2017/03/how-blockchain-is-changing-finance.

Tardi, C. January 14, 2022. "Why Has Gold Always Been Valuable." *Investopedia*. www.investopedia.com/articles/investing/071114/why-gold-has-always-had-value.asp#:~:text=Gold's%20value%20is%20ultimately%20a,gold%20as%20a%20valuable%20commodity.

Teague, J. June 7, 2022. "Starting a DAO in the USA? Steer Clear of DAO Legislation." *The Defiant*. https://thedefiant.io/starting-a-dao-in-the-usa-steer-clear-of-dao-legislation.

Team Luno. May 22, 2021. "How Many Satoshis Make a Bitcoin?" *Luno*. https://discover.luno.com/how-many-satoshis-make-a-bitcoin/.

Technopedia. June 29, 2021. "Web 1.0." *Technopedia.* www.techopedia.com/definition/27960/web-10.

Tehcnopedia. March 31, 2017. "Semantic Web." *Technopedia.* www.techopedia.com/definition/27961/semantic-web.

Thales. December 29, 2021. "Digital Identity Trends—5 Forces That Are Shaping 2022." *Thales.* www.thalesgroup.com/en/markets/digital-identity-and-security/government/identity/digital-identity-services/trends#:~:text=Usually%20issued%20or%20regulated%20by,as%20defined%20by%20national%20law.

The Conversation. April 2, 2020. "Why Undocumented Immigrants Still Fear the 2020 Census." *The Conversation.* https://theconversation.com/why-undocumented-immigrants-still-fear-the-2020-census-132842.

The Conversation. August 24, 2021. "When You Buy an NFT, You Don't Completely Own It—Here's Why." *The Conversation.* https://theconversation.com/when-you-buy-an-nft-you-dont-completely-own-it-heres-why-166445.

The Creative Penn. November 5, 2021. "Creatokia. The World of Digital Originals (NFTs) With Jens Klingelhöfer and John Ruhrmann." *The Creative Penn.* www.thecreativepenn.com/2021/11/05/creatokia-digital-originals-nfts/.

The Crystal Marketing Team. October 7, 2021. "2021 Crypto Regulations in South-East Asia." *Crystal.* https://crystalblockchain.com/articles/2021-crypto-regulations-in-south-east-asia/.

The Editors of Encyclopedia Britanica. 2022. "Greenback Movement." *Encyclopedia Britanica.* www.britannica.com/event/Greenback-movement (accessed October 13, 2022).

The Editors of Encyclopedia Britannica. 2022. "Resumption Act of 1875." *Encyclopedia Britannica.* www.britannica.com/topic/Resumption-Act-of-1875 (accessed October 13, 2022).

The European Press Review. October 16, 2021. "Major Pros and Cons of Cryptocurrency in 2021." *The European Press Review.* www.europeanbusinessreview.com/major-pros-and-cons-of-cryptocurrency-in-2021/.

The Investopedia Team. May 26, 2022. "2008 Recession: What the Great Recession Was and What Caused It." *Investopedia.* www.investopedia.com/terms/g/great-recession.asp.

The Neeva Team. March 10, 2022. "Bringing Transparency to Web3: Neeva.xzy, the Web3 Search Engine." *Neeva.com.* https://neeva.com/blog/neeva-xyz-the-web3-search-engine.

The Royal Society. 2022. "What Is Machine Learning?" *The Royal Society.* https://royalsociety.org/topics-policy/projects/machine-learning/videos-and-background-information/ (accessed August 24, 2022).

TheVERSEverse. 2022. "TheVERSEverse mission." *theVERSEverse.* https://theverseverse.com/mission/ (accessed July 4, 2022).

Thomas, L. September 22, 2021. "TIME Announces 'TIMEPieces' NFT Collection." *NFT Now*. https://nftnow.com/news/time-magazine-timepieces-nft-collection/.

Thomas, M. June 6, 2022. "30 Internet of Things Examples You Should Know." *Built In*. https://builtin.com/internet-things/iot-examples.

Tidy, J. November 13, 2022. "The Fall of the FTX 'King of Crypto' Sam Bankman-Fried." *BBC News*. www.bbc.com/news/technology-63612489.

Tiffany, K. February 6, 2019. "Flickr Will Soon Start Deleting Photos—and Massive Chunks of Internet History." *Vox*. www.vox.com/the-goods/2019/2/6/18214046/flickr-free-storage-ends-digital-photo-archive-history.

Tighe, D. August 30, 2022. "How Often Do You Swipe Your Loyalty Card for Top-Up Shopping?*" *Statista*. www.statista.com/statistics/1125748/loyalty-card-usage-rate-for-top-up-shopping-in-the-uk-by-income/.

Tilbe, A. July 23, 2022. "Web3 and AI: Top 3 Most Important Machine Learning Methods." *Illumination*. https://medium.com/illumination/web3-and-ai-top-3-most-important-machine-learning-methods-d1cf4374a965.

Time PR. March 18, 2022. "Time Releases First-Ever Full Magazine Issue as an NFT on the Blockchain Featuring a Cover Story on Ethereum Co-Founder Vitalik Buterin." *Time Spotlight Story Press Room*. https://time.com/6158525/time-releases-first-ever-nft-magazine-issue/#:~:text=Founder%20Vitalik%20Buterin-,TIME%20Releases%20First%2DEver%20Full%20Magazine%20Issue%20as%20an%20NFT,Ethereum%20Co%2DFounder%20Vitalik%20Buterin&text=On%20Wednesday%2C%20March%2023,an%20NFT%20on%20the%20blockchain.

Tokened. 2022. "Tokenization Solution for Loyalty." *Tokened*. https://tokend.io/loyalty/ (accessed October 21, 2022).

Torrey, T. March 1, 2020. "The Cost of Getting Copies of Your Medical Records." *Very Well*. www.verywellhealth.com/cost-of-getting-copies-of-your-medical-records-2615313.

Treehouse Technology Group. 2022. "How Blockchain Can Revolutionize the Concert-Goer Experience." *Treehouse Technology Group* (Blog). https://treehousetechgroup.com/blockchain-and-concert-experience/#:~:text=Blockchain-based%20ticketing%20platforms%20can,with%20ticketing%20sites%20like%20TicketMaster (accessed April 6, 2022).

TRG Datacenters. September 28, 2021. "The Most Popular NFT's of 2021." *TRG Datacenters*. www.trgdatacenters.com/the-most-popular-nfts-of-2021/.

Tucker, E., L. Whitehurst, G. Johnson, and F. Hussein. Updated November 22, 2023. "Largest Crypto Exchange Binance Fined $4 Billion, CEO Pleads Guilty to Not Stopping Money Laundering." *The Associated Press*. https://apnews.com/article/cryptocurrency-exchange-binance-justice-department-settlement-sec-8314e9697b98cfe3a9827c78e5720914.

Tuwiner, J. April 9, 2022. "Bitcoin Confirmations." *BuyBitcoinWorldwide.com.* https://buybitcoinworldwide.com/confirmations/.

Tuwiner, J. July 15, 2022. "79+ Blockchain Statistics, Facts, and Trends (2022)." *Buy Bitcoin Worldwide.* https://buybitcoinworldwide.com/blockchain-statistics/.

U.S. Census History. 2022. "What Is the Connection Between the U.S. Census Bureau and IBM?" *United States Census.* www.census.gov/history/www/faqs/innovations_faqs/what_is_the_connection_between_the_census_bureau_and_ibm.html#:~:text=Hollerith%20left%20the%20Census%20Bureau,International%20Business%20Machines%20(IBM).&text=company%20he%20founded%20eventually%20became%20known%20as%20IBM (accessed January 18, 2022).

U.S. Food and Drug Administration. September 26, 2022. "Drug Supply Chain Security Act (DSCSA)." *U.S. Food and Drug Administration.* www.fda.gov/drugs/drug-supply-chain-integrity/drug-supply-chain-security-act-dscsa#:~:text=The%20Drug%20Quality%20and%20Security,distributed%20in%20the%20United%20States.

UKTN. February 24, 2021. "Bitcoin and the Challenges for Financial Regulation." *UKTN.* www.uktech.news/bitcoin-and-the-challenges-for-financial-regulation.

USA.gov. 2021. "Consumer Financial Protection Bureau." *USA.gov.* www.usa.gov/federal-agencies/consumer-financial-protection-bureau (accessed December 15, 2021).

Usercentrics. December 16, 2021. "The EU's General Data Protection Regulation (GDPR)—An overview." *Usercentrics.* https://usercentrics.com/knowledge-hub/the-eu-general-data-protection-regulation/#:~:text=What%20is%20the%20General%20Data,has%20been%20collected%20or%20processed.

van der Crabben, J. April 28, 2011. "Coinage." *World History Encyclopedia.* www.worldhistory.org/coinage/.

van Oordt, M.R.C. and W. Bolt. May 14, 2019. "Speculation and the Price of Virtual Currency." *VOXEU.* https://cepr.org/voxeu/columns/speculation-and-price-virtual-currency.

VAVE. October 24, 2020. "Real Estate Tokenization—An Overview of the New Investment Trend." *VAVE* (Blog). https://vave.io/blog/real-estate-tokenization/real-estate-tokenization-an-overview-of-the-new-investment-trend/.

Vazirani, A.A., O. O'Donoghue, D. Brindley, and E. Meinert. February 12, 2019. *Implementing Blockchains for Efficient Healthcare: Systematic Review.* National Library of Medicine. www.ncbi.nlm.nih.gov/pmc/articles/PMC6390185/#ref27.

Vazirani, A.A., O. O'Donoghue, D. Brindley, and E. Meinert. October 7, 2018. *Implementing Blockchains for Efficient Healthcare: Systematic Review.* National Library of Medicine. www.ncbi.nlm.nih.gov/pmc/articles/PMC6390185/www.jmir.org/2019/2/e12439/.

VeriDoc Global. February 27, 2019. "Theme Park Tickets and VeriDoc Global's Blockchain Solution." *VeriDoc Global*. https://veridocglobal.medium.com/theme-park-tickets-and-veridoc-globals-blockchain-solution-a-winning-combination-c731f8befbd0.

Veriff. July 26, 2022. "What Is KYC In crypto?" *Veriff* (Blog). www.veriff.com/blog/what-is-kyc-in-crypto.

Veselov, V. June 9, 2014. "Computer AI Passes Turing Test in 'World First'." *BBC News*. www.bbc.com/news/technology-27762088.

Victor, Y. May 11, 2020. "Exystayz: Unleashing the Full Potentials of Global Holiday Rental Using Blockchain Technology." *Medium.com*. https://medium.com/@Mexite3yo/ezystayz-unleashing-the-full-potentials-of-global-holiday-rental-using-blockchain-technology-e9775f6e4432.

Voatz. 2022. "How Voatz Works." *Voatz*. https://voatz.com/type/5-how-voatz-works/ (accessed March 9, 2022).

Voatz. November 11, 2022. "Voatz Successfully Completes Its 2022 Elections in the US & Canada." *Voatz*. https://voatz.com/2022/11/11/2022-elections-in-the-us-canada-successfully-completed/.

Vuleta, B. September 19, 2022. "What Is Common Law?" *Legaljobs* (Blog). https://legaljobs.io/blog/what-is-common-law/.

Wagner, L. October 12, 2022. "What Is SHA-256?." *Boot.dev* (Blog). https://blog.boot.dev/cryptography/how-sha-2-works-step-by-step-sha-256/.

Wanguba, J. 2022. "How Many Cryptocurrencies Have Failed in 2022?" *E-Crypto News*. https://e-cryptonews.com/how-many-cryptocurrencies-have-failed/#:~:text=Mostly%2C%20they%20come%20in%20the, Coinopsy%20which%20tracks%20such%20failures (accessed November 15, 2022).

Waterworth, K. September 19, 2022. "Investing in NFT Real Estate." *The Motley Fool*. www.fool.com/investing/stock-market/market-sectors/financials/non-fungible-tokens/nft-real-estate/#:~:text=NFTs%20in%20the%20real%20estate,in%20fact%2C%20own%20a%20thing.

Watson, A. August 8, 2022. "Local Newspaper Losses in the U.S. 2004–2022." *Statista*. www.statista.com/statistics/944134/number-closed-merged-newspapers/#:~:text=A%20report%20on%20local%20news,to%201%2C500%20to%20under%201%2C250.

Wegrzyn, K.E. and E. Wang. August 19, 2021. "Types of Blockchain: Public, Private, or Something in Between." *Foley & Lardner LLP* (Blog). www.foley.com/en/insights/publications/2021/08/types-of-blockchain-public-private-between.

Wenstrom, E. May 12, 2021. "NFTs for Books: How This Emerging Tech Can Reward Authors & Readers." *Book Riot*. https://bookriot.com/nfts-for-books/.

Western Union. August 16, 2018. "When Will My Receiver Get the Money?" *Western Union*. https://wucare.westernunion.com/s/article/When-can-the-

receiver-pick-up-the-money-I-sent?language=en_US#:~:text=Money%20
in%20Minutes%20service%20for,could%20vary%2C%20depending%20
on%20country.

Whipps, H. November 16, 2007. "The Profound History of Coins." *Live Science.*
www.livescience.com/2058-profound-history-coins.html.

White-Gomez, A. January 27, 2022. "Why You Need to Know About the Bacon
Protocol." *One37PM.* www.one37pm.com/nft/what-is-the-bacon-protocol.

Whittaker, M. July 29, 2022. "What Is Bitcoin Halving." *Forbes Advisor.* www
.forbes.com/advisor/investing/cryptocurrency/bitcoinhalving/#:~:text=
The%20Bitcoin%20halving%20is%20when,counteract%20inflation%20
by%20maintaining%20scarcity.

Wikipedia. 2022. "Net Neutrality by Country." *Wikepedia.* https://en.wikipedia
.org/wiki/Net_neutrality_by_country#Summary (accessed September 7, 2022).

Wikipedia. 2022. "Greenback (1860s Money)." *Wikipedia.* https://en.wikipedia
.org/wiki/Greenback_(1860s_money) (accessed October 13, 2022).

Wikipedia. 2022. "Internet of Things." *Wikipedia.* https://en.wikipedia.org/wiki/
Internet_of_things (accessed August 25, 2022).

Wikipedia. 2021. "American Recovery and Reinvestment Act of 2009." *Wikipedia.*
https://en.wikipedia.org/wiki/American_Recovery_and_Reinvestment_Act_
of_2009#:~:text=The%20approximate%20cost%20of%20the,billion%20
between%202009%20and%202019.https://en.wikipedia.org/wiki/
American_Recovery_and_Reinvestment_Act_of_2009%23:~:text=The
approximate cost of the,billion between 2009 and 2019 (accessed December
15, 2021).

Wikipedia. 2022. "AOL Explorer." *Wikipedia.* https://en.wikipedia.org/wiki/
AOL_Explorer#:~:text=AOL%20Explorer%2C%20previously%20
known%20as,Microsoft's%20Trident%20browser%20engine   (accessed
August 10, 2022).

Wikipedia. 2022. "AOL." *Wikipedia.* https://en.wikipedia.org/wiki/AOL#:~:
text=AOL%20was%20one%20of%20the,1993%20began%20adding%20
internet%20access (accessed August 10, 2022).

Wikipedia. 2021. "Bitcoin." *Wikipedia.* https://en.wikipedia.org/wiki/Bitcoin
(accessed November 2, 2021).

Wikipedia. 2022. "Brave (Web Browser)." *Wikipedia.* https://en.wikipedia.org/
wiki/Brave_(webbrowser) (accessed November 4, 2022).

Wikipedia. 2022. "Electric Energy Consumption." *Wikipedia.* https://en
.wikipedia.org/wiki/Electric_energy_consumption (accessed October 26, 2022).

Wikipedia. 2022. "Fork (Blockchain)." *Wikipedia.* https://en.wikipedia.org/
wiki/Fork_(blockchain) (accessed February 2, 2022).

Wikipedia. 2021. "Greenback (1860s Money)." *Wikipedia.* https://en.wikipedia
.org/wiki/Greenback_(1860s_money) (accessed November 12, 2021).

Wikipedia. 2021. "History of Amazon." *Wikipedia.* https://en.wikipedia.org/wiki/History_of_Amazon (accessed November 23, 2021).

Wikipedia. 2022. "History of the Legal Profession." *Wikipedia.* https://en.wikipedia.org/wiki/History_of_the_legal_profession (accessed March 16, 2022).

Wikipedia. 2022. "IBM and the Holocaust." *Wikipedia.* https://en.wikipedia.org/wiki/IBM_and_the_Holocaust (accessed January 18, 2022).

Wikipedia. 2022. "Initial Exchange Offering." *Wikipedia.* https://en.wikipedia.org/wiki/Initial_exchange_offering#:~:text=Initial%20exchange%20offering%20(IEO)%20is,its%20reserve%20for%20Tether%20tokens (accessed February 9, 2022).

Wikipedia. 2022. "Internet Access." *Wikipedia.* https://en.wikipedia.org/wiki/Internet_access (accessed August 15, 2022).

Wikipedia. 2021. "John C. Biggens." *Wikipedia.* https://en.wikipedia.org/wiki/John_C._Biggins (accessed November 12, 2021).

Wikipedia. 2022. "Meta." *Wikipedia.* https://en.wikipedia.org/wiki/Meta (accessed August 15, 2022).

Wikipedia. 2021. "Shell Money." *Wikipedia.* https://en.m.wikipedia.org/wiki/Shell_money (accessed November 5, 2021).

Wikipedia. 2022. "Smart Contract." *Wikipedia.* https://en.wikipedia.org/wiki/Smart_contract#:~:text=Since%20the%202015%20launch%20of,a%20blockchain%20or%20distributed%20ledger (accessed September 27, 2022).

Wikipedia. 2022. "Voterverified Paper Audit Trail." *Wikipedia.* https://en.wikipedia.org/wiki/Voterverified_paper_audit_trail#:~:text=In%20the%20United%20States%2C%2027,statewide%20or%20in%20local%20jurisdictions (accessed March 9, 2022).

Wikipedia. 2021. "Wall Street Reform." *Wikipedia.* https://en.wikipedia.org/wiki/Wall_Street_reform (accessed December 14, 2021).

Wikipedia. 2022. "Web 2.0." *Wikipedia.* https://en.wikipedia.org/wiki/Web_2.0 (accessed August 15, 2022).

Wikipedia. 2021. "Wire Transfer." *Wikipedia.* https://en.wikipedia.org/wiki/Wire_transfer#:~:text=The%20first%20widely%20used%20service,on%20its%20existing%20telegraph%20network.&text=Because%20the%20earliest%20wire%20transfers,still%20used%20in%20some%20countries (accessed November 12, 2021).

Williamson, M. February 9, 2022. "NFT Real Estate in the Metaverse. The Next Big Thing?" *Finance Magnates.* www.financemagnates.com/cryptocurrency/nfts-markets-in-2022-from-trading-volumes-to-real-estate/.

Willings, S. July 27, 2021. "Most of Spotify's Top 0.8% of Artists Earn Less Than $50k in Streaming Revenue." *MusicTech.* https://musictech.com/news/most-of-spotifys-top-0-8-of-artists-earn-less-than-50k-in-streaming-revenue/.

Wimbush, S. April 2, 2020. "Blockchain Technology: Improving Law Offices or Decreasing the Need for Lawyers." *The Race to the Bottom* (Blog). www .theracetothebottom.org/rttb/2020/4/1/blockchain-technology-improving-law-offices-or-decreasing-the-need-for-lawyers.

Wiseman, R. January 21, 2022. "NFTs for Writers: New Options to Publish in a Digital World." *Novlr.* www.novlr.org/the-reading-room/nfts-for-writers-new-ways-to-publish-in-a-digital-world.

Wojno, M. March 9, 2022. "Crypto Mortgage Lender Milo Secures $17M Financing to Expand Operations, Enabling Crypto Holders to Buy Real Estate." *ZDNet.* www.zdnet.com/finance/blockchain/crypto-mortgage-lender-milo-secures-17m-financing-to-expand-operations-enabling-crypto-holders-to-buy-real-estate/.

Wolfson, R. April 7, 2022. "Grammys 2022: NFTs Hot Topic of Discussion Among Musicians and Industry Experts." *Cointelegraph.* https://cointelegraph .com/news/grammys-2022-nfts-hot-topic-of-discussion-amongst-musicians-and-industry-experts.

Wolfson, R. July 28, 2022. "Decentralized Storage Providers the Web3 Economy, But Adoption Still Underway." *Cointelegraph.* https://cointelegraph.com/ news/decentralized-storage-providers-power-the-web3-economy-but-adoption-still-underway.

World Crypto Index. 2022. "What Is a Decentralized Search Engine and How Does It Work." *World Crypto Index.* www.worldcryptoindex.com/ decentralized-search-engines/#:~:text=With%20a%20decentralized%20 search%20engine,it%20with%20a%20private%20key (accessed November 30, 2022).

World Travel & Tourism Council. 2022. "Economic Impact Reports." *World Travel & Tourism Council.* https://wttc.org/research/economic-impact (accessed April 2, 2022).

Wright, K. January 19, 2022. "Fintech Startup Milo Is Offering 30-Year Crypto Mortgages'." *Cointelegraph.* https://cointelegraph.com/news/fintech-startup-milo-is-offering-30-year-crypto-mortgages.

Writer's Digest. 2022. "How Long Does It Take to Get a Book Published?" *Writers Digest.* www.writersdigest.com/getting-published/how-long-does-it-take-to-get-a-book-published#:~:text=With%20our%20rules%20established%20 above,they%20plan%20their%20production%20schedule (accessed July 4, 2022).

XR Today Team. August 1, 2022. "What Are the Seven Layers of the Metaverse?" *XR Today.* www.xrtoday.com/virtual-reality/what-are-the-seven-layers-of-the-metaverse/.

YCharts. 2022. "Bitcoin Price." *YCharts.* https://ycharts.com/indicators/bitcoin_ price (accessed October 13, 2022).

Ye Han, J. February 20, 2018. "How Blockchain Technology Is Transforming the Legal Industry." *Bloomberg Law.* https://news.bloomberglaw.com/tech-and-telecom-law/how-blockchain-technology-is-transforming-the-legal-industry.

Young, M. October 7, 2020. "75 Crypto Exchanges Have Closed Down so Far in 2020." *Cointelegraph.* https://cointelegraph.com/news/75-crypto-exchanges-have-closed-down-so-far-in-2020.

Zapotochnyi, A. October 19, 2022. "What Are Smart Contracts?" *Blockgeeks.* https://blockgeeks.com/guides/smart-contracts/.

Žavcer, G. June 21, 2022. "Cancel Culture and Censorship: Freeing the Content Through Web3." *DCD.* www.datacenterdynamics.com/en/opinions/cancel-culture-and-censorship-freeing-the-content-through-web3/.

ZenLedger. May 17, 2022. "Decentralized Exchange Vs Centralized Exchange: A Comparison." *Zen Ledger* (Blog). www.zenledger.io/blog/decentralized-exchange-vs-centralized-exchange.

Zhang, S. July 28, 2018. "Big Pharma Would Like Your DNA." *The Atlantic.* www.theatlantic.com/science/archive/2018/07/big-pharma-dna/566240/.

About the Author

Sylvain Metz is an award-winning former newspaper reporter and editor from Jackson, Mississippi, now living in Essen, Germany, with his wife, Funda, and their dog, Andie, where he works as a freelance writer and English teacher.

Index

Airbnb, 118
Altcoins, 148–149
America Online (AOL), 228
Application-specific integrated circuits (ASICs), 147
Artificial intelligence (AI), 239–241
Art, NFTs and, 193–194
Asset-backed tokens, 153–155
Asymmetrical encryption, 13–14
Axle Infinity, 206

Bacon Protocol, 213
BankChain, 25
Bank Secrecy Act (BSA), 184
Basic attention tokens (BATs), 108, 109
bHome, 213
Bitcoin, 10, 11, 37–41, 45, 128, 131, 145–148
Bitcoin mining, 47, 50–51
Bit gold, 15
Blind Signature, 141
Blockchain, xv, xvi, xvii, 9–10, 235–236
  banks, 95–98
  block, elements of, 27–29
  components, 17
  consensus, 39–41
  consortium blockchains, 25
  cost reductions, 22
  and government, 128
    India, 90–91
    for people, 81–82
    property, 87–89
    Republic of Georgia, 89–90
    United States, 91–93
    voting, 82–87
  and health care, 67–70
    medical community, 65–66
    medical fraud, 67
    patients as medical collaborators, 63–65
    recordkeeping, 61–63
    supply chain, 66–67

hybrid blockchains, 25–26
and identity, 71–73
  decentralized, 75–80
  online, 73–75
  reboot, 75
issue, 45
loans, 98–99
mempools, 33–35
nodes, 35–36
origin, 10–16
and practice of law, 111–115
private blockchains, 25
proof of authority (PoA), 41, 42
proof of stake (PoS), 41–42
proof-of-work (PoW), 36–39
  carbon emissions, 49–52
  energy consumption, 47–49
proponents, 18
and print media, 105–109
public blockchains, 24–25
to raise capital, 99–100
and real estate, 101–102
  liquidity, 103
  tokenization, 102
security, 18–21, 100
smart contracts, 29–30
stability, 23
storage, 43–45
and supply chain
  energy, 57–59
  quality monitoring, 56–57
  shipping, 60
  working conditions monitoring, 56–57
timestamps, 30–31
transaction, 31–33
transparency, 21–22
travel and entertainment, 117–18
  concerts and events, 120
  rental property, 118–120
  theme parks, 121
types, 24–26
Blockpharma, 66–67

Books, NFTs and, 195–197
Brave browser, 109, 251

Carbon emissions, 49–52
Census technology, 3
Centers for Disease Control and
    Prevention (CDC), 66
Centralized exchanges (CEX), 160,
    161
Chain of custody, 93
Client puzzle function, 15
Cloud storage, 251–252
Coins, 135, 149–150
Cold wallet/cold storage, 170–172
Colonial Pipeline, 23
CompuServe, 228
Concerts, 120
Congi, 98
Consensus, 39–41
Consortium blockchains, 25
Creatokia, 197
Credit cards, 139, 140
Crypto.com, 202
Cryptocurrency, xv, 95, 97, 119
    advantages, 186
    altcoins, 148–149
    bitcoin, 145–148
    coins and tokens, 149–150
    critics of, 179
    evolution of swap, 133–134,
        141–142
        money, in modern era,
        139–140
        paper money, 136–139
        salt for gold, 134–136
    exchange collapses, 177
    failures, 177–178
    fast cash, 162–163
    fraud, 178–179
    government regulation, 179–184
    money laundering, 178–179
    overview, 127–128
    regulation, 175–176
    stablecoins, 149
    taxes, 163–164
    trading tools
        custodial/noncustodial wallet,
        168–172
        wallets, 167–168
    value, 129–132

Cryptography, 13
    asymmetrical encryption, 13–14
    symmetric encryption, 13–14
    types, 13–14
Custodial/noncustodial wallet,
    168–172

Debit card, 140
Decentralized apps, 241, 242
Decentralized Autonomous
    Organizations (DAOs),
    237–239
Decentralized exchanges (DEX), 160,
    161
Decentralized identifiers (DIDs),
    75–77
Decentralized identity, 75–80
Decentralized networks, 236–237
Decentralized peer-to-peer network, 17
Decentralized search engines, 221
Demand Notes, 138
DIDs. See Decentralized identifiers
    (DIDs)
Digital Services Act (DSA), 5
Digital signature, 14
Digital wallet, 76
Diners Club card, 140
doc.ai app, 63
Double spending, 145
Drug Chain Supply Chain Security
    Act (DSCSA), 57

Eavesdropping, 2
Eidoo Hybrid Exchange, 160
Energy, 57–59
Energy consumption, 47–49
Equity token offerings (ETOs), 99
Ethereum blockchain, 119–120
European Convention on Human
    Rights, 1950, 5
European Securities and Markets
    Authority (ESMA), 183
EU-wide anti-money laundering
    authority (AMLA), 181, 182
Events, 120
EzyStayz, 119
Ezy token, 119

Fair Data Society, 249
Fiat money, 138

Field-programmable gate array
    (FGPA), 147
Fork, 20
Fractional shares, 211–212
Free speech, 232, 253
Front-running, 33–34
FTX, 177
Full nodes, 35

Gaming, NFTs and, 205–208
General Data Protection Regulation
    (GDPR), 5, 6
Gold, 135, 137, 138
Government
    blockchain and, 128
        India, 90–91
        for people, 81–82
        property, 87–89
        Republic of Georgia, 89–90
        United States, 91–93
        voting, 82–87
Graphic processing units (GPUs), 147
Graphics interchange formats (GIFs),
    199
Greenbacks. See U.S. Note

Hard fork, 21
Hash, 11–13, 129
Hashcash, 11, 36
Hassle-free sharing, 163
Health care
    blockchain and, 67–70
        medical community, 65–66
        medical fraud, 67
        patients as medical collaborators,
            63–65
        recordkeeping, 61–63
        supply chain, 66–67
Health Insurance Portability and
    Accountability Act of 1996
    (HIPPA), 62
Hybrid blockchain, 25–26, 90–92
Hybrid exchange, 160

IBM food trust, 25
Identity
    blockchain and, 71–73
        decentralized, 75–80
        online, 73–75
        reboot, 75

Initial coin offerings (ICOs), 99–100
Initial exchange offerings (IEOs), 99,
    100
Integra Ledger, 113
Internet of things (IoT), 243–244
Interoperability, 79, 254
Investment banks, 95

Keccak-256, 37
Known Traveler Digital Identity, 77–78

Legal Tender Act, 1862, 138
Legolas Hybrid Exchange, 160
Liquidity, 103, 216
Loans, 98–99

Machine learning, 241–242
Markets in Crypto Act (MiCA), 183
Matrix, 249
Medical community, 65–66
Medical fraud, 67
Mempools, 33–35
Merkle tree, 43, 44
Metal money, 139
Metaverse, 244–245
Mining nodes, 35
Mintable, 202
Mobility, 79
Money, in modern era, 139–140
Money laundering, 178–179, 182–184
Mortgages, 212–214
Music, NFTs and, 194–195

Neeva.xyz, 247
Net neutrality, 255–256
Nodes, 35–36
Nonfungible tokens (NFTs), 157,
    203–204
    advantages and disadvantages,
        215–218
    and art, 193–194
    books and literature, 195–197
    buying/selling, 201–203
    collectables, 199–201
    and gaming, 205–208
    graphics interchange formats (GIFs),
        199
    images, 199
    liquidity, 216
    and music, 194–195

overview, 189–191
perspective, 192–193
and poetry, 198
as real estate, 209–211
    fractional shares, 211–212
    mortgages, 212–214
    taxes, 217–218
Nyan Cat, 199

OMNI Real Estate Token ($ORT),
    211
Online identity, 73–75
OpenLaw, 113
OpenSea, 202
Opera, 251

Paper money, 136–139
Peer-to-peer electronic cash system,
    128
PeerTube, 248
Personal Information Protection and
    Electronic Documents Act, 6
Play-2-earn (P2E) games, 206
Poetry, NFTs and, 198
Practice of law, blockchain and,
    111–115
Print media, blockchain and,
    105–109
Privacy, 1–7, 78–79
Private blockchain, 25, 90, 91
Proof of authority (PoA), 41, 42, 235
proof of stake (PoS), 41–42
Proof-of-work (PoW), 11, 36–39
    carbon emissions, 49–52
    energy consumption, 47–49
Proof-of-Work function, 15
Property, 87–89
Public blockchain, 24–25, 90, 91
Punch card system, 3

Qurrex Hybrid Exchange, 160

Ransomware, 23
Real estate
    blockchain and, 102–103
    nonfungible tokens (NFTs) as,
        209–211
        fractional shares, 211–212
        mortgages, 212–214

Recordkeeping, 61–63
The Redemption Act, 1875, 138
Rental property, 118–120
Reward tokens, 153, 155, 156

Satoshis, 146
Secretum, 249–250
Secure benchmark function, 15
Secure Hash Algorithm 256-bit
    (SHA-256), 11, 12, 37, 146,
    147
Securities, 100
Security, 18–21, 79
Security/equity tokens, 153, 154
Security token offerings (STOs), 99,
    100
Semantic Web, 233–234
SHA-256. See Secure Hash Algorithm
    256-bit (SHA-256)
Sharding, 43
Signature, 14
Silver coins, 135
Smart cards, 62
Smart contracts, 15, 29–30, 113–115,
    209, 210
Social media, 248
Stablecoins, 149, 159, 213
Status, 250
Storage, 43–45, 93
StoragJ, 252
SuperRare, 202
Supply chain
    blockchain and, 66–67
        energy, 57–59
        quality monitoring, 56–57
        shipping, 60
        working conditions monitoring,
            56–57
    food supply tracking, 54–55
Symmetric encryption, 13–14

Taxes
    cryptocurrency, 163–164
    nonfungible tokens (NFTs),
        217–218
Theme parks, 121
theVERSEverse, 198
Time, 199–200
TIMEPieces NFT collection, 200

Timestamps, 30–31
Token economy, 151–153
    cryptocurrency tokens, 153–157
Tokenization, 102
Tokens, coins *vs.*, 149–150
Trading card games (TCGs), 206
Trading tools, 167–173
Traditional banking, 95
Transaction, 31–33, 123
Transparency, 21–22
Transparent digital ledger, 21–22
Transparent distributed ledgers, 27
Travala, 119
Travel and entertainment
    blockchain and, 117–18
        concerts and events, 120
        rental property, 118–120
        theme parks, 121
Trust, defined, 143
Trustless, 24
Two-factor identification method, 169

U.S. Note, 130, 137
Usenet, 228
Utility tokens, 153, 154

Virtual Assets Regulatory Authority
        (VARA), 236
Virtual worlds, NFTs and, 207–208

Voatz, 85–87
Voting, 82–87

Walled gardens, 9, 232
Wallets, 167–168
Web 1.0, 227–230
Web 2.0, 230–232
Web 3.0, 200, 222–223, 232–233
    blogs, 249
    browsers, 250–251
    cloud storage, 251–252
    control, 253–254
        net neutrality, 255–256
    messaging, 249–250
    overview, 221–222
    search engines, 247
    social media, 248
    videos, 248–249
    vision, 224–225
Web3.storage, 252
Webjet of Australia, 119
WebTV, 229
Winding Tree, 119–120
World wide web (www), 222–223
    internet speed, 223–224
    Semantic Web, 233–234
    Web 1.0, 227–230
    Web 2.0, 230–232
    Web 3.0, 232–233

OTHER TITLES IN THE COLLABORATIVE INTELLIGIENCE COLLECTION

Jim Spohrer and Haluk Demirkan, Editors

- *Journey to the Metaverse* by Antonio Flores-Galea
- *Doing Digital* by Ved Sen
- *Breakthrough* by Martin Fleming
- *How Organizations Can Make the Most of Online Learning* by David Guralnick
- *Teaching Higher Education to Lead* by Sam Choon-Yin
- *Business and Emerging Technologies* by George Baffour
- *How to Talk to Data Scientists* by Jeremy Elser
- *Leadership in The Digital Age* by Niklas Hageback
- *Cultural Science* by William Sims Bainbridge
- *The Future of Work* by Yassi Moghaddam, Heather Yurko, Haluk Demirkan, Nathan Tymann and Ammar Rayes
- *Advancing Talent Development* by Philip Gardner and Heather N. Maietta
- *Virtual Local Manufacturing Communities* by William Sims Bainbridge
- *T-Shaped Professionals* by Yassi Moghaddam, Haluk Demirkan and James Spohrer
- *The Interconnected Individual* by Hunter Hastings and Jeff Saperstein

Concise and Applied Business Books

The Collection listed above is one of 30 business subject collections that Business Expert Press has grown to make BEP a premiere publisher of print and digital books. Our concise and applied books are for...

- Professionals and Practitioners
- Faculty who adopt our books for courses
- Librarians who know that BEP's Digital Libraries are a unique way to offer students ebooks to download, not restricted with any digital rights management
- Executive Training Course Leaders
- Business Seminar Organizers

Business Expert Press books are for anyone who needs to dig deeper on business ideas, goals, and solutions to everyday problems. Whether one print book, one ebook, or buying a digital library of 110 ebooks, we remain the affordable and smart way to be business smart. For more information, please visit www.businessexpertpress.com, or contact sales@businessexpertpress.com.

www.ingramcontent.com/pod-product-compliance
Lightning Source LLC
LaVergne TN
LVHW020846190325
806302LV00007B/84